# Information, Sensation, and Perception

# Information, Sensation, and Perception

Kenneth H. Norwich

Institute of Biomedical Engineering,
Department of Physiology, and
Department of Physics
University of Toronto
Toronto, Ontario, Canada

**ACADEMIC PRESS, INC.**
A Division of Harcourt Brace & Company

San Diego   New York   Boston   London   Sydney   Tokyo   Toronto

Copyright © 1993 by ACADEMIC PRESS, INC.

All Rights Reserved.
No part of this publication may be reproduced or transmitted in any form or by any
means, electronic or mechanical, including photocopy, recording, or any information
storage and retrieval system, without permission in writing from the publisher.

Academic Press, Inc.
1250 Sixth Avenue, San Diego, California 92101-4311

*United Kingdom Edition published by*
Academic Press Limited
24–28 Oval Road, London NW1 7DX

Library of Congress Cataloging-in-Publication Data

Norwich, Kenneth H.
    Information, sensation, and perception  /  Kenneth H. Norwich.
        p.    cm.
    Includes index.
    ISBN 0-12-521890-7
    1. Perception--Mathematical models.  2. Senses and sensation-
-Mathematical models.  I. Title.
BF311 .N68   1993
152. 1--dc20                                           93-16692
                                                          CIP

PRINTED IN THE UNITED STATES OF AMERICA
93  94  95  96  97  98    BC    9  8  7  6  5  4  3  2  1

To my wife, Barbara,
Supportive from $t = 0$

# Contents

# 4   Information of Events with Discrete Outcomes: Methods of Communication Theory and Psychology

# 5   Information of Events with Discrete Outcomes: Applications in Communications Science and in Psychology

# 6   Information of Events with Discrete Outcomes: Methods of Physics

# 7   The Information of Events with Continuous Outcomes

# 8   The Entropy of the Normal Distribution

# 9    Modeling the $H$-Function

# 10    Derivation of the Law of Sensation

# 11    Sensory Adaptation

# 12   Differential Thresholds, Weber Fractions, and JNDs

# 13   Simple Reaction Times and the Blondel–Rey Law

## 14   Odds and $n$'s, and the Magical Number Log $(2\pi)$ Bits of Information

## 15   Boltzmann and Berkeley

# 16 Physiological Consequences of the Relativity of Perception

# 17 Extrapolations and Speculations

# Preface

I recall that as I lay in my room with a migraine headache in December 1958, an idea came to mind. There was, naturally, a certain period of time required for development of this idea, which accounts for the modest delay in bringing it to print, but here it sits before you now. In the interim, I have published a number of papers on the subject in various journals. However, there are gaps between the papers and there is a body of knowledge that must be assimilated before these papers can even be read. With this book, I have tried to fill these gaps and provide the fundamental body of basic knowledge. The idea has matured through the years, so that my early papers on the subject now seem to me as quaint, primitive, and sometimes a trifle embarrassing. This book updates things.

I present here a theory of perception based on the premise that a perceiver is necessary if there is to be a world external to this perceiver. Couched in other language, the existence of the world is relative, in some way, to the perceiver of that world. My debt to George Berkeley is supreme.

Taking this philosophy of perceptual relativity as a given, my first problem was to find a mathematical structure that would support it. After rather a lot of searching I did find a candidate for such a mathematical structure—one that did not dissolve in the next migraine—and my problem was then to test or validate it.

I chose the field of sensory science (neurophysiology and psychophysics) as a proving ground because this field is replete with empirical equations—that is, equations that describe experimental findings, but which are without any known theoretical basis. If my candidate for mathematical structure is a good one, it should permit derivation, from this mathematical base, of all (or many) of the empirical equations of sensory science and should provide a degree of conceptual unity to the field of sensory science.

Please note that I have avoided using the term *mathematical model* for the structure in question. I have the feeling that a mathematical model is something created by the modeler that can be modified to suit his or her desires (like clay in a potter's hands). I have no such feelings regarding the mathematical structure presented here. I feel more as if I have "unearthed" the structure or, at best, discovered it. It was there all along, and I just found it. It is not really mine to modify at my whim. It is too simple and too fundamental a concept.

For whom is this book intended? I think it is for those with a keen desire to understand what is meant by *perception* or *sensation*—not specifically *this* perceptual phenomenon or *that* sensory mechanism, but something closer to the fundamental nature of the perceptual process, the conscious apprehension of the world by a living (or nonliving!) creature. But before you say to yourself "That's me for sure!" (you would never say to yourself "That is I!") you had better consider the overhead. If your background is largely in the physical sciences, is your desire powerful enough to impel you to study—not just read—the purely physiological and psychological chapters of this book before proceeding to the more physically oriented material? And if your background is in biology or psychology, are you prepared to take the time to brush up on, or learn *de novo*, the necessary basic mathematics? You do not need a lot of mathematical knowledge to get through this book, but you do need at least one course on basic calculus and some introductory mathematical statistics. Experience has shown me that it is *absolutely mandatory* for comprehension of this material that one understands (a) logarithms and exponentials and (b) the Taylor series in one variable. With respect to the latter, you should be able to expand, for example, $e^x$ or $\ln(1 + x)$, $-1 < x \leq 1$, in a Taylor series. Not exactly higher mathematics, but at least this level is required to follow what is contained on these pages.

The book is intended for psychophysicists and physicists, for sensory physiologists, for engineers and computer scientists interested in perceptual phenomena, and for anyone with a desire to explore sensation and perception from a new perspective. The material in this book has formed part of a course given yearly to senior undergraduates in the Department of Physiology and to students in the School of Graduate Studies at the University of Toronto. Among the offerings of this book are explanations of why both Fechner's and Stevens' laws are valid, to differing degrees, in different circumstances; why we can react more rapidly to a more intense stimulus; and how perception in the biological sense can be related to "quantum observation," as expressed in quantum mechanics.

Chapter 1 provides some orientation. Chapter 2 introduces the *entropic theory of perception*, which, I hope, will encourage you to study the next six chapters of background material in depth. Chapters 3 through 8 provide background in sensory science, thermodynamics and statistical mechanics, and information theory. You may choose from these chapters to complement your background. For example, a physics major does not require my "crash course" in thermodynamics. Chapter 3 provides basic sensory science, and it has been my experience that many sensory scientists are not too familiar with these quantitative aspects of their field. When fortified by the material in Chapters 3 through 8, you should find no difficulty with Chapter 9, where the fundamental equations of the entropy theory of perception are developed. My journal papers often *started* at the level of Chapter 9, making the assumption that the reader could provide the necessary background.

Chapters 10 through 14 are heavily numerical, providing the experimental testing of the theory. No act of faith is required of you to accept the validity of the theory that has been developed. Scores of experimental records and graphs are presented in the book. Armed only with a pocket calculator you can confirm or deny the capability of the theory to explain the data. Predictions are also made which transcend the available data.

Fundamentally, I present here a single equation, $F = kH$, and a mathematical structure for $H$. I demonstrate that most of the empirical equations of psychophysics follow from this single equation. I entreat you to judge the equation not on its ability to generate any one sensory law, such as Fechner's law or the power law of sensation, which might be improved by the ad hoc addition of terms, but by the totality of its capabilities—the ability of a single equation to accomplish multiple tasks.

A parallel theme, begun later in the book, is the development of the *perceptual unit*, a structure that can, *of itself*, perceive, or be aware. The approach taken here is, in a sense, complementary to that of the neural network modelers. In the neural network approach, it is hoped that higher mental functions may emerge from the interplay of a large number of very simple units. In the entropic approach, the germ of higher mental function is encapsulated in a single perceptual unit.

Chapters 15 and 16 give the history of development of the entropic idea. That is, chronologically, these chapters would be Chapters 1 and 2. However, I wanted you to sample the power of $F = kH$ before learning of the origins of the idea.

Chapter 17 is a flight of fancy. While it is easy to read as a stand-alone chapter since there are no equations, I fervently hope that you will not do so. The sole claim of this chapter is that *it issues from*, or is an extrapolation of, the more restricted form of the entropy theory which makes up the rest of the book, and which I have striven so hard to validate using experimental data. Only when the extent of validity of the core theory is established in your mind can you attain the perspective from which to judge the merits of the extrapolations offered in the final chapter. Chapter 17 may provide material for fireside discussion, but you must not emerge from reading this book with the impression that it was about cochlear implants or Darwinian evolution. I invoke the metaphor of a dessert, which is last in a meal but does not contain the greatest part of its nourishment.

The book deals with sensation in general and not with any particular organ of sensation. It demonstrates how one may derive many of the mathematical laws of sensation *without reference to the mechanism of sensory transduction*. How is such a thing possible? Surely you have to know how the organ works before you can make a mathematical statement about its function! Not so. Laws of the "conservation" type, such as found in thermodynamics, permit one to formulate mathematical constraints without knowledge of specific mechanisms.

By way of analogy, consider a rectangular grid of streets as shown in the map below.

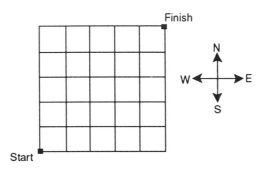

The grid is divided into 25 squares, representing city blocks. The north–south streets are all one-way streets leading north, and the east–west streets are all one-way streets leading east. An automobile begins at START and reaches its destination at FINISH.

(a) What distance was traversed by the automobile as it traveled from START to FINISH, without violating the one-way laws?

(b) What route was taken by the automobile as it traveled from START to FINISH?

Clearly the answer to (a) is 10 blocks, and the answer to (b) is unknown. We know the total distance covered (analogous to a conservation law), but we do not know the exact route (or "mechanism"). In the same way we shall be able to discover, to some degree, how a taste or light receptor responds to its specific stimulus by observing the total amount of information it receives from its stimulus (cf. total number of blocks traveled), but we may not be able to say anything about the anatomy or specific physiological mechanism of the receptor (cf. exact route taken by the automobile).

I am grateful to a number of my colleagues and students for their support and assistance in the writing of this book. In particular I thank (mathematician) Beatrice Aebersold for proofreading the first 12 chapters with special attention to mathematical accuracy. I am grateful to Professor Lawrence Ward for many discussions on the entropy theory and for his insightful comments on the difficult Chapter 13. I give special thanks to (physicist) Willy Wong for his commentary on the quantum physical sections of this book, for his help in carrying out many of the curve fits, and for assistance with the computer programming that was needed to prepare many of the diagrams. As always, the author bears full responsibility for the material as presented.

I am most grateful to the Natural Sciences and Engineering Research Council of Canada for their support of much of the research on the entropy theory of perception.

# 1

# Introduction

*"You have been in Afghanistan, I perceive." Sherlock Holmes had just been introduced to Dr. John Watson and his perception was the result of the following chain of deductive and inductive reasoning: By introduction, a medical man; By observation, of military bearing. Therefore, likely an army doctor. By observation, dark skin with white wrists. Therefore, sun-tanned; therefore, probably just back from the tropics. By observation, haggard face with stiff arm. Therefore, probably wounded. General knowledge: War in Afghanistan.*
*"Perception": Army surgeon from Afghanistan.*

## PERCEPTION

A great perceiver was Sherlock Holmes. Or was he an observer? Few people would volunteer the definitive distinction between these terms, but that is the sort of activity we must undertake if we are to examine the very pith and core of the process of perception—which is a cardinal aim of this book.

If you discriminate between the loudness of two tones, are you engaging in an act of perception?

If you read on your monitor that an atom in an excited state has just released a photon or light particle, have you *perceived* the quantum event?

If a source of light is made 1000 times more intense (that is, releases 1000 times more energy per unit time in the form of light), it may appear only about 10 times brighter. Does this phenomenon have anything to do with the rapidity with which you can stop your car at a stoplight?

Will extraterrestrial creatures (if they exist) be limited, as terrestrial creatures are, to receive about $\log_2(2\pi)$ bits of information by perceiving a flash of light?

Is there a correction factor required in the theory of evolution introduced by the evolution of the creatures who are, themselves, formulating the theory of evolution?

Does the now-vanished odor of wet paint which permeated the room only a moment ago have anything to do with the optical illusion produced by the Necker cube shown in Figure 17.1?

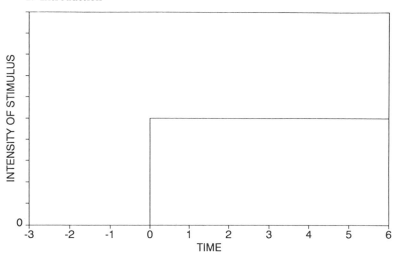

FIGURE 1.1   The type of stimulus dealt with in this book is in the form of a step function in intensity applied at $t = 0$. It is represented by

$$\text{Intensity} = 0, \quad t < 0$$
$$= I, \quad t > 0.$$

Can we possibly construct machines that perceive, or only machines that observe? (That distinction again.)

Is is possible the Fechner's and Stevens' laws are just different approximations of the same sensory law?

The answer that I suggest to each of the above questions is "Yes." I raise these titillating issues prematurely and out of sequence in an unabashed attempt to capture your imagination and to illustrate the process of unification within and among the sciences that we shall pursue through our study of perception. I am also raising these "glamorous" questions now so that you may keep them in mind as we proceed through some rather hard slogging in the early chapters of the book.

We shall spend much of our effort, particularly in the central chapters, in the study of rather simple, "atomistic" aspects of perception. We shall confine our attention to stimuli of the simplest kind: signals of the "intensity" type, such as the intensity of a light signal or the density of an odorant gas. Moreover, the discussion will remain confined to stimuli that are applied in the form of a step function (Figure 1.1). Only in the later chapters will we relax that restriction.

This is a theoretical treatise. The general approach, I think, is that of the physicist. A year of calculus and the introductory concepts of statistics will take you a long way, and many psychologists around the world have been able to get to the heart of the theory. In some cases, detailed mathematical arguments have been relegated to "boxes" or appendices. There is a distinction between the material placed in boxes and that in

appendices. The material in the boxes is necessary for thorough understanding of the theory, while that in the appendices can be skipped or the
conclusions taken for granted. However, I wanted the complete mathematical argument to be present in this book.

Occasionally, I have found it convenient to assign two different equation numbers to the same equation when it appears in different parts of
the text. To remind the reader of the dual assignment I have used a
slash. For example (A4.7)/(4.21) means that Equation (A4.7) is identical
to Equation (4.21).

Although the development presented is completely theoretical, in the
sense that no new experimental data are given, all derived equations are
validated using measured data obtained from the published literature or
by courtesy of a colleague. In this latter respect—the fastidious insistence
upon testing theoretical results against measured data—the current
work differs from many other theoretical studies on perception.

In the course of this book, I discuss many of the sensory systems, not
just a single modality. The feature that I invoke to unify the senses is the
concept of "information." Although temperature receptors, mechanoreceptors and light receptors each transduce a particular form of energy
into neural signals (action potentials), all receptors transmit information
from the so-called "external world" to the central nervous system. So
information is a universal currency in which we shall trade. Psychologists, in particular, often respond that information has already been
weighed as a tool for exploring the senses and been found wanting.
However, the manner in which I apply the theory of information here is
very different from anything advanced in the 1950s and 1960s. One
could, I suspect, dispense totally with the terms information and "information theory," and proceed directly from the statistical mechanical
treatment of entropy as introduced by Ludwig Boltzmann toward the end
of the nineteenth century. I felt, though, that Boltzmann's methods
might seem too remote and Claude Shannon's information theoretical
terminology would sound somewhat more familiar. So I have tried, where
possible, to use familiar Shannonian terms such as "channel," "transmission of information," and "bit."

The ideas that I present in this book arose many years ago when I first
studied the philosophical work of George Berkeley, in particular, "A
Treatise Concerning the Principles of Human Knowledge." But I am
afraid to *begin* this book with Berkeley, because many people would
approach his work with preconceptions, which I am anxious to alter. So I
state the assumptions fundamental to my view of perception in the early
chapters without describing explicitly how I came to formulate them.
Then, later in the book, I confess my debt to the venerable philosopher
and show the lineage of my thinking.

Philosophically, the current work is complementary to that put forward by the late David Marr who stated: "From a philosophical point of
view, the approach that I describe is an extension of what have some-

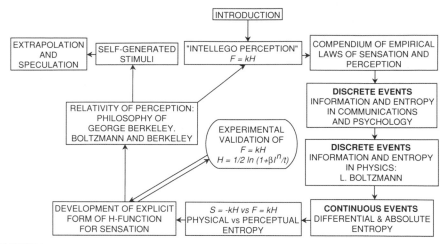

FIGURE 1.2   Flow diagram for this book. We begin on a philosophical note, but soon become technical. As we approach the end, we again become philosophical as we try to place the subject matter in perspective.

times been called representational theories of mind. On the whole, it rejects the more recent excursions into the philosophy of perception, with their arguments about sense-data, the molecules of perception, and the validity of what the senses tell us; instead, this approach looks back to an older view, according to which the senses are for the most part concerned with telling one what is there'' (Marr, 1982). In this book by contrast, we indeed, query the relationship between percepts and the mind that perceives. As we shall see, this will lead us to view the mind in an unusual manner. The philosophy is discussed, however, only after we have glimpsed the rather extraordinary power of the new view of perception. Figure 1.2 may help to clarify the order of approach.

Since my readers will have different educational backgrounds, I have included chapters dealing with more elementary material that may be familiar to some and not to others. I devote quite some space (about three chapters) to developing the rudiments of information theory, all of which can be skipped over by you if you're knowledgeable in these matters. I have also devoted Chapter 3 to the description of various physiological and psychological experiments dealing with the special senses. These experiments are the ones on which we later test our theoretical structure; they are, so to speak, grist for the mill. Although the chapter that deals with experiments is intended primarily for the psychophysically naïve, there are facets of the classical analysis of experiments that are, in my experience, not familiar to all practicing psychophysicists. The final chapter, dealing with extrapolations, extends far beyond the atomistic percepts associated with stimuli of the intensity type. Here we relax our requirement for mathematical rigor and give free vent to imagination.

Figure 1.2 is a flow diagram that guides us through the book. Note that the flow of thought is cyclical, beginning with the selection (not derivation) of an equation, $F = kH$, and finally comes full cycle back to this same block, but now with a philosophical basis for the equation. We might note also that the central block, dealing with experimental validation, occupies some five chapters (10 through 14 inclusive). Please note also that the final two blocks on the left-hand side of the flow diagram should be approached in sequence. That is, they should be read *after* the remainder of the book has been digested.

Let me now state, as explicitly as I can, one of the main objectives of this book. Throughout the past century and a half, rather a large number of *empirical equations* have been formulated by psychologists and physiologists studying sensory phenomena. Empirical equations are equations based purely on measurement. They are convenient descriptions of data, but descriptions for which there has been no general explanation. One of the earliest of these empirical equations is Weber's law, $\Delta I/I = $ constant.[1] Another is the Plateau–Brentano–Stevens power law, $F = kI^n$ etc. In this book, as well as in the various journal papers to which it refers, I *derive* these hitherto empirical laws from a small set of assumptions. In fact I try to derive, from the same set of assumptions, *all* the sensory laws relating three fundamental psychophysiological[2] variables. *Unification* of the laws of sensation is one of my primary objectives.

To the physicists among my readership, *unification* needs no further elaboration; the concept of unification of the fundamental physical forces, etc., is abundantly clear. However, I have found that to the biological and social scientists this term is far from familiar. So with the latter group in mind, let me try to demonstrate both the *meaning* and the *power* behind the process of unification. I proceed by using an analogy.

## THE MEANING AND IMPORT OF UNIFICATION OF THE LAWS OF SCIENCE

I am choosing the analogy of the ideal gas law, which most readers will have encountered at some time in their elementary physics or chemistry courses. Let us consider the experiment represented by Figure 1.3. A quantity of gas is contained within a cylinder. The gas can be compressed by driving a piston inward or rarefied by pulling the piston outward. No molecules of gas can escape from the cylinder. The ideal gas law (or Boyle–Gay-Lussac law) states that

$$PV = nRT, \tag{1.1}$$

where $P$ is the pressure of the gas, $V$ is the volume it occupies, $n$ is the number of moles of gas, $R$ is the gas constant, and $T$ the absolute

FIGURE 1.3    A quantity of gas contained within a cylinder. A piston serves to compress or decompress the gas, but no molecules can escape.

temperature. Let us confine the discussion to a single mole of gas in order to simplify the equation.

Consider, now, three simple experiments that we can perform on the gas. Each experiment will involve studies on the three state variables, $P$, $V$, and $T$.

In the first experiment we maintain the volume of the gas at a constant value (by fixing the piston in place), and we study the manner in which pressure changes with temperature. From Equation (1.1) we obtain

$$P \propto T, \tag{1.2}$$

pressure varies directly with temperature (Figure 1.4), which we recognize as Charles' law.

In the second experiment, we hold the temperature of the gas at a constant value, and we study how pressure changes with volume. From Equation (1.1),

$$P \propto 1/V, \tag{1.3}$$

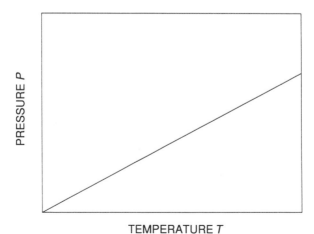

FIGURE 1.4    Charles' law for an ideal gas. Pressure varies with absolute temperature when volume is held constant.

pressure varies inversely with volume, which we recognize as Boyle's law.

In the third experiment, we again hold volume constant, but now we proceed somewhat differently. Recalling that $n = 1$, we differentiate Equation (1.1) with respect to $P$:

$$\frac{dT}{dP} = \frac{V}{R}.$$

Representing the differentials, $dP$ and $dT$, by their respective finite differences,

$$\Delta T = \frac{V}{R} \Delta P.$$

Finally, dividing by $T$, we obtain

$$\frac{\Delta T}{T} = \left( \frac{V}{R} \Delta P \right) \frac{1}{T},$$

or

$$\frac{\Delta T}{T} \propto \frac{1}{T}. \tag{1.4}$$

That is, suppose that we conduct an experiment in which volume is held constant and pressure is changed by a small, but always constant amount, $\Delta P$. Then the fractional change in temperature, $\Delta T/T$, will, by Equation (1.4), vary inversely with $T$, as shown in Figure 1.5.

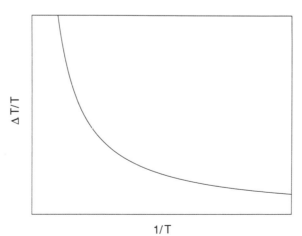

FIGURE 1.5   The volume of an ideal gas is held constant. When pressure is changed by a fixed amount, $\Delta P$, the fractional change in temperature, $\Delta T/T$, varies inversely with temperature, $T$.

Three experiments; three variables. The reason for selecting these particular experiments is that they can be considered as analogs of certain well-known psychophysical experiments: the demonstration of the "law of sensation," of the principle of adaptation, and of the Weber fraction, respectively. We shall deal with the psychophysical experiments in Chapter 3, but, for the moment, let us fix our attention on the analogs. They illustrate some valuable lessons.

## Unification

The first thing to observe is that the single, parent equation, $PV = RT$ ($n = 1$), embraces all three types of experiment: $P \propto T$, $P \propto 1/V$, and $\Delta T/T \propto 1/T$. Knowledge of the parent equation permits us to derive each of the three daughter equations and hence, to predict the results of each of the three types of experiment. Not only does it predict the results of the three selected experiments, but, presumably, of all the experiments ever performed and of all the experiments that ever *will* be performed (within certain limits) involving the variables $P$, $V$, and $T$. That is, the parent or master equation is a great unifying concept.

## Physical Insight

The equation $PV = RT$ might have carried out its unifying function even if it had remained an empirical equation: a rule that just happened to work. However, with the advent of the branch of physics called *kinetic theory*, it became possible to *derive* this equation from the assumed kinetic properties of molecules. The emergence of $PV = RT$ from the kinetic theory of molecules enhanced confidence in the molecular model of matter that was still debated at the beginning of the twentieth century. Thus, the ability to derive a master or unifying equation from a mathematical model of a physical system builds confidence in the veracity of the model.

## Conservation Laws

The derivation of $PV = RT$ from kinetic theory was even more re-markable because of an extraordinary feature of this derivation. The derivation does not in any way require knowledge of the intermolecular forces or even of the volume occupied by a molecule. It requires only laws of the conservation or balance type; namely, the conservation of mass (or particles) in a closed chamber and the conservation of energy in an elastic collision when the gas is in thermal equilibrium. These conservation laws, coupled with the Newtonian concept of force as rate of change of momentum and the principle of equipartition of energy, permit the derivation[3] of $PV = RT$. Detailed knowledge of the intermolecular forces is not needed for the argument.

## LAWS OF CONSERVATION AND LAWS OF MECHANISM

When the nature of the forces between molecules became known, our understanding of gas dynamics was, of course, enhanced. Our model of the gaseous state would not be complete if it did not contain provision for both elements: *conservation* or balance laws and *mechanistic* laws governing forces. These two types of law are complementary; they work together. There is absolutely no antagonism between them.

To underscore the complementary nature of laws of conservation and of mechanism, I offer a further example. Suppose that some chemical reaction is depicted as follows:

$$\text{reagents} \rightarrow \text{products}.$$

Without knowing any details of the mechanism of the reaction, we can invoke the law of conservation of mass, which states that (in the absence of nuclear reactions)

$$\text{total mass of reagents} = \text{total mass of products}$$

If, at a later time, we come to understand the mechanism or explicit form of the reaction, we can write,

$$A + B \rightarrow C + D$$
$$\text{reagents} \rightarrow \text{products}.$$

We then understand the reaction explicitly, in terms of specified molecular components, but we shall not, in the process, have invalidated the law of conservation of mass. The law of conservation *required* a corresponding law of mechanism to complete the picture; the two laws work together.

Why am I dwelling on the relationship between these two types of law? This becomes clearer as we move forward. We derive, in later chapters, a master or parent equation for the process of sensation. This master or parent law, from which we derive, and therefore unify, many of the laws of sensation and perception, is a law of the conservation type. It states, effectively, that the information content of a stimulus is relayed, with negligible loss, to the sensory receptor and thence to the brain. That is, it is an equation of information balance. It must be understood clearly that this law of conservation,

$$\text{information of stimulus} = \text{information relayed to brain},$$

does not in any way concern mechanism. That is, one must still work toward understanding the mechanism of operation of the sensory receptors; but such mechanisms *complement* and do not replace the principle of information balance. Enough said.


## NOTES

1. Don't worry if these laws are unfamiliar. They will be defined in due course.
2. Neologism: psychophysical + physiological = psychophysiological.
3. Need I say that a few details have been omitted?


## REFERENCES

Berkeley, G. 1975. *Philosophical Works* (Introduction and Notes by M. R. Ayers). Dent, London.

Marr, D. 1982. *Vision*. Freeman, San Francisco.

# 2

## Perception as a Choice among Alternatives

PERCEPTION: UNDEFINED

In order to define a word, we try to express it in terms of other words whose meanings are more familiar. For example, Webster's definition of a pen is "Any instrument for writing with ink.... ." This process is fine as far as it goes, but certain words denote ideas that seem to defy expression in simpler form. Of this genre is *perception*, which Webster's approaches valiantly as "The act of perceiving; apprehension with the mind or the senses. ..." However, comprehending *mental apprehension* may be no simpler than comprehending perception itself. Coren and Ward (1989) wisely opt in favor of an operational definition: "Someone who is interested in the study of perception is interested in our conscious experience of objects and object relationships." So if we understand what is meant by consciousness we can infer the meaning of perception. The difficulty in definition does not in any way deter us from using the word. The noun perception seems to be growing in popularity, particularly among journalists. Have you noticed how frequently you hear of "a growing perception of ..." or "my perception of the situation is that ... "? I must admit that despite the plethora of books on the subject, and the unquestioned erudition of their authors, I often introduce perception to my students using exactly the same example my grade 2 teacher, Jenny Snider, used for me when I was 7 years old.

"My friend asked me the time," she told me, "and I looked at my watch."

"So what is the time?" reiterated her friend.

"Oh!" replied my teacher. "I looked at my watch, but I didn't perceive the time!"

Although she had *mentally apprehended* her watch, and was definitely *conscious* of having done so, she nonetheless, had not *perceived* the time.

So, definitions set aside, what is the salient feature of perception? What characterizes this form of human activity? Does it lie uniquely within the province of the sciences of physiology and psychology? Is it shared by animals? Can we build automata, robots, that will also partake in this activity?

I am going to argue that the crux of the process of perception was appreciated by the ancients; that perception can be treated as legitimately by physics as by psychology; that animals perceive; and that if we construct our robots with sensory systems embracing both active and passive components (to be discussed later), these robots will, in principle, be able to perceive.

Let's start with the ancients—at least with the ancient Romans. I was miffed, a few years ago, when I learned from the Department of Classics at the University of Toronto that the Roman-in-the-street would not likely have said "percipio" if he or she meant "I perceive" (I had dutifully ferreted this out of a Latin dictionary), but rather "intellego." Wherefore intellego? Well, etymologically the word is made up of two simpler Latin words: *inter* meaning *between* and *lego* meaning *I choose* or *gather*. To *perceive* was, then, *to choose between* alternatives.

I like it: *To choose between*. I like it because it codifies what I believe is a fundamental concept underlying and unifying perceptual phenomena: making a choice among alternatives. For example, if you perceive that the color is blue, you have chosen blue from among other possible colors: red, orange, green . . . . If Mrs. Snider had perceived that it was 10 o'clock, then she had selected 10 from among the possibilities 1 through 12. When she looked at her watch without making this selection, she, of course, failed to perceive the time. When the TV anchorperson remarked that there was a perception among meteorologists that a global greenhouse (warming) effect was imminent, the implication was that "greenhouse" was selected from among at least the possibilities "greenhouse," "icehouse," or "no effect."

Perception involves a selection from among alternatives, but this property of perception does not, in itself, involve the idea of consciousness. For example, a simple Meccano model might select long metal strips from among an assortment of long and short strips, but we would be hard pressed to attribute to it any form of consciousness. We shall do the best we can with the concept of consciousness as the theory unfolds.

Perception, as an *intellego* activity, implies something important. It implies that the *percept* (which we shall take to mean *that which is perceived*) must always be found among a set of alternatives contained within the memory of the perceiving system. Thus, for example, if I perceive that an apple is large, it is because I retain in my memory a record of apples of various sizes, and I can make the selection of "large" from among them.[1] Since perception is dependent on the memories of the perceiving system, it follows that if different perceiving systems have different memories, they will perceive differently. Within the sphere of the very simple stimuli that we shall be considering, it means, for example, that a sensory system for perceiving the brightness of light can perceive only those levels of brightness that are contained within its "memory." It is certainly tempting to ask: Well, how did one perceive these aboriginal brightnesses? In this matter, I again beg the reader's patience. We shall return to this question in due course.

As a consequence of the above, we can say that perception is *relative* to the memory of the perceiving system. Perception is, therefore, *relative* intellego in nature: intellego insofar as it chooses among alternative and relative in that it depends on the state of the perceiving system.

We should also observe that the intellego concept allows for approximate perception. That is, you might select not just one member of a set of alternatives but several members. For example, you might perceive that a color is either orange or red (but not green or blue), and I may perceive that your age lies between 35 and 40 (but you are definitely not a teenager). Perception can, therefore, denote a reduction in the number of alternatives without arriving at a unique remaining possibility.

## INFORMATION: DEFINED

We are all familiar with the term "information" in the semantic or verbal sense. For example: The newspaper contains a lot of information. Or: I lack the information needed to reach a destination. However, the term information is usually assigned a meaning in the generic sense, which removes it from any particular context. Following the seminal work by Shannon (1948) and by Wiener (1948), information is defined as a reduction in uncertainty. Suppose that an event may occur in one of many ways; that is, it has many possible outcomes. We might say that we are *uncertain* about the outcome. For example, if a coin is tossed, it can fall heads or tails, so that there is some momentary uncertainty about the outcome. After the outcome is known, the uncertainty vanishes, or is resolved, and the perceiver[2] of the event receives a quantity of information equal to the vanished uncertainty. *Information theory* provides a way of quantifying the initial uncertainty and, therefore, quantifying the information received. The uncertainty preceding the occurrence of an event is usually termed *entropy*, so that the quantity of information received is equal to the reduction in entropy. One must be careful not to confuse this type of entropy, which is information theoretical entropy, with *physical* or *thermodynamic entropy*, a quantity used extensively in physics and chemistry.[3] While there is a relationship between the two entropies, which we explore later on, the entropy used in this book is generally of the information theoretical type. The symbol $H$ designates entropy.

In the coin-tossing example, there were only two possible outcomes but, in general, an event *with discrete outcomes* can have $x$ possible outcomes, where $x$ is a positive integer.[4] Suppose that the probability of the $i$th possible outcome is $p_i$. Then entropy, $H$, is defined by the equation

$$H = - \sum_{i=1}^{x} p_i \log p_i. \tag{2.1}$$

That is, $H$ is composed of a weighted sum of the logarithms of the probabilities of the outcomes. The base of the logarithms used is arbitrary. We shall generally use natural logarithms (ln), logarithms to the base $e$, because natural logs are simpler to deal with in many mathematical operations. The "unit" of $H$ will be the *natural unit*. When logarithms to the base 2 are used, the unit of $H$ becomes the *bit*. It is a simple matter to convert from one unit to another[5]:

$$\text{bits} = \text{natural units}/\ln 2. \tag{2.2}$$

Therefore, when entropy, $H$, is reduced totally, that is, when one of the $x$ outcomes is perceived to occur, the amount of information, $\mathscr{I}$, that is received is given simply by

$$\mathscr{I} = H. \tag{2.3}$$

To take a simple example, if the event is the selection of one card from a shuffled deck of 52, the probabilities $p_i$ are all equal to $1/52$ so that

$$H = -(1/52)\log(1/52) \cdots -(1/52)\log(1/52)$$
$$= -52/52 \log(1/52) = \log 52.$$

If we use natural logs, $H = \ln 52 = 3.95$ natural units $= 3.95/\ln 2$ or 5.70 bits of information. From this example we can infer the general theorem that the entropy of an event with $x$ outcomes, all of which are equally probable, is equal to $\log x$.

It is, of course, possible that there is some interfering factor that prevents the perceiver from determining the outcome of an event with complete certainty and, therefore, the number of possible outcomes may not be reduced to one, single possibility. That is, some residual uncertainty may remain. For example, the event may be hearing a spoken numeral between 1 and 9. Suppose that each of the 10 possible numerals are equally probable so that (analogous to the playing card example above) the entropy equals $\log 10$. However, the spoken words "five" and "nine" are easily confused, so it may be that even after the event has occurred (the spoken numeral is heard) there is still some residual uncertainty about whether it was "five" or "nine." The entropy has been reduced from $\log 10$ to $\log 2$, but not to $\log 1 = 0$. In this case, $\mathscr{I} < H$: the transmitted information is less than the total original entropy (Brillouin, 1964).

Note also the dependence of information receipt, $\mathscr{I}$, on the set of values of the *a priori* probabilities, $p_i$. Different values for $p_i$ will give rise to quite different values for $\mathscr{I}$. For example, suppose I toss a coin that you think is a fair coin with equal probabilities for head and tail, but that I know is biased. I know, from the manner in which the coin was constructed, that it will fall heads on $2/3$ of the tosses and tails on only $1/3$ of the tosses. Then

$$H_{\text{you}} = -(1/2)\log(1/2) - (1/2)\log(1/2) = 1 \text{ bit},$$

while

$$H_{\text{me}} = -(2/3)\log(2/3) - (1/3)\log(1/3) = 0.92 \text{ bit}.$$

I have received less information than you have although we both perceived the outcome of the same event. The reason why I received *less* information is not as important as the fact that we received *different amounts*. Our respective previous life experiences have determined our value for the *a priori* probabilities and, hence, for the received information. Received information is, in this respect, not an absolute quantity.

The reader may already have appreciated the parallelism between the concept of relative intellego perception and that of information by entropy reduction, which is the subject of the next section.


## INFORMATION AND PERCEPTION

The relative intellego nature of perception, as we have seen, implies that perception involves a selection of one or several choices from among many and that the choices available depend upon the history and memory of the perceiving system. We have also learned that a measure of information is obtained by making a selection of one or several possible outcomes of an event from among many possible outcomes and that the quantity of information is calculated from the *a priori* probabilities, which are, in turn, dependent upon the history and memory of the recipient of the information. From this parallelism it may be seen that information theory provides a natural means to measure the "quantity" or "amount" of perception. Let's take a few examples. On a macroscopic scale, if I perceive that you are wearing your brown jacket (from your wardrobe of two, equally worn jackets) my percept is "worth" $\log_2 2$, or one bit of information, while if I perceive that you are wearing your green tie from your holdings of 8, equally worn ties, my percept is "worth" $\log_2 8$, or three bits of information (the selections are assumed independent since you are an academic and are, therefore, unlikely to match tie with jacket). In order to apply this idea at the microscopic scale of perception at this stage in our development of information theory, let us pretend that for some hypothetical creature, light intensity is perceived only in discrete levels: intensity level 1 (lowest level), intensity level 2 (a little more intense), ... intensity level $x$ (most intense possible level). For a particular percept, the probabilities of the respective light intensity levels are known to be $p_1, p_2, \ldots, p_x$. Then the quantity of information associated with the percept of exactly one of these intensity levels is equal to $-p_1 \log p_1 - p_2 \log p_2 \ldots -p_x \log p_x$. Information theory is a natural means of quantifying a percept.

We should note in passing that one can also quantify an approximate percept. Continuing the example of light intensities, let us suppose that there were originally 10 identifiable light intensity categories, so that the uncertainty before the act of perception is given by

$$H_{\text{before}} = -\sum_{i=1}^{10} p_i \log p_i.$$

If, just for convenience of discussion, all the $p_i$ were equal, then

$$H_{\text{before}} = \log 10.$$

Suppose, now, that the process of perception serves to reduce the number of intensity categories to three rather that to a single category, and that the three are equally probable. Then

$$H_{\text{after}} = \log 3.$$

That is, information received, $\mathscr{I}$, is given by

$$\mathscr{I} = H_{\text{before}} - H_{\text{after}}$$
$$= \log 10 - \log 3. \tag{2.4}$$

In all cases, information received is relative to the number of intensity categories and their respective *a priori* probabilities.

The above example does not indicate exactly the manner in which we shall be carrying out calculations later on, but it does introduce the general idea.

We might observe, at this point, that information theory also provides a natural means of quantifying what might be called "quantum perception." In quantum physics, the anticipation of a measurement is associated with a wavefunction, which is a mathematical construct representing a number of possible outcomes to the measurement. Each possible outcome can be assigned a probability. When the measurement is actually made, the wavefunction "collapses," leaving only a single possihility. In this respect, it can be seen that one could assign an information content to the quantum measure.

Suppose that a quantum system consists of a *mixture* of two possible states, which we can designate as $|\psi_1\rangle$ and $|\psi_2\rangle$. A measurement performed on the system will disclose one or other of the two states. The probability of $|\psi_1\rangle$ is $p_1$ and the probability of $|\psi_2\rangle$ is $p_2$. The information content of this percept is then

$$\mathscr{I} = -p_1 \log p_1 - p_2 \log p_2. \tag{2.5}$$

A *superposition* of quantum states (vis-à-vis a mixture) will give rise to a more complicated set of probabilities, but the principle is the same. Quantum mechanical perception (usually called "observation") can be seen to be an instance of what we have called intellego perception, the selection of one from several possibilities.


## THE GIST OF THE ENTROPIC THEORY OF PERCEPTION

Hitherto, we have made no biological commitment. We have calculated H-functions for various simple perceptual situations, but we have not yet related the entropy, $H$, to any biological function. In the example of light intensity explored above, we calculated that $\log 10 - \log 3$ units of information were gained in the process of perception; but we have not specified any significance of this information to the perceiving organism. Indeed, why *should* there be any significance? I argue in various ways throughout this book that there is a great deal of biological significance.

The fundamental equation put forward is

$$F = kH, \tag{2.6}$$

where $k$ is a constant, greater than zero, and $F$ is a *perceptual variable*. An example of $F$, albeit not one of which I am overly fond, is the subjective magnitude of a stimulus. Drawing again upon the example of perception of light intensities, the physical intensity of a steady light source could be measured in watts (leaving aside more complex photometric units). From the physical intensity we can calculate, in the manner shown above, the value of the entropy, $H$. Multiplying $H$ by a constant, we obtain $F$, which is the subjective magnitude of the light stimulus, or simply the *brightness* of the light. The value of the constant, $k$, is determined by the scale on which the investigator wishes to measure brightness.

Just to render the idea a little more concrete, let us take a numerical example. Let's continue to suppose that some organism can perceive only discrete intensities of light, rather than a continuum of intensities as we human beings can. Suppose that after a brief exposure to a light stimulus, the organism can determine that the *intensity* of the light, that is the power of the light source, is one of 30, 40, or 50 watts, with equal probabilities of $1/3$ assigned to each. Its perceptual entropy or uncertainty, as obtained from Equation (2.1), is equal to $\log_2 3 = 1.58$ bits. Suppose that a scale of brightness is set up with $k = 1$. Since $F = kH$ from Equation (2.6), the brightness of the source would be equal to $1 \times \log_2 3 = 1.58$ scale units. Undoubtedly, this calculation will raise a number of questions in the mind of the thoughtful reader,[6] but let's give the ideas time to unfold naturally.

While this example does capture the gist of the idea that will be developed, the restriction of light sensitivity to discrete values is artificial, and the reader should resist comparing the result with the well-known laws of human sensation that apply to continuously variable stimuli.

A second example of a perceptual variable, $F$, is the impulse rate, or the rate at which action potentials propagate, in a primary sensory afferent neuron. Imagine a single light detector dissected out of the retina of an animal, still attached to its sensory neuron. For example, a single omatidium from the eye of the *Limulus* crab was investigated some years ago by Hartline and Graham (1932). The investigator can then stimulate the photoreceptor *in vivo* and measure the frequency of action potentials (electrical spikes) that propagate down the attached primary sensory neuron (nerve fiber). From the physical intensity of the stimulating light we are able to calculate the value of the entropy, $H$ (although we have not yet described explicitly how this can be done) and equate this value to a constant, $k$, multiplied by the impulse frequency, $F$. So, for example, if $H = 3$ bits and $k = 10$ [impulses $\cdot$ s$^{-1}$bit$^{-1}$], the impulse frequency, $F = kH = 30$ impulses or action potentials per second. The key is, of course, to be able to evalaute $H$ for continuously distributed light signals.

We have now carried the idea of the previous section one step further. In the previous section, we showed that a percept could be quantified using information theory. In this section we can begin to understand the psychophysical (e.g., brightness) and physiological (e.g., impulse rate) impact of the quantified percept on the biological organism. Brain and neuron respond "in proportion to" the entropy of the stimulus.

Equation (2.6), $F = kH$, is a conjecture which we explore in some depth. Its origins and justification have to await the final chapters of the book, but where does this equation lead? We shall see that it leads toward the unification of the "laws" of sensation. That is, it permits us to derive from a single equation many of the empirical laws of sensation, such as Fechner's and Weber's laws. It also permits us to make a number of predictions—some of them rather unexpected—about the behavior of the senses. It provides some critical links between biology and physics, and may even provide some insights into the form and meaning of some of the laws of physics. Parenthetically, it also has something to say about practical matters, such as the construction of cochlear implants for the hearing impaired. However, most important in my opinion, $F = kH$

codifies the manner in which the brain and central nervous system apprehend the "external world." In the generally held world view (recall D. Marr's remarks), the brain serves essentially to encode and discriminate "that which is out there." $F = kH$, however, casts doubt on that rather simple view. $F$ is, in fact, the sensory language of the brain; it encodes the electrical signals that are carried from the sensory receptors to the brain. $H$, however, is not just a mathematical transcription of elements of the external world. If it were, we would, indeed, have a Marr world view, because the brain picture, $F$, would just be a map of the external world picture, $H$. The mapping process external → brain would represent a completely objective process. However, $H$ is an *uncertainty*; it reflects not what the world *is*, but rather what the sensory receptors *think* the world is. $F = kH$ implies that we only perceive those aspects of the external world that do not conform to our expectation and, hence, of which we are uncertain. Moreover, and most startling, when our uncertainty vanishes ($H = 0$), so do our perceptions ($F = 0$).

I recognize that a lot of ideas have been introduced in this chapter, and rather succinctly. Before exploring these ideas further, I recommend that we take a one-chapter digression to discuss certain aspects of the experimental investigations of sensation and perception. We pick up the thread of $F = kH$ again in later chapters. The reader for whom *information theoretical entropy* is a new concept might like to peruse a primer on the subject before proceeding, or to read about and beyond the subject from an expert like J. R. Pierce (1980).

## NOTES

1. Let us ignore the case where I observe an "apple" that is larger than any apple I have ever seen before and I must decide if it is really an exceptional specimen of the apple species or some other kind of fruit. Such considerations would take us too far afield.
2. I have used the word "perceiver" without yet justifying it, but the reader may realize immediately why I have done so.
3. I like Peters' term, *intropy*, for *in*formation *t*heoretical ent*ropy* (Peters, 1975).
4. We later consider events whose outcomes lie on a continuum, such as the intensity of a sound; but for the moment we deal only with those events that have discrete outcomes, such as the roll of a die, whose outcome may be simply one of 1, 2, 3, 4, 5, or 6.
5. To convert $H$ from units calculated in logs base $a$ to units calculated in logs base $b$, we use the algebraic identity

$$\log_a y = \log_b y / \log_b a .$$

(Think of the mnemonic: $y/a = (y/b)/(a/b)$. Therefore, $\log_2 y = \log_e y/\log_e 2$.

6. In the matter of the hypothetical organism that can perceive only discrete intensities of light,

$$F = kH$$

with $k = 1$ becomes

$$F(\text{brightness}) = H(\text{entropy or uncertainty}).$$

Therefore, after a brief exposure of $t_0$ seconds to a light stimulus, the organism's photoreception system retains the uncertainty of three possible discrete light intensities: 30, 40, or 50 watts, each intensity associated with a probability of $1/3$. Therefore,

$$F = H = \log_2 3 = 1.58 \text{ "bits" of brightness.}$$

After a little thought, however, the reader may conclude that this process is patently wrong. After all, it is possible that a second stimulus will be less intense, and after the $t_0$ seconds of exposure, the organism's photoreception system will again experience the uncertainty of three discrete light intensities: this time 10, 20, and 30 watts. Again we would have

$$F = H = \log_2 3 = 1.58 \text{ bits of brightness.}$$

That is, the less-intense light stimulus would appear equally as bright as the more-intense stimulus, which is counterintuitive. Indeed, when we turn again in Chapter 16, to the hypothetical case of an organism which can perceive only discrete intensities, we tolerate the consequence within the entropy theory that all stimuli appear equally bright. However, at the present stage in our study, we attempt to avoid this strange result by not probing too deeply. Resolution of this paradox, at least superficially, is found in what has been called the "Fullerton–Cattell law," an empirical law cited by G. S. Fullerton and J. McK. Cattell in 1892: "The error of observation tends to increase as the square root of the magnitude, the increase being subject to variation whose amount and cause must be determined for each special case." The law was generalized by Guilford (1932) to read (using our symbols)

$$\Delta I = kI^n,$$

where $I$ is the intensity of the light stimulus, and $\Delta I$ is the magnitude of the uncertainty after $t_0$ seconds. $k$ and $n$ are constants that are greater than zero. That is, the range of observable stimulus intensities increases with the $n$th power of the mean intensity. As applied to our problem, suppose that the sensory receptor takes several samples of its stimulus. We apply Guilford's law to mean that the range of light intensities, $\Delta I$, recorded by the receptor for the smaller stimulus is smaller than the range of light intensities recorded for the larger stimulus. Since the larger stimulus left the photoreceptor system with an uncertainty of three light intensities, the smaller stimulus would leave the receptor with an uncertainty of two light intensities, say 10 and 20 watts, or even with the certain result of a single intensity. Therefore, for the less intense light stimulus,

$$F = H = \log_2 2 = 1 \text{ bit of brightness},$$

or

$$F = H = \log 1 = 0 \text{ (imperceptible stimulus)}.$$

*That is, the greater stimulus appeared brighter than the smaller stimulus, not directly because it was more intense, but because it engendered greater entropy or uncertainty at the level of the photoreceptor system.* Applying Guilford's law inappropriately, as we have done above, to an isolated sensory receptor is a teaching device only. This law is derived later, in effect, when we come to treat the Weber fraction theoretically.

## REFERENCES

Brillouin, L. 1964. *Science, Uncertainty and Information.* Academic Press, New York.

Coren, S., and Ward L. M. 1989. *Sensation and Perception*, 3rd ed. Harcourt, Brace, Jovanovich, San Diego.

Guilford, J. P. 1932. A generalized psychophysical law. *Psychological Review* **39**, 73–85.

Hartline, H. K., and Graham, C. H. 1932. Nerve impulses from single receptors in the eye. *Journal of Cellular and Comparative Physiology*, **1**, 277–295.

Peters, J. 1975. Entropy and information: Conformities and controversies. In *Entropy and Information in Science and Philosophy* (L. Kubá and J. Zeman, Eds.) Elsevier, Amsterdam.

Pierce, J. R. 1980. *An Introduction to Information Theory: Symbols, Signals and Noise*, 2nd ed., Dover, New York.

Shannon, C. E. 1948. A mathematical theory of communication. *Bell System Technical Journal* **27**, 379–423.

Slepian, D., Ed. 1974. *Key Papers in the Development of Information Theory.* IEEE Press, New York. (Note: All the papers of Shannon referenced in this book can be found conveniently bound together in this book.)

Wiener, N. 1948. *Cybernetics.* The Technology Press, MIT, Cambridge, MA.

# 3

# The Empirical Laws
# of Sensation
# and Perception

In this chapter, we set down the weighty ballast of philosophy and information theory and examine the somewhat lighter matter of the empirical rules of sensation and perception. By *empirical* laws we mean (Webster's dictionary) laws "making use of, or based on, experience, trial and error, or experiment, rather than theory or systematized knowledge." For somewhat more than 100 years, beginning (probably) with the work of Weber, empirical laws of sensation have been formulated. These algebraic rules, based essentially on laboratory observations, relating only occasionally to each other, and not derived theoretically from laws in other sciences, have dominated the scientific literature. Each empirical law stands as a universe unto itself: it neither is derived from any simpler principle nor leads to the generation of other laws. Each law has absolute dominion over its own territory. Such is the state of scientific polytheism that we now describe.

The reason for introducing these laws early in the book is that they provide, so to speak, grist for the mill. We shall endeavor, as the informational theory of sensation is developed, to provide theoretical derivations for all of these empirical laws. It is probably better to introduce them earlier and in a group, rather than later as they are invoked.

Some of the empirical laws carry the names of their originator; some, such as "the exponential decay" of this or that quantity are just rules of thumb. We are not concerned with all of these rules, but only a subset of them. In particular, we shall be interested in those empirical laws that govern the relationship between three fundamental variables: $I$, the steady intensity of a stimulus; $t$, the time since onset of the stimulus, or, occasionally, the duration of this stimulus; and $F$, the perceptual variable related to the stimulus. $F$, you will recall, was defined in Chapter 2. As mentioned in the Introduction to Chapter 1, all stimuli with which we shall be concerned here are steady, or constant stimuli, given in the form of a step function (Figure 1.1). While stimuli that vary with time are of very definite interest, for example those that may vary sinusoidally, their formal treatment is more difficult within this informational or entropic theory, and such progress as has been made with these stimuli is not reported here. Neither do we grapple with the effects of multiple stimuli that are applied concurrently. So we do not deal, for example, with the sweetness of a solution of two types of sugar or with the effect of a masking sound on a pure tone.

With these restrictions in mind, let us examine eight types of experiment performed by physiologists, psychologists, and physicists that give rise to well-known empirical equations of sensation. In each case in which the perceptual variable, $F$, occurs, recall from Chapter 2 that it can be interpreted both psychophysically, as a subjective magnitude (e.g., brightness), and physiologically, as a rate of impulse propagation in a neuron. In Chapter 13, we begin to distinguish mathematically between these two interpretations.

## THE LAW OF SENSATION

When $F$ is interpreted psychophysically, this law is sometimes referred to as "the psychophysical law".

Ernst Heinrich Weber (1795–1878) (pronounce Vay'ber) was a German physiologist who was professor of anatomy and later of physiology at Leipzig (Gregory and Zangwill, 1987). He drew attention to the ratio $\Delta I/I$, where $\Delta I$ is the smallest difference between two stimulus intensities that can be discriminated. Wrote Weber (in translation)[1]: "...in observing the difference between two magnitudes, what we perceive is the ratio of the difference to the magnitudes compared" (Drever, 1952). Together with Fechner, he asserted, after much experimentation on lifting weights,

$$\Delta I/I = \text{constant}, \tag{3.1}$$

where the constant is known as *Weber's constant*. We call the empirical law (3.1) "Weber's law".

Gustav Theodor Fechner (1801–1887) (pronounce Fech'-ner, ch as in loch) was a German physicist who is remembered largely for his work *Elemente der Psychophysik* (1860). Fechner augmented Equation (3.1) by equating the constant on the right-hand side with $\Delta F$, a just noticeable difference in sensation (the $F$ is my symbol, not Fechner's). More specifically, the equation attributed to him is

$$\Delta I/I = \Delta F/a, \tag{3.2}$$

where both $a$ and $\Delta F$ are constants. Implicit in Equation (3.2) is that a variable, $F$, can legitimately be defined to quantify human sensation or feeling. Assigning numerical measure to a sensation is rather an audacious suggestion. Equation (3.2) then asserts that if the physical magnitude of a stimulus is changed by $\Delta I$, where $\Delta I$ is the smallest change detectable by a human subject, then the corresponding change in sensation, $\Delta F$, will always be constant. The just noticeable difference is abbreviated to jnd. Fechner's argument is often stated as follows.

If $\Delta I$ and $\Delta F$ are small changes in $I$ and $F$, respectively, they may be replaced in Equation (3.2) by $dI$ and $dF$, respectively.

$$dI/I = dF/a. \tag{3.3}$$

Integrating both sides of Equation (3.3),

$$F = a \ln I + b, \qquad b \text{ constant}, \tag{3.4}$$

or

$$F = a' \log I + b, \tag{3.4a}$$

where $a'$ is constant and the logarithm may be taken to any convenient base, say 10. That is, when $F$ is plotted against the logarithm of $I$, the result expected is a straight line. This is *Fechner's law*, or the *Weber–Fechner law*. A discussion of "Fechnerian integration" and related topics is given by Baird and Noma (1978, Chap. 4). The problem of measuring the quantity, $F$, is very taxing and has occupied psychophysicists for many years. This problem is discussed in an introductory manner by Coren and Ward (1989) and in more detail by Baird and Noma (1978). More about early attempts to quantify sensation, and about the legitimacy of Fechnerian integration, is given in the first chapter of Marks' book (1974).

The result of Fechner's law is that if "suitable" measure for $F$ can be found, a graph of $F$ against the logarithm of $I$ (to any base) is expected to produce a straight line. That is, for a given modality, plotting experimental values of $F$ against the corresponding values for the logarithm of $I$ should give the result that the data points lie on a straight line whose slope is $a'$ and whose $y$-intercept is $b$. Fechner's law might be called a *semilogarithmic law*, because data array linearly when $F$ is plotted on a linear scale while $I$ is plotted on a logarithmic scale. There are many examples in the published literature of measured data that conform to Fechner's law.

While $F$ was interpreted psychophysically by Fechner, we recall again from Chapter 2 that $F$ may also be interpreted neurophysiologically as the frequency of impulses in a sensory neuron. In the well-known paper by Hartline and Graham (1932) also cited in Chapter 2, a single light receptor (omatidium) from the horseshoe crab (*Limulus*) was dissected out together with its primary afferent neuron. The receptor could be stimulated with light of varying intensity, $I$, and the resulting impulse frequency, $F$, in the attached neuron, measured. The authors showed that Fechner's law was obeyed. There is evidence, therefore, that Fechner's law, a form of the law of sensation is valid to a degree using either interpretation of the perceptual variable, $F$.

Plateau was a Belgian physicist, contemporary with Fechner. He is often given credit for conceiving the *power law of sensation*, an alternative to the semilogarithmic law of Fechner (Plateau, 1872). This power law is given explicitly by Equation (3.7) below. F. Brentano (1874) attempted to derive this power law beginning from Weber's law. In the twentieth century, this power law of sensation found its most enthusiastic exponent in the person of S. S. Stevens. While I did state above, admittedly, that each of these empirical laws remained independent of all other such laws, there have, nonetheless, been attempts made over the years to link them together. I think that these attempts at deriving the laws are laudable and I present some of them in these pages. Usually, however, it was found necessary to add *other* empirical relations in order to complete the derivation.

The derivation of the Plateau–Brentano–Stevens power law of sensation beginning from Weber's law is attributed to Brentano (Stevens, 1961) and proceeds as follows. Suppose that the physical magnitude of the stimulus, $I$, and the subjective magnitude of the stimulus, $F$, both obey Weber's law. Then from Equation (3.1),

$$\Delta I/I = c_1,$$

and

$$\Delta F/F = c_2,$$

where $c_1$ and $c_2$ are both constants. Then by combining these equations,

$$\Delta I/I = (1/n)\Delta F/F, \tag{3.5}$$

where $n = c_2/c_1$. Equations (3.1) and (3.5) are, of course, quite different. Again replacing the finite differences by their corresponding differentials,

$$dI/I = (1/n)dF/F.$$

Assuming the legitimacy of Fechnerian integration, we obtain

$$\ln F = n \ln I + \ln k, \tag{3.6}$$

where $\ln k$ is a constant of integration. This equation can be converted immediately into the form

$$F = kI^n. \tag{3.7}$$

This power law of sensation stands in contrast to Fechner's semilogarithmic law. It is important to observe that by taking logarithms *to any base* of both sides of Equation (3.7) we obtain

$$\log F = n \log I + B, \qquad (3.8)$$

where $B$ is constant. That is, the Plateau–Brentano–Stevens law might be described as a *full logarithmic law* (cf. Fechner's semilogarithmic law) because data are expected to array themselves along a straight line when both $F$ and $I$ are plotted on logarithmic scales. The slope of this straight line is the power function exponent, $n$.

Many modalities of sensation have been analyzed by means of the power law (3.7), and characteristic values of the exponent, $n$ (or rather, characteristic ranges of values for $n$), have been tabulated for each modality. For example, for the intensity of sound, $n \simeq 0.3$ for tones of 1000 Hz. For a complete list of exponents governing the various modalities the reader is referred to the texts, such as Coren and Ward (1989). Stevens spent many years demonstrating that when $F$ was measured by the process of "magnitude estimation" (a free-wheeling assignment of numbers to match the magnitudes of human sensations) the power law (3.7) was the law of best fit. To capture the day, Stevens (1970) replotted the *Limulus* data of Hartline and Graham of 1932 on a log–log graph (that is, he made a full logarithmic plot rather than a semilogarithmic plot as Hartline and Graham had done), and what emerged was a straight line as impressive as that obtained by Hartline and Graham. Surely, then, the power law of sensation was "the correct" law of sensation and could lay claim to the title of the psychophysical law!

So, indeed, it may be, but feeling that Fechner might desire a posthumous reply, I played the inverse game. I selected data measured by Stevens (1969) for the sense of taste of saltiness (sodium chloride solution). Stevens had showed from a plot of the logarithm of magnitude estimation vs. the logarithm of concentration of solution that these data strongly supported the power law of sensation. In Figure 3.1 the same data are plotted in a Fechner semilogarithmic graph: magnitude estimation (not its logarithm) is plotted against the logarithm of concentration of the solution. The result is quite a decent straight line, thereby affirming Fechner's law!

*Is it possible that the two forms of the law of sensation given by Equations (3.4) and (3.8), Fechner's law and the Plateau–Brentano–Stevens law, are really mathematically equivalent over some range of I-values?* To this question we shall certainly return. In the interim, the reader interested in pursuing Fechner vs. Stevens is referred to the very scholarly review of the subject by L. Krueger (1989) or to Krueger's more condensed review (1990).

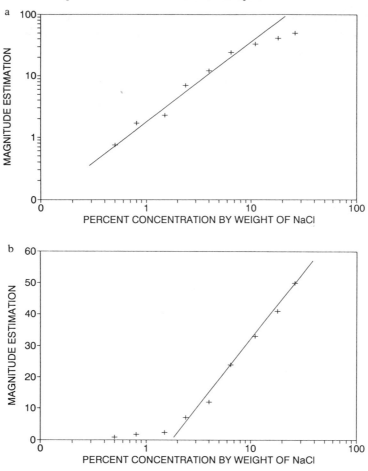

FIGURE 3.1  (a) Data from S. S. Stevens (1969). Magnitude estimation of the taste of saltiness of solutions of sodium chloride of different concentrations. In this log–log plot, the data are seen to fall nearly on a straight line, except for the two or three *most* concentrated solutions, whose magnitude estimates fall *below* the straight line. This is the type of graph preferred by Stevens. (b) The same data as shown in (a) are plotted here in a semilog plot. Note that the data again fall very nearly on a straight line, except for the two or three *least* concentrated solutions, whose magnitude estimates fall *above* the straight line. This is the type of graph preferred by Fechner.

We have been using the perceptual variable, $F$, with both the psychophysical and the physiological interpretations. In this regard, one must take note of the papers of G. Borg and his colleagues (for example, Borg *et al.*, 1967). Taking advantage of the fact that in the human being, sensory nerve fibers mediating taste from the anterior two-thirds of the surface of the tongue pass backward toward the brain in the nerve called the *chorda tympani* and that this nerve is surgically accessible as it passes through the middle ear, Borg *et al.* carried out a series of experiments. Two days before surgery was to be performed on the ear, psychophysical experiments were carried out with solutions of citric acid (sour), sodium chloride (salt), and sucrose (sweet), as well as with various other solutions. The method of magnitude estimation was used and the results were plotted on log–log scales. In this way the power function exponents were obtained as the slopes of the observed straight lines. During the course of surgery performed on the middle ear, the investigators were able to measure the electrical responses in the exposed fibers of the chorda tympani to the application of these same solutions to the surface of the tongue. These data, also, were plotted on log–log scales. The power function exponents were found to be very similar to the corresponding exponents measured in the psychophysical experiments. Therefore, Borg *et al.* demonstrated, at least for the sense of taste, the legitimacy of using the same variable, $F$, with both the psychophysical and the neurophysiological interpretations.

We cannot, of course, generalize the above conclusions to include all other sensory modalities. For example, in the case of audition, the loudness of a tone cannot be mapped onto or associated with the impulse rate in a single auditory neuron. We also see later that the time scale of neuronal events differs markedly from the time scale of psychophysical events.

We proceed, in the mathematical development that follows, as if each primary sensory afferent neuron functions independently and in parallel with all other primary sensory afferents, although we realize that this approximation cannot be taken too far. And we pretend, until Chapter 13, that subjective magnitudes always parallel the corresponding neural impulse rates as they do in the experiments of Borg *et al.* The mathematical work proceeds somewhat more fluently with these assumptions, but we understand that in the final analysis fuller recognition must be made of the distinction between psychophysics and neurophysiology. In the coming chapters, we usually treat $F$ as a psychophysical variable because the experimental data available for testing the validity of our equations are much more numerous. I do, however, confess my uneasiness with the general process of assigning numbers, subjectively, to one's sensations. I use the results of these experiments involving subjective magnitudes because, at least at the beginning of our studies, they provide a convenient way of testing the theory. As the theory develops further, however, we work with experiments in which subjective magnitude plays a lesser role or no role at all.

Finally, let me stress that in the above analysis of the law of sensation we have ignored the variable, $t$, the time since onset of the stimulus. *Time* is a poor relative in papers describing experiments on subjective magnitudes; it is a variable that is always prominent in the conduct of the experiments, but is often not reported by the investigators. We treat $t$ as a constant in these experiments. That is, we assume in all experiments that the same period of time has elapsed between the onset of the stimulus and the measurement of $F$. If this were not the case, the effects of adaptation (see below) would wreak havoc. We also assume that new stimuli have been applied only after the sensory receptor has had time to recover completely from previous stimuli; that is, we presume that the sensory receptors are "unadapted." Please note, therefore, that the law of sensation is obtained from the three cardinal variables, $F$, $I$, and $t$, by holding $t$ constant and relating $F$ to $I$.

We have also assumed tacitly, in the above discussion, that a unique algebraic form of the psychophysical law exists and governs many of the modalities of sensation. There are those who maintain that a unique psychophysical law is chimerical, that none exists. For example, Weiss (1981) argues, quite properly, that the algebraic form of any psychophysical law must depend on the manner in which the physical intensities, $I$, are measured. If we decided to measure the concentrations of odorants using the pC scale (the negative logarithm of the concentration of the odorant), then the psychophysical law, both the Fechner and the Stevens forms, would be patently wrong. Weiss is quite right. However, we show later on that there is a condition with which all measures of stimulus intensity must comply if they are to give rise to a universal psychophysical law: namely the logarithm of stimulus variance must be a linear function of the logarithm of stimulus magnitude; that is, $\sigma^2 \propto I^n$. This rule will be complied with (approximately) when concentrations of odorants or solutions are measured on linear scales, but not if they are measured on logarithmic or other scales. My reasons for affirming its existence become clearer as we proceed. We return to Weiss' objection in Chapter 10.

## ADAPTATION

The term adaptation seems to mean different things to different people. I use the term in two senses, the first of which is best introduced by example. Suppose you walk into a room dominated by the pungent odor of fresh paint, or perhaps into a kitchen enveloped by the heavy odor of cabbage cooking. In either case the odor is very prominent when you first enter the room, but weakens with time, and after a few moments may become virtually undetectable. We say that you have *adapted* to the olfactory stimulus. The phenomenon is often quite dramatic. When you first experienced the adaptation effect as a child did you not think that the stimulus itself had vanished? Certainly some adults I have spoken with still believe this to be true. "After a few minutes, the paint doesn't smell any more," a housepainter once told me. However, the stimulus is certainly still present; only our sensation of it has diminished. This type of adaptation might be called *psychophysical adaptation*.

It is important to observe that not all modalities of sensation seem to adapt, or if they do adapt, do so incompletely. The rate of adaptation may also vary considerably. Olfactory receptors, of course, do adapt and often adapt completely or *to extinction*. That is, odor simply disappears after a short period. Taste receptors adapt, but not necessarily to extinction; that is, the sweet taste from the sugar solution in your mouth may become less intense, but will not disappear completely. Temperature receptors behave in much the same fashion. Mechanoreceptors are classified by the speed with which they adapt, and their speed of adaptation specializes them as velocity receptors, vibration receptors, etc. (Schmidt, 1978). Pain receptors do adapt to some extent. As you can imagine, a lot of work has been done on this subject. However, often pain persists and the sufferer requires chemical analgesia. Light receptors may not seem to adapt under normal circumstances. For example, the page you are reading is not fading. However, when you step from a dark room into bright sunlight, you may be temporarily blinded. After a few moments, the eye does light adapt and the world seems less bright (in a very literal sense!). Of course, we do not stay adapted forever; after the stimulus has been removed for a period of time, we "de-adapt" so that, for example, we may reenjoy the scent of hydrogen sulfide gas.

The second meaning which I import to the term adaptation is *increase in threshold*. A *threshold* for sensation is the stimulus of least intensity which one can detect. Thresholds tend to increase as adaptation proceeds and to decrease as de-adaptation occurs. For example, if you wish to detect visual stimuli of very low intensity, flashes of light consisting of only a few photons, a good strategy is to remain in a very dark room for about 30 minutes. The eye de-adapts (usually referred to as *dark adaptation*) so that the retinal photodetectors called *rods* can decrease their threshold of detection. The change in light intensity threshold (*luminance threshold*), $\Delta I$, has been related to the *adapting luminance*, $I$, by Weber's law (Dowling, 1987):

$$\Delta I / I = \text{constant}. \qquad (3.1)$$

So the two meanings to be associated with adaptation are psychophysical and threshold shift. By and large, I deal with psychophysical adaptation. I regard adaptation as a phenomenon (again) involving two of the three cardinal variables. In the case of psychophysical adaptation, intensity, $I$, is held constant while the perceptual variable, $F$, changes with the time since stimulus onset, $t$. By and large, the psychophysical adaptation curve has the shape illustrated in Figure 3.2.

We recall that the law of sensation was regarded as the mathematical relationship between $F$ and $I$ with $t$ held constant. Now, taking the effects of adaptation into account, we see that for many modalities, $F$ will

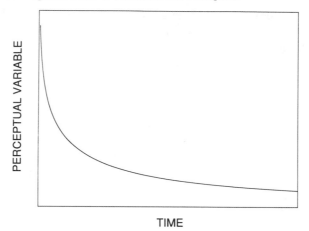

TIME

FIGURE 3.2   Psychophysical adaptation curve (schematic). A perceptual variable (e.g., magnitude estimate) declines monotonically with the time since stimulus onset. Stimulus intensity is held constant.

be smaller when $t$ is larger. Therefore, in a full logarithmic plot (power law of sensation) of $F$ vs. $I$, the straight line obtained will shift downward on the graph when $t$ is greater. For example, the neural response of a pressure receptor (impulses per second) to a constant-force stimulus (newtons) results in a series of nearly parallel straight lines (Schmidt, 1978, p. 88). This effect is illustrated in Figure 3.3. The reason why the straight lines are parallel emerges as we conduct our theoretical analysis.

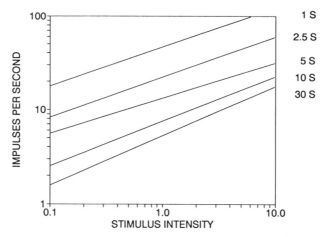

FIGURE 3.3   After Schmidt, 1978. Neural response of a pressure receptor on a log–log plot. Each straight line represents the "law of sensation" for a receptor at a specified time of adaptation (1 s, 2.5 s, . . . ). Clearly, the greater the adaptation time, the greater the downward shift of the straight line. We shall understand later why the lines are nearly parallel.

The subject of auditory adaptation requires some further remarks. While there seems to be near-universal agreement that psychophysical adaptation does occur (for example, apparently pulsating tones are more easily detected than are steady tones), the extent of this adaptation is not completely clear (to me). However, there are two representations of auditory adaptation that are quite clear. The first is very rapid neuro-physiological adaptation in the guinea pig auditory nerve reported by Yates *et al.* (1985). These investigators recorded the response of guinea pig ganglion cells to 100-ms tone bursts, in the form of peristimulus and poststimulus time histograms. The result was a rapid decline in the frequency of action potentials during the first 50 ms following the start of the tone stimulus. There is also a classical paper by Galambos and Davis (1943) purporting to show pronounced adaptation in single auditory nerve fibers of the cat. However, in a later note (1948), the authors queried their own work suggesting that the electrical effects measured may have issued from other neurons.

A second very clear manifestation of auditory adaptation, this time in the human being, was discovered by Hood in 1950. Hood's method involves the comparing of loudness in one ear, which is being adapted to a tone, with that in the opposite ear, which is receiving very little sound. Specifically, this is how the effect is measured. A tone of constant intensity is presented to the *adapting ear*. It is this ear which is being tested for a decrease in loudness sensation. An intermittent tone is presented to the opposite or *test ear*. The subject must adjust the intensity of the tone in the test ear to balance the loudness between both ears. It is found that the adapting ear adapts with respect to the test ear.

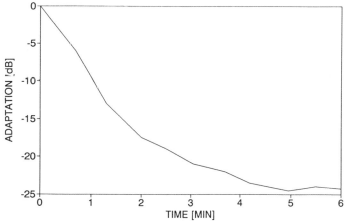

FIGURE 3.4  SDLB (simultaneous dichotic loudness balance) data of Small and Minifie (1961 Figure 3c, p. 1030). One ear, stimulated by means of a steady tone, adapts with respect to the other ear, which is stimulated only intermittently.

Note that in this clever measure of adaptation, the investigator does not record the subjective magnitude, or loudness of the tone, but rather records the objective or physical magnitude of the adaptation process. That is, he or she records the decrease in intensity of sound in decibels[2] required to produce a balance between ears. A graph of decibel adaptation vs. time, using the data of Small and Minifie (1961), is given in Figure 3.4. It may be seen that about 30 dB of adaptation are recorded when one ear is tested with respect to the other. This process is called the technique of *simultaneous dichotic loudness balance*. Note that it, too, relates two of the three cardinal variables: $I$, the physical intensity of the tone (giving rise to decibels of adaptation) and $t$, the time since onset of the tone. We study the adaptation process theoretically in Chapter 11.

## THE WEBER FRACTION

We have already encountered Weber's fraction, $\Delta I/I$, which is usually measured as the ratio of the smallest detectable difference between two stimuli, to the lower of the two stimuli. $\Delta I$ has also been called the *differential threshold* or *limen for intensity discrimination*. We saw in the formation of Equation (3.1) that Weber and Fechner believed that $\Delta I/I$ was constant over the physiological range of perceptible $I$. However, later work by other investigators showed this not to be the case. For most, if not all, modalities of sensation the Weber fraction is maximum for the lowest intensities and falls progressively as $I$ increases. For the middle range of intensities, $\Delta I/I$ is nearly constant, approximating Weber's law (3.1). For high values of $I$, approaching the maximum (nonpainful) level of stimulation, $\Delta I/I$ again rises for many modalities. This terminal rise in the Weber fraction is certainly found for the sense of taste (Lemberger, 1908; see Figure 3.5(a) and the sense of vision (König and Brodhum, as reported in Nutting, 1907, Table 1; Hecht, 1934, Figure 3.6), and possibly also for the sensation of temperature (Pütter, 1922). High-intensity rise in the Weber fraction may also be a feature of auditory intensity discrimination (McConville *et al.* 1991), although this is far from certain.

Again, although most authors do not report the duration of stimuli used in measurements of intensity discrimination, it will be assumed that the duration is kept constant for all stimuli. Thus, the graph of $\Delta I/I$ vs. $I$ is obtained by holding $t$, one of the three cardinal variables, constant and plotting the relationship between the other two variables. The reader may object that only one of the remaining two variables is evident, namely $I$; the other variable, $F$, is not present. Actually, the variable, $F$, *is* present but is just not visible. Recall that $\Delta I$ refers to the change in intensity, $I$, that corresponds to one just noticeable difference in sensation. This jnd in sensation can be written in the form $\Delta F$. Therefore, the

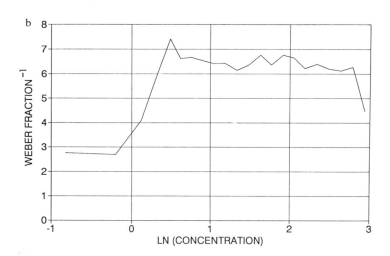

FIGURE 3.5   (a) Data of Lemberger (1908) for differential threshold of taste of sucrose. Weber fraction plotted against concentration of tasted solution. Note the features of the curve: fall in Weber fraction for low intensities to a plateau region that extends from about 2 to 16% solution, followed by a terminal rise as the physiological maximum is approached. Lemberger actually provided three additional data points showing that for very high concentrations Weber fractions become very great (discrimination is poor as maximum concentration is approached). (b) Same data as in (a). Inverse Weber fraction is plotted against ln (concentration). The number of rectangles beneath the curve between concentrations $a$ and $b$ is equal to the number of jnd's between $a$ and $b$.

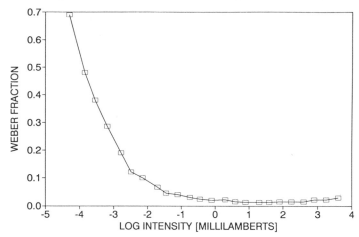

FIGURE 3.6    Data of König for differential threshold of light intensities. Weber fraction is plotted against intensity of light. Manifests the same features as the corresponding curve for taste (Figure 3.5a).

expression for Weber fraction, if written out more fully would be

$$\frac{\Delta I}{\Delta F}\bigg/ I,$$

the change in stimulus intensity per jnd divided by the lower of the two intensities.

The experimental process whereby the Weber fraction is measured is of interest to us. There is not one single definitive value of $\Delta I$ for which a distinction between signal intensities can be made. Rather, $\Delta I$ must be inferred statistically from the experimental data. The experimental protocol might be as follows. The subject might be presented with two stimulus signals sequentially and required to indicate which of the two was more intense. The difference between intensities can be designated $\delta I$. This procedure might be repeated many times with the same two stimuli, sometimes with the more-intense stimulus presented first and sometimes with the less-intense first. The proportion of correct discriminations, $C$, can then be computed. But $C$ is a function of the difference in intensities, $\delta I$. That is, $C$ is $C(\delta I)$. In order to define $C(\delta I)$ over a range of values of $\delta I$, the experiment can be repeated with the lower of the two stimulus signals at the same value as before, but with $\delta I$ changed. $C(\delta I)$ can again be computed. This process is repeated until the function $C(\delta I)$ has been defined for a range of values of $\delta I$. The graph of $C$ vs. $\delta I$ often obtained is sigmoid in shape, as shown in Figure 3.7.

The value of $\delta I$ to be taken as $\Delta I$, "the" limen for intensity discrimination, is largely arbitrary, but $\Delta I$ is commonly taken as the value of $\delta I$

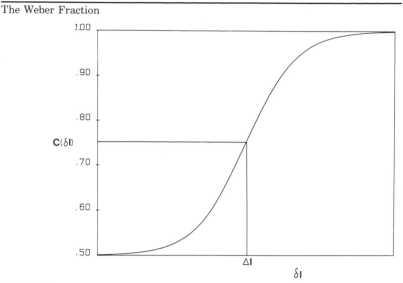

**FIGURE 3.7**  Statistical measurement of the differential threshold, $\Delta I$. Proportion of correct discriminations, $C(\delta I)$, plotted against intensity difference, $\delta I$. Define $\Delta I$ as the value of $\delta I$ for which $C(\delta I)$ equals 0.75.

for which $C$ is equal to 0.75; that is, $\Delta I$ is the stimulus increment that will permit a correct discrimination between intensities 75% of the time. $\Delta I$ is, of course, a function of $I$, so it must be determined at all requisite stimulus intensity levels. As you can see, there is a lot of experimental work involved in the determination of one Weber fraction curve with $I$ ranging from threshold to maximum physiological intensity. A method for measuring the difference limen that is, perhaps, more classical is described by Coren and Ward (1989, pp. 33–35).

The purpose of including the above experimental protocol in this book is primarily to demonstrate the *arbitrariness* of the function $\Delta I(I)$ ($\Delta I$ as a function of $I$). If the criterion for discrimination is changed from 0.75 to 0.5, for example, the function $\Delta I(I)$ will change accordingly. Therefore—and this is a feature we draw upon later—$\Delta I$, the limen for intensity discrimination, is not a unique quantity. If $\Delta I$ is to appear as a variable in a theoretically derived equation, its lack of uniqueness must be compensated for. We deal with this problem when it arises.

Let us turn our attention now back to the graph of $\Delta I$ vs. $I$, where $I$ extends over the full range of physiological values, from threshold to the verge of pain. The extent of the full physiological range will vary considerably depending on the modality of sensation. For example, for the sense of taste, $I_{max}/I_{min} \simeq 10^2$, while for the sense of hearing, $I_{max}/I_{min} \simeq 10^{11}$ (or greater). The value of $\Delta I/I$ may approach (or exceed?) unity for values of $I$ close to threshold and descend to values nominally in the range 0.1–0.5 in the middle range of $I$. If $\Delta I/I$ tends toward a plateau or constant value in this middle region, the constant will be referred to as Weber's constant, with reference to Equation (3.1).

It is rare, but always noteworthy, when people succeed in deriving a sensory law from another, more basic law, without the addition of major assumptions: the apparent complexity of the universe is demonstrably diminished. In this regard, it is worthwhile to see how Ekman (1959) was able to derive an expression for the Weber fraction from a variant of the power law of sensation. Ekman added one additional constant, $a$, to the power law, Equation (3.7), to obtain the equation

$$F = k(I + a)^n. \tag{3.9}$$

It transpires that the constant $a$ must be greater than zero (see Equation (3.10) below), which makes the interpretation of Equation (3.9) somewhat difficult. If we differentiate $F$ with respect to $I$, we find

$$\frac{dF}{dI} = \frac{nF}{I + a}.$$

Introducing an approximation using finite differences and solving for the Weber fraction,

$$\Delta I/I = \frac{a\,\Delta F/nF}{I} + \frac{\Delta F}{nF}.$$

At this point, Ekman found it necessary to introduce an additional equation,

$$\Delta F = cF,$$

which we have seen before in the derivation of the power law of sensation. Combining the last two equations we obtain

$$\Delta I/I = \frac{ac/n}{I} + c/n, \tag{3.10}$$

or simply

$$\Delta I/I = A/I + B, \tag{3.10a}$$

where $A$ and $B$ are constants greater than zero. More of the history of this equation is given in Chapter 12.

Equation (3.10) does, indeed, describe the shape of the Weber fraction, showing that it has large values for small values of the intensity, $I$, and that it descends toward a constant plateau value of $B$ for larger values of $I$. Apparently, Fechner himself proposed a modification of Equation (3.1) to Equation (3.10). Note that Equation (3.10) does not allow a high-intensity rise in the Weber fraction.

From the graph of $\Delta I/I$ vs. $I$, can we calculate the total number of jnd's, $N$, which, when stacked one on the other, would extend from threshold to maximum physiological intensity? In principle, $N$ can be measured directly (see Lemberger, 1908) by making $N$ measurements; however, in practice, this is often impossible and one must calculate $N$ from fewer than $N$ measurements. $N$ may be calculated from the equation,

$$N = \int_{I_{\text{thresh}}}^{I_{\max}} \frac{dI}{\Delta I}. \tag{3.11}$$

The idea is that $dI/\Delta I$ is the number of jnd's that "fit into" a small intensity range, $dI$. If we then integrate from the value of intensity at threshold, $I_{\text{thresh}}$, to the maximum physiological value of $I$, $I_{\max}$, we shall obtain $N$, the total number of jnd's.

Since $\Delta I$ has been measured for a number of intensities, $I$, we can calculate $1/\Delta I$ for these intensities. Equation (3.11) states that $N$ is equal to the area of the curve formed by plotting $1/\Delta I$ against $I$ for the full range of $I$. One can then plot the graph and find the area by numerical integration using, for example, the trapezoidal rule or Simpson's rule (see, for example, Press *et al.*, 1986). If $I$ has a large range of values, such as in the senses of vision and hearing, Equation (3.11) may be difficult to employ, and I recommend a minor modification. Since

$$d(\ln I) = dI/I,$$

$$dI/\Delta I = \frac{d(\ln I)}{\Delta I/I}$$

and Equation (3.11) may be written in the form

$$N = \int_{\ln I_{\text{thresh}}}^{\ln I_{\max}} \frac{d(\ln I)}{\Delta I/I}. \tag{3.12}$$

That is, $N$ is equal to the area of the curve obtained by plotting the reciprocal of the Weber fraction, $(\Delta I/I)^{-1}$, against the natural logarithm of $I$. Such a graph has been made from Lemberger's data in Figure 3.5b, and the reader can easily estimate the area by counting the number of large squares beneath the curve (about 21 jnd's).

If a plateau region exists in the Weber fraction curve, say between the intensity levels $I_{\text{low}}$ and $I_{\text{high}}$, then Equation (3.12) can be used to calculate, in a very simple way, the total number of jnd's, $N_{\text{plateau}}$, between these limits. Since $\Delta I/I =$ Weber's constant in this plateau region, this quantity may be removed from under the integral sign:

$$N_{\text{plateau}} = \frac{1}{\text{Weber constant}} \int_{\ln I_{\text{low}}}^{\ln I_{\text{high}}} d(\ln I) \tag{3.13}$$

$$N_{\text{plateau}} = \frac{1}{\text{Weber constant}} \ln(I_{\text{high}}/I_{\text{low}}),$$

or

$$N_{\text{plateau}} = \frac{\ln 10}{\text{Weber constant}} \log_{10}(I_{\text{high}}/I_{\text{low}}). \tag{3.14}$$

For example, referring to Figure 3.5b, if we approximate the plateau region in Lemberger's data as extending between sucrose concentrations of 1 to 16, then, since the Weber constant $\simeq 0.14$ and

$$N_{\text{plateau}} = \frac{\ln(16/1)}{0.14} = 19.8 \text{ jnd's.}$$

One final word on Weber fractions. When dealing with the sense of hearing, the variable, $I$, is sometimes used to represent mean sound pressure, $p$, and sometimes to represent mean sound intensity which varies as $p^2$. Therefore,

$$\Delta I/I = \Delta p^2/p^2 \simeq 2p\Delta p/p^2 = 2\Delta p/p. \tag{3.15}$$

Note also the power law for sound intensity,

$$F = kI^n \rightarrow kp^{2n}, \tag{3.16}$$

so that the power function exponent for sound pressure is twice that for sound intensity.

## The Analogs

Let us digress briefly from our review of sensory experiment to consider again the ideal gas analog introduced in Chapter 1. Recall the three state variables, $P$, $V$, and $T$ and the three equations involving these variables derived from the ideal gas law, Equation (1.1):

$$P \propto T \qquad \text{Charles' law} \tag{1.2}$$

$$P \propto 1/V \qquad \text{Boyle's law} \tag{1.3}$$

$$\Delta T/T \propto 1/T \tag{1.4}$$

To obtain Equation (1.2) we held $V$ constant; to obtain Equation (1.3) we held $T$ constant; and to obtain Equation (1.4) we again held $V$ constant and considered the result when $\Delta P$ was also constant.

Compare the idea gas equations with the psychophysical experiments that we have been discussing. Our three variables are now $t$ (time since stimulus onset), $I$ (intensity of stimulus), and $F$ (perceptual variable). To obtain the law of sensation, we held $t$ constant and obtained a graph where $F$ increases monotonically with $I$ (Figure 3.1; cf. Equation (1.2)). To study adaptation phenomena we held $I$ constant and obtained a graph where $F$ decreased monotonically with $t$ (Figure 3.2; cf. Equation (1.3)). To study difference discrimination we again held $t$ constant and found for constant $\Delta F$ that $\Delta I/I$ varied as a function of $I$ (Figure 3.5; cf. Equation (1.4)).

The primary reason for introducing the $PVT$ analogs is to aid (psychophysicists and biologists primarily) in regarding the three sensory experiments not as independent entities but rather as different experiments performed with the same three variables; $I$, $t$, and $F$. Once this conceptual leap has been made, one has less difficulty understanding how a single equation, analogous to $PV = RT$, can serve to *unite* the three types of experiment. And unification is basically what this book is about.

Just as $PV = RT$ can be written as $P = P(T, V)$, the hypothetical unifying sensory equation can be written formally as

$$F = F(I, t), \tag{3.17}$$

where the explicit form of the function, $F(I, t)$, has yet to be developed. When $t$ is held constant (that is, $t = t' =$ constant), then

$$F = F(I, t') \tag{3.18}$$

will describe the law of sensation (presumably in both the full logarithmic and the semilogarithmic forms). When $I$ is held constant (that is $I = I' =$ constant), then

$$F = F(I', t) \tag{3.19}$$

will describe adaptation phenomena. When both $t$ and $\Delta F$ are held constant (that is, $t = t'$ and $\Delta F = \Delta F'$), then

$$\Delta I/I = g(t', \Delta F'; I) \tag{3.20}$$

will describe the Weber fraction; $g$ is some function yet to be defined. In the coming chapters we work toward the derivation of the critical function $F(I, t)$. We can, actually, be a little more explicit even at the present time. Since we have introduced the relationship

$$F = kH, \tag{2.6}$$

where $k$ is constant, in Chapter 2, we know that the critical function, $F$, can be expressed in the form

$$F(I, t) = kH(I, t) \tag{3.21}$$

Our problem is, then, to derive the algebraic form of the function $H(I, t)$.

## THRESHOLD EFFECTS: THE LAWS OF BLONDEL AND REY, OF HUGHES, AND OF BLOCH AND CHARPENTIER

We move forward in time, now, from the mid-nineteenth century (Weber and Fechner) to the late nineteenth and early twentieth century. In 1885, Bloch and Charpentier stated their law governing the minimum quantity of light energy required for detection by an observer. In separate papers published in *Comptes Rendus de la Société de Biologie*, they argued that $I_{\text{thresh}}$, the minimum perceptible light intensity, is a function of the duration $t$, of the light signal. In fact, for values of $t$ less than about 0.1 s

$$I_{\text{thresh}} \cdot t = \text{constant}. \tag{3.22}$$

That is, the simple arithmetic product of $I_{\text{thresh}}$ with $t$ is constant. Since $I_{\text{thresh}}$ can be measured in units of power (e.g., joules per second), the Bloch–Charpentier constant represents a minimum energy for signal detection. However, when $t$ exceeds some upper bound, the law is violated. There is a minimum value for $I_{\text{thresh}}$ below which no light stimulus is perceptible.[3] Let us call this value $I_{\infty}$. Then

$$I_{\text{thresh}} \geq I_{\infty}. \tag{3.23}$$

The same law seems to hold for the sense of hearing, although I am not quite sure who first observed it. A graph published recently in the *Handbook of Perception and Human Performance* (Scharf and Buus, 1986) contains the collective data of Garner (1947), Feldtkeller and Oetinger (1956), and Zwislocki and Pirodda (1965). This graph shows that the threshold shift (in decibels)[2] of 1000-Hz tone bursts is a linearly decreasing function of the logarithm of time, for $t$ less than 0.3 seconds. That is

$$10 \log_{10}(I_{\text{thresh}}/I_{\infty}) = -k \log_{10} t + \text{constant}, \qquad k > 0.$$

If one measures the value of $k$ from the graph, it is found that $k$ is very nearly equal to 10. That is, representing the constant on the right-hand side of the above equation by $10 \log_{10} a$, we obtain to a good approximation

$$I_{\text{thresh}} / I_\infty = a/t$$

or

$$I_{\text{thresh}} \cdot t = a I_\infty, \tag{3.24}$$

Which is, again, the Bloch–Charpentier law. $a$ can be estimated from the data to be about 0.16 s.

Moving forward a little in time to 1912, Blondel and Rey addressed the issue of the mathematical relationship between $I_{\text{thresh}}$ and $t$ for larger values of $t$; that is, for values of $t$ greater than that for which the Bloch–Charpentier law was valid. The empirical relationship they discovered, which has been confirmed by many other studies, is the following:

$$\frac{I_{\text{thresh}}}{I_\infty} = 1 + \frac{a}{t}. \tag{3.25}$$

The constant $a$, usually now known as the Blondel–Rey constant, has a value of about 0.21 s. As Blondel and Rey pointed out, when $t$, the duration of the stimulus, is small, the second term on the right-hand side of Equation (3.25) becomes much greater than 1, and consequently

$$\frac{I_{\text{thresh}}}{I_\infty} \simeq \frac{a}{t},$$

which retrieves the Bloch–Charpentier law. Equation (3.25) is, therefore, a more general empirical equation embracing the earlier law.

I have found the proceedings of a symposium on flashing lights chaired by J. G. Holmes (1971) to be a valuable source of information on this subject.

Not to be outdone by the vision researchers, J. W. Hughes (1946) published his research on the auditory threshold of brief tones and showed that the Blondel–Rey equation was valid also for tones of various frequencies between 250 and 4000 Hz. Hughes drew the readers' attention to the similarity between Equation (3.25) and the equation giving the threshold electrical current which passes through a nerve cell membrane, as a function of the time needed to achieve threshold or firing of the neuron (the "chronaxie equation of Lapicque"). Hughes does not seem to give sufficient data in his paper for the evaluation of the constant, $a$, for audition. However, since again the equation goes over into the Bloch–Charpentier law for brief $t$, one might estimate $a$ to have the value of about 0.16 second (see Equation (3.24)).

I am not aware of Hughes' work having been replicated, but Plomp and Bouman (1959) have extended Hughes' studies.

## SIMPLE REACTION TIME

The subject's finger is poised above a button that will register the exact time it is pressed. On her ears are headphones. The instant she hears a tone through the headphones she will press the button. The time between the beginning of the tone and the pressing of the button is called the simple reaction time. In general (Coren and Ward, 1989), the reaction time is the time between the onset of a stimulus (auditory, visual, gustatory . . . ) and the subject's overt response.

A feature that makes the simple reaction time particularly interesting is its peculiar relationship to the intensity of the stimulus: The more intense the stimulus, the shorter the reaction time. This relationship between reaction time $t_r$, and stimulus intensity is shown in Figure 3.8 (Chocholle, 1940). There is, of course, a threshold intensity below which the stimulus cannot be detected.

There are various physiological events that transpire during the reaction time. A neuronal signal must travel from the sensory receptor(s) to the brain passing one or more synapses, a motor signal must proceed down to muscle, and muscle must contract to actuate the finger. The study of these components dates back at least to the time of Helmholtz. We return later to muse, briefly, over this sequence of events.

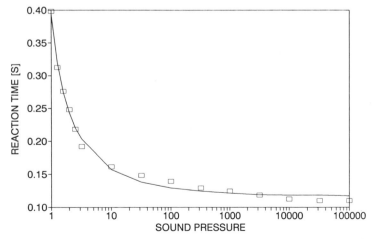

FIGURE 3.8   Data of Chocholle (1940). Reaction time plotted against sound pressure. The smooth curve is discussed later in the text.

We see, though, that on the whole, the relation between reaction time and stimulus intensity is, again, a relationship between the two variables, $I$ and $t$. However, $t = t_r$ is not necessarily the time since stimulus onset (the sense in which $t$ has been used before), but rather is the time taken by the subject to react to the stimulus. This leads us later into somewhat darker waters.

Simple reaction time, too, has its associated empirical equations, the best known of which are probably those of Piéron. Although Piéron formulated several empirical relations between $t_r$ and $I$, the one with which we are most concerned is (Piéron, 1914, 1952)

$$t_r = t_{r\,\min} + CI^{-n}, \qquad (3.26)$$

where $C$ and $n$ are constants that are greater than zero, and $t_{r\,\min}$ is the smallest possible value of $t_r$, obtained for the maximum physiological value of $I$. It can be seen that Equation (3.26) describes the type of curve depicted in Figure 3.8. Moreover, an extraordinary observation has been made, particularly for simple reaction times to auditory and visual stimuli: the value of the exponent, $n$, in Equation (3.26) is close to, but usually less than, the value of $n$ found in the power law of sensation (Fig. 14.2),

$$F = kI^n. \qquad (3.7)$$

Why in the world should this be so? Is it pure coincidence?

We demonstrate later, using the unifying equation (3.21) in its explicit form, that both Equation (3.7) and Equation (3.26) can be derived from the same "parent" equation and that the exponent, $n$, can be expected to be similar in magnitude in both equations.

However, despite all that we attempt to do, "simple" reaction time retains some secrets that we are not able to fathom.

Just a general remark here before proceeding. It should be recognized that all of the preceding empirical equations represent means or averages taken on many, many trials involving many individual subjects. There are large intersubject differences and no attempt has been made, in these pages, to tabulate them. Neither are we able, in the theoretical exposition that follows, to make allowance for these differences. Rather, we are content just to be able to derive the equations for the means.


## THE POULTON–TEGHTSOONIAN LAW

In a well-known paper published in 1971, R. Teghtsoonian, working with data assembled by E. C. Poulton (1967), made an extraordinary observation. He observed a relationship between the power function exponents, $n$ (Equation 3.7), for different sensory modalities and the logarithm of the physiological range spanned by these modalities. For

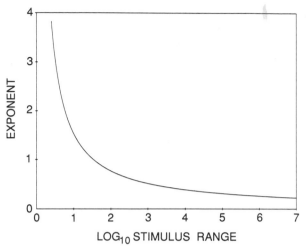

FIGURE 3.9   Schematic of graph by Teghtsoonian using data assembled by Poulton. Power function exponent plotted against $\log_{10}$ stimulus range = 1.53. The data array themselves along a rectangular hyperbola.

example, audition has the exponent value of about 0.3 (sound intensity at 1000 Hz), and auditory intensity spans a range of about $10^9$, so that $\log_{10}$ (range) $\simeq 9$. The sense of taste gives rise to an exponent much closer to 1.0, while it spans only about 2 decades of concentrations (intensities), so that $\log_{10}$(range) $\simeq 2$. Higher exponents are associated with a smaller range and vice versa.[4] In fact, when Teghtsoonian plotted a graph of $n$ vs. log(range) (shown schematically in Figure 3.9), he found that the data lay on a rectangular hyperbola whose equation was

$$(n)(\log_{10} \text{ range}) = 1.53. \qquad (3.27)$$

In our explorations, we shall derive Equation (3.27) in the course of theoretical studies of the Weber fraction.

## A VERY APPROXIMATE LAW OF OLFACTORY THRESHOLDS

An empirical equation was discovered by Laffort et al. (1974) and elaborated by Wright (1982). It is a law that holds only very approximately, but may be worth mentioning here anyway.

Let $I_\infty$ be the lowest detectable concentration of an odorant. Now define

$$p_{ol} = -\log_{10} I_\infty. \qquad (3.28)$$

Laffort et al. discovered a hyperbolic relationship between $n$ and $p_{ol}$

quite similar to Equation (3.27):

$$(n)(p_{ol}) = \text{constant}. \qquad (3.29)$$

This relationship has not always been confirmed by other investigators.


## THE FERRY–PORTER LAW AND TALBOT'S LAW

The final empirical law we shall discuss here was formulated by Ferry (1892) and Porter (1902) and deals with flashing lights. It refers to an experiment in which a subject is observing a flashing light, or a rotating disk with black and white sectors. The frequency of the flashing light is held constant. Let us suppose that the on time of the light is equal to the off time. The frequency of flashing is slowly increased. At a certain frequency the subject reports that the light no longer appears intermittent but rather appears to be steady. The frequency of flashing may then be slowly decreased until the light again appears intermittent. In this way, a *critical fusion frequency* or *critical flicker frequency* (CFF) for the light of a given wavelength for a given intensity is established. The experiment may then be repeated for a number of different intensities of light, keeping the wavelength constant.

It is found that the critical fusion frequency increases with increasing intensity of the light, up to a certain maximum intensity. The shape of the graph of CCF vs. $I$ is influenced by the regions of the retina on which the image of the light falls and also shows the effects of the two types of light receptors, rods and cones, that are found in the human retina. However, CFF, over a wide range of intensities, is found to increase linearly with the logarithm of the intensity (Figure 3.10). That is

$$\text{CFF} = a \log I + b, \qquad a, b \text{ constant}. \qquad (3.30)$$

This semilogarithmic law is called the *Ferry–Porter law*.

One should note here again that, as with so many of the preceding empirical laws of sensation, we deal with a relationship between the intensity of the stimulus and the duration of time over which the stimulus is applied (the on time of the light in each cycle).

At frequencies that exceed the critical fusion frequency, the effective luminance (intensity) of a flashing light is independent of frequency and is equal to the average over time of the real luminance. This phenomenon is called *Talbot's law*.

With this law we conclude our tour of the empirical laws of sensation. We have not, by any means, exhausted the stock of such laws: many, many more of them exist. However, all eight laws are dealt with in a theoretical sense in the course of this book.

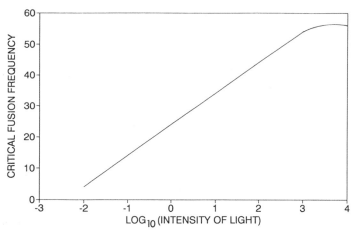

FIGURE 3.10   Schematic demonstration of the Ferry–Porter law. Critical fusion frequency for a flickering light source is related linearly to the logarithm of the intensity of the light, to a saturable limit. The curve drawn is characteristic of the type obtained when the observed light falls on the fovea.


## NOTES

1. A word to the wise... what Weber actually wrote in Latin is "in observando discrimine rerum inter se comparatarum, non differentiam rerum, sed rationem differentiae ad magnitudinem rerum inter se comparatarum, percipimus" (cited by Drever, 1952).

2. Decibels (dB): Let $x$ and $x_0$ be any two numbers. We can use $x_0$ as a reference with respect to which $x$ is reported. For example, we could report all values of $x$ as multiples of $x_0$:

$$q_1 = x_1/x_0, \qquad q_2 = x_2/x_0 \ldots .$$

The decibel system reports $x$ as a logarithm of the $q$s. For example,

$$dB_1 = 10 \log_{10} q_1 = 10 \log_{10} x_1/x_0;$$

$$dB_2 = 10 \log_{10} q_2 = 10 \log_{10} x_2/x_0 \ldots$$

In general

$$dB = 10 \log_{10} x/x_0.$$

Why do we use the dB system? Why not just report $x$ as $x$? Sometimes the values of $x$ we are interested in become very large or very small; for example $x_1 = 10^{-7}$, or $x_2 = 10^8$. It is then convenient to choose a handy value of $x_0$ (say $x_0 = 1$) and use the dB system. Then

$$x_1 = 10 \log_{10} 10^{-7} = -70 \text{ dB}$$

$$x_2 = 10 \log_{10} 10^8 = 80 \text{ dB}.$$

Note that you can always use the dB value to solve backward to obtain the original $x$ value. For example, what $x$ value corresponds to $y$ dB?

$$y = 10 \log_{10} x$$

$$\log_{10} x = y/10$$

$$x = 10^{y/10}.$$

3. Modern signal detection theory addresses the problem of threshold detection probabilistically, but we do not introduce SDT in this book.
4. The values given for "range" are low. There is an arbitrary element involved in specifying the upper limit of the range.

## REFERENCES

Baird, J. C., and Noma, E. 1978. *Fundamentals of Scaling and Pyschophysics*. Wiley, New York.

Bloch, A. M. 1885. Expériences sur la vision. *Comptes Rendus de la Société de Biologie, Series 8*, **37**, 493–495.

Blondel, A., and Rey, J. 1912. The perception of lights of short duration at their range limits. *Transactions of the Illuminating Engineering Society*, **7**, 625–662.

Borg, G., Diamant, H., Ström, L., and Zotterman, Y. 1967. The relation between neural and perceptual intensity: A comparative study on the neural and psychophysical response to taste stimuli. *Journal of Physiology* **192**, 13–20.

Brentano, F. 1874. *Psychologie vom Empirischen Standpunkt*, Vol. 1. Dunker and Hunblot, Leipzig.

Charpentier, A. 1885. *Comptes Rendus de la Société de Biologie, Series 8*, **2**, 5.

Chocholle, R. 1940. Variations des temps de réaction auditifs en fonction de l'intensité à diverses fréquences. *Année Psychologique* **41**, 65–124.

Coren, S., and Ward, L. M. 1989. *Sensation and Perception*, 3rd ed. Harcourt, Brace, Jovanovich, San Diego.

Dowling, J. E. 1987. *The Retina: An Approachable Part of the Brain*, Chap. 7. Belknap Press of Harvard Univ. Press, Cambridge, MA.

Drever, J. 1952. *A Dictionary of Psychology*. Penguin, Harmondsworth, Middlesex, England.

Ekman, G. 1959. Weber's law and related functions. *The Journal of Psychology* **47**, 343–352.

Fechner, G. T. 1966. *Elements of Psychophysics*. (D. H. Howse and E. L. Boring, Eds.; H. E. Adler, Translator). Holt, Reinhart & Winston, New York. Published originally in 1860.

Ferry, E. S. 1892. Persistence of vision. *American Journal of Science* 44 (series 3), 192–207.

Galambos, R., and Davis, H. 1943. The response of single auditory-nerve fibers to acoustic stimulation. *Journal of Neurophysiology* **6**, 39–57.

Galambos, R., and Davis, H. 1948. Action potentials from single auditory-nerve fibers? *Science* **108**, 513.

Gregory, R. L., and Zangwill, O. L. 1987. *The Oxford Companion to the Mind*. Oxford Univ. Press, Oxford.

Hartline, H. K., and Graham, C. H. 1932. Nerve impulses from single receptors in the eye. *Journal of Cellular and Comparative Physiology* **1**, 277–295.

Hecht, S. 1934. *A Handbook of General Experimental Psychology*. Clark Univ. Press, Worcester, MA.

Holmes, J. G., Symposium Chairman. 1971. *The Perception and Application of Flashing Lights*. Univ. of Toronto Press, Toronto. Published originally by Adam Hilger, Ltd., Great Britain.

Hood, J. D. 1950. Studies in auditory fatigue and adaptation. *Acta Oto-Laryngologica Supplementum* **92**, 1–57.

Hughes, J. W. 1946. The threshold of audition for short periods of stimulation. *Proceedings of the Royal Society of London Series B* **133**, 486–490.

König, A., and Brodhun, E. 1889. Experimentelle Untersuchungen über die psychophysische Fundamentalformel in Bezug auf den Gesichtsinn. *Sitzber. d. Akad. d. Wiss., Berlin*, 641.

Krueger, L. E. 1989. Reconciling Fechner and Stevens: Toward a unified psychophysical law. *Behavioral and Brain Sciences* **122**, 251–267.

Krueger, L. E. 1990. Toward a unified psychophysical law and beyond. In *Ratio Scaling of Psychological Magnitudes* (Bolanowski and Gescheider, Eds.) Erlbaum.

Laffort, P., Patte, F., and Etcheto, M. 1974. Olfactory coding on the basis of physicochemical properties. *Annals of New York Academy of Sciences* **237**, 193–208.

Lemberger, F. 1908. Psychophysische Untersuchungen über den Geschmack von Zucker und Saccharin (Saccharose und Krystallose). *Pflügers Archiv für die gesammte Physiologie des Menschen and der Tiere*. **123**, 293–311.

Marks, L. E. 1974. *Sensory Processes: The New Psychophysics*. Academic Press, New York.

McConville, K. M. V., Norwich, K. H., and Abel, S. M. 1991. Application of the entropy theory of perception to auditory intensity discrimination. *International Journal of Biomedical Computing* **27**, 157–173.

Nutting, P. G. 1907. The complete form of Fechner's law. *Bulletin of the Bureau of Standards* **3**, 59–64.

Piéron, H. 1914. II Recherches sur les lois de variation des temps de latence sensorielle en fonction des intensités excitatrices. *L'Année Psychologique t.* **20**, 17–96.

Piéron. H. 1920–1921. III Nouvelles recherches sur l'analyse du temps de latence sensorielle et sur la loi qui relie ce temps a l'intensité de l'excitation. *L'Année Psychologique t.* **22**, 58–142.

Piéron, H. 1952. *The Sensations: Their Functions, Processes and Mechanisms*, p. 353. Yale Univ. Press, New Haven.

Plateau, J. A. F. 1872. Sur la mesure des sensations physiques, et sur la loi qui lie l'intensité de ces sensations à l'intensité de la cause excitante. *Bulletins de l'Académie Royale des Sciences, des Lettres, et des Beaux-Arts de Belgique* **33**, 376–388.

Plomp, R., and Bouman, M. A. 1959. Relation between hearing threshold and duration for tone pulses. *The Journal of the Acoustical Society of America* **31**, 749–758.

Porter, T. C. 1902. Contribution to the study of flicker II. *Proceedings of the Royal Society London* **70A**, 313–329.

Poulton, E. C. 1967. Population norms of top sensory magnitudes and S. S. Stevens' exponents. *Perception and Psychophysics* **2**, 312–316.

Press, W. H., Flannery, B. P., Teukolsky, S. A., and Vetterling, W. T. 1986. *Numerical Recipes: The Art of Scientific Computing*. Cambridge Univ. Press, Cambridge.

Püter, A., 1922. Die Unterschiedsschwellen des Temperatursinnes. *Zeitschrift für Biologie* **74**, 237–298.

Scharf, B., and Buus, S. 1986. Audition I: Stimulus, physiology, threshold. In *Handbook of Perception and Human Performance* (K. R. Boff, L. Kaufman, and J. P. Thomas, Eds.), Fig. 14.27, pp. 14–31 Wiley, New York.

Schmidt, R. F. 1978. Somatovisceral sensibility. In *Fundamentals of Sensory Physiology* (R. F. Schmidt, Ed.). Springer, New York.

Small, A. M., Jr., and Minifie, F. D. 1961. Effect of matching time on perstimulatory adaptation. *The Journal of the Acoustic Society of America* **33**, 1028–1033.

Stevens, S. S. 1961. To honor Fechner and repeal his law. *Science* **133**, 80–86.

Stevens, S. S. 1969. Sensory scales of taste intensity. *Perception and Psychophysics* **6**, 302–308.

Stevens, S. S. 1970. Neural events and the psychophysical law. *Science* **170**, 1043–1050.

Teghtsoonian, R. 1971. On the exponents in Stevens' law and the constant in Ekman's law. *Psychological Review* **78**, 71–80.

Weiss, D. J. 1981. The impossible dream of Fechner and Stevens. *Perception* **10**, 431–434.

Wright, R. H. 1982. In *The Sense of Smell*, Chap. 18, Fig. 2. CRC Press, Boca Raton, FL.

Yates, G. K., Robertson, D., and Johnstone, B. M. 1985. Very rapid adaptation in the guinea pig auditory nerve. *Hearing Research* **17**, 1–12.

# 4

# Information of Events with Discrete Outcomes: Methods of Communication Theory and Psychology

We were introduced to the concept of *information* in Chapter 2, where the distinction was made (note 4) between discrete and continuous outcomes to an event. An event with only discrete outcomes is one such as the toss of a coin, which can land only heads or tails. An event with continuous outcomes is one such as the time of a response, which can, in principle, take on an infinity of values. In this chapter we consider only events of the former type, and we analyze, using two parallel and equivalent methods, how information is transferred during these events. The reader is reminded that the word information, if it is not qualified by an adjective, will always refer to that quantity which is measured by information theoretical entropy (sometimes called *communications entropy*). In Chapter 2 we glimpsed the way in which the information or entropy concept was to be employed in the analysis of sensory events: a natural law will be formulated giving perceptual response (such as the rate of action potential propagation in a sensory neuron) as a mathematical function of the entropy of a stimulus. If information, and hence entropy, were only an arbitrary creation of communications engineers, fabricated as a convenient means of measuring the efficiency of transmitting a message in a telephone cable, it would be surprising indeed that nature would use the same measure in sensory neurons. Therefore, we proceed in Chapter 6 to examine how the information concept, masquerading in different garb, was introduced into physics by Ludwig Boltzmann more than half a century before Shannon's paper on the theory of communication, and how information (or, equivalently, informational entropy) was woven into the fabric of physical law. As the story unfolds, we see that the entrance of informational entropy as a primary variable of neurophysiology seems to be an extension of its role as a primary variable in physics.

## PICKING UP THE THREAD

We suppose that some event may happen in $N$ discrete ways. For example, a election may result in only 1 winner from among 12 candidates who are running. We may say, therefore, that the election event has $N = 12$ possible discrete outcomes. The uncertainty that prevails before the election results are known is measured using the entropy, $H$, that was defined by Equation (2.1)

$$H = - \sum_{i=1}^{N} p_i \log p_i \qquad (4.1)$$

where $p_i$ is the probability of the $i$th outcome. That is, $H$ is a weighted sum of the logarithms of the *a priori* probabilities. Of course, the probabilities must sum to unity; that is,

$$\sum_{i=1}^{N} p_i = 1. \qquad (4.2)$$

Therefore, the election uncertainty is given by

$$H = - \sum_{i=1}^{12} p_i \log p_i,$$

where $p_1$ is the *assumed* probability that candidate 1 will be elected, etc. We note that, in contrast to the earlier example of tossing a coin or rolling a die where the *a priori* probabilities were possibly determined geometrically, the probabilities in this example are established by various subjective means (perhaps augmented by the results of preelection polls). When the results of the election become known, the uncertainty vanishes, and information about the election takes its place. The information about which candidate won the election is equal to the preexisting uncertainty, so that

$$\mathscr{I} = H. \qquad (4.3)$$

We recall that the base of the logarithms used is arbitrary; and also that when all the probabilities are equal (say equal to $p$), then

$$H = \log N, \qquad (4.4)$$

where

$$N = 1/p. \qquad (4.5)$$

We might ask the very natural question: Given some value for the number of possible outcomes, $N$, which values for $p_i$ will render $H$ maximum? For example, suppose we deal with an event with two possible

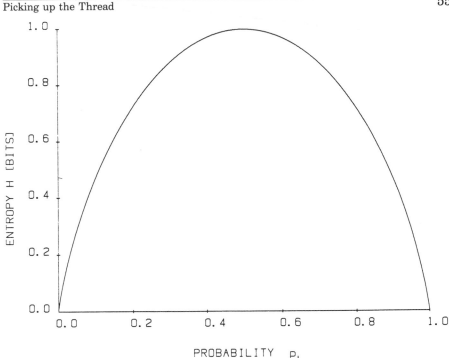

FIGURE 4.1  Entropy of an event with two possible outcomes, as a function of the probability, $p_1$, of one of these outcomes. $p_2 = 1 - p_1$. Note that entropy is maximum for $p_1 = p_2 = \frac{1}{2}$.

outcomes whose probabilities are $p_1$ and $p_2$. Then, as a consequence of Equation (4.2), $p_2 = 1 - p_1$. What value of $p_1$ will then produce a maximum value for $H$? From Equation (4.1),

$$H = -p_1 \log p_1 - (1 - p_1)\log(1 - p_1). \qquad (4.6)$$

We shall take $\lim_{p_1 \to 0} p_1 \log p_1 = 0$. Then we may see that for $p_1 = 0$, $H = 0$, and for $p_1 = 1$, $H = 0$. This result is quite reasonable since, when $p_1 = 0$, $p_2 = 1$, the second outcome is a certainty and, therefore, uncertainty, $H$, vanishes. $H$ is similarly equal to zero for $p_1 = 1$, when the first outcome is a certainty. The mathematical function $H(p_1)$ must, therefore, be equal to zero for the two extreme values of $p_1$. Moreover, because of the symmetry in the variables $p_1$ and $p_2$, the function must be symmetrical about the line $p_1 = \frac{1}{2}$. The complete graph of $H$ vs. $p_1$ is shown in Figure 4.1, where $H$ is seen to be maximum for $p_1 = p_2 = \frac{1}{2}$.

Consider now the general case of an event with $N$ possible outcomes. Then $H$ is given by Equation (4.1) subject to the constraint expressed by Equation (4.2). In order to extremize $H$, that is to find its relative maxima and minima, we introduce a Lagrangian multiplier, $\lambda$, to produce the expression

$$G = - \sum_{i=1}^{N} p_i \ln p_i + \lambda \left( \sum_{i=1}^{N} p_i - 1 \right). \qquad (4.7)$$

That is, we set up the expression

$$G = \text{entropy} + \text{Lagrangian multiplier} \times \text{constraint}.$$

The values of $p_i$ for which $H$ is an extremum subject to the normalization constraint is found by differentiating $G$ partially with respect to each of the $p_i$ and equating the derivatives to zero:

$$\frac{\partial}{\partial p_k} \left[ - \sum_{i=1}^{N} p_i \ln p_i + \lambda \left( \sum_{i=1}^{N} p_i - 1 \right) \right] = 0$$

$$-1 - \ln p_k + \lambda = 0$$

$$\ln p_k = \lambda - 1$$

$$p_k = e^{\lambda - 1}, \qquad \text{for all } p_k. \qquad (4.8)$$

That is, all $p_i$ are equal and must be equal to $1/N$ for an extremum.

In principle, we are not yet finished, since we must show that the extremum for $H$ when $p_i = 1/N$ is, in fact, a maximum. For the completion of the proof, the reader is referred to Raisbeck (1963).

So the entropy, $H$, is maximum when the outcomes of the event are equally probable, as we saw in the example in Figure 4.1. In other words, we are most uncertain when an event is equally likely to occur in various possible ways, and we derive the greatest possible amount of information from observing the outcome of such an event. Just for the fun of it, Figure 4.2 depicts an event with three possible outcomes with probabilities $p_1$, $p_2$, and $p_3$. Since $p_3 = 1 - p_1 - p_2$, $H$ can be plotted along the $z$-axis as a function of the two variables, $p_1$ and $p_2$. $H$ is maximum for $p_1 = p_2 = p_3 = \frac{1}{3}$.

Just a note on the appropriateness of the log-function as a means of expressing information. Suppose we toss a fair coin. Then the head–tail information we obtain is $\log_2 2 = 1$ bit. If we toss the coin a second time, we receive an additional 1 bit of information. Therefore, the total amount of information that we receive by observing the results of two sequential tosses is 2 bits. Suppose, now, that we place two coins in a closed box, shake the box, and observe the results of the simultaneous toss. How much information do we receive? Well, there are four equally probable outcomes to the simultaneous toss: HH, HT, TH, TT. Therefore, the quantity of information received is equal to $\log_2 4 = 2$ bits, the same

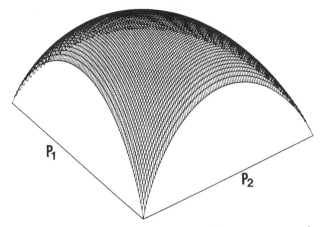

$P_1$

$P_2$

FIGURE 4.2 Entropy of an event with three possible outcomes, as a function of the probabilities $p_1$ and $p_2$ of these outcomes. Entropy, $H$, is given by $H = -\Sigma_{i=1}^{3} p_i \log p_i$. Since $p_3 = 1 - p_1 - p_2$,

$$H = -p_1 \log p_1 - p_2 \log p_2 - (1 - p_1 - p_2)\log(1 - p_1 - p_2).$$

The graph shows $H$ as a function of $p_1$ and $p_2$. However, appearances can be deceiving. In the graph shown, the origin is actually remote from the viewer and the $p_1$- and $p_2$- axes come toward him/her. The viewer's eye is situated below the $p_1$-$p_2$ plane and the surface is concave, not convex (as it appears). $H$ is, of course, maximum at $p_1 = p_2 = p_3 = \frac{1}{3}$.

amount we received by tossing the two coins sequentially. Any other result would have been untenable.

## A CHANNEL OF COMMUNICATION

We consider now some means of transmitting a message between two stations. The means is arbitrary. It could be electrical or optical, such as that used for a telephone, or even acoustical such as that used for ordinary speech. In order to simplify the initial discussion, suppose that only two symbols are transmitted: 1 or 0; that is, messages consist purely of strings of 0's and 1's. Let us suppose, also, that our channel transmits without error, so that each time the transmitter sends 0, the receiver gets 0, etc. For purposes of illustration, suppose that the probability of transmitting 0 is 0.2 and the probability of transmitting 1 is 0.8 (Figure 4.3). We can represent the probabilities of symbols (0, 1) for the transmitter (source) by the vector (0.2, 0.8), and the probabilities of symbols (0, 1) for the receiver by the same vector (0.2, 0.8). The transmitter, or *source entropy* is given by

$$H_{\text{source}} = -\sum_{i=1}^{2} p_s \log p_s = -0.2 \log 0.2 - 0.8 \log 0.8.$$

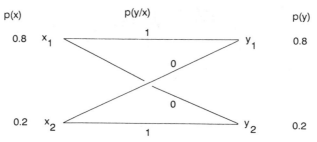

FIGURE 4.3   Information transmission in a noiseless channel. The probability of transmission of $x_1$ equals 0.8 and, since $p(y_1|x_1) = 1$, probability of receipt of $y_1$ equals 0.8, etc.

Similarly, the *receiver entropy* is given by

$$H_{\text{receiver}} = - \sum_{i=1}^{2} p_r \log p_r = -0.2 \log 0.2 - 0.8 \log 0.8.$$

The information received by the receiver is then

$$\mathcal{I} = H_{\text{source}} = H_{\text{receiver}}. \tag{4.9}$$

Now the realities of communication are such that interference, or noise, usually affects the transmission of signals through a channel, resulting in errors at the receiver. That is, the transmission of a zero will sometimes result in the receipt of a one and vice versa. In this case, the information received, $\mathcal{I}$, will not be equal to $H_{\text{source}}$ or to $H_{\text{receiver}}$. We now develop equations governing the information received when a signal is received from such a noisy channel. Only a little in the way of basic mathematics is required: some facility with iterated summation operators such as $\sum_{j=1}^{n}\sum_{k=1}^{n}$, and the definition of conditional probability. We deal with signals transmitted, for which we use the symbol $x_j$, and signals received, for which we shall use the symbol $y_k$. Let us generalize our lexicon of transmitted symbols from 2 to $n$. Then, for example, $p_j(x_1)$ represents the probability of transmitting signal $x_1$, and $p_k(y_3)$ represents the probability of receiving signal $y_3$. In general, then, $p_j(x_j)$ represents the probability of transmitting the signal $x_j$, and $p_k(y_k)$ represents the probability of receiving the signal $y_k$. To simplify the nomenclature, we can drop the subscripts following the $p$ without introducing any ambiguity: $p(x_j)$ means $p_j(x_j)$ etc. We define $p(x_j|y_k)$ as the *conditional probability* of $x_j$ given $y_k$; that is, the probability that signal $x_j$ was transmitted given that signal $y_k$ was received. $p(y_k|x_j)$ is defined analogously. We further define $p(x_j, y_k)$ as the *joint probability* that $x_j$ was transmitted and $y_k$ received. From the definition of conditional

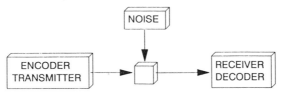

FIGURE 4.4    Schema for a noisy channel.

probability emerge two fundamental equations that we use on various occasions,

$$p(x_j, y_k) = p(x_j|y_k) \cdot p(y_k) \qquad (4.10)$$

$$p(x_j, y_k) = p(y_k|x_j) \cdot p(x_j), \qquad (4.11)$$

where the dot signifies ordinary multiplication.

The sequence of events is now depicted by the well-known diagram shown in Figure 4.4.

A key feature of the noisy channel is what one might call *residual uncertainty*. The simple coin-tossing paradigm involved, ostensibly, no noise, so that when we observed the outcome of a toss to be "heads," there were no lingering doubts that perhaps it was really "tails" and we had misread the face of the coin. For this reason, we could write simply

$$\mathscr{I} = H = -\Sigma p \ln p.$$

In the more general case, however, receipt of the signal $y_k$ still leaves some residual uncertainty; $p(x_j|y_k)$ gives the probability, not always zero, that some signal other than $x_k$ may have been transmitted. Therefore, $\mathscr{I}$ is no longer simply equal to $-\Sigma p(x_j)\ln p(x_j)$. In fact $\mathscr{I}$ is less than this amount due to the residual uncertainty. In general, for noisy channels

$$\mathscr{I} = H_{\text{before}} - H_{\text{after}}. \qquad (4.12)$$

That is, the transmitted information is equal to the difference between the source entropy or uncertainty, $H_{\text{before}}$, given as usual by $-\Sigma p(x_j)\ln p(x_j)$, and the residual entropy, $H_{\text{after}}$.

The noisy channel will now be analyzed mathematically in two different ways: (a) by the methods of communication theory and (b) by the methods of mathematical psychology. The two methods lead to identical results, but there is something to be learned by examining both methods.

The "minimalist" reader may certainly skip over the next section and proceed directly to the section on psychological methods (The Noisy Channel II).

## THE NOISY CHANNEL I

*The information about a transmitted ensemble of signals contained in the received ensemble of signals*

Equation (4.1), which introduced us to the entropy concept, is a weighted average of the logarithms of the probabilities of the possible outcomes. We now go back a step—actually recede to a step more elementary than Equation (4.1)—and examine the individual possible outcomes, rather than their average. However, we carry out this examination within the context of a noisy channel.

Following Middleton (1960), let us generalize the example of Figure 4.3 to include the presence of noise. Again we revert to the case of only two possible signals, but now we allow the possibility of mistakes (Figure (4.5), Box 4.1). $x_1$ and $x_2$ designate the transmitted signals, $y_1$ and $y_2$ the corresponding received signals. As before, let $p(x_1) = 0.8$ and $p(x_2) = 0.2$. Various nonzero conditional probabilities, $p(x_j|y_k)$, selected arbitrarily, are indicated on the diagram:

$$p(y_1|x_1) = 5/8$$
$$p(y_2|x_1) = 3/8$$
$$\overline{\text{sum to 1.}}$$

Similarly

$$p(y_1|x_2) = 1/4$$
$$p(y_2|x_2) = 3/4$$
$$\overline{\text{sum to 1.}}$$

$p(y_k)$, the probability of receiving $y_k$ is given by the equation

$$p(y_k) = p(x_1, y_k) + p(x_2, y_k)$$
$$= p(y_k|x_1) \cdot p(x_1) + p(y_k|x_2) \cdot p(x_2) \qquad (4.13)$$

Thus

$$p(y_1) = (5/8)(0.8) + (1/4)(0.2) = 0.55$$
$$p(y_2) = (3/8)(0.8) + (3/4)(0.2) = 0.45.$$

The $p(y_k)$ are entered in Figure 4.5.

BOX 4.1    Signals transmitted with probability $p(x)$ and received with probability $p(y)$s

$p(y_k) = \sum_{j=1}^{2} p(x_j, y_k)$, therefore,

$p(y_1) = p(x_1, y_1) + p(x_2, y_1)$

$= p(y_1|x_1) \cdot p(x_1) + p(y_1|x_2) \cdot p(x_2)$,

Equation (4.13),

$= (5/8 \times 0.8) + (1/4 \times 0.2) = 0.55$

$p(y_2) = p(x_1, y_2) + p(x_2, y_2)$

$= p(y_2|x_1) \cdot p(x_1) + p(y_2|x_2) \cdot p(x_2)$

$= (3/8 \times 0.8) + (3/4 \times 0.2) = 0.45$

Having obtained the $p(y_k)$ we can now calculate the $p(x_j|y_k)$.

$p(x_1|y_1) = p(y_1|x_1) \cdot p(x_1)/p(y_1) = (5/8) \times (0.8)/(0.55) = 0.90\dot{9}$

$p(x_2|y_1) = p(y_1|x_2) \cdot p(x_2)/p(y_1) = (1/4) \times (0.2)/(0.55) = 0.090\dot{9}$

$p(x_1|y_2) = p(y_2|x_1) \cdot p(x_1)/p(y_2) = (3/8) \times (0.8)/(0.45) = 0.66\dot{6}$

$p(x_2|y_2) = p(y_2|x_2) \cdot p(x_2)/p(y_2) = (3/4) \times (0.2)/(0.45) = 0.33\dot{3}$

We can now calculate the mutual informations from Equations (4.16) and (4.17).

$\mathscr{I}_m(x_j|y_k) = \mathscr{H}(x_j) - \mathscr{H}(x_j|y_k)$

$= -\log p(x_j) + \log p(x_j|y_k) = \log \dfrac{p(x_j|y_k)}{p(x_j)}$

$\mathscr{I}_m(x_1|y_1) = \log \dfrac{p(x_1|y_1)}{p(x_1)} = \log(0.909/0.8) = 0.128$ n.u.

$\mathscr{I}_m(x_2|y_1) = \log \dfrac{p(x_2|y_1)}{p(x_2)} = \log(0.0909/0.2) = -0.788$ n.u.

$\mathscr{I}_m(x_1|y_2) = \log \dfrac{p(x_1|y_2)}{p(x_1)} = \log(0.666/0.8) = -0.182$ n.u.

$\mathscr{I}_m(x_2|y_2) = \log \dfrac{p(x_2|y_2)}{p(x_2)} = \log(0.333/0.2) = 0.511$ n.u.

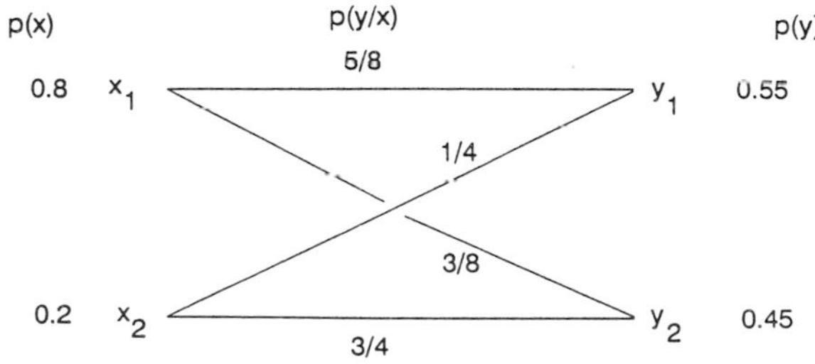

FIGURE 4.5    Information transmission in a noisy channel (cf. Figure 4.3 for a noiseless channel). The probabilities 5/8, 1/4, 3/8, 3/4 are conditional probabilities, $p(y|x)$. The values for $p(y)$ are calculated from $p(x)$ and $p(y/x)$ in the text above.

We now make the following definitions:

$$\mathscr{H}(x_j) = -\log p(x_j) = \text{initial or } a \text{ priori uncertainty}$$
$$\text{of the receiver about occurrence of } x_j$$

(4.14)

$$\mathscr{H}(x_j|y_k) = -\log p(x_j|y_k) = \text{final or } a \text{ posteriori uncertainty}$$
$$\text{of the receiver about occurrence of } x_j$$
$$\text{after } y_k \text{ has been received.}$$

(4.15)

For example, a "zero" was received $(y_k)$, but was a "one" really transmitted $(x_j)$? Then introducing the idea expressed by Equation (2.4) and (4.12) that

$$\text{Information} = H_{\text{before}} - H_{\text{after}},$$

we have

$$\mathscr{I}_m(x_j|y_k) = \mathscr{H}(x_j) - \mathscr{H}(x_j|y_k) \qquad (4.16)$$

$$= \log[p(x_j|y_k)/p(x_j)] \qquad (4.17)$$

from Equations (4.14) and (4.15). $\mathscr{I}_m$ is known as the *mutual information* of $x_j$ and $y_k$.

The purpose of the example of Figure 4.5 is to calculate $\mathscr{I}_m(x_j|y_k)$ for all pairs $(j, k)$; therefore, we need values of $p(x_j|y_k)$. We can calculate this conditional probability using the values for $p(x_j)$, $p(y_k)$, and $p(y_k|x_j)$ that have been entered in the diagram. Equating the right-hand sides of Equations (4.10) and (4.11),

$$p(x_j|y_k) = p(y_k|x_j)p(x_j)/p(y_k). \qquad (4.18)$$

The details of the calculations are given in Box 4.1, and the results are summarized below:

$$\mathscr{I}_m(x_1|y_1) = 0.128 \text{ natural units (n.u.)}$$

$$\mathscr{I}_m(x_2|y_1) = -0.788 \text{ n.u.}$$

$$\mathscr{I}_m(x_1|y_2) = -0.182 \text{ n.u.}$$

$$\mathscr{I}_m(x_2|y_2) = 0.511 \text{ n.u.}$$

We notice a strange phenomenon: $\mathscr{I}_m(x_2|y_1)$ and $\mathscr{I}_m(x_1|y_2)$ have negative values. The receiver has obtained negative information; his uncertainty about the transmitted signal is *greater* having received a signal than it was before the signal was transmitted. This result occurs when the conditional probability for $x$, for example, $p(x_2|y_1)$, is less than the original probability for $x$, $p(x_2)$.

The example of Figure 4.5 can be expanded to include $n > 2$ possible signals.

The mutual information, $\mathscr{I}_m(x_j|y_k)$, is interesting heuristically, but our primary concern is the *average* information gain by the receiver. In the case of the noiseless channel we dealt with this matter by taking the *expectation E*, of the logs of the transmission probabilities (see for example, Freund and Walpole (1980) or any standard text on probability),

$$H = -E[\log p_i] = -\sum_{i=1}^{n} p_i \log p_i \qquad (4.1)$$

We approach the noisy channel in the same way, *mutatis mutandis*.

Let us define

$$H(X) = E[\mathscr{H}(x)] = -\sum_{j=1}^{n} p(x_j)\log p(x_j). \qquad (4.19)$$

$H(X)$, the source entropy (cf. Equation (4.9) above), is the average *a priori* uncertainty about occurrence of $x$ (before any $x_j$ occurs). Recalling the result of Equation (4.8), we see that $H(X)$ will be maximum when all $p(x_j)$ are equal.

In a similar fashion, we can define the *conditional entropy*, $H(X|Y)$, for the set of transmitted $x_j$ given the received set $y_k$.

$$H(X|Y) = E_{xy}[\mathscr{H}(x|y)] = -\sum_{j=1}^{n}\sum_{k=1}^{n} p(x_j, y_k)\log p(x_j|y_k). \quad (4.20)$$

That is, the logarithms of the probabilities of $x_j$ given $y_k$ are averaged by means of a weighted sum of the joint probabilities of the occurrence of $x_j$ and $y_k$. $H(X|Y)$ is, then, the average *a posteriori* uncertainty about the set of $x_j$ after the set $y_k$ has been received. It represents the information lost in transmission and is sometimes known as the *equivocation*.

Again using the principle expressed by Equations (2.4), (4.12), and (4.16) we write

$$\boxed{\mathscr{I}(X|Y) = H(X) - H(X|Y).} \qquad (4.21)$$

$\mathscr{I}(X|Y)$ is the average mutual information; or the average information about the ensemble of transmitted signals, $X$, contained in the ensemble of received signals, $Y$; or the average transmitted information. It will be referred to simply as the *transmitted information*. Expressing Equation (4.21) in words

transmitted information

     = source entropy − equivocation

     = source entropy − information loss due to errors in transmission

Equation (4.21) is an explicit form of Equation (4.12). Written in full,

$$\mathscr{I}(X|Y) = -\sum_{j=1}^{n} p(x_j)\log p(x_j) + \sum_{j=1}^{n}\sum_{k=1}^{n} p(x_j, y_k)\log p(x_j|y_k).$$

$$(4.21a)$$

An alternative formulation of this equation is (see Appendix)

$$\mathscr{I}(X|Y) = -\sum_{j=1}^{n} p(x_j)\log p(x_j) + \sum_{k=1}^{n} p(y_k)\sum_{j=1}^{n} p(x_j|y_k)\log p(x_j|y_k).$$

$$(4.21b)$$

It can be shown that $\mathscr{I}(X|Y)$ is always equal to or greater than zero.[1] When the channel is noiseless, $p(x_j, y_k) = 0$ for all $j \neq k$, so that from Equation (4.20), $H(X|Y) = 0$ and Equation (4.21) becomes effectively identical to (4.1).

In the same way we define

$$H(X, Y) = -\sum_{j=1}^{n}\sum_{k=1}^{n} p(x_j, y_k)\log p(x_j, y_k), \qquad (4.22)$$

where $H(X, Y)$ is the *joint entropy* of the ensembles. Analogously we can define the receiver entropy, $H(Y)$, and the information, $\mathscr{I}(Y|X)$. Various interesting relationships among these variables emerge, for which the reader is referred to the standard textbooks on communication theory.

The derivation of Equation (4.21) was our primary aim in this section. We now reorient ourselves and examine the noisy channel from the point of view of the psychologist of the 1950s.

## THE NOISY CHANNEL II

*The information required for a categorical judgment. The "confusion" matrix*

It was but 3 years after the appearance of Shannon's seminal work that Garner and Hake (1951) published their well-known paper entitled "The Amount of Information in Absolute Judgments." We derive Equation (4.21) again, but now within the context of a Garner–Hake experiment involving human judgments, rather than by analysis of the transmission of signals through a channel. Actually, there is no salient difference between these two paradigms, but it is instructive to look at the same problem in a different way

The idea of an experiment involving judged categories can be illustrated with the following simple example. Suppose that there are three rods whose lengths are 10, 20, and 30 cm. A subject is shown the 10-cm rod and told that it has a length of 10 cm; he or she is then shown the 20-cm rod and told that it has a length of 20 cm, etc. Thereafter, the experimenter draws the rods from the table and shows them to the subject, who tries to identify the rod as 10, 20, or 30 cm by visual examination. The subject is not permitted to measure the rods. However, the chances are good that he or she will never make a mistake; the 10-cm rod will always be identified as 10-cm long, etc. Let us call the actual rod presented to the subject *the stimulus* (the 10-cm rod will be stimulus 1; the 20-cm rod, stimulus 2; and the 30-cm rod, stimulus 3), and let us call the subject's identification or reply, *the response* (the identification *this rod is rod* 1 will be *response* 1, etc.) Suppose the experiment continues until 100 stimulus–responses have been made. We can represent the stimuli by $x_j$, $j = 1, 2, 3$, and the responses by $y_k$, $k = 1, 2, 3$. That is, $x_2$ will represent a trial where the subject is presented with the 20-cm rod for identification, and $y_3$ will represent the act of the subject in identifying the 30-cm rod. The results of such an experiment will probably look much like those shown in Table 4.1. In this example the 10-cm rod stimulus was given 33 times ($x_1 = 33$) and correctly identified 33 times ($y_1 = 33$). It was never incorrectly identified as the 20- or the 30-cm rod. The 20-cm rod was given 34 times, etc. The columns and rows are each summated and, of course, the sum of sums for rows and the sum of sums for columns are each equal to 100. In the *stimulus–response matrix* depicted by the Table 4.1 only the diagonal elements are nonzero.

Suppose that the three rods are now cut to 20, 22, and 24 cm, and the experiment is repeated. The subject is now going to make mistakes in identification. A possible stimulus—response matrix is shown in Table 4.2. In this hypothetical experiment the stimulus $x_1$, the 20-cm rod, was presented 33 times in all, was correctly identified only 21 times, and was

TABLE 4.1   Three Rods of Lengths 10, 20, and 30 cm

| Stimulus categories, $x_j$ | Response categories, $y_k$ | | | Totals |
| | $y_1 = 10$ cm | $y_2 = 20$ cm | $y_3 = 30$ cm | |
|---|---|---|---|---|
| $x_1 = 10$ cm | 33 | 0 | 0 | 33 |
| $x_2 = 20$ cm | 0 | 34 | 0 | 34 |
| $x_3 = 30$ cm | 0 | 0 | 33 | 33 |
| Totals | 33 | 34 | 33 | 100 |

TABLE 4.2    Three Rods of Lengths 20, 22 and 24 cm

| Stimulus categories, $x_j$ | Response categories, $y_k$ | | | Totals |
|---|---|---|---|---|
| | $y_1 = 20$ cm | $y_2 = 22$ cm | $y_3 = 24$ cm | |
| $x_1 = 20$ cm | 21 | 7 | 5 | 33 |
| $x_2 = 22$ cm | 8 | 24 | 2 | 34 |
| $x_3 = 24$ cm | 5 | 9 | 19 | 33 |
| Totals | 34 | 40 | 26 | 100 |

identified as $y_2$ on 7 occasions and as $y_3$ on 5 occasions. The stimulus–response matrix is no longer diagonal. The nonzero off-diagonal elements represent mistakes in identification (cf. errors in signal transmission). It would seem clear that a stimulus–response matrix (sometimes called a "confusion" matrix), is, in principle, the same as a transmission–receipt matrix for a standard communication channel such as a telephone; in place of "stimulus" read "signal transmitted" and in place of "response" read "signal received."

There are three restrictions to the type of category experiment with which we shall be dealing. First, we are concerned only with those experiments dealing with stimuli of the "intensity" type, such as the intensity of light or of sound or the concentration of a solution or the magnitude of a force. That is we shall *not* be concerned with stimuli such as the length of rods, although they served as a simple introduction to the confusion matrix. Second, we are interested primarily in the set of stimuli that span the totality of the physiological range, from threshold to maximum nonpainful stimulus; for example, auditory stimuli will extend from threshold to about $10^{10}$ or $10^{11}$ times threshold. The upper limit to the range of stimuli is often hard to define. Third, we are concerned primarily with the results obtained from "trained" subjects; that is, with subjects who have had as much time as desired to practice and learn which stimulus corresponds to which category. We speak more about the design of these experiments after we discuss the methods of analysis.

Let us now generalize the discussion of the stimulus–response matrix. Except for some minor changes in nomenclature, we follow the method of Garner and Hake. Although the number of stimulus categories need not, in principle, be equal to the number of response categories, we take them to be equal, just for simplicity.

Let $N$ be the total number of trials, or the number of times a stimulus was presented to a given subject in the course of a single experiment. Then $N_{jk}$ is the number of times a stimulus in category $j$ was given and identified to be response category $k$. That is, $N_{35}$ is the number of times stimulus category 3 was given by the investigator but identified or judged (incorrectly) to be (response) category 5. The $N_{jk}$ can be tabulated as in

TABLE 4.3   Generalized Stimulus–Response Matrix

| Stimulus categories | Response categories | | | | Total |
|---|---|---|---|---|---|
| | $y_1$    $y_2$ | $y_k$ | | $y_n$ | |
| $x_1$ | $N_{11}$  $N_{12}$ | $N_{1k}$ | | $N_{1n}$ | $N_{1.}$ |
| $x_2$ | $N_{21}$  $N_{22}$ | $N_{2k}$ | | $N_{2n}$ | $N_{2.}$ |
| $x_j$ | $N_{j1}$  $N_{j2}$ | $N_{jk}$ | | $N_{jn}$ | $N_{j.}$ |
| $x_n$ | $N_{n1}$  $N_{n2}$ | $N_{nk}$ | | $N_{nn}$ | $N_{n.}$ |
| Total | $N_{.1}$  $N_{.2}$ | $N_{.k}$ | | $N_{.n}$ | $N$ |

Table 4.3. The sum of all elements in the $k$th column equals $N_{.k}$ That is

$$\sum_{j=1}^{n} N_{jk} = N_{.k}.$$ (4.23)

Similarly, the sum of all elements in the $j$th row equals $N_{j.}$. That is

$$\sum_{k=1}^{n} N_{jk} = N_{j.}.$$ (4.24)

The total number of stimuli given is equal to the total number of responses made:

$$\sum_{k=1}^{n} N_{.k} = \sum_{j=1}^{n} N_{j.} = N$$ (4.25)

We can define the joint probability $p(x_j, y_k)$ by

$$p(x_j, y_k) = N_{jk}/N$$ (4.26)

We can also define the following probabilities, *a posteriori*, using $N_{.k}$, $N_{j.}$ and $N$:

$$p(x_j) = N_{j.}/N$$ (4.27)

$$p(y_k) = N_{.k}/N$$ (4.28)

Similarly, we can define the conditional probabilities

$$p(x_j|y_k) = N_{jk}/N_{.k},$$ (4.29)

which is the conditional probability of stimulus $x_j$ given response $y_k$ and

$$p(y_k|x_j) = N_{jk}/N_{j.},$$ (4.30)

which is the conditional probability of response $y_k$ given stimulus $x_j$. Each of the equations (4.26), (4.29), and (4.30) provides the elements for

TABLE 4.4a    Dividing Each Element of the Stimulus–Response Matrix in Table 4.3 by $N$ (Equation (4.26)) Produces a Matrix of Conditional Probabilities, $p(x_j, y_k)$

| Stimulus categories | Response categories | | |
| --- | --- | --- | --- |
| | $y_1$ | $y_k$ | $y_n$ |
| $x_1$ | $p(x_1, y_1)$ | $p(x_1, y_k)$ | $p(x_1, y_n)$ |
| $x_2$ | $p(x_2, y_1)$ | $p(x_2, y_k)$ | $p(x_2, y_n)$ |
| $x_j$ | $p(x_j, y_1)$ | $p(x_j, y_k)$ | $p(x_j, y_n)$ |
| $x_n$ | $p(x_n, y_1)$ | $p(x_n, y_k)$ | $p(x_n, y_n)$ |

TABLE 4.4b    Dividing Each Element of the Stimulus–Response Matrix in Table 4.3 by $N_{.k}$ (Equation (4.29)) Produces a Matrix of Conditional Probabilities, $p(x_j|y_k)$

| Stimulus categories | Response categories | | |
| --- | --- | --- | --- |
| | $y_1$ | $y_k$ | $y_n$ |
| $x_1$ | $p(x_1|y_1)$ | $p(x_1|y_k)$ | $p(x_1|y_n)$ |
| $x_2$ | $p(x_2|y_1)$ | $p(x_2|y_k)$ | $p(x_2|y_n)$ |
| $x_j$ | $p(x_j|y_1)$ | $p(x_j|y_k)$ | $p(x_j|y_n)$ |
| $x_n$ | $p(x_n|y_1)$ | $p(x_n|y_k)$ | $p(x_n|y_n)$ |

TABLE 4.4c    Dividing Each Element of the Stimulus–Response Matrix in Table 4.3 by $N_{j.}$ (Equation (4.30)) Produces a Matrix of Conditional Probabilities, $p(y_k|x_j)$

| Stimulus categories | Response categories | | |
| --- | --- | --- | --- |
| | $y_1$ | $y_k$ | $y_n$ |
| $x_1$ | $p(y_1|x_1)$ | $p(y_k|x_1)$ | $p(y_n|x_1)$ |
| $x_2$ | $p(y_1|x_2)$ | $p(y_k|x_2)$ | $p(y_n|x_2)$ |
| $x_j$ | $p(y_1|x_j)$ | $p(y_k|x_j)$ | $p(y_n|x_j)$ |
| $x_n$ | $p(y_1|x_n)$ | $p(y_k|x_n)$ | $p(y_n|x_n)$ |

a new matrix, which are shown in Tables 4.4a–4.4c. We observe that all of the elements in the matrices shown in Tables 4.3 and 4.4 can be evaluated from the data collected in an experiment on categorical judgments performed in the manner described above.

Recalling again the two defining equations for conditional probability,

$$p(x_j, y_k) = p(x_j|y_k) \cdot p(y_k) \tag{4.10}$$

$$p(x_j, y_k) = p(y_k|x_j) \cdot p(x_j). \tag{4.11}$$

The above two equations are verified by the *a posteriori* Equations (4.26) to (4.30). For example, using Equations (4.28) and (4.29), we can evaluate the right-hand side of Equation (4.10):

$$p(x_j|y_k) \cdot p(y_k) = \frac{N_{jk}}{N_{\cdot k}} \cdot \frac{N_{\cdot k}}{N} = \frac{N_{jk}}{N}.$$

By Equation (4.26), the left-hand side of (4.10) is given by $N_{jk}/N$, as required.

We require, now, one final definition. Let

$$P(x_j, y_k) = p(x_j) \cdot p(y_k). \qquad (4.31)$$

We can interpret the quantity $P(x_j, y_k)$ as the probability of occurrence of two independent events. These independent events occur with probabilities $p(x_j)$ and $p(y_k)$. For example, if a coin is tossed on two occasions, the outcomes of the two tosses are independent. The probability of heads on the first toss is $\frac{1}{2}$ and the probability of heads on the second toss is $\frac{1}{2}$. Therefore the probability of heads on both tosses equals $\frac{1}{2} \times \frac{1}{2} = \frac{1}{4}$. However, the outcome $y_k$ is, in general, not independent of the outcome $x_j$. That is, response $y_k$ is not, in general, independent of the applied stimulus, $x_j$. In fact, we believe that the outcome of stimulus events and response events are quite closely related. If $x_j$ and $y_k$ were independent or "uncoupled" for some observer, $P(x_j, y_k)$ would give the probability of concurrence of the two outcomes. He or she would, however, be the poorest possible observer, since his or her responses would be totally unrelated to the corresponding stimulus (see, however, the problem for the reader in Chapter 5, Psychology: Categorical Judgments).

Now, we have defined the joint entropy of this stimulus–response system by Equation (4.22)

$$H(X, Y) = - \sum_{j=1}^{n} \sum_{k=1}^{n} p(x_j, y_k) \log p(x_j, y_k). \qquad (4.22)$$

Therefore, we can define the *maximum* joint entropy by

$$H(X, Y)_{\max} = - \sum_{j=1}^{n} \sum_{k=1}^{n} P(x_j, y_k) \log P(x_j, y_k). \qquad (4.32)$$

The maximum entropy corresponds to the most "disordered" system, which, in turn, corresponds to the system in which input (stimulus) and output (response) are totally uncorrelated. In such a system joint entropy is equal to $H(X, Y)_{\max}$. In such a system no information about the stimulus is transmitted to the subject since he or she does not associate a given response with any particular stimulus.

We can now present an alternative to Equations (4.12) and (4.21), which stated that the average information about the ensemble of transmitted signals or stimuli contained in the ensemble of received signals or responses is given by

$$\mathscr{I}(X|Y) = H(X) - H(X|Y) \qquad (4.21)$$

$$= H_{\text{before}} - H_{\text{after}} \qquad (4.12)$$

We now introduce as an equivalent mathematical statement

$$\mathscr{I}(X|Y) = H(X,Y)_{\text{max}} - H(X,Y). \qquad (4.33)$$

The quantities on the right-hand side can be evaluated using Equation (4.22) and (4.32), which, in turn, can be evaluated from the measured results. Equation (4.33) is, perhaps, more easily understood intuitively than (4.21). When $H(X,Y)$ takes on its maximum value (transmitted and received signals independent), the transmitted information, $\mathscr{I}(X|Y)$, equals zero as required. When $H(X,Y)$ takes on its minimum value, $\mathscr{I}(X|Y)$ is maximum. But $\mathscr{I}(X|Y)$ is maximum when no errors in identification are made; that is, when the matrix elements $N_{jk} = 0$ for $j \neq k$. We can see from Table 4.1 that under these conditions, Equation (4.33) reduces to

$$\mathscr{I}(X|Y) = H(X). \qquad (4.34)$$

With reference now to Equation (4.21), we see that $\mathscr{I}(X|Y)$ is maximum when the equivocation, $H(X|Y)$ is equal to zero, when we have

$$\mathscr{I}(X|Y) = H(X). \qquad (4.34)$$

So we obtain the same asymptotic result from (4.21) and (4.33). Therefore, on first glance, Equation (4.21) and (4.33) seem to exhibit similar properties. The interested reader is referred to the Appendix for a detailed proof that these equations are actually identical.

Equation (4.21) may be written in words:

Information transmitted = stimulus entropy − stimulus equivocation.

$$(4.35)$$

We may now add a symmetrical equation,

$$\mathscr{I}(X|Y) = H(Y) - H(Y|X) \qquad (4.36)$$

or, expressed in words,

information transmitted = receiver entropy − receiver equivocation.

$$(4.37)$$

## SUMMARY

Amid the maelstrom of equations in this chapter, let us keep in mind that what we have done is, in the final analysis, very simple. We have demonstrated in two ways (using the paradigm of a transmission line and of an experiment on categorical judgments) that information transmitted for a noisy channel, $\mathscr{I}(X|Y)$, may be calculated from Equations (4.21) and (4.36):

$$\mathscr{I}(X|Y) = H(X) - H(X|Y)$$
$$= H(Y) - H(Y|X) \text{ bits per signal or bits per stimulus.}$$

Some of the probabilities used to calculate $\mathscr{I}(X|Y)$ may be known *a priori*, such as the $p(x_j)$, the probability of transmission of a signal or of application of a stimulus. Other probabilities may only be known *a posteriori*, after an experiment has been conducted. We run through an example of the calculation of $\mathscr{I}(X|Y)$ in the next chapter.

The above equations have been derived from two ostensibly distinct, but nonetheless equivalent, starting points. We began with

$$\mathscr{I}(X|Y) = H_{\text{before}} - H_{\text{after}}, \tag{4.12}$$

and alternatively with

$$\mathscr{I}(X|Y) = H(X, Y)_{\text{max}} - H(X, Y). \tag{4.33}$$

Both viewpoints led to the same conclusion.

We note, finally, that when the equivocation, $H(X|Y)$, is equal to zero, we obtain

$$\mathscr{I}(X|Y) = H(X), \tag{4.34}$$

which is the information transmitted for a noiseless channel, as expressed by Equation (4.1).

## THE BOTTOM LINE

In order to calculate the average mutual information, $\mathscr{I}(X|Y)$, one may use either Equation (4.21a) or (4.21b). Either of these equations may be conveniently utilized in a computer program, such as the one given in Chapter 5.

## APPENDIX: THE EQUIVALENCE OF EQUATIONS (4.21) AND (4.33)

$$\mathscr{I}(X|Y) = H(X) - H(X|Y) \tag{4.21}$$

and

$$\mathscr{I}(X|Y) = H(X, Y)_{\text{max}} - H(X, Y) \tag{4.33}$$

are identical.

Beginning with Equation (4.33), we expand the right-hand side using Equations (4.22) and (4.32):

$$\mathcal{I}(X|Y) = -\sum_{j=1}^{n}\sum_{k=1}^{n} P(x_j, y_k)\log P(x_j, y_k)$$

$$+ \sum_{j=1}^{n}\sum_{k=1}^{n} p(x_j, y_k)\log p(x_j, y_k). \qquad (A4.1)$$

The first double-summation on the right-hand side can be simplified by introducing Equation (4.31), the defining equation for $P(x_j, y_k)$:

$$-\sum_{j=1}^{n}\sum_{k=1}^{n} P(x_j, y_k)\log P(x_j, y_k)$$

$$= -\sum_{j=1}^{n}\sum_{k=1}^{n} p(x_j)p(y_k)\log\left[p(x_j)p(y_k)\right]$$

$$= -\sum_{j=1}^{n}\sum_{k=1}^{n} p(x_j)p(y_k)\log p(x_j) - \sum_{j=1}^{n}\sum_{k=1}^{n} p(x_j)p(y_k)\log p(y_k)$$

$$= -\sum_{j=1}^{n} p(x_j)\log p(x_j) \sum_{k=1}^{n} p(y_k) - \sum_{j=1}^{n} p(x_j) \sum_{k=1}^{n} p(y_k)\log p(y_k).$$

Since $\sum_{j=1}^{n} p(x_j) = 1 = \sum_{k=1}^{n} p(y_k)$,

$$-\sum_{j=1}^{n}\sum_{k=1}^{n} P(x_j, y_k)\log P(x_j, y_k)$$

$$= -\sum_{j=1}^{n} p(x_j)\log p(x_j) - \sum_{k=1}^{n} p(y_k)\log p(y_k)$$

$$= H(X) + H(Y) \qquad (A4.2)$$

by Equation (4.19) and its analog.

Continuing with the second double summation on the right-hand side of Equation (A4.1),

$$\sum_{j=1}^{n}\sum_{k=1}^{n} p(x_j, y_k)\log p(x_j, y_k)$$

$$= \sum_{j=1}^{n}\sum_{k=1}^{n} p(y_k)p(x_j|y_k)\log\left[p(y_k)p(x_j|y_k)\right]$$

using Equation (4.11),

$$= \sum_{j=1}^{n} \sum_{k=1}^{n} p(y_k)\log p(y_k) \cdot p(x_j|y_k) + \sum_{j=1}^{n} \sum_{k=1}^{n} p(y_k)p(x_j|y_k)\log p(x_j|y_k)$$

$$\text{(A4.3)}$$

$$= \sum_{k=1}^{n} p(y_k)\log p(y_k) \sum_{j=1}^{n} p(x_j|y_k) + \sum_{j=1}^{n} \sum_{k=1}^{n} p(y_k)p(x_j|y_k)\log p(x_j|y_k)$$

$$= \sum_{k=1}^{n} p(y_k)\log p(y_k) + \sum_{j=1}^{n} \sum_{k=1}^{n} p(x_j, y_k)\log p(x_j|y_k) \qquad \text{(A4.4)}$$

(since $\sum_{j=1}^{n} p(x_j|y_k) = 1$)

$$= -H(Y) - H(X|Y), \qquad \text{(A4.5)}$$

where

$$H(Y) = -\sum_{k=1}^{n} p(y_k)\log p(y_k) = \text{receiver entropy} \qquad \text{(A4.6)}$$

and

$$H(X|Y) = -\sum_{j=1}^{n} \sum_{k=1}^{n} p(x_j, y_k)\log p(x_j|y_k) = \text{source equivocation.}$$

$$\text{(4.20)}$$

Combining Equations (A4.1), (A4.2), and (A4.5), we have

$$\mathscr{I}(X|Y) = H(X) + H(Y) - H(Y) - H(X|Y)$$
$$\mathscr{I}(X|Y) = H(X) - H(X|Y). \qquad \text{(A4.7)/(4.21)}$$

We observe that Equation (A4.7) is identical to Equation (4.21). This equation gives the average mutual information, or the average information about the

$$\text{ensemble of} \left| \begin{array}{c} \text{transmitted signals} \\ \text{stimuli} \end{array} \right| X,$$

contained in the

$$\text{ensemble of} \left| \begin{array}{c} \text{received signals} \\ \text{responses} \end{array} \right| Y,$$

or the *average transmitted information*.

Therefore, we have converted the right-hand side of Equation (4.33) into the right-hand side of Equation (4.21), showing that the equations are identical.

If we evaluate the second double summation on the right-hand side of Equation (A4.1) using the conditional probability $p(y_k|x_j)$, we can obtain in the same way Equation (4.36). Finally we should note that if we write

$$p(x_j, y_k) = p(y_k)p(x_j|y_k), \qquad (4.11)$$

introduce this quantity into Equation (4.20), and reverse the order of summation, we have

$$H(X|Y) = -\sum_{k=1}^{n} p(y_k) \sum_{j=1}^{n} p(x_j|y_k)\log p(x_j|y_k) \qquad (A4.8)$$

which is an alternative formulation of $H(X|Y)$. This equation was used to derive Equation (4.21b).

## NOTES

1. There are very few "it can be shown that"'s in this book. Personally, I regard that phrase with a degree of suspicion; I suspect the author really can't prove it, and this is his way of getting off the hook. But what really elevates suspicion to the point of certainty is when the author writes "It can *easily* be shown that." How many hours I have whiled away just to prove things that one author or another had found so obvious that it was not worth demonstrating! Would it have taken me that long if it could be *"easily shown"*? Certainly not! I'm sure the author is bluffing. All of them are. It can't be me.

## REFERENCES

Freund, J. E., and Walpole, R. E. 1980. *Mathematical Statistics*. Prentice–Hall, Englewood Cliffs, NJ.

Garner, W. R., and Hake, H. W. 1951. The amount of information in absolute judgments. *Psychological Review* **58**, 446–459.

Middleton, D. 1960. *An Introduction to Statistical Communication Theory*. McGraw–Hill, New York.

Raisbeck, G. 1963. *Information Theory: An Introduction for Scientists and Engineers*. MIT Press, Cambridge.

Shannon, C. E., and Weaver, W. 1949. *The Mathematical Theory of Communication*. Univ. Illinois Press, Urbana.

# 5

## Information of Events with Discrete Outcomes: Applications in Communications Science and in Psychology

### COMMUNICATIONS SCIENCE

We have now developed some of the fundamental equations governing information transmitted in the presence of noise. The type of source we have considered is one in which successive symbols emitted are statistically independent of each other. For example, if the alphabet of transmitted symbols is just the ordinary English alphabet, the probability $p(h)$ of emitting the letter $h$ from the source is independent of the previous letter emitted. However, experience tells us that this assumption of independence is unrealistic. For example if the preceding letter was $s$ or $c$, the probability of $h$ following would seem to be greater than if the preceding letter was, say, $a$ or $b$, since there are, surely, more words containing the combination sh or ch than ah or bh. The type of source we have modeled is called a *zero memory source*. Suppose that the 26 letters of the English alphabet and the "blank" symbol are equally probable. An upper limit to the source entropy by Equation (4.4) is, then,

$$H(X) = \log_2 27 = 4.75 \text{ bits per letter.}$$

In fact, a more realistic estimate places $H(X)$ between 0.6 and 1.3 bits per letter (Pierce, 1980). Nonetheless, bearing in mind the limitations of the zero memory model, we can begin to appreciate the applicability of our equations.

The application of information theory by communications engineers is based on the equivalence of the *bit* with the *binary digit*. If a noiseless channel can transmit $C$ on-or-off pulses per second, then it can transmit $C$ binary digits per second; and if each binary digit carries one bit of information, the channel can transmit $C$ bits per second. We may say that the *channel capacity* is $C$ bits per second.

Suppose the source entropy for the noiseless channel is $H(X)$ bits per symbol. Then if the channel capacity is $C$ bits per second, the output of the source can be *coded* in such a way that the channel can transmit an average of $C/H$ symbols per second. The average rate of transmission cannot exceed this value of $C/H$. The above theorem is due to Shannon.

We cannot discuss here the science and art of coding; it would take us too far afield. The reader is referred to the texts on information theory, which treat the matter of coding very thoroughly.

For the case of the discrete noisy channel we refer to Equation (4.21),

$$\mathscr{I}(X|Y) = H(X) - H(X|Y). \tag{4.21}$$

Suppose that all quantities in this equation are measured in units of bits per second. The channel capacity, $C$, is equal to the maximum possible value of the rate of transmission for the channel, $\mathscr{I}(X|Y)_{\max}$ [bits per second]. Shannon's fundamental theorem for a noisy channel is as follows. Choose a value of $\mathscr{I}(X|Y) = \mathscr{I}$. If $\mathscr{I} < C$ there exists a coding system such that the output of the source can be transmitted over the channel with an arbitrarily small frequency of errors (or an arbitrarily small equivocation).

Clearly, the above is of great interest to communications engineers. A primary application of information theory in communications science is, therefore, the calculation of channel capacity. Knowledge of channel capacity, then, leads to the development of efficient codes for the transmission of messages.

Perhaps the real power of information theory in communications comes with the analysis of channels that transmit continuous rather than discrete signals; that is, continuous waveforms rather than just discrete zeros and ones and the like. For such continuous or "analog" channels, using the known ratio of signal-to-noise power and the bandwidth of the channel, one can calculate *a priori* the value of the channel capacity. Therefore, one can calculate the greatest number of bits per second transmissible by the channel from a knowledge of two physical parameters. The nature of such a calculation awaits our introduction to the information of events with continuous outcomes (Chapter 8), but we can certainly appreciate its significance even at this stage.

## PSYCHOLOGY: CATEGORICAL JUDGMENTS

We have seen in Chapter 4 the manner in which psychologists utilized the information transmission function (Equations (4.21) and (4.33)) to calculate the amount of information (in bits per stimulus) transmitted in

TABLE 5.1   Stimulus–Response Matrix

| Stimulus categories | Response categories | | | | | |
|---|---|---|---|---|---|---|
| | $y_1$ | $y_2$ | $y_3$ | $y_4$ | $y_5$ | $N_{j.}$ |
| $x_1$ | 20 | 5 | 0 | 0 | 0 | 25 |
| $x_2$ | 5 | 15 | 5 | 0 | 0 | 25 |
| $x_3$ | 0 | 6 | 17 | 2 | 0 | 25 |
| $x_4$ | 0 | 0 | 5 | 12 | 8 | 25 |
| $x_5$ | 0 | 0 | 0 | 6 | 19 | 25 |
| $N_{.k}$ | 25 | 26 | 27 | 20 | 27 | 125 |

an experiment on categorical judgments. Many different types of categorical experiment were performed evaluating $\mathscr{I}(X|Y)$, for example, for brightness, hue, position of a pointer in a linear interval, loudness, pitch, odor intensity, taste intensity, etc. Stimuli of the simplest type, such as loudness or pitch, have been termed "one-dimensional," while position of a dot in a square would be called "two-dimensional" because both horizontal and vertical coordinates must be identified by the subject. Similarly, identification of colors of equal luminance has been termed two-dimensional, since the colors can vary both in hue and in saturation. We shall confine our discussion to one-dimensional stimuli.

In Chapter 4, we discussed the general theory of measuring transmitted information, $\mathscr{I}(X|Y)$, for an experiment on categorical recognition or judgment. Let us now take a specific numerical example of a stimulus–response or confusion matrix and evaluate $\mathscr{I}(X|Y)$ using Equation (4.21) or (4.21a). Consider the hypothetical experiment whose stimulus–response matrix is given in Table 5.1. Dividing each matrix element by the sum of all the elements, which is 125, will give the matrix of joint probabilities, Table 5.2. Table 5.3 gives the matrix of conditional probabilities, $p(y_k|x_j)$, calculated from Equation (4.30). Also entered in this table are $p(x_j)$ and $p(y_k)$, evaluated from Equations (4.27) and (4.28). Table 5.4 gives the matrix of conditional probabilities, $p(x_j|y_k)$, calcu-

TABLE 5.2   Matrix of Joint Probabilities $p(x_j, y_k)$

| | $y_1$ | $y_2$ | $y_3$ | $y_4$ | $y_5$ |
|---|---|---|---|---|---|
| $x_1$ | 0.16 | 0.04 | 0 | 0 | 0 |
| $x_2$ | 0.04 | 0.12 | 0.04 | 0 | 0 |
| $x_3$ | 0 | 0.048 | 0.136 | 0.016 | 0 |
| $x_5$ | 0 | 0 | 0 | 0.048 | 0.152 |

1

TABLE 5.3    Matrix of Conditional Probabilities $p(y_k|x_j)$

|        | $y_1$ | $y_2$ | $y_3$ | $y_4$ | $y_5$ | $p(x_j) = N_{j.}/125$ |
|--------|-------|-------|-------|-------|-------|-----------------------|
| $x_1$  | 0.80  | 0.20  | 0     | 0     | 0     | 0.20                  |
| $x_2$  | 0.20  | 0.60  | 0.20  | 0     | 0     | 0.20                  |
| $x_3$  | 0     | 0.24  | 0.68  | 0.08  | 0     | 0.20                  |
| $x_4$  | 0     | 0     | 0.20  | 0.48  | 0.32  | 0.20                  |
| $x_5$  | 0     | 0     | 0     | 0.24  | 0.76  | 0.20                  |
| $p(y_k) = N_{.k}/125$ | 0.200 | 0.208 | 0.216 | 0.160 | 0.216 | 1 |

lated from Equation (4.29). From Equation (4.19),

$$H(X) = -5(0.2\ln 0.2) = 1.60944 \text{ natural units.}$$

Multiplying the elements of Table 5.2 by the logarithms of the corresponding elements of Table 5.4 (recalling that $0\log 0 = 0$) gives $H(X|Y)$ (Equation (4.20)).

$$H(X|Y) = 0.77518 \text{ natural units.}$$

From Equation (4.21), transmitted information per stimulus

$$\mathscr{I}(X|Y) = 1.60944 - 0.77518 = 0.83426 \text{ natural units.}$$

$$0.83426/\ln 2 = 1.2036 \text{ bits.}$$

The above represents rather a lot of work, even with the use of a calculator, although there were only five categories. Alternatively, a spreadsheet can be used with calculations performed using macros. Once you understand the principles involved, you may wish to use a computer program like the one written in Basic provided below. The program uses standard matrix notation, so that $C(I, J)$ represents $N_{ij}$, which is the

TABLE 5.4    Matrix of Conditional Probabilities $p(x_j|y_k)$

|        | $y_1$ | $y_2$   | $y_3$    | $y_4$ | $y_5$    |
|--------|-------|---------|----------|-------|----------|
| $x_1$  | 0.80  | 0.19231 | 0        | 0     | 0        |
| $x_2$  | 0.20  | 0.57692 | 0.185185 | 0     | 0        |
| $x_3$  | 0     | 0.23077 | 0.629629 | 0.1   | 0        |
| $x_4$  | 0     | 0       | 0.185185 | 0.6   | 0.296296 |
| $x_5$  | 0     | 0       | 0        | 0.3   | 0.703703 |

number in the $i$th row and $j$th column of the original stimulus–response matrix.

```
10 'MARCH 26, 1991; K. H. NORWICH
20 'CALCULATES TRANSMITTED INFORMATION FROM A CONFUSION
       MATRIX.
30 'INFORMATION, IXGY = IYGX, OR I(X¦Y) = I(Y¦X), IS CALCULATED FROM
40 'EQUATION 4.21.
50 '
60 INPUT "NUMBER OF ROWS = ";M
70 INPUT "NUMBER OF COLUMNS = ";N
80 DIM C(M,N): 'CONFUSION MATRIX
90 DIM PJ(M,N): 'JOINT PROBABILITY MATRIX
100 DIM PXGY(M,N): 'MATRIX OF CONDITIONAL PROBABILITIES, X Given Y
110 DIM PYGX(M,N): 'MATRIX OF CONDITIONAL PROBABILITIES, Y Given X
120 DIM SUMX(N): ' N.k
130 DIM SUMY(M): ' Nj.
140 '
150 PRINT "ENTER DATA FOR PRIMARY CONFUSION MATRIX"
160 FOR X = 1 TO M
170   FOR Y = 1 TO N
180     PRINT "C(";X;Y;") = ";
190     INPUT C(X,Y)
200     TOTAL = TOTAL + C(X,Y)
210   NEXT Y
220 NEXT X
230 '
240 'CALCULATE Nj. AND N.k AND JOINT PROBABILITY MATRIX
250 FOR X = 1 TO M
260   FOR Y = 1 TO N
270     SUMY(X) = SUMY(X) + C(X,Y)
280     SUMX(Y) = SUMX(Y) + C(X,Y)
290     PJ(X,Y) = C(X,Y)/TOTAL
300   NEXT Y
310 NEXT X
320 '
330 'CALCULATE SOURCE AND RECEIVER ENTROPIES
340 FOR X = 1 TO M
350   HX = HX − (SUMY(X)/TOTAL)*LOG(SUMY(X)/TOTAL)
360 NEXT X
370 FOR Y = 1 TO N
380   HY = HY − (SUMX(Y)/TOTAL)*LOG(SUMX(Y)/TOTAL)
390 NEXT Y
400 '
410 'CALCULATE SOURCE AND RECEIVER ENTROPIES AND MATRICES OF
       CONDITIONAL PROBS
420 FOR X = 1 TO M
430   FOR Y = 1 TO N
440     PYGX(X,Y) = C(X,Y)/SUMY(X)
450     PXGY(X,Y) = C(X,Y)/SUMX(Y)
460   NEXT Y
470 NEXT X
480 '
490 'CALCULATE H(X¦Y) AND H(Y¦X)
500 FOR X = 1 TO M
510   FOR Y = 1 TO N
520     IF PXGY(X,Y) = 0 THEN 540
530     HXGY = HXGY − PJ(X,Y)*LOG(PXGY(X,Y))
540     IF PYGX(X,Y) = 0 THEN 560
```

```
550   HYGX = HYGX – PJ(X,Y)*LOG(PYGX(X,Y))
560  NEXT Y
570 NEXT X
580 '
590 'CALCULATE INFORMATION BY TWO FORMULAS
600 IXGY = HX – HXGY:   'EQUATION (4.21)
610 IYGX = HY – HYGX:   'EQUATION (4.36)
620 '
630 ' PRINT OUT SOURCE AND RECEIVER ENTROPIES,
640 'EQUIVOCATIONS AND INFORMATION TRANSMITTED, I(X¦Y) = I(Y¦X)
650 PRINT "SOURCE ENTROPY = "; HX; "NATURAL UNITS, OR"; HX/LOG(2); "
     BITS"
660 PRINT "RECEIVER ENTROPY = "; HY; "NATURAL UNITS, OR"; HY/LOG(2);
     " BITS"
670 PRINT "SOURCE EQUIVOCATION = "; HXGY; "NATURAL UNITS, OR";
     HXGY/LOG(2);   " BITS"
680 PRINT "RECEIVER EQUIVOCATION = "; HYGX; "NATURAL UNITS, OR";
     HYGX/LOG(2);   " BITS"
690 PRINT "I(X¦Y) = "; IXGY; " NATURAL UNITS, OR" ;IXGY/LOG(2); " BITS"
700 PRINT "I(Y¦X) = "; IYGX; " NATURAL UNITS, OR" ;IYGX/LOG(2); " BITS"
710 END
```

Both for fun and for further insight, you might like to consider the following problem. Suppose that in an experiment on categorical judgments there are $n$ categories. In the resulting stimulus–response matrix there are only $n$ nonzero elements. No two of the nonzero elements occupy the same row or the same column. Suppose, further, that all of the diagonal elements, $N_{ii}$, are zero. That is, our hapless subject did not correctly identify even one stimulus! For example, if $n = 3$, the matrix may look like this:

|  | Response $y$ | | |
|---|---|---|---|
| | 0 | $a$ | 0 |
| Stimulus $x$ | 0 | 0 | $b$ |
| | $c$ | 0 | 0 |

$a, b, c > 0.$

Every time a stimulus from category 1 was given, it was consistently identified as belonging to category 2; every time a stimulus from category 2 was given, it was consistently identified as belonging to category 3; etc.

What values would you expect for the equivocations $H(X|Y)$ and $H(Y|X)$? Derive the equivocations mathematically or calculate them using the computer program. What does this strange result mean?

Turning now to another matter, how will $\mathcal{I}(X|Y)$, the measured transmitted information, vary with the number of categories, $n$, in an experiment on categorical judgments of one-dimensional stimuli? Let us regard the stimulus probabilities, $p(x_j)$, since they are under control of the experimenter, as equally probable so that $p(x_j) = 1/n$. Therefore, the source or stimulus entropy, $H(X)$ (Equation (4.19)), is equal to $\log_2 n$ bits. Let us also select the range of stimuli to extend from the minimum perceptible stimulus to the maximum perceptible stimulus (below the threshold for pain). We can now draw a graph of transmitted information, $\mathscr{I}(X|Y)$, against stimulus entropy, $H(X)$. We should recall here Equation (4.21):

$$\mathscr{I}(X|Y) = H(X) - H(X|Y). \qquad (4.21)$$

Clearly, when $n = 1$, $H(X) = 0$ and $\mathscr{I}(X|Y) = 0$; if there is only one category, no information can be transmitted since there was no prior uncertainty. Suppose that $n = 2$ and that the two stimulus categories lie at opposite ends of the spectrum of stimulus values, category 1 bordering the threshold value and category 2 bordering the greatest possible stimulus value if this can be defined. For stimuli of the intensity type, the greatest stimulus intensity would be close to the maximum allowable physiological value. In this experiment ($n = 2$), it is unlikely that stimuli would be confused. The equivocation would be close to zero, so that $\mathscr{I}(X|Y) = H(X) \cong 1$ bit. Thus, for the first two values of $n$ considered, $\mathscr{I}(X|Y)$ has been equal or very nearly equal to $H(X)$.

Now let us increase $n$ to 3 by adding a category between the high and low extremes. Will the subject make any mistakes in identifying categories? Occasionally, perhaps. However, with $n$ equal to 4 categories, mistakes will probably be made; $H(X|Y)$ will be greater than zero and $\mathscr{I}(X|Y)$ will be less than $H(X)$. As $n$ increases, $\mathscr{I}(X|Y)$ will continue to rise, but less than the rise in $H(X)$ and, thus, will fall below the straight line $\mathscr{I}(X|Y) = H(X)$. The graph obtained experimentally is shown schematically in Figure 5.1. $\mathscr{I}(X|Y)$ approaches an asymptote at about 2.5 bits of information per stimulus ($\mathscr{I}(X|Y)_{\max}$). While the position of this asymptote is not invariant, it does not change dramatically for different types of stimulus. For example, for pitch $\mathscr{I}(X|Y)_{\max}$ is about 2.5 bits per stimulus (Pollack, 1952, 1953); for auditory intensity, 2.3–2.5 bits per stimulus (Garner, 1953); and for taste 1.7–1.9 bits per stimulus (Beebe-Center et al., 1955). When you think about it, this is quite surprising. Why should there be a common upper limit to our ability to make "absolute" or categorical judgments? If we set $H(X|Y)$ equal to zero in Equation (4.21) we can write

$$\mathscr{I}(X|Y)_{\max} = H(X)_{\max} - 0. \qquad (5.1)$$

Suppose we also set

$$H(X)_{\max} = \log_2(n_{\max}), \qquad (5.2)$$

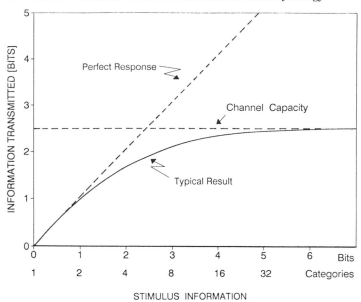

STIMULUS INFORMATION

FIGURE 5.1  Schematic graph representing the information transmitted in an experiment on categorical judgments. The abscissa contains the stimulus entropy, $H(X)$, measured in number of equally probable categories, and in bits as $\log_2$ (*number of equally probable categories*). The ordinate contains the information transmitted, $\mathscr{I}(X|Y)$, as calculated from Equation (4.21). The straight line $\mathscr{I}(X|Y) = H(X)$ represents the "best" possible performance, with equivocation equal to zero. Typically, the experimentally obtained curve falls progressively below the line of best performance and approaches $\mathscr{I}(X|Y)_{\max}$, which is the channel capacity, drawn at about 2.5 bits per stimulus.

since stimulus categories are equally probable. Therefore

$$n_{\max} = 2^{\mathscr{I}(X|Y)\max} = 2^{2.5} = 5.7 \text{ categories.} \qquad (5.3)$$

That is, it is "as if" 5.7 (equally probable) categories can be identified without error. Hence Miller's famous paper "The Magical Number Seven, Plus or Minus Two: Some Limits on Our Capacity for Processing Information (1956). Later studies, particularly on categorical judgments of "intensities," might suggest that the number is closer to 6 than 7, and, in a flight of fancy, we later speculate on the merits of $2\pi \simeq 6.3$.

The value of $\mathscr{I}(X|Y)$ has been termed the channel capacity by analogy with the use of this term in communications science. The measurement of channel capacity for categorical judgments has been subjected to a great deal of analysis. For example, "edge effects" must be considered: the enhanced ability of subjects to categorize stimuli at the extreme values. "Practice effect" refers to the ability of subjects to increase $\mathscr{I}(X|Y)_{\max}$ by prolonged practice or to the augmented channel capacity of experts; for example, it seems that wine tasters possess an enhanced ability to identify tastes. "Feedback effect" refers to the subject's being told, after making a judgment, whether it was correct etc. Anomolous results may emerge if $\mathcal{I}(X|Y)_{max}$ is computed from an averaged confusion matrix rather than a matrix representing a subject's performance on a single occasion.

Values of $\mathcal{I}(X|Y)_{max}$ measured from two-dimensional stimuli are greater than those measured from one-dimensional stimuli, but usually not twice as great. For example, $\mathcal{I}(X|Y)_{max}$ for a pointer in a linear interval has been measured to be 3.25 bits (Hake and Garner, 1951), while $\mathcal{I}(X|Y)_{max}$ for a pointer in a square equals about 4.6 bits $\neq 2 \times$ 3.25 bits (Klemmer and Frick, 1953).

I shall have a good deal to say in this book about one-dimensional stimuli of the intensity type, such as the intensity of sound or the concentration of a solution that is to be tasted. I shall approach the question of the maximum information transmitted per stimulus in quite a different way; that is, I suggest a rather different way of measuring the channel capacity.

## THE CONCEPTUAL BASIS FOR THE APPLICATION OF INFORMATION THEORY AS DEVELOPED IN THE 1950s

To review:

In the 1950s, both communications engineers and psychologists began to utilize information theory to calculate channel capacities. Stripped to its conceptual bones, the process was as follows. An entity called "information," whose magnitude could be calculated from the properties of a channel of communication, was defined. Each channel was tagged or labeled with a number called the channel capacity, which represented the greatest amount of information that could be transmitted per symbol (or per stimulus) using this channel. This channel capacity was then utilized in different ways by the respective disciplines; the engineers used it as a guide for coding, the psychologists as a means of analyzing perceptual processes.

Two features of information theory as it was employed by these disciplines should be recognized: (i) its nonunique nature and (ii) its extrinsic nature. These two properties, as we shall see, are not totally independent.

(i) Shannon's seminal paper on what is now called "information theory" was entitled, modestly, "A Mathematical Theory of Communication"; it was not entitled "The Mathematical Theory of Communication." There was wisdom in Shannon's selection of the indefinite article, since there are other possible measures of information. Perhaps the most celebrated is *Fisher's information* (Fisher, 1949). Fisher defined information to be proportional to the reciprocal of variance. For example, a calculated quantity is subject to random error and, as a result, has variance $\sigma^2$. If the experiment or measurement is then repeated $N$ times, the variance will be reduced to $\sigma^2/N$. Therefore, for large $N$, variance becomes small. The reciprocal of variance is, therefore, a measure of information provided by measurements (see, for example, Bell, 1968). There are other, more general measures of entropy and information (see, for example, Renyi, 1970; Van der Lubbe *et al.*, 1984). Many people, myself included, think that Shannon's measure is the most natural and most useful but, admittedly, it is not unique. Consider also *algorithmic information content* or *algorithmic randomness* of a physical entity, which is defined by Zurek (1990) as "the size (in bits) of the most concise message (e.g., of the shortest program for a universal computer) which describes that entity with requisite accuracy."

(ii) By "extrinsic" I refer to the tag or label that is pinned on the communications channel, branding it with a stated channel capacity. Because there are other possible measures of information it is, in principle, possible to label the channel with a different number, representing an alternative measure. The point is, though, that our calculations or predictions of the physical operation of the channel are unaffected by the information label we put upon it. That is, the physical theory of channel function is independent of which mathematical equation we use to assess its efficiency in transmitting information. The physical system is, so to speak, oblivious of the measure of information used by the engineer or psychologist to appraise it.

There is a tendency across all disciplines by those who apply the information measure to do so in a manner in which the measure is nonunique and extrinsic. For example, Norbert Wiener, in his famous book *Cybernetics* (1948), introduced the world to the logarithmic measure of information with the following sentences: "We know *a priori* that a variable lies between 0 and 1, and *a posteriori* that it lies on the interval $(a, b)$ inside $(0, 1)$. Then the amount of information we have from our *a posteriori* knowledge is

$$- log_2 \frac{measure\ of\ (a, b)}{measure\ of\ (0, 1)}."$$

The measure is nonunique: we could select other measures of the amount of information given by knowing the position of a point in a line. The measure is also extrinsic to the line interval $(a, b)$, in the sense that we could adopt a different measure of information, and this would not in any way affect our measure of the interval $(a, b)$. The measure of $(a, b)$ is totally unaffected by the method we use to assess its information content. The nonuniqueness and extrinsic properties are related.

G. Gatlin (1972) advocated a measure of the information content of a chain of DNA. The maximum possible entropy of a length of DNA is calculated *a priori* by assuming that at each position in the molecule the four bases adenine, guanine, thymine, and cytosine were equally probable. The *a posteriori* entropy is then calculated after analyzing the DNA molecule and measuring the actual base frequencies. The difference between *a priori* value and *a posteriori* value is then taken as a measure of the information content of the molecule. Again the measure is nonunique, since we could devise other measures of information content of DNA (e.g., the number of amino acids in the corresponding protein structure?), and extrinsic because the biochemistry of DNA does not seem to depend on or change with an information measure.

All this is, of course, not surprising, but I raise the issue here in order to contrast the information scientist's use of the information measure with the physicist's use of the information measure. We shall see in the next chapter that the physicist's measure of information is, indeed, (i) unique and (ii) intrinsic to the system. That is, the physicist may not make an arbitrary selection from among the various mathematical functions that measure information, and, if he or she should select an alternative measure, the calculated or predicted behavior of the system under study (cf. communications channel) would differ from the observed behavior. The calculated information enters as a variable into the dynamics of the physical system.

## REFERENCES

Beebe-Center, J. G., Rogers, M. S., and O'Connell, D. N. 1955. Transmission of information about sucrose and saline solutions through the sense of taste. *Journal of Psychology* **39**, 157–160.

Bell, D. A. 1968. *Information Theory and Its Engineering Applications*, 4th ed. Pitman, London.

Fisher, R. A. 1949. *The Design of Experiments*, 5th ed., p. 182. Oliver & Boyd, Edinburgh.

Garner, W. R. 1953. An informational analysis of absolute judgments of loudness. *Journal of Experimental Psychology* **46**, 373–380.

Gatlin, G. 1972. *Information Theory and Living Systems*. Columbia Univ. Press, New York.

Hake, H. W., and Garner, W. R. 1951. The effect of presenting various numbers of discrete steps on scale reading accuracy. *Journal of Experimental Psychology* **42**, 538–566.

Klemmer. E. T., and Frick, F. C. 1953. Assimilation of information from dot and matrix patterns. *Journal of Experimental Psychology* **45**, 15–19.

Miller, G. A. 1956. The magical number seven, plus or minus two: Some limits on our capacity for processing information. *Psychological Review* **63**, 81–97.

Pierce, J. R. 1980. *An Introduction to Information Theory: Symbols, Signals and Noise*, 2nd ed., p. 103. Dover, New York.

Pollack, I. 1952. The information of elementary auditory displays. *Journal of the Acoustical Society of America* **24**, 745–749.

Renyi, A. 1970. *Probability Theory*. Vol. IX, Sect. 6, North-Holland, Amsterdam.

Van der Lubbe, J. C. A., Boxma, Y., and Boekee, D. E. 1984. A generalized class of certainty and information measures. *Information Sciences* **32**, 187–215.

Wiener, N. 1948. *Cybernetics*. Wiley, New York.

Zurek, W. H. 1990. Algorithmic information content, Church-Turing thesis, physical entropy and Maxwell's demon. In *Complexity, Entropy and the Physics of Information* (W. H. Zurek, Ed.) pp. 73–89. Addison-Wesley, Redwood City, California.

# 6

## Information of Events
## with Discrete Outcomes:
## Methods of Physics

ORIENTATION

It is important to understand the manner in which the concept of information is applied in physics, because it is closely aligned with the manner in which we shall be applying information in the analysis of sensory systems. In a way, it is not proper to speak of "the applications of information theory in physics," because the statistical entropy concept was introduced into physics by Boltzmann more than half a century before Wiener and Shannon's treatises and the coining of the term "information theory." Physicist Leon Brillouin wrote two books dealing with the information concept in science (1962 and 1964). The earlier of the two books is the one more commonly cited; however, the later of the two books I find the more useful.

This chapter is designed to give the gist of how the information idea is used in physics. In the pages to follow, the first and second laws of thermodynamics will be presented as they were understood in the nineteenth century. It will be shown how Carnot engines operating under constraint of the second law gave rise to Clausius' inequality and how this inequality can be used to introduce the concept of *physical* or *thermodynamic entropy*. Change in physical entropy will be shown to be calculable from macroscopic measurements made in the laboratory. Physical entropy will then be expressed from the perspective of statistical mechanics—that is, in terms of the probabilistic behavior of molecules—and linked with *information theoretical entropy*. The interdiction of "It can be shown that" (Chapter 4, note 1) will be suspended here as we try to compress a rather lengthy subject into a few pages. The reader is encouraged to capture the flow of ideas rather than the details of the proofs. I acknowledge my supreme debt in preparing this chapter to F. W. Sears' text on thermodynamics and statistical mechanics (1953). It was from Professor Sears' book that I first learned thermodynamics as a student; it is in this book that I search again and again for inherent jewels and errant joules. I also recommend the texts by Zemansky (1943) and Zemansky and Dittman (1981).

## THE FIRST LAW OF THERMODYNAMICS

The development of thermodynamics preceded the establishment of the atomic theory of matter, so that the formulations of the first and second laws of thermodynamics in the nineteenth century were made largely while matter and energy were regarded as continua. The first law of thermodynamics is an expression of the principle of conservation of energy. A quantity called the *internal energy* of a system was formulated, which we shall represent by $U$. Any change in $U$ is produced by the difference between the heat, $Q$, flowing *into* the system and work, $\mathscr{W}$, done *by* the system. That is

$$dU = d'Q - d'\mathscr{W}. \tag{6.1}$$

The primes indicate that $d'Q$ and $d'\mathscr{W}$ are not exact differentials; that is, no meaning can be attached to terms such as "the heat in the system." The difference between the two inexact differentials $d'Q$ and $d'\mathscr{W}$ is equal to the exact differential, $dU$. We say that the internal energy is a determinant of the *state* of the system.

Dividing Equation (6.1) by the number of moles in the system, we can write

$$du = d'q - d'w. \tag{6.2}$$

Internal energy, then, reflects a balance between heat flow into, and work done by, the system. The first law is, in effect, an accounting principle for energy.

The first law of thermodynamics is certainly adequate, in itself, to account for many physical processes. For example, suppose that our system consists of two metal blocks at different temperatures that are in contact with each other, but insulated thermally from their environment. Since the system is thermally insulated, $d'Q = 0$; and if we permit the system to do no work, $d'\mathscr{W} = 0$. By the first law, $dU = 0$. It is common experience that heat will flow from the block at the higher temperature to the block at the lower temperature until both blocks reach the same temperature. The first law simply acknowledges the legitimacy of the redistribution of heat between the blocks while conserving internal energy.

Suppose now that we *begin* with the two blocks at the same temperature and in contact with each other. Is it possible that heat will flow from one block to the other, leaving the first block at a lower temperature and the second at a higher temperature? Since no heat leaves the system and no work is done, $dU$ remains equal to zero, and so the first law does not prohibit such occurrences. However, experience tells us that this phenomenon never occurs. From this example and similar considerations, it is recognized that the first law alone is not adequate to account for all thermodynamic phenomena. Another state variable like the internal energy is required.

## THE SECOND LAW OF THERMODYNAMICS

Hence, one expression of the *second* law of thermodynamics, due to Clausius, is the following:

No process is possible whose sole result is the removal of heat from a reservoir at one temperature (lower) and the absorption of an equal quantity of heat at a higher temperature.[1]

## THE CARNOT CYCLE / ENGINE

Clausius was aided by the work of Sadi Carnot (1824; please see Carnot, 1977) who abstracted the properties of heat engines. Carnot understood even before the formulation of the first law that just as mechanical work is done by water falling from a higher to a lower level, so, too, mechanical work can be done when heat flows from a heat reservoir at a higher temperature to a heat reservoir at a lower temperature. He also understood that the heat engine is best analyzed with reference to a cyclical process where a gas or some other "working substance" is passed through a sequence of compressions and expansions. The heat engine is known as a *Carnot engine*, and the associated cycle as the *Carnot cycle*.

Let the heat issuing from the hot reservoir be $Q_1$, that entering the cold reservoir be $Q_2$, and the work done *by* the working substance (let's call it the *system*) be $\mathscr{W}$. These processes are illustrated in Figure 6.1. The Carnot engine can operate in reverse, so that heat $Q_2$ may be absorbed from the cooler reservoir into the system, coupled with work, $\mathscr{W}$, done by the system, and heat $Q_1$ released at the hotter reservoir. When operating in the latter fashion, the system is known as a Carnot refrigerator. The algebraic signs of $Q_1, Q_2$, and $\mathscr{W}$ are taken with respect

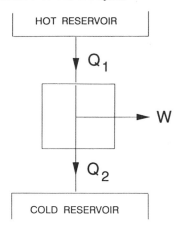

**CARNOT ENGINE**

FIGURE 6.1   Carnot engine. Heat $Q_1$ flows from a heat reservoir at a higher temperature to a system (working substance). Heat $Q_2$ flows from the system to a heat reservoir at a lower temperature. Work $\mathscr{W}$ is done by the system. Carnot refrigerator. Heat $Q_2$ is drawn from the cooler reservoir, work $\mathscr{W}$ is done on the system. Heat $Q_1$ is delivered to the warmer reservoir.

to the system; that is, $Q_1 > 0$ when heat flows from the hotter reservoir to the system, $Q_2 < 0$ when heat flows from the system to the colder reservoir, and $\mathscr{W} > 0$ when the system does positive work on the outside world. The Carnot engine is a reversible[2] engine.

The exchanges of energy depicted in Figure 6.1 occurred during a Carnot cycle, after which the internal energy of the system was left unchanged. Therefore, from the first law as expressed by Equation (6.1), the changes in heat minus the change in work must equal zero, or

$$Q_1 + Q_2 - \mathscr{W} = 0,$$

or

$$\mathscr{W} = Q_1 + Q_2. \tag{6.3}$$

These results are independent of the working substance, which is the substance undergoing the Carnot cycle.

Lord Kelvin then utilized the ratio of $Q_1$ to $Q_2$ to *define* the temperature of the reservoirs:

$$\frac{Q_1}{T_1} + \frac{Q_2}{T_2} = 0. \tag{6.4}$$

It is possible to show that when the working substance is an ideal gas,

Equation (6.4) can be derived using the ideal gas law, Equation (1.1), and the first law of thermodynamics, Equation (6.3). The Kelvin temperature is numerically equal to the absolute temperature.

We note that the second law of thermodynamics has not yet been brought to bear on the Carnot engine/refrigerator.

## THE CLAUSIUS INEQUALITY

Armed now with a verbal statement of the second law, and Equation (6.4) relating heat flows from two heat reservoirs and the respective temperatures of these reservoirs, we can appreciate the development of Clausius' inequality.

We consider any arbitrarily chosen process in which a system is carried through a closed cycle (involving expansions, contractions, heat loss, heat gain, positive work done by the system, positive work done on the system), such that its end state is identical with its initial state (pressure, volume, and temperature of a fixed quantity of matter returned to their original values). Then it can be shown with the aid of Carnot engines (that is, the first law of thermodynamics), using Equation (6.4), and using the second law of thermodynamics that

$$\sum_{i=1}^{\substack{\text{all} \\ \text{reservoirs}}} \frac{Q_i}{T_i} \leq 0, \tag{6.5}$$

where $T_i$ are the temperatures of the reservoirs and $Q_i$ are the heat flows as seen by the system (that is, $Q_i$ is positive when heat proceeds from the heat reservoir toward the system). When only infinitesimally small quantities of heat are exchanged with infinitely many heat reservoirs, we may pass to the integral form

$$\int \frac{d'Q}{T} \leq 0. \tag{6.6}$$

Both (6.5) and (6.6) express the *Clausius inequality*, which is valid whether the cyclic process is reversible or irreversible.[2] The simplest example to illustrate (6.5) is the flow of, say, $Q$ joules from a higher temperature reservoir, $T_{\text{high}}$, to a lower temperature reservoir, $T_{\text{low}}$. Then the summation on the left-hand side of (6.5) is just

$$\frac{Q}{T_{\text{high}}} + \frac{-Q}{T_{\text{low}}} = Q\left[\frac{1}{T_{\text{high}}} - \frac{1}{T_{\text{low}}}\right] \text{joule/deg},$$

which must be less than zero as demanded by the right-hand side of (6.5).

## PHYSICAL ENTROPY

The term *entropy* was introduced by Clausius in 1854 to mean a transformation (Greek, *trepein*, to turn). We are now in position to understand what this term means and how it may be calculated.

While the Clausius inequality was derived for a cyclic system that was either reversible or irreversible, we now consider just a reversible system. Suppose our system cycles first forward and then backward returning to its starting point. Let $d'Q_f$ be the heat flowing into the system in its forward cycle, and $d'Q_b$ the heat in its reverse cycle. Then because of the reversible nature of the system

$$d'Q_f = -d'Q_b \qquad (6.7)$$

and the temperature, $T$, of the heat reservoir is equal to that of the system. Using the contour integral $\oint$ to represent integration around a cycle, we have from (6.6)

$$\oint \frac{d'Q_f}{T} \leq 0$$

and

$$\oint \frac{d'Q_b}{T} \leq 0. \qquad (6.8)$$

Introducing (6.7) into (6.8) we see that the only way (6.8) can be true is if the equality sign holds, so that

$$\oint_{rev} \frac{d'Q}{T} = 0, \qquad (6.9)$$

where rev indicates that the process is reversible. We are following the argument of Sears (1953) very closely.

We can now show that $d'Q/T$ is an exact differential. Consider an arbitrary closed path for the reversible cycle, represented schematically in Figure 6.2. $A$ and $B$ are any two points on the contour; path $I$ leads from $A$ to $B$ and path $II$ from $B$ to $A$. Then

$$\oint_{rev} \frac{d'Q}{T} = \underbrace{\int_A^B \frac{d'Q}{T}}_{\text{along path } I} + \underbrace{\int_B^A \frac{d'Q}{T}}_{\text{along path } II} = 0. \qquad (6.10)$$

If path $II$ were traversed in the opposite direction then, as a consequence

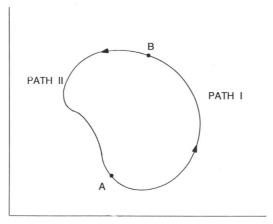

FIGURE 6.2    Reversible cycle.

of the reversibility of the reaction,

$$\int_B^A \frac{d'Q}{T} = -\int_A^B \frac{d'Q}{T}. \qquad (6.11)$$

along path II      along path II

Inserting this result into Equation (6.10), we have

$$\int_A^B \frac{d'Q}{T} = \int_A^B \frac{d'Q}{T}. \qquad (6.12)$$

along path I      along path II

That is, the integral between two points $A$ and $B$ has the same value along all reversible paths. Therefore, $d'Q/T$ is an exact differential and may be represented by $dS$:

$$\int_A^B \frac{d'Q}{T} = \int_A^B dS = S_B - S_A. \qquad (6.13)$$

That is, the value of the integral depends not on the path, but only on its end points. *S is called the physical* or *thermodynamic entropy of the system.*

In this chapter we must distinguish explicitly between "physical" and "informational" entropy.

The second law of thermodynamics for a reversible process, therefore, permits the mathematical statement

$$dS = \frac{d'Q}{T}.$$ (6.14)

Specific entropy, $s$, can be obtained by dividing $S$ by the number of moles in the system:

$$ds = d'q/T$$ (6.15)

(cf. Equation (6.2)). The units of entropy are, of course, joule $\cdot$ deg$^{-1}$ or joule $\cdot$ deg$^{-1}$ $\cdot$ mole$^{-1}$.

## THE PRINCIPLE OF INCREASE OF PHYSICAL ENTROPY

In Figure 6.3 a cyclical process is depicted wherein an isolated system proceeds from $A$ to $B$ irreversibly by some natural process and is then returned from $B$ to $A$ reversibly. The cycle as a whole is irreversible. By the Clausius inequality (6.6),

$$\oint \frac{d'Q}{T} = \underbrace{\int_A^B \frac{d'Q}{T}}_{\substack{\text{irreversible} \\ \text{path}}} + \underbrace{\int_B^A \frac{d'Q}{T}}_{\substack{\text{reversible} \\ \text{path}}} < 0.$$

The quantity $d'Q/T$ in the first integral is not an exact differential because the process is irreversible, but $d'Q$ in the first integral is equal to

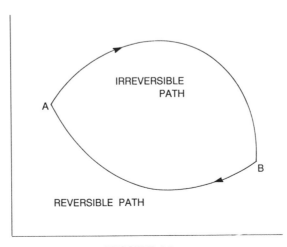

FIGURE 6.3

zero because the system is isolated and does not exchange heat with its surroundings. The first integral is, therefore, equal to zero. The second integral does represent a reversible process, so its value is equal to $S_A - S_B$. Therefore

$$S_A - S_B < 0$$

$$S_B > S_A. \tag{6.16}$$

The thermodynamic entropy of the system in state $B$ is greater than its entropy in state $A$. Since the process was arbitrary, we learn as a consequence of the second law of thermodynamics that *the thermodynamic entropy of an isolated system increases in every natural (irreversible) process.*


## THE LABORATORY MEASURE OF PHYSICAL ENTROPY CHANGE

Change in physical entropy is a measurable, nearly palpable quantity that is measured in joules/degree or joules/degree · mole. For example, a change in phase (solid to liquid or liquid to gas) is carried out at a constant temperature, while the phases remain in equilibrium with each other. When the phase change is carried out reversibly, $d'Q$, the heat absorbed, is the latent heat of fusion or vaporization, and the temperature will be the melting or boiling point, respectively. To take a specific instance, consider the melting of ice. The latent heat of fusion of water is equal to 79.70 cal/g at one atmosphere. The entropy change as ice melts can be found as follows.

Heat change $\Delta q = (79.70 \text{ cal/g})(4.18 \text{ joule/cal})(18 \text{ g/mole})$

$$= 600. \times 10^1 \text{ joule/mole.}$$

Ice melts at $0°C = 273°K$.

Entropy change $\Delta s = \Delta q/T = 6000/273 = 22.0$ joule/deg · mole.

As another example, if a solid is heated from temperature $T_1$ to $T_2$,

$$dq = C\,dT,$$

where $C$ is specific heat per mole. Then, calculating on the basis of a reversible reaction,

$$ds = dq/T = C\,dT/T$$

$$\Delta s = \int_{T_1}^{T_2} C\,dT/T = C \ln(T_2/T_1) \text{ joule/deg · mole.}$$

Et cetera.

## SUMMARY OF SECTION ON CLASSICAL THERMODYNAMICS

This is not a treatise on thermodynamics. The purpose of the preceding pages is to demonstrate (i) that changes in thermodynamic entropy are calculated from standard laboratory measurements of macroscopic variables made by calorimeters and thermometers and (ii) that thermodynamic entropy was defined before the atomic theory of matter was established, and so calculations of entropy change can be made without reference to atoms and molecules.

*As we proceed, it is seen that direct comparison can be made between the thermodynamic variable, S, and the perceptual variable, F, that has been defined in Chapter 2.*


## STATISTICAL MECHANICS: $\mu$-SPACE AND PHASE POINTS

The atomic theory of matter, conceived in the West in the fifth century BCE in Greece by Democritus and Leukippus, matured some 2300 years later in the nineteenth century. Physicists and chemists, employing the principles of *kinetic theory*, sought to translate the laws of macroscopic physics and chemistry into terms of atoms and molecules. Using a gas as a model, it is not difficult to see how the macroscopic variable, pressure, can be interpreted as many molecules colliding with a surface and changing their direction of motion. The rate of change of momentum of the molecules as they strike the surface constitutes a force, and the force per unit area is measured macroscopically as pressure. Temperature can be interpreted as a measure of the average kinetic energy of molecules comprising the gas. Physical entropy, however, is somewhat more difficult to express in terms of the properties of gas molecules. This task was achieved by the Austrian physicist, Ludwig Boltzmann, using the methods of what we now call *statistical mechanics*. The term was first coined by Gibbs in 1901.

Statistical mechanics concerns itself not with the motions and collisions of individual molecules, but with the properties of large assemblies of molecules, which it treats probabilistically. In order to do so, it is necessary to utilize spaces consisting of more than the usual three dimensions. Let's take a simple example from everyday life. Suppose that a helicopter is located 100 meters above a heliport and is proceeding at constant altitude in a northwesterly direction at 80 kilometers per hour. The helicopter's three spatial coordinates are given by (i) its altitude and (ii) the longitude and (iii) latitude of the heliport; its three coordinates in *velocity space* are given by (i) its vertical speed (0) and its horizontal speed in the directions (ii) north and (iii) west. Therefore, we see that even if the orientation of the helicopter (which direction it is facing and its inclination to the horizontal) is ignored, it still requires six coordinates, three in ordinary space and three in velocity space, to define its position and motion completely. This six-dimensional space is needed to define the position and velocity of a molecule, irrespective of its orientation. Three coordinates, $x, y, z$, define a molecule's position is configuration space, and three coordinates, $v_x, v_y, v_z$, define its position in velocity space. One speaks of the hyperspace needed to define the position and motion of a molecule as a *phase space*, and the particular six-dimensional space described above as a type of $\mu$-*space* ("$\mu$" Green *mu*, for *molecule*).[3] One also speaks of the coordinates of a *representative point* $(x, y, z, v_x, v_y, v_z)$ of a type of molecule in $\mu$-space.[4] Such a representative point is called a *phase point*.

We can now subdivide $\mu$-space into small, six-dimensional elements of volume, $\delta v_\mu = \delta x \, \delta y \, \delta z \, \delta v_x \, \delta v_y \, \delta v_z$, which we call *cells* in $\mu$-space. We can number the cells $1, 2, 3, \ldots i, \ldots$ and let $N_i$ be the number of phase points in the $i$th cell. The density of points in the $i$th cell is, then, $N_i / \delta v_\mu$.

## MACROSTATES AND MICROSTATES

We imagine our gas confined to a rigid container whose walls do not permit the exchange of either molecules or energy. We deal with the equilibrium situation.

Specification of which cell is occupied by each molecule in our system would completely define a *microstate* of the system. For example, molecule 1 is in cell 1507, molecule 2 is in cell 2,345,678 ... would define a specific microstate. However, clearly the macroscopic or observable properties of the gas do not permit the specification of a unique microstate. For example, the density of the gas will depend only on the total number of molecules contained in one cubic meter of gas and will tell us little about which individual molecule occupies which cell in $\mu$-space. The macroscopic properties of the gas will, in general, depend only on the numbers, $N_i$, the number of phase points that lie in each cell in $\mu$-space. Complete specification of the $N_i$ will define a *macrostate* of the system.

Clearly, many microstates make up one macrostate. For example, we could take one molecule from $N_1$ and place it in $N_2$, and one from $N_2$ and place it in $N_1$, producing a new microstate but leaving the macrostate unchanged. The number of microstates that make up a given macrostate is called the *thermodynamic probability* of that macrostate, and is commonly represented by $W$. It is not difficult to compute $W$ given the values of $N_i$. To take a simple example, suppose that there are only five cells in

$\mu$-space: $N_1 = 2$, $N_2 = 1$, $N_3 = 1$, $N_4 = 0$, $N_5 = 0$. That is, the first cell contains two phase points, the second and third cells each contain a single point, while the fourth and fifth cells contain no points at all. In this example we shall have only four phase points which can be designated $a$, $b$, $c$, and $d$. The only possible distributions of the four phase points in the five cells are shown in Table 6.1. From combinatorial theory, the value of $W$ is given by $W = 4!/2! \, 1! \, 1! \, 0! \, 0!$, where $0!$ can be taken equal to one (refer to a standard text on probability such as Freund and Walpole). That is, $W = 12$ microstates per macrostate.[5] Laboratory observation cannot distinguish one microstate from another. We can say that the *uncertainty* pertaining to a macrostate is a function of the number of microstates associated with it.

In general, if there are $N$ representative points, the number of microstates is given by

$$W = \frac{N!}{N_1! \, N_2! \, N_3! \dots}, \qquad (6.17)$$

where

$$N = \sum_i N_i. \qquad (6.18)$$

Recall that we have, by definition, a system with constant total energy. Moreover, we confine the system to have a constant volume and to be in a state of equilibrium. The totality of microstates whose total energy is so constrained comprise what Gibbs has termed a *microcanonical ensemble*. Desloge (1966) offers a particularly clear description of microstates and ensembles.

TABLE 6.1    Microstates Corresponding to a Single Macrostate

| Cell | Microstates | | | | | | | | | | | |
|------|----|----|----|----|----|----|----|----|----|----|----|----|
|      | 1  | 2  | 3  | 4  | 5  | 6  | 7  | 8  | 9  | 10 | 11 | 12 |
| $N_1$ | ab | ac | ad | bc | bd | cd | ab | ac | ad | bc | bd | cd |
| $N_2$ | c  | b  | b  | a  | a  | a  | d  | d  | c  | d  | c  | b  |
| $N_3$ | d  | d  | c  | d  | c  | b  | c  | b  | b  | a  | a  | a  |
| $N_4$ | —  | —  | —  | —  | —  | —  | —  | —  | —  | —  | —  | —  |
| $N_5$ | —  | —  | —  | —  | —  | —  | —  | —  | —  | —  | —  | —  |

*Note.* There are four phase point: $a, b, c, d$. A total of 12 microstates correspond to the single macrostate where two particles are contained within phase cell $N_1$, one particle within phase cells $N_2$ and $N_3$, and zero particles within the two remaining phase cells $N_4$ and $N_5$.

# THE BASIC ASSUMPTION OF STATISTICAL MECHANICS

*All microstates of a system that have the same energy are equally probable.* This statement has been called (for example, Jackson 1968) the basic assumption of statistical mechanics. With reference, then, to our microcanonical ensemble, all microstates expressed by Equation (6.17) are equally probable. Therefore (Equation (4.4)), the information theoretical entropy of the macrostate is given by

$$H_I = \ln W. \tag{6.19}$$

$H_I$ encodes the uncertainty of the human perceiver about which particular microstate gives rise the a specified macrostate.

Boltzmann then postulated that physical entropy, $S$, will be proportional to (what we now call) information theoretical entropy, $H_I$. That is[6]

$$S = k_B H_I, \tag{6.20}$$

or expressed alternatively,

$$S = k_B \ln W. \tag{6.21}$$

This remarkable equation, that equates the macroscopic, observable variable, $S$, to $\ln W$, the uncertainty about which molecular microstate makes up a macrostate, is inscribed on Boltzmann's gravestone, although he apparently never wrote it in this form. The $k_B$ is known as *Boltzmann's constant*. Not surprisingly, not all physicists are happy about the interpretation of $\ln W$ as a human uncertainty, because it seems to be injecting a subjective quantity into Equation (6.21), which is an equation of physics and, therefore, an objective entity completely free from human influence. To avoid such quasi-subjectivity, $\ln W$ is simply taken to be the natural log of the thermodynamic probability, $W$. Period.

We have seen before how a macroscopic variable can be expressed as a measure of uncertainty, or information theoretical entropy,

$$F = kH_I. \tag{2.6}$$

We are now beginning to fill in the history of Equation (2.6). Let us continue with the development of statistical mechanics in order to appreciate the utility of Equations (6.20) and (6.21).

We shall need to use Stirling's approximation for evaluating $\ln x!$, where $x$ is a large, positive integer. Stated here without proof,

$$\ln x! \simeq x \ln x - x. \tag{6.22}$$

The proof is not difficult, and the reader is referred to the texts. Taking logarithms of both sides of Equation (6.17),

$$\ln W = \ln N! - \sum_i \ln N_i!$$

Applying Stirling's approximation,

$$\ln W = (N \ln N - N) - \left( \sum_i N_i \ln N_i - \sum_i N_i \right)$$

$$= N \ln N - \sum_i N_i \ln N_i \qquad (6.23)$$

using Equation (6.18).

We recall that the system is in a state of equilibrium, which we might designate by a maximum value of the thermodynamic probability, $W$. That is, the change in $W$ at equilibrium produced by the aggregate of all the small changes in the occupancies $N_i$ resulting from motions of the phase points in $\mu$-space will equal zero. Expressing this variation mathematically using Equation (6.23),

$$\delta \ln W = \delta(N \ln N) - \delta \sum_i N_i \ln N_i = 0.$$

That is

$$0 - \sum_i \ln N_i \, \delta N_i - \sum_i N_i \, \delta \ln N_i = 0.$$

But

$$\sum_i N_i \, \delta \ln N_i = \sum_i (N_i/N_i) \, \delta N_i = \sum_i \delta N_i = 0,$$

since the total number of particles does not change. Therefore (dropping the subscript under the summation sign for simplicity),

$$\sum \ln N_i \, \delta N_i = 0. \qquad (6.24)$$

This equation, then, expresses the maximum value of $W$ at equilibrium. We introduce, now, the constraints imposed by the microcanonical ensemble. First, the total number of molecules, $N$, remains constant. Taking the variation of $N$,

$$\delta N = \sum \delta N_i = 0. \qquad (6.25)$$

Second, the total energy of the system remains constant. If the energy of the $i$th cell is designated by $w_i$, the total internal energy will be given by

$$U = \sum w_i N_i. \qquad (6.26)$$

The variation of the internal energy is also equal to zero, so that

$$\delta U = \sum w_i \, \delta N_i = 0. \tag{6.27}$$

Introducing three Lagrangian multipliers of undetermined value, we combine Equations (6.24), (6.25), and (6.27) to give

$$\sum (\ln N_i + \ln A + \beta w_i) \, \delta N_i = 0. \tag{6.28}$$

Since the $\delta N_i$ are independent, each coefficient is independent, so that

$$\ln N_i + \ln A + \beta w_i = 0,$$

or

$$N_i = (1/A)\exp(-\beta w_i) \tag{6.29}$$

which is the celebrated Maxwell–Boltzmann energy distribution.

$$\sum N_i = N = (1/A) \sum \exp(-\beta w_i) = Z/A.$$

That is

$$Z = \sum \exp(-\beta w_i), \tag{6.30}$$

where $Z$, which is known as the *partition function*, stands for the German word *Zustandssumme*, usually translated as "sum of states." Since

$$1/A = N/Z,$$

(6.29) becomes

$$N_i = \frac{N}{Z}\exp(-\beta w_i) \tag{6.31}$$

giving the number of phase points in the $i$th cell in the state of maximum thermodynamic probability.

We are almost home.

Substituting the value of $N_i$ from (6.31) into (6.23),

$$\ln W = N \ln N - \sum N_i(\ln N - \ln Z - \beta w_i)$$

$$= N \ln N - \ln N \sum N_i + \ln Z \sum N_i + \beta \sum w_i N_i.$$

Now

$$\sum N_i = N \qquad \text{and} \qquad \sum w_i N_i = U,$$

so that

$$\ln W = N \ln N - N \ln N + N \ln Z + \beta U.$$

Since

$$S = k_B \ln W, \tag{6.21}$$

$$S = k_B N \ln Z + k_B \beta U. \tag{6.32}$$

Using simple thermodynamic arguments, it can be shown that $k_B\beta$ is equal to the reciprocal of temperature, so that

$$S = Nk_B \ln Z + U/T. \tag{6.33}$$

Using the partition function, we have been able to "identify" the thermodynamic entropy, $S$, with a statistical function of molecular behavior in a gas. Again, using Equations (6.26) with (6.30) and (6.31), the internal energy can also be identified with statistical properties of molecules:

$$U = Nk_B T^2 \frac{d(\ln Z)}{dT}. \tag{6.34}$$

The relationship $S = k_B \ln W$ has been the key that permitted the mapping of macroscopic thermodynamics onto the microscopic function of (invisible) molecules in a gas.

The value of $W$ is the maximum value consistent with constant energy, volume, and number of particles. To continue the example of Table 6.1, suppose that cell $N_1$ contained phase points with energy $w_1 = 1$, $N_2$ with energy $w_2 = 2$, $N_3$ with energy $w_3 = 3$, $N_4$ with energy

TABLE 6.2    Illustration that Different Macrostates
Are Compatible with the Same Total Energy

| Cell | Energy | Configuration (macrostate) | |
| --- | --- | --- | --- |
| | | Configuration $A$ | Configuration $B$ |
| $N_1$ | 1 | 2 | 3 |
| $N_2$ | 2 | 1 | 0 |
| $N_3$ | 3 | 1 | 0 |
| $N_4$ | 4 | 0 | 1 |
| $N_5$ | 5 | 0 | 0 |
| Total energy = | | 7 | 7 |
| Number of microstates = | | $\dfrac{4!}{2!1!1!0!0!} = 12$ | $\dfrac{4!}{3!0!0!1!0!} = 4$ |

*Note.* Total energy for configuration $A$ is obtained from (2 phase points) (energy = 1) + (1 phase point)(energy = 2)... = 7 units of energy. Similarly, the total energy for configuration $B$ is 7 units. Although both configurations of four phase points have total energy equal to 7, configuration $A$ is the more spread out or disordered and, therefore, has the greater number of microstates or "thermodynamic probability."

4, and $N_5$ with energy 5. Then the macrostate with two phase points in cell 1, one point in cell 2, one in cell 3, and none in cells 4 and 5, has a total energy of $(2)(1) + (1)(2) + (1)(3) + (0)(4) + (0)(5) = 7$. $W$ for this configuration was shown to be equal to 12. However another way of obtaining a macrostate with total energy 7 would be $N_1 = 3$, $N_2 = 0$, $N_3 = 0$, $N_4 = 1$, and $N_5 = 0$ (see Table 6.2). $W$ for this new configuration would be equal to

$$\frac{4!}{3!\,0!\,0!\,1!\,0!} = 4.$$

That is, the configuration $(2, 1, 1, 0, 0)$ has a greater value of $W$ than the configuration $(3, 0, 0, 1, 0)$ and would, therefore, be closer to the maximum value of $W$ for the given total energy of 7 units. The reader might like to check this configuration for maximum $W$ approximately, using $N_i$-values from Equation (6.29) with $\beta = 1$.

## PHYSICAL ENTROPY AND DISORDER

The quantity $W$ permits us to relate physical entropy to "disorder," which is its usual interpretation in the lay literature. The more phase cells occupied by the gas in configuration space ($x$–$y$–$z$-space), the greater is the physical entropy, $S$. Dissemination of phase points throughout a larger volume signifies larger $W$, more disorder, and greater physical entropy.

We can illustrate this idea by calculating the change in thermodynamic entropy in the isothermal, reversible expansion of one mole of an ideal gas from volume $V_1$ to volume $V_2$. If we allow that the internal energy of an idea gas is independent of its volume, then from the first law of thermodynamics, Equation (6.1),

$$d'Q = d'\mathscr{W} = pdV.$$

From the ideal gas law, Equation (1.1), $pdV = (RT/V)\,dV$. From the second law of thermodynamics,

$$dS = \frac{d'Q}{T} = \frac{pdV}{T} = \frac{R}{V}\,dV,$$

so that

$$\Delta S = \int_{V_1}^{V_2} \frac{R}{V}\,dV = R\ln\frac{V_2}{V_1}. \tag{6.35}$$

Now let us calculate the same quantity, $\Delta S$, from statistical mechanics. Suppose that $V_1$ comprises $n_1$ cells of volume $\delta v$ so that $V_1 = n_1\,\delta v$. Similarly, $V_2 = n_2\delta v$. There are $n_1$ ways of putting one molecule into $V_1$,

$n_1^2$ ways of putting two molecules in $V_1, \ldots, n_1^{N_0}$ ways of putting Avogadro's number, $N_0$, molecules into $V_1$. Therefore, $W_1 = n_1^{N_0}$. Similarly, $W_2 = n_2^{N_0}$. Since $S = k_B \ln W$,

$$\Delta S = k_B \ln \Delta W = k_B \ln n_2^{N_0} - k_B \ln n_1^{N_0}$$

$$= k_B N_0 \ln(n_2/n_1)$$

$$= R \ln(n_2/n_1)$$

since $R = k_B N_0$ (where $R$ is the gas constant, $k_B$ is Boltzmann's constant, and $N_0$ is Avogadro's number). That is,

$$\Delta S = R \ln\left(\frac{V_2/\delta v}{V_1/\delta v}\right)$$

or

$$\Delta S = R \ln \frac{V_2}{V_1} \tag{6.36}$$

exactly as before in (6.35).

Thus, we can see clearly how the critical equation, $S = k_B \ln W$, permits the mapping of macroscopic thermodynamics onto the properties of molecules.


## APPLICATIONS OF ENTROPY CHANGE IN CHEMISTRY

We recall from inequality (6.16) that the physical entropy of an isolated system increases in every natural (irreversible) process. We now understand with reference to the molecular representation of entropy that the increase in thermodynamic entropy can be interpreted as a progression from a *more*-ordered to a *less*-ordered state. In chemistry, this principle of increasing physical entropy is applied to determine whether a system will change spontaneously. If a change, such as that produced by chemical reaction, will result in an increase in physical entropy, the reaction is likely to go forward (see, for example, Hargreaves and Socrates, 1973).


## THE PURPOSE OF THIS CHAPTER

In this chapter we have made a survey of the concept of physical entropy as it was born into classical thermodynamics and as it was translated, largely through the work of Boltzmann, into statistical mechanics. Physical entropy was seen, through the $S = k_B \ln W = k_B H_I$ relationship, to be proportional to the information theoretical entropy, in the equilibrium state. Through the use of $S \propto H_I$, classical macroscopic thermodynamics became interpretable completely in terms of the properties of molecules. The mapping process was not completed during Boltzmann's lifetime.

We learned from Chapter 5 that the information concept, as it has been applied in communications science and psychology and biochemistry, is nonunique and extrinsic to the system. By contrast, the use of the information measure in physics is both unique and intrinsic. The measure

$$H_I = \ln W \qquad (6.19)$$

is a unique measure of uncertainty. No other measure is acceptable. No other measure will permit the mapping of thermodynamics onto statistical mechanics. That is, if $H_I = \ln W$ is correct, our calculations of physical events will be correct; but if $H_I = \ln W$ were incorrect, we would get wrong answers. Our calculations of the thermodynamic entropy, internal energy, free energy, etc. would be wrong. $H_I = \ln W$ is "intrinsic" in the sense that this equation enters physics as a natural law. It is an integral part of physics.

There is yet another way of viewing the two statements,

$$\mathcal{I}(X|Y) = H(X) - H(X,Y) \qquad (4.21)$$

and

$$H_I = \ln W. \qquad (6.19)$$

Both statements, the first about $\mathcal{I}(X|Y)$ and the second about $H_I$, might be called *metastatements* (Greek, *meta*: after). That is, Equation (4.21) arose in the case of a channel transmitting a message, or making a *statement*. The statement is arbitrary; for example, "The weather is fine today." Then Equation (4.21) is a metastatement because it talks *about* the statement. It tells us how much information is transmitted by the statement without actually telling us what the statement is. Similarly, $H_I = \ln W$ is a metastatement, giving us the uncertainty that any particular microstate is associated with a macrostate. The corresponding statement would be "We have microstate $bc, a, d, —, —$" (see Table 6.1). However, the statement is hidden from us. Instead, embedded as an integral part of our physical law is the metastatement "The uncertainty about which particular microstate is present in the maximum value of $W$ consistent with constraints. ..."

The contrasts and comparisons made above are important, because when I propose Equation (2.6)[7]

$$F = kH_I,$$

I suggest its use in the physicist's sense rather than in the communication scientist's sense. That is, I propose $H_I$ as a *unique* measure, *intrinsic* to the physiological function of an organism. Moreover, by its use I propose that sensory messages that are relayed neuronally to the brain are, in reality, metastatements about the so-called external world. That is, the brain will receive only messages that express the state of uncertainty of the peripheral sensory receptors about the world external, but will never receive messages that directly describe the state of this world. For example, the conscious brain will not receive a message about the brightness of a light, but only about how uncertain the eye is about how bright the light is (Norwich, 1977).

These ideas now set the stage for development of the perceptual theory. There is, however, one more topic we must study by way of background before developing the perceptual model: the informational entropy of continuous distributions.

## NOTES

1. Clausius' statement of the second law of thermodynamics can be shown to be equivalent to Kelvin's statement of the second law (Sears, 1953). *No process is possible whose sole result is the abstraction of heat from a single reservoir and the performance of an equivalent amount of work*. That is, heat cannot be totally converted into work.

2. A reversible process is one carried out with the system effectively in equilibrium with its environment: a succession of equilibrium states. Pressure, temperature, and density of each portion of the system remain uniform.

3. $\mu$-space may have more than six dimensions if one allows for the internal configuration of the molecule.

4. Often, the coordinates are $x, y, z$, and $p_x, p_y, p_z$, where the latter three coordinates are the momenta of the particle, $mv_x, mv_y, mv_z$.

5. Note that we do not consider permutations within a cell; representative points $ab$ and $ba$ within a phase cell are considered identical.

6. Equation (6.20), as we have written it, is, of course, an anachronism. $H_I$ was not "born," so to speak, until the time of Wiener and Shannon. Boltzmann did, indeed, have an $H$-function, but we shall not introduce it at this time.

7. The "$k$" in this equation is a constant, but not Boltzmann's constant.

## REFERENCES

Brillouin, L. 1962. *Science and Information Theory*, 2nd ed. Academic Press, New York.
Brillouin, L. 1964. *Scientific Uncertainty and Information*. Academic Press, New York.
Carnot, S. 1977. *Reflections on the Motive Power of Fire* (E. Mendoza, ed.). Peter Smith, Gloucester, MA.

Desloge, E. A. 1966. *Statistical Physics*. Holt, Rinehart, & Winston, New York.

Freund, J. E., and Walpole, R. E. 1980. *Mathematical Statistics*, 3rd ed., Prentice–Hall, Englewood Cliffs, NJ.

Hargreaves, G., and Socrates, G. 1973. *Elementary Chemical Thermodynamics*. Butterworths, London.

Jackson, E. A. 1968. *Equilibrium Statistical Mechanics*. Prentice–Hall, Englewood Cliffs, NJ.

Norwich, K. H. 1977. On the information received by sensory receptors. *Bulletin of Mathematical Biology* **39**, 453–461.

Sears, F. W. 1953. *An Introduction to Thermodynamics, the Kinetic Theory of Gases, and Statistical Mechanics*, 2nd ed. Addison-Wesley, Reading, MA.

Zemansky, M. W. 1943. *Heat and Thermodynamics*. McGraw–Hill, New York.

Zemansky, M. W., and Dittman, R. H. 1981. *Heat and Thermodynamics: An Intermediate Textbook*, 6th ed. McGraw–Hill, New York.

# 7

## The Information of Events with Continuous Outcomes

### PROBABILITY DENSITY

We have studied in some detail the entropy of events with $N$ possible *discrete* outcomes, whose *a priori* probabilities are $p_1, p_2, \ldots, p_N$:

$$H = - \sum_{i=1}^{N} p_i \log p_i. \tag{2.1}$$

The entropy of a potential winner of a lottery, when a single selection will be made from among $m$ tickets which have been sold, is governed by the *a priori* probabilities,

$$p_{\text{Lisa}} = (\text{Number of tickets purchased by Lisa})/m,$$

$$p_{\text{Harry}} = (\text{Number of tickets purchased by Harry})/m, \ldots.$$

The identifying feature of this type of problem is that there are a finite number of outcomes (e.g., Lisa wins, Harry wins,...) and an associated discrete *probability function*, defined by the *pure numbers* $p_{\text{Lisa}}$, $p_{\text{Harry}} \cdots$.

We can study the intensities (densities) of low levels of illumination by means of such discrete, probability functions. For example, the probability that one photon (light particle) will arrive at a rod (a type of light receptor) in some fixed interval of time is $p(\mathbf{x} = 1)$. The probability that two will arrive is $p(\mathbf{x} = 2)$, etc. The boldface character $\mathbf{x}$ signifies a *random variable* that may take on the values $1, 2, \ldots$. Equation (2.1) might be written

$$H = - \sum_i p(\mathbf{x} = x_i) \log p(\mathbf{x} = x_i). \qquad (7.1)$$

The probability function governing photon arrival is the Poisson function or distribution,

$$p(\mathbf{x} = z) = \frac{e^{-\lambda}\lambda^z}{z!}, \qquad z = 0, 1, 2, \ldots \qquad (7.2)$$

which provides the probability that exactly $z$ photons will arrive in a given interval of time. The parameter, $\lambda$, is the mean or average number of photons.

However, when the level of illumination becomes greater, photons are continually bombarding the retina of the eye, and intensity changes become, effectively, continuous. It is no longer possible to measure the effects of individual photons; we can no longer speak meaningfully of the probability that exactly $x_i = z$ photons will arrive. Rather we introduce a different kind of function called a *probability density function*, $p(x)$, such that $p(x)\Delta x$ is the probability that the intensity of light (measured on a continuous scale) lies between the values $x$ and $x + \Delta x$, for small $\Delta x$. Statisticians do not seem overly fond of such definitions and prefer something like the following:

The probability that a random variable, $\mathbf{x}$, will take on a value between $a$ and $b$ is given by

$$\int_a^b p(x)\, dx. \qquad (7.3)$$

The density $p(x)$ will have the dimensions $[x^{-1}]$, so that $p(x)\, dx$ is a dimensionless probability. That is, $p(x)\, dx$ can be compared with the quantity $p(\mathbf{x} = x)$:

$$p(\mathbf{x} = x) \leftrightarrow p(x)\, \Delta x. \qquad (7.4)$$

We can compare the normalization requirements for the two types of function. For the probability function,

$$\sum_i p(\mathbf{x} = x_i) = 1 \qquad (7.5)$$

and for the probability density function $p(x) \geq 0$,

$$\int_{-\infty}^{\infty} p(x)\, dx = 1. \qquad (7.6)$$

## THE DIFFERENTIAL ENTROPY OF A PROBABILITY DENSITY FUNCTION

Well—if we can calculate the entropy of a (discrete) probability function using Equation (2.1), can we not simply substitute into Equation (7.1) replacing the $p(\mathbf{x} = x)$ by $p(x)\Delta x$? Let us take this approach and see.

Substituting relation (7.4) into Equation (7.1),

$$H = -\sum_i p(x_i)\,\Delta x\,\log(p(x_i)\,\Delta x)$$

$$= -\sum_i p(x_i)\log p(x_i)\,\Delta x - \left(\sum_i p(x_i)\,\Delta x\right)\log \Delta x. \qquad (7.7)$$

Then, since $\sum_i p(x_i)\,\Delta x = 1$, in the limit as $\Delta x \to 0$

$$H = -\int_{-\infty}^{\infty} p(x)\log p(x)\,dx - \lim_{\Delta x \to 0}\log \Delta x. \qquad (7.8)$$

However, the second term on the right-hand side approaches negative infinity as $\Delta x \to 0$. That is, for any probability density function, $p(x)$, $H$ will be infinite.

Equation (7.8) seems to be telling us that as the number of rectangles into which a continuous probability density function can be divided is increased progressively (refer Figure 7.1), the measure of "uncertainty" becomes larger without limit. Why does this phenomenon arise?

In order to understand the problem, it is useful to consider an example. Suppose that the probability density function $p(x)$ represents the height of adult males in some population. Let $x$ be measured in centimeters. Then $p(x)\Delta x = p(175)(1)$ equals the probability that the height of a man selected at random from the population will be found to be between 175 and $175 + 1$ cm. We could fragment the continuous probability density function into a number of narrow rectangles (say 250) with $\Delta x = 1$ cm and calculate $H$ from Equation (7.1):

$$H_1 = -\sum_{i=1}^{250} p(\mathbf{x} = x_i)\log p(\mathbf{x} = x_i). \qquad (7.9)$$

Two hundred and fifty centimeters is just a convenient upper limit for height. Then $H_1$ equals the value of the integral in Equation (7.8) minus $\log \Delta x$, which is just equal to the value of the integral since $\Delta x = 1$. We could, however, carry the process further and divide the continuous probability density function into rectangles with width $\Delta x = 1$ mm $= 0.1$

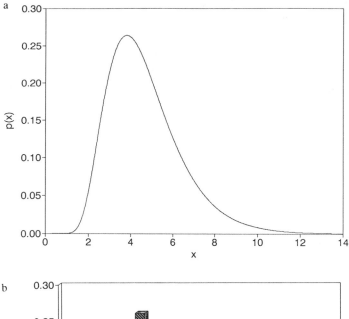

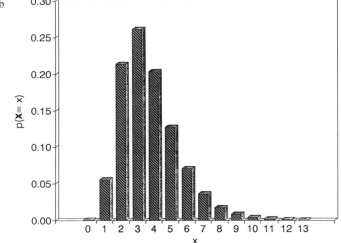

FIGURE 7.1   The smooth curve in (a) is the graph of the probability density function $p(x)$. The area under the curve is normalized to 1. One cannot, using the density function alone, obtain a proper measure of the information transmitted by making a measurement of the quantity, $x$. The probability function in (b) was obtained by fragmenting the smooth density function into rectangles of unit width. The probability function is also normalized to 1: $\sum_{x=0}^{13} p(\mathbf{x} = x) = 1$. One can, indeed, obtain a measure of the information transmitted by making a measurement of the quantity, $x$, and using Equation (7.1). However, the amount of information calculated will depend on the number of rectangles into which the smooth density function is divided.

cm, and evaluate $H$ as

$$H_2 = - \sum_{i=1}^{2500} p(\mathbf{x} = x_i) \log p(\mathbf{x} = x_i). \qquad (7.10)$$

As before, we equate $H_2$ to the value of the integral in Equation (7.8) minus $\log \Delta x$, and we find that $H_2$ is equal to the value of the integral minus $\log 0.1$, which is a greater entropy than before! We appear to be more uncertain about the height of the next male sample who will be drawn from the population. That is,

$$H_2 > H_1. \qquad (7.11)$$

So the process would, apparently, continue. If $\Delta x = 0.1$ mm, $H$ would increase again and eventually reach infinity. The infinity arises because of the infinite number of choices we should have as $\Delta x \to 0$. As such, we would receive an infinite quantity of information when the entropy was reduced by making a measurement of a man's height. It is essentially a question of resolution. We assumed first that a height of 176 cm is distinguishable from a height of 175 cm; then we assumed that 175.1 cm is distinguishable from 175 cm; then we assumed that 175.01 cm is distinguishable from 175 cm, etc. If no limit is placed on the resolution of heights possible, then infinite information will be transmitted by any actual measurement of height. This argument, can, perhaps, be made more concrete by use of a simple computer program.

In the following program, written in BASIC, a normal probability distribution with zero mean and unit variance has been taken. That is, $p(x) = N(x; 0, 1)$. This continuous probability density is first divided into rectangles of width 1, then of width 0.5, 0.25. ... Entropy is measured from the corresponding (discrete) histograms as in Equations (7.9) and (7.10) and is then calculated theoretically using Equation (7.8). We shall see in Chapter 8 that the integral in Equation (7.8) is equal to $\frac{1}{2}\ln(2\pi) + \frac{1}{2}$. It can be seen that the measured value of entropy agrees well with the theoretical value and that fragmentation into rectangles still preserves the normalization of the density (area = 1). The value of entropy increases, apparently without limit, as the width of the rectangles decreases.

From a practical point of view, the above argument of decreasing the value of $\Delta x$ without limit is ludicrous. There is a limit to the precision with which the height of a person can be measured. Small changes in posture, fluctuations in intervertebral spacing, etc. produce such a limit. Probably the precision of the measurement is not as small as 0.1 mm. Therefore, there is little point to measuring $H$ with $\Delta x < 0.1$ mm, and, therefore, we do not obtain an infinite quantity of information from a measurement of height.

```
10 'PROGRAM IN BASIC TO ILLUSTRATE THAT DIVIDING A CONTINUOUS
      PROBABILITY DENSITY FUNCTION INTO A PROGRESSIVELY GREATER
      NUMBER OF RECTANGLES RESULTS IN A DISCRETE ENTROPY
      (H = -SUM P LOG P) THAT INCREASES WITHOUT LIMIT.
20 PRINT " ENTROPY", " ENTROPY", " WIDTH OF", "   AREA"
30 PRINT "(MEASURED)", "(THEORETICAL)", " RECTANGLE"
40 '
50 DEL = 1: 'WIDTH OF RECTANGLES BEGINS AT 1.
60 '
70 'SELECT A GAUSSIAN FUNCTION WITH UNIT VARIANCE
80 DEF FNA(X)= (1/SQR(2*3.1416))*EXP(-X*X/2)
90 '
100 'CALCULATE THE AREA UNDER THE GAUSSIAN FUNCTION AND THE
       VALUE OF ENTROPY, H.
110 '
115 WHILE 1
120          H = 0: AREA = 0
130          FOR X = -10 TO 10 STEP DEL
140               AREA = AREA + FNA(X)*DEL
150               H = H - DEL*FNA(X)*LOG(DEL*FNA(X))
160          NEXT X
170'
180          'THEORETICALLY, H EXCEEDS THE VALUE OF THE
             DIFFERENTIAL ENTROPY, (.5*LOG(2*Pi) + .5), BY THE NEGATIVE
             LOG OF THE WIDTH OF THE RECTANGLE.
190          HTHEOR = .5*LOG(2*3.1416) + .5 - LOG(DEL)
200          PRINT H, HTHEOR, DEL, AREA
210'
220          'DECREASE THE WIDTH OF THE RECTANGLES BY A FACTOR OF 2
             AND REPEAT...
230          DEL = DEL/2
240 WEND

RUN
```

| ENTROPY (MEASURED) | ENTROPY (THEORETICAL) | WIDTH OF RECTANGLE | AREA |
|---|---|---|---|
| 1.418938 | 1.41894 | 1 | .9999989 |
| 2.112085 | 2.112087 | .5 | .9999988 |
| 2.805231 | 2.805234 | .25 | .9999988 |
| 3.498378 | 3.498381 | .125 | .9999989 |
| 4.191524 | 4.191528 | .0625 | .9999988 |
| 4.88467 | 4.884676 | .03125 | .9999989 |
| 5.577818 | 5.577823 | .015625 | .9999982 |
| 6.270962 | 6.27097 | .0078125 | .9999981 |
| . | . | . | . |
| . | . | . | . |
| . | . | . | . |

There is nothing unique about our example of measuring height. Every measurement of a quantity that is continuously distributed is limited in precision either by the nature of the measuring apparatus or by the properties of the measured quantity itself. Therefore, neither $H$ nor the amount of information received from the measurement will be infinite. Let us have another look at Equation (7.8).

The integral $-\int_{-\infty}^{\infty} p(x)\log p(x)\, dx$, which appears in Equation (7.8), is known as a *differential entropy* (McEliece, 1977). You may be thinking, as I did when I first encountered the differential entropy, that it is a natural extension of Equation (7.1) into the continuous domain, and would be a natural way of expressing the uncertainty associated with a probability density function. Life, however, is not this simple. The differential entropy, as we have seen, is only one of two expressions that evolve from the $H$-function for discrete random variables when $p(\mathbf{x} = x)$ is replaced by $p(x)\,dx$. Therefore, numerical values of the differential entropy are not, in themselves, a reflection of our earlier notions of uncertainty. The differential entropy may even turn out to have a negative value. Moreover, the differential entropy is not "coordinate-free"; its value will depend on the units in which $x$ is measured. For example, if $p(x)$ is, again, the probability density function for heights of people, $x$ may be measured in centimeters so that

$$H_{\text{centimeter}} = -\int_{-\infty}^{\infty} p(x) \log p(x)\, dx. \qquad (7.12)$$

Suppose, however, that values of the random variable are measured in meters, and let $g(y)$ be the new probability density function for heights. Then, using the theorem for change of variable (refer, for example, Freund and Walpole, 1980),

$$g(y) = p(x)\left|\frac{dx}{dy}\right|. \qquad (7.13)$$

But $x = 100y$ (that is, 1 m = 100 cm), so that $|dx/dy| = 100$. Hence

$$g(y) = 100\, p(x).$$

Then (leaving out the limits of integration)

$$H_{\text{meter}} = -\int g(y)\log g(y)\, dy = -\int 100\, p(x)\log(100\, p(x))\frac{dx}{100}$$

$$= -\int p(x)\log p(x)\, dx - \int p(x)\log(100)\, dx$$

$$H_{\text{meter}} = H_{\text{centimeter}} - \log 100, \qquad (7.14)$$

(Shannon and Weaver, 1964, p. 91). That is, the differential entropy is neither a measure of uncertainty in keeping with our previous notions of uncertainty, nor is it even independent of the units of measurement of values of the random variable. This example is illustrated in Figure 7.2.

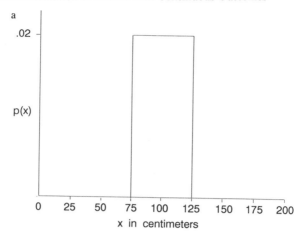

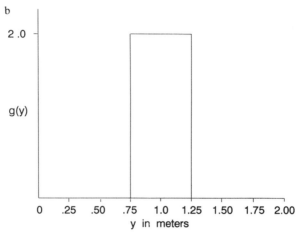

FIGURE 7.2   We suppose that the probability density function for heights of adult males in some (strange) population is governed by the uniform distribution: $p(x) = 0.02$, $75 \leq x \leq 125$, where $x$ is measured in centimeters. We note that $p(x)$ is normalized so that $\int_{-\infty}^{\infty} p(x)\, dx = (0.02)(50.0) = 1.0$. Another density function governing the same random process is the uniform distribution $g(y)$, defined by $g(y) = 2.0$, $0.75 \leq y \leq 1.25$, where $y$ is measured in meters. Again, note that $g(y)$ is normalized so that $\int_{-\infty}^{\infty} g(y)\, dy = (2.0)(0.50) = 1.0$. The differential entropy of $p(x)$ can be evaluated explicitly: $H_{\text{centimeter}} = -(0.02 \log 0.02)(125 - 75) = -\log 0.02 = \log 50$. The differential entropy of $g(y)$ can also be evaluated explicitly: $H_{\text{meter}} = -(2.0 \log 2.0)(1.25 - 0.75) = -\log 2.0 = \log 0.5$. That is, $H_{\text{meter}} = H_{\text{centimeter}} - \log 100$, as given by Equation (7.14). The above illustrates that differential entropy is not independent of the units in which the random variable is measured.

## THE ABSOLUTE ENTROPY

We have been dealing with a probability density function, $p(x)$. Suppose we now consider some other probability density function, $q(x)$, defined on $x$. Treating $q(x)$ in exactly the same manner as $p(x)$, we obtain for its entropy using Equation (7.8),

$$H' = -\int q(x)\log q(x)\,dx - \lim_{\Delta x \to 0} \Delta x. \qquad (7.15)$$

Subtracting $H'$ from $H$,

$$H - H' = -\int p(x)\log p(x)\,dx - \left(-\int q(x)\log q(x)\,dx\right) \quad (7.16)$$

since the two $\Delta x$-terms cancel. $H - H'$, the difference between two differential entropies, is known as the *absolute entropy*. In contrast to the differential entropy, the absolute entropy *is* coordinate-free. That is, $H_{abs} = H - H'$ will have the same value regardless of the units in which values of the random variable are measured. This may be illustrated from the centimeter–meter example of the previous section. When measuring in units of centimeters,

$$H_{abs\atop centimeter} = -\int p(x)\log p(x)\,dx + \int q(x)\log q(x)\,dx.$$

When measuring in units of meters,

$$H_{abs\atop meter} = \left[-\int p(x)\log p(x)\,dx - \log 100\right] - \left[-\int q(x)\log q(x)\,dx - \log 100\right]$$

$$= H_{abs\atop centimeter}$$

For a more general proof refer, for example, to the text by S. Goldman (1953).

So the absolute entropy is coordinate-free; but what, if anything, has it to do with the transmission of information? We recall that for a noisy channel it was necessary to represent the information transmitted per symbol as the difference between two $H$-functions:

$$\mathcal{I} = H_{before} - H_{after}. \qquad (4.12)$$

That is, information was obtained as the difference between the uncertainty that existed before the measurement was made and the uncertainty that remained after the measurement had been made. The noise in the channel limited the accuracy with which it was possible to transmit a symbol. We now call upon this idea again in the attempt to adapt the absolute entropy for the measurement of information.

We recall from the example of measuring heights that the measurement was limited in its precision by various anatomical factors such as fluctuating intervertebral spacings. These factors limiting the precision of a measurement play the part of a noise that limits the amount of information transmitted. The probability density function for height may, therefore, be regarded as a density function for "pure" height compounded with "noise" (read, perhaps, as "pure signal" with noise). In Equation (7.16) for absolute entropy, then, let us regard $p(x)$ as $p_{SN}(x)$ (that is, $p_{\text{signal-noise}}(x)$), and $-\int p_{SN}(x)\log p_{SN}(x)\,dx$ as the differential entropy of signal together with noise.

What role, then, is played by the differential entropy

$$-\int q(x)\log q(x)\,dx?$$

A reasonable suggestion is that $q(x)$ be the density function for noise alone, which we might represent by $p_N(x)$. Then, by conjecture, the absolute entropy is equal to the information "content" of a measurement, by which we mean the information received by the measurer when the measurement is made. That is,

$$\mathscr{I} = H_{\text{abs}} = -\int p_{SN}(x)\log p_{SN}(x)\,dx + \int p_N(x)\log p_N(x)\,dx. \quad (7.17)$$

It is apparent that Equation (7.17) possesses at least one necessary asymptotic property. That is, as $p_{SN} \to p_N$ (pure signal vanishes), $\mathscr{I} = H_{\text{abs}} \to 0$, meaning that no information is received, which makes sense, because in these circumstances there is no discernible signal. Further investigation of Equation (7.17) as a measure of information will have to await a discussion of the means of evaluating $p_{SN}$.

We might speculate that what has been done by the subtraction process in Equation (7.17) is to convert a continuous probability density function, $p_{SN}$, which might be represented by Figure 7.1a (and from which we obtain, obstensibly, an infinite quantity of information) into a histogram of the type shown in Figure 7.1b, from which we can obtain a proper measure of information. The effect of the subtraction process in Equation (7.17) is to "discretize" the continuous density function. The width of the bars in the histogram are determined by the noise level, or the limitation to our measurement of values of $x$. If we represent Equation (7.17) as

$$\mathscr{I} = H_{SN} - H_N \quad (7.18)$$

we might compare it to the explicit form of the information equation for a discrete, noisy channel:

$$\mathscr{I}(X|Y) = H(X) - H(X,Y). \tag{4.21}$$

Although the comparison is not perfect, the equivocation, $H(X,Y)$ seems to play the part of the differential entropy of noise.

## CONVOLUTION

It was stated above that $p_{SN}(x)$ is the probability density function for pure signal compounded with noise, without suggesting a procedure for obtaining it. The method used is one of convolution. Suppose that $p_S(x)$ and $p_N(x)$ are density functions for signal and noise, respectively. We recall that $p_{SN}(x)\,\Delta x$ is the probability of finding a value of signal-plus-noise whose total lies between the values of $x$ and $x + \Delta x$. Thus, for example, $p_{SN}(10)\,\Delta x$ is the probability that $x_S + x_N = 10$ very nearly. There are, however, infinitely many ways by which $x_S + x_N = 10$:

$$x_S = 14, \qquad x_N = -4, \qquad x_S + x_N = 10$$

$$x_S = 13, \qquad x_N = -3, \qquad x_S + x_N = 10$$

$$\vdots$$

$$x_S = 10, \qquad x_N = 0, \qquad x_S + x_N = 10$$

$$\vdots$$

$$x_S = -5, \qquad x_N = 15, \qquad x_S + x_N = 10$$

$$\vdots$$

Thus, if we let $x = x_S + x_N$ and $x' = x_N$, then $x_S = x - x'$. Therefore,

$$\overset{x_S + x_N}{\swarrow} \qquad\qquad \overset{x_S}{\swarrow} \qquad\qquad \overset{x_N}{\swarrow}$$

$$p_{SN}(x)\,\Delta x = \sum_{x'=-\infty}^{\infty} p_S(x - x')\,\Delta x \cdot p_N(x')\,\Delta x'. \tag{7.19}$$

The probabilities $p_S(x - x')\,\Delta x$ and $p_N(x')\,\Delta x'$ are multiplied to give the probability of concurrence of the two independent events, and the products are added to give the total probability of these mutually exclusive events. Taking Equation (7.19) to the limit as $\Delta x \to 0$,

$$p_{SN}(x) = \int_{-\infty}^{\infty} p_S(x - x') p_N(x')\,dx'. \tag{7.20}$$

Equations (7.19) and (7.20) could equally well have been written with the arguments of the two functions interchanged. The integral in Equation (7.20) is known as a *convolution integral*, and it its found in many branches of mathematics.[1]

Using Equation (7.20), we can, in principle, obtain $p_{SN}$ explicitly, by convolving the two functions $p_S$ and $p_N$. The integration can often be carried out analytically.

We can now, in principle, evaluate $\mathscr{I}$, the information contained in a measurement made of a variable that is distributed continuously, from knowledge of the two probability density functions, $p_S$ and $p_N$:

(a) Using Equation (7.20) we obtain $p_{SN}(x)$.
(b) Using Equation (7.17)/(7.18) we obtain $\mathscr{I}$.

## APPLICATIONS IN PERCEPTUAL STUDIES

There are very, very few investigators who have found it desirable to use the information from "continuously distributed" probability density functions (sometimes referred to as "information from analog channels") in studies of perception. Such analog information will, however, be required almost exclusively in the sensory studies in this book. It is well to remember that while differential entropy is not a proper measure of information, any difference between two differential entropies evaluated for the same random variable, $x$, may indeed be a correct measure of information. The differential entropy that is subtracted need not always represent the obfuscation of a noise. For example, consider two absolute entropies

$$H_{abs1} = H_{diff1} - H_{noise} \qquad (7.21)$$

$$H_{abs2} = H_{diff2} - H_{noise}. \qquad (7.22)$$

Then

$$H_{abs1} - H_{abs2} = H_{abs} = H_{diff1} - H_{diff2}. \qquad (7.23)$$

$H_{abs}$ is found as the difference between two differential entropies, neither of which represents noise. We shall have occasion to obtain an absolute entropy as the difference between two differential entropies, the second of which will be labeled "reference":

$$H_{abs} = H_{diff} - H_{reference} \qquad (7.24)$$

$H_{reference}$ may or may not be a noise in the usual sense, but it will, nonetheless, limit the precision with which a sensory measurement can be made. (Please refer also to Chapter 16.)

$H_{abs}$ becomes a little more tangible when it is evaluated for specific probability density functions. The object of the next chapter is to evaluate

$H_{abs}$ when the differential entropies from which it is obtained issue from the normal or Gaussian distribution.

## NOTES

1. "Convolution" (Latin, *con*: together + *volvere*: to roll). Perhaps better is "folded back." As the dummy variable $x'$ increases, the argument of $p_{SN}(x')$ increases, while that of $p_S(x - x')$ decreases.

## REFERENCES

Freund, J. E., and Walpole, R. E. 1980. *Mathematical Statistics*. Prentice-Hall, Englewood Cliffs, NJ.

Goldman, S. 1953. *Information Theory*. Prentice–Hall, Englewood Cliffs, NJ.

McEliece, R. J. 1977. *The Theory of Information and Coding: A Mathematical Framework for Communication*. Addison–Wesley, Reading, MA.

Shannon, C. E., and Weaver, W. 1964. *The Mathematical Theory of Communication*. Univ. of Illinois Press, Urbana.

# 8

## The Entropy of the Normal Distribution

### INTRODUCTION

The "normal distribution" or "Gaussian distribution" or Gaussian probability density function is defined by

$$N(x;\mu,\sigma) = \frac{1}{(2\pi\sigma^2)^{1/2}} e^{-(x-\mu)^2/2\sigma^2}. \tag{8.1}$$

This density function, which is symmetrical about the line $x = \mu$, has the familiar bell shape shown in Figure 8.1. The two parameters, $\mu$ and $\sigma^2$, each have special significance; $\mu$ is the mean and $\sigma^2$ the variance of the distribution. All probability density functions must be normalized to unity, and it is shown in most textbooks on advanced calculus that

$$\int_{-\infty}^{\infty} N(x;\mu,\sigma)\, dx = 1. \tag{8.2}$$

The expectation of $x$, $E(x)$, is equal to the mean; that is,

$$E(x) = \int_{-\infty}^{\infty} xN(x;\mu,\sigma)\, dx = \mu. \tag{8.3}$$

The expectation of $(x - \mu)^2$, $E(x - \mu)^2$, is equal to the variance; that is,

$$E(x - \mu)^2 = \int_{-\infty}^{\infty} (x - \mu)^2 N(x;\mu,\sigma)\, dx = \sigma^2. \tag{8.4}$$

The latter two equations, if unfamiliar, may be found in all textbooks on mathematical statistics, or may be verified directly by the reader.

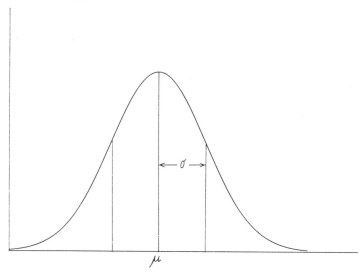

**FIGURE 8.1**   The normal distribution with mean, $\mu$, and variance $\sigma^2$: $N(x; \mu, \sigma)$. About $\frac{2}{3}$ of the area under the curve lies within one standard deviation, $\pm\sigma$, of the mean.

The differential entropy of the normal distribution can be found without difficulty. From the definition of differential entropy given in Chapter 7, and using Equation (8.1),

$$H = -\int_{-\infty}^{\infty} (2\pi\sigma^2)^{-1/2} e^{-(x-\mu)^2/2\sigma^2} \ln\left[(2\pi\sigma^2)^{-1/2} e^{-(x-\mu)^2/2\sigma^2}\right] dx$$

$$H = \tfrac{1}{2}\ln(2\pi\sigma^2)\int_{-\infty}^{\infty} (2\pi\sigma^2)^{-1/2} e^{-(x-\mu)^2/2\sigma^2}\, dx$$

$$+ \frac{1}{2\sigma^2}\int_{-\infty}^{\infty} (2\pi\sigma^2)^{-1/2}(x-\mu)^2 e^{-(x-\mu)^2/2\sigma^2}\, dx.$$

Introducing Equations (8.2) and (8.4),

$$H = \tfrac{1}{2}\ln(2\pi\sigma^2) + \tfrac{1}{2}.$$

Writing $\tfrac{1}{2}$ as $(\tfrac{1}{2}\ln e)$,

$$H = \tfrac{1}{2}\ln(2\pi e\sigma^2), \tag{8.5}$$

which is the simple result we sought. We note that the differential entropy of the Gaussian probability density function depends only on the variance and not on the mean.

It has often been demonstrated (for example, Goldman, 1953) that for a given, fixed value of variance, $\sigma^2$, the probability density with the greatest value of $H$ is the Gaussian density.

For an $n$-dimensional Gaussian density defined by

$$N(x_1, x_2, \ldots; \mu_1, \mu_2, \ldots \sigma_1, \sigma_2 \ldots)$$

$$= \prod_{i=1}^{n} \left(2\pi e \sigma_i^2\right)^{-1/2} \exp\left[-\frac{(x_i - \mu_i)^2}{2\sigma_i^2}\right] \tag{8.6}$$

the differential entropy is

$$H = (n/2)\ln 2\pi e \left(\sigma_1^2 \sigma_2^2 \cdots \sigma_n^2\right)^{1/n} \tag{8.7}$$

as shown by McEliece (1977). In the limiting case, for $n = 1$, Equation (8.7) reduces to (8.5).

## CONVOLUTION OF TWO GAUSSIANS

Suppose that a pure signal is described by $N(x; \mu_S, \sigma_S)$, and its obfuscating noise by $N(x; \mu_N, \sigma_N)$. Then, as shown by Equation (7.20), the density function resulting from pure signal in the presence of noise is provided by the convolution

$$p_{SN}(x) = \int_{-\infty}^{\infty} N(x - x'; \mu_S, \sigma_S) N(x'; \mu_N, \sigma_N) \, dx'. \tag{8.8}$$

In fact, when we carry out the convolution of two Gaussians, the result is a third Gaussian density whose mean is the sum of the means of the two component functions and whose variance is the sum of the variances of the two component functions. That is,

$$p_{SN} = N\left(x; \mu_S + \mu_N, \left(\sigma_S^2 + \sigma_N^2\right)^{1/2}\right). \tag{8.9}$$

The full demonstration of (8.9) is not usually given in the textbooks because it is rather tedious, but it is provided in the Appendix for completeness. Writing Equation (8.9) explicitly,

$$p_{SN} = \left[2\pi\left(\sigma_S^2 + \sigma_N^2\right)\right]^{-1/2} \exp\left[-\frac{\left[x - (\mu_S + \mu_N)\right]^2}{2\left(\sigma_S^2 + \sigma_N^2\right)}\right]. \tag{8.10}$$

Using Equations (8.5) and (8.10), we can now write down directly the differential entropy of the two component densities and of the convolution of the two Gaussian components:

$$H_S = \tfrac{1}{2}\ln\left(2\pi e \sigma_S^2\right) \tag{8.11}$$

$$H_N = \tfrac{1}{2}\ln\left(2\pi e \sigma_N^2\right) \tag{8.12}$$

and

$$H_{SN} = \tfrac{1}{2}\ln\left[2\pi e\left(\sigma_S^2 + \sigma_N^2\right)\right]. \tag{8.13}$$

## INFORMATION

Following Equation (7.17), we represent the information of a measurement as a difference (Shannon, 1948):

$$\mathscr{I} = H_{SN} - H_N$$

$$= \tfrac{1}{2}\ln\left[2\pi e\left(\sigma_S^2 + \sigma_N^2\right)\right] - \tfrac{1}{2}\ln\left[2\pi e \sigma_N^2\right] \tag{7.18}$$

$$\mathscr{I} = \tfrac{1}{2}\ln\left[1 + \sigma_S^2/\sigma_N^2\right] \text{ natural units per signal.} \tag{8.14}$$

Remember that (7.18) was put forward as a "reasonable" candidate for the information obtained by making a measurement of a variable that was distributed continuously. Equation (8.14) is just a specific instance of (7.18) where the respective density functions are Gaussian. Equation (8.14) demonstrates various properties that would support its candidacy for an information function. $\mathscr{I}$ increases monotonically with increasing $\sigma_S$; the greater the standard deviation of the measured signal, the more uncertain we are about what the signal is, the more information we obtain from the measurement. Moreover, $\mathscr{I}$ increases monotonically with *decreasing* $\sigma_N$; the smaller the obfuscating factor, the greater the information obtained from the measurement. And of course, when $\sigma_S^2 = 0$, $\mathscr{I} = \ln 1 = 0$; when the signal (effectively) vanishes, no information is obtained. Or, looked at in another way, when the measurement is certain ($\sigma_S = 0$), no information is obtained.

A brief derivation of Equation (8.14) and its relation to "Shannon's second theorem" is provided by Beck (1976).

In the sensory analysis that follows, it will be helpful to interpret $\mathscr{I}$ as an information, because information is rather a tangible quantity that may conjure a picture in our minds. However, the informational interpretation of Equation (8.14) is not mandatory; no problem of a mathematical nature will be encountered by regarding $\mathscr{I}$ in this equation as simply the difference between differential entropies. In fact, since we shall hold $\sigma_N^2$ to be constant, $\mathscr{I}$ may be regarded simply as a differential entropy plus a constant, which definitely conjures no picture. The application of the function $\mathscr{I}$ in the analysis of sensory events will proceed in either case, with informational or entropic interpretation. Information is just a useful "currency" in which we can visualize a sensory neuron as trading. It is rather a concrete matter to state that a certain afferent neuron has relayed $b$ bits of information to the brain. However, although less concrete, it is equally valid to say simply that a sensory receptor served by this afferent has reduced its entropy by $b$ bits. But we are getting a little ahead of our story.

## MORE ON THE INTERPRETATION OF THE INFORMATION FROM CONTINUOUS SOURCES

Using Equation (8.14), we can continue from Chapter 7 the attempt to interpret the information from continuous probability densities into the more intuitive information from discrete probability functions. You will remember that the probability density function for noise was used to limit the number of discrete rectangles into which the probability density for the signal might be divided: the less intense the noise, the greater the number of rectangles, and the greater the value of the (discrete) entropy. The process of dividing into narrower and narrower rectangles had to be limited by some natural constraint, so that a unique value of (discrete) entropy could be obtained. The problem was one of "discretizing" the continuum.

For the normal distribution, Equation (8.4) illustrates how the continuous distribution can be rendered, in effect, discrete. Suppose we regard $\sigma_S^2/\sigma_N^2 \gg 1$. Then Equation (8.14) becomes effectively

$$\mathscr{I} = \tfrac{1}{2}\ln\!\left(\sigma_S^2/\sigma_N^2\right). \tag{8.15}$$

But $\sigma_S$ and $\sigma_N$ are the standard deviations of the probability density functions for signal and noise, respectively. If we regard $\sigma_S/\sigma_N$, rounded to the nearest integer $= n$, as the equivalent number of equally probable outcomes to the measurement event, then from the usual equation for discrete entropy,

$$H = \ln(\sigma_S/\sigma_N) = \ln(n). \tag{8.16}$$

From (8.15), of course, $\mathscr{I} = H$. This idea is shown schematically in Figure 8.2.

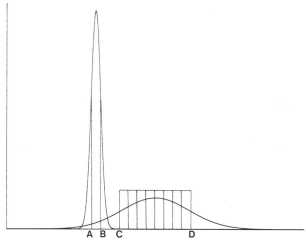

**FIGURE 8.2** Squaring the normal curve (sort of), or "discretizing" the continuum. Two normal distributions are shown, the one on the right-hand side representing the pure signal, and the other representing the noise signal. $AB$ designates the region between $-\sigma_N$ and $+\sigma_N$, and $CD$ designates the region between $-\sigma_S$ and $+\sigma_S$ (see Figure 8.1). It is seen that $CD$ can be divided into eight rectangles of width $AB$. We can then regard the eight rectangles as a histogram defining eight equally probable, discrete, outcomes to an event. The information obtained from a measurement of the outcome is equal to $\ln(\sigma_S/\sigma_N) =$ $\ln(4/0.5) = \ln 8$, which is approximately equal to the outcome of the original continuous event, $\frac{1}{2}\ln[1 + (\frac{1}{2}CD)^2/(\frac{1}{2}AB)^2]$. We can see that as the noise variance, $\sigma^2$, becomes smaller, $\sigma$ becomes smaller, more $AB$'s fit into CD, and the information is greater.

## THE CENTRAL LIMIT THEOREM

Suppose that $\mathbf{x}_1, \mathbf{x}_2, \ldots \mathbf{x}_n$ constitute a random sample drawn from an infinite population. We say that $\mathbf{x}_1, \mathbf{x}_2, \ldots \mathbf{x}_n$ constitute a *random sample of size n*. Let

$$\bar{\mathbf{x}} = (\mathbf{x}_1 + \mathbf{x}_2 + \cdots + \mathbf{x}_n)/n \qquad (8.17)$$

be the sample mean. The Central Limit Theorem states that if random samples of size $n$ are drawn from a large or infinite population with mean $\mu$, and variance $\sigma^2$, the sample mean, $\bar{\mathbf{x}}$ is approximately distributed normally with mean $\mu$, and variance $\sigma^2/n$. Note that the theorem makes no mention of the nature of the population from which samples are drawn. Even if the population is far from a "normal" or "Gaussian" population, the sample means will still be distributed normally for sample size $\geq 30$. If, however, the population is not too different from normal, the distribution of means will be normal for values of $n$ much smaller than 30. The populations we consider in our sensory work are expected to fall into the latter category.

Statistically, no mention need be made about how a sample of size $n$ is obtained. However, in our scientific applications of the Central Limit Theorem, it is indeed necessary to consider how the sample was obtained. In fact, a measuring device will reach into the large or infinite population and sequentially make $n$ measurements, $x_1, x_2, \ldots x_n$. I refer to each of these measurements as *one sampling*. That is, *it is necessary to make n samplings (or measurements) of the population to obtain one sample of size n*. The language is a little unwieldy, but I hope it is clear.

We have seen, now, that if the original population has variance $\sigma^2$, the means of samples of size $n$ are normally distributed with variance $\sigma^2/n$. Therefore, the differential entropy of the original distribution is given by Equation (8.5) directly, while the differential entropy of the distribution of means of samples of size $n$ is obtained from Equation (8.5) by replacing $\sigma^2$ by $\sigma^2/n$:

$$H_{\text{mean}} = \tfrac{1}{2} \ln(2\pi e \sigma^2/n). \tag{8.18}$$

If the precision of the measurement of the means (net result of sampling + computation) is limited by Gaussian noise with variance $\sigma_N^2$, the information obtained from such a measurement is given by Equation (8.14) with $\sigma_S^2$ replaced by $\sigma_S^2/n$:

$$\mathscr{I} = \frac{1}{2} \ln\left[1 + \frac{\sigma_S^2/n}{\sigma_N^2}\right] \quad \text{natural units per measurement.} \tag{8.19}$$

Thus it would appear that the information received by obtaining a measurement of the mean of 10 samplings ($n = 10$) is *less* than the information received by making a measurement based on a single sampling from the population ($n = 1$). However, this is not the interpretation I wish to pursue.

If one looks at the information given by Equation (8.19) as a function of $n$, the sample size, it is seen that $\mathscr{I}$ is maximum for $n = 1$, and $\mathscr{I} \to 0$ for $n \to \infty$. When $n \to \infty$, the sample variance, $\sigma^2/n \to 0$, implying that one has near-perfect knowledge of the population mean. We have incorporated the idea of Fisher's information (Chapter 5) into Shannon's structure. However, Equation (8.19) was not given by Shannon. I interpret

$$H(n) = \mathscr{I}(n) = \frac{1}{2} \ln\left[1 + \frac{\sigma_S^2/n}{\sigma_N^2}\right] \tag{8.19a}$$

as the information which *can still be gained* about the population mean after $n$ samplings of a population have produced a single sample of size $n$. That is, $\mathscr{I}(n)$ is an absolute entropy; an uncertainty about the value of the population mean; and a *potential information* that may be received as the process of sampling continues. That is, with increasing $n$, uncertainty and potential information decrease, while information about the population mean increases. This interpretation of Equation (8.19) will be pursued in the next chapter when we come to model the process of sensation.

The difference in potential information, and, therefore, the gain in information, when the sample size is increased from $n_1$ to $n_2$ is given by $H(n_1) - H(n_2)$. The reader might like to show that for $\sigma_S^2/(n_2\sigma_N^2) \gg 1$, the gain in information is equal to $\ln\sqrt{n_2/n_1}$ (cf. Equation (11.10)).

## ANALOG CHANNELS

You may remember that in Chapter 5 we left some unfinished business. We discussed the applications of information from discrete systems to communications engineering, but we could not, at that time, examine continuous or analog systems. However, we are now in a position to do so.

Communications systems deal usually with signals such as electrical potentials (voltages) that are transmitted with complex waveforms having, effectively, zero mean value. Equation (8.14) gives information in natural units per sample (of a complex signal). The well-known *sampling theorem* (Shannon, 1949) states that if a function contains no frequencies higher than $W$, it is completely determined by giving its ordinates at a series of points spaced $1/(2W)$ seconds apart. The theorem has also been generalized to include the case where the frequency band does not start at zero but at some higher value. $W$ is then a bandwidth. Therefore, if we divide the right-hand side of Equation (8.14) [natural units of information per sample] by $1/(2W)$ [seconds per sample] we obtain

$$C = W \ln\left(1 + \sigma_S^2/\sigma_N^2\right) \text{ natural units per second.} \qquad (8.20)$$

Shannon has shown (1949), using an argument involving the volumes of spheres in hyperspace, that $C$ is the channel capacity of the channel. If we divide (8.20) by $\ln 2$ we get, of course, bits per second.

The ratio of variances is usually written as $P/N$, the signal-to-noise ratio, so that

$$C = W \ln(1 + P/N). \qquad (8.21)$$

This equation, then, gives the greatest rate at which an analog channel with a given signal-to-noise ratio and Gaussian noise ("white thermal noise") can transmit information. (Remember that the Gaussian distribution has the greatest differential entropy for a given variance.) As an example (from Raisbeck), if an audio circuit for the transmission of speech has a signal-to-noise ratio $P/N$ equal to 36 dB, and the bandwidth, $W$, is 4500 Hz, we can immediately calculate the channel capacity, $C$. Since $P/N = 10^{3.6}$ (note 2, Chapter 3),

$$C = (4500/\ln 2)\ln(1 + 10^{3.6}),$$

or about 50,000 bits per second.

## APPENDIX: CONVOLUTION OF TWO GAUSSIAN FUNCTIONS

The convolution of the two Gaussian functions $N(x; \mu_S, \sigma_S)$ and $N(x; \mu_N, \sigma_N)$ that is given formally in Equation (8.8) is now carried out explicitly.

$$p_{SN}(x) = \int_{-\infty}^{\infty} \frac{1}{2\pi\sigma_S\sigma_N} \exp\left(\frac{-(x - x' - \mu_S)^2}{2\sigma_S^2}\right)\exp\left(\frac{-(x' - \mu_N)^2}{2\sigma_N^2}\right) dx'.$$

Changing variable, we set

$$Z = x' - \mu_N.$$

$$p_{SN}(x) = \int_{-\infty}^{\infty} \frac{1}{2\pi\sigma_S\sigma_N} \exp\left(\frac{-(x - Z - \mu_S - \mu_N)^2}{2\sigma_S^2}\right)\exp\left(\frac{-Z^2}{2\sigma_N^2}\right) dZ.$$

Setting

$$X = x - \mu_S - \mu_N, \tag{A8.1}$$

$$p_{SN}(x) = \frac{1}{2\pi\sigma_S\sigma_N} \int_{-\infty}^{\infty} e^{-(X-Z)^2/2\sigma_S^2} e^{-Z^2/2\sigma_N^2} dZ$$

$$= \frac{1}{2\pi\sigma_S\sigma_N} e^{-X^2/2\sigma_S^2} \int_{-\infty}^{\infty} \exp\left(\frac{2XZ}{2\sigma_S^2} - \frac{Z^2}{2\sigma_S^2} - \frac{Z^2}{2\sigma_N^2}\right) dZ$$

$$= \frac{1}{2\pi\sigma_S\sigma_N} e^{-X^2/2\sigma_S^2} \int_{-\infty}^{\infty} \exp\left\{-\left\{2\left[\frac{-X}{2\sigma_S^2}\right]Z + \left[\frac{1}{2\sigma_S^2} + \frac{1}{2\sigma_N^2}\right]Z^2\right\}\right\} dZ$$

$$= \frac{1}{2\pi\sigma_S\sigma_N} e^{bX} \int_{-\infty}^{\infty} e^{-(aZ^2 + 2bZ)} dZ,$$

where

$$a = \frac{1}{2}\left(\frac{1}{\sigma_S^2} + \frac{1}{\sigma_N^2}\right), \quad \text{and} \quad b = -\frac{X}{2\sigma_S^2}. \tag{A8.2}$$

$$p_{SN}(x) = \frac{1}{2\pi\sigma_S\sigma_N} e^{bX} \int_{-\infty}^{\infty} e^{b^2/a} e^{-a(Z+b/a)^2} dZ.$$

Changing variable by setting $u = Z + b/a$, $du = dZ$,

$$p_{SN}(x) = \frac{1}{2\pi\sigma_S\sigma_N}e^{bX}e^{b^2/a}\int_{-\infty}^{\infty}e^{-au^2}\,du\,.$$

Since $\int_{-\infty}^{\infty}e^{-au^2}\,du = \sqrt{\pi/a}$, $a > 0$ (see any discussion of the error function),

$$p_{SN}(x) = \frac{\sqrt{\pi/a}}{2\pi\sigma_S\sigma_N}e^{bX+b^2/a}\,. \tag{A8.3}$$

$b^2/a$ can be evaluated from Equation (A8.2):

$$b^2/a = \frac{X^2}{4\sigma_S^4}\left/\frac{1}{2}\left(\frac{1}{\sigma_S^2} + \frac{1}{\sigma_N^2}\right)\right. = \left(\frac{\sigma_N^2}{\sigma_S^2 + \sigma_N^2}\right)\frac{X^2}{2\sigma_S^2}\,.$$

Completing the algebra,

$$bX + b^2/a = -X^2/2(\sigma_S^2 + \sigma_N^2)\,. \tag{A8.4}$$

From the definition of $a$ in (A8.2),

$$\frac{\sqrt{\pi/a}}{2\pi\sigma_S\sigma_N} = \frac{1}{\sqrt{2\pi(\sigma_S^2 + \sigma_N^2)}}\,. \tag{A8.5}$$

Substituting Equations (A8.4) and (A8.5) into (A8.3), and returning the value for $X$ from (A8.1), we obtain the required result,

$$p_{SN} = \left[2\pi(\sigma_S^2 + \sigma_N^2)\right]^{-1/2}\exp-\left[\frac{[x - (\mu_S + \mu_N)]^2}{2(\sigma_S^2 + \sigma_N^2)}\right]\,. \tag{8.10}$$

## REFERENCES

Beck, A. H. W. 1976. *Statistical Mechanics, Fluctuations, and Noise.* Arnold, London.

Goldman, S. 1953. *Information Theory.* Prentice–Hall, Englewood Cliffs, NJ.

McEliece, R. J. 1977. *The Theory of Information and Coding: A Mathematical Framework for Communication.* Addison-Wesley, Reading, MA.

Raisbeck, G. 1963. *Information Theory: An Introduction for Scientists and Engineers.* MIT Press, Cambridge, MA.

Shannon, C. E. 1948. A mathematical theory of communication. *Bell System Technical Journal* **27**, 623–656.

Shannon, C. E. 1949. Communication in the presence of noise. *Proceedings of the IRE* **37**, 10–21.

# 9

## Modeling the *H*-Function

It is time to pick up the thread of the argument that was begun in Chapter 2. The fundamental equation (2.6) was proposed,

$$F = kH, \qquad (2.6)/(9.1)$$

where $F$ is a perceptually related variable such as subjective magnitude or impulse frequency in a sensory neuron, $k$ is a constant that is greater than zero, and $H$ is the entropy of a stimulus. Since $H$ can be regarded as an uncertainty, or perhaps as a potential for receipt of information, $F$ is a measure of this uncertainty or potential to receive information. Therefore, Equation (2.6)/(9.1) states that a quantity, $F$, which can be measured in the laboratory, is, in effect, a measure of uncertainty. In Chapter 2, it was suggested that the "denomination" of this uncertainty —that is, the quantity which is uncertain—is the exact value of the physical magnitude or intensity of the stimulus. This process of setting a measurable quantity proportional to an uncertainty no doubt strikes some people as enigmatic, to say the least. However, we may recall that we have already encountered this process in Chapter 6 in our survey of statistical mechanics. Boltzmann discovered that

$$S = k_{\mathrm{B}} \ln W = k_{\mathrm{B}} H_I, \qquad (6.20), (6.21)$$

where $S$ is the thermodynamic entropy of a gas under equilibrium conditions, and $k_{\mathrm{B}}$ is now known as Boltzmann's constant. The denomination of the uncertainty, $H$, is the exact microstate corresponding to a given macrostate. A measurable quantity had been set equal to an uncertainty.

"Aha!" you may be thinking.

"So $F = kH$ is modeled after $S = k_{\mathrm{B}} H_I$!"

Would that I possessed such insight. There seems to be no direct link connecting physical entropy, $S$, with, for example, neural impulse rate as measured by $F$. There certainly have been studies involving the thermodynamic entropy of neural processes (e.g., Margineanu, 1972), but these studies have not, to my knowledge, been related to perceptual function. However, we draw the equations $F = kH$ and $S = k_B H_I$ quite closely together in Chapter 15.

"Then what reasoning led you to postulate $F = kH$?" you may ask. A rather different sort of reasoning, closer to the philosophy of Berkeley than to the physics of Boltzmann.

Now is a good time to look back at Figure 1.2, which gives the order of exposition. We have proceeded to the right, across the top of the flow diagram, down the right-hand side, and partway across the bottom. We are now moving toward the block at the lower left corner. The center block (validation) will take us through a number of chapters. We shall then proceed up the left-hand side of the diagram to reach Berkeley, with whose concept of "relative perception" we really began.

At the level of Chapter 2, we had developed only the concept of entropy or information of events with discrete outcomes. So, in order to introduce Equation (9.1), it was necessary to postulate the existence of an organism that could perceive only discrete stimuli. That is, the organism could determine only that the stimulus assumed the values $I_1, I_2, \ldots, I_n$, but could not perceive a continuum of intensities.[1] Then, if the probabilities of occurrence of the stimuli were equal, $H = \log n$, and $F = kH = k \log n$: $F$ was proportional to the logarithm of the number of equally probable stimulus intensities. This discrete representation certainly produces some conceptual problems, which I tried to mitigate, tentatively, in note 6 to Chapter 2. The discrete representation, however, was intended primarily as a vehicle to introduce Equation (9.1). A more realistic interpretation of (9.1) requires that $H$ be a measure of entropy in a system with continuous outcomes; that is a system where intensity, $I$, can vary continuously. For this reason, we took a long digression through Chapters 4, 5, 7, and 8. We should now be in possession of the conceptual apparatus necessary to proceed.

## THE SENSORY RECEPTOR AS A QUANTUM DETECTOR

Many of the ideas developed here were put forward by the author in 1977.

The sensory stimulus belongs most properly to the microscopic or quantum world. Fewer than 10 molecules of an odorant may be detected by the olfactory receptor(s). About 15 photons may be required to see a flash of light (Barlow and Mollon, 1982, p. 127). Certainly when operating at these near-liminal levels, the sensory detector can be regarded as a "quantum detector." However, the sensory afferent neuron issuing from these receptors, and most particularly the brain to which these neurons report, does not seem to be equipped to detect individual quanta (molecules, photons...). Let me elaborate.

As stated before, we are concerned in this book primarily with constant stimuli of the intensity type; that is, with stimuli of light, sound, concentration, etc. that are presented in the form of step functions (Figure 1.1). However, to be more precise it should be said that we deal with stimuli whose *mean or average value* is constant, since most stimuli of the intensity type consist of a multitude of small particles or bundles of energy whose density is changing on a moment to moment basis (Figure 9.1). For example, if it is stated that the stimulus is an $0.1M$ solution of sucrose, what is meant is that the bottle of stock solution contains 0.1 mole of sucrose per liter of solution. However, due to random movements of sucrose molecules in solution, a very small sample of this solution will seldom consist of exactly the stated concentration. The concentration of a very small sample will fluctuate about the value of $0.1M$. Therefore, the sensory receptors, which sample only very small quantities of the stimulus solution, *will detect variable concentrations of sucrose even when the stimulus is (macroscopically) constant* (Figure 9.1). Similarly, the photoreceptor, even when stimulated by a macroscopically constant light stimulus, will record a fluctuating photon density.

Not all the sensory stimuli that we deal with can be reduced to a density fluctuation diagram such as Figure 9.1, but the principle of

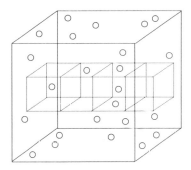

FIGURE 9.1   The large cube represents a large sample of a fluid containing 24 particles. Imagine the boundaries of this cube as impermeable so that, although particles are free to move about, they cannot escape from the large container. Particles move about randomly within this cube. The small cubes represent small samples of the fluid such as might be obtained by a sensory receptor. The boundaries of the small cubes (in dotted lines) are just imagined boundaries, so that particles are free to move in and out. Due to random movements of the particles, one of the small cubes contains no particles, two of them contain one particle, and one contains three particles. In this way, a sensory receptor may obtain $0, 1, 2, 3, \ldots$ particles in any one process of sampling.

fluctuation about the mean will still prevail. For example, if we apply a sudden, constant load to a tendon which activates a stretch receptor, there will be a period of transient oscillation, followed, probably, by small, sustained fluctuations about the mean force, produced by muscle and elastic elements. Similarly, sound waves which activate the hearing mechanism consist of fluctuations in air pressure, etc.

The receptors are quantum receptors and, therefore, detect quantum fluctuations. However, the brain, which receives the report of sensory receptors, is not made aware of quantum fluctuations. The message the brain receives concerns the level of the steady, macroscopic stimulus, which is the mean of the signals detected by the receptors. The fluctuating environment of the sensory receptor is translated, presumably by a process of averaging, into a smooth report received at the brain. Since the message of the sensory receptors is usually relayed to the brain by means of a neural frequency code, it is expected that this frequency will also, usually, encode a smoothed or averaged signal (although, of course, we cannot be sure[2]).

## SAMPLING THE STIMULUS POPULATION

The receptor will be regarded as drawing samples from the stimulus population which, in turn, will be regarded as an infinite population. Each sample will provide one value of the density of the stimulus. For concentration, density equals the number of molecules per sampled fluid volume; for light, density equals the number of photons per volume of light beam sampled. The samples are identically and independently distributed. Hence, if the original population of densities had mean, $\mu$, and variance $\sigma_S^2$ ("$S$" designates "stimulus"), the mean of $m$ samplings of the population will be a sample of size $m$, which, by the central limit theorem, will tend toward the normal distribution with mean, $\mu$, and variance, $\sigma_S^2/m$, as $m$ increases (see Chapter 8).

At what rate does a sensory receptor make samplings of its stimulus population? We do not know. We know only that such samplings must be occurring. In the absence of any definitive knowledge, I suggest a sort of null conjecture: namely that the rate of sampling is constant, so that at time, $t$,

$$m = [t/t_s], \qquad (9.2)$$

where $t_s$ is the time between samples, and $[t/t_s]$ designates the greatest integer not greater than $t/t_s$. In a continuous representation,

$$m = \alpha t \qquad \alpha \text{ constant} > 0. \qquad (9.3)$$

$$\alpha = dm/dt, \qquad (9.4)$$

or

$$\text{sampling rate} = dm/dt. \tag{9.5}$$

Clearly, for $m$ small, the approximation of number of samplings, $m$, by the continuous variable, $t$, will weaken; and additionally, for small $m$ the acceptability of the central limit theorem weakens. Therefore, the validity of the model for $H$ as a function of $t$ that we are developing will extend only beyond some minimum value for the variable, $t$.

The differential entropy of the distribution of means is

$$H_S = -\int p \ln p \, dx, \tag{9.6}$$

or explicitly (from Equation (8.18)),

$$H_S = \tfrac{1}{2}\ln(2\pi e \sigma_S^2/m), \tag{9.7}$$

where $p$ is the normal distribution with variance $\sigma^2/m$. We do not know the factors operating within the receptor system that limit the precision with which a mean may be measured. However, we understand from Chapter 7 that in the absence of such a "noise" distribution, no finite value for information can be distinguished.

## THE REFERENCE SIGNAL

Let us, therefore, assume the existence of "Gaussian white noise," which is just an interfering signal whose probability density is normal. Since the term noise is usually regarded in the pejorative, let us designate this signal as *reference* instead. It is a stimulus signal without which information would not be measurable. Accordingly, its variance will be designated by $\sigma_R^2$, and its differential entropy by

$$H_R = \tfrac{1}{2}\ln(2\pi e \sigma_R^2). \tag{9.8}$$

The absolute entropy received per stimulus, $H$, is then given by

$$H = H_{S+R} - H_R = \tfrac{1}{2}\ln[2\pi e(\sigma_S^2/m + \sigma_R^2)] - \tfrac{1}{2}\ln(2\pi e \sigma_R^2). \tag{9.9}$$

$$H = \tfrac{1}{2}\ln(1 + \sigma_S^2/m\sigma_R^2). \tag{9.10}$$

In the theory that follows we shall take $\sigma_R^2$ to be constant for a given modality of sensation. Introducing Equation (9.3),

$$H = \tfrac{1}{2}\ln(1 + \sigma_S^2/\sigma_R^2 \alpha t). \tag{9.11}$$

Since $F = kH$ from Equation (9.1), we have

$$F = \tfrac{1}{2}k\ln(1 + \sigma_S^2/\sigma_R^2 \alpha t). \tag{9.12}$$

RELATIONSHIP BETWEEN VARIANCE AND MEAN

Equation (9.12), then, relates the perceptual variable, $F$, to $\sigma_S^2$, the variance of the stimulus population, and $t$, the duration of the stimulus. Unfortunately, in this form, the equation is still not readily applicable in the analysis of experiments, because $\sigma_S^2$ is not usually known. In the laboratory, we measure the mean stimulus value, $\mu$, but usually not the variance. It is, therefore, necessary to introduce a relationship between mean and variance of the form

$$\sigma_S^2 = f(\mu); \tag{9.13}$$

that is, $\sigma_S^2$ is some function of mean stimulus intensity, $\mu$. However, in formulating such an equation it is necessary to bear in mind where $\sigma_S^2$ is being "measured," and where $\mu$ is being measured. $\sigma_S^2$ is the stimulus variance "as seen by" the sensory receptor; it is the variance obtained by the receptor's sampling of its stimulus environment. On the other hand, $\mu$, the population mean, is estimated by the investigator as $I$, the intensity of the constant stimulus (that is, $\mu = I$), at some convenient location within the laboratory. For example, $\sigma_S^2$ for audition may be measured at the hair cells within the cochlea in the inner ear, while $\mu = I$ = sound intensity is usually measured by a sound level meter at the outer ear. Hence, $\sigma^2$ incorporates fluctuation arising from both the physical stimulus and the biological receptor. Therefore, the character of the function, $f(\mu)$, is not obvious, although in the case of audition some idea may be obtained from the work of Rhode (1971). I selected for $f(\mu)$, empirically, a simple power function, so that

$$\sigma_S^2 \propto \mu^n, \qquad n \text{ constant} > 0, \tag{9.14}$$

or, since $\mu = I$,

$$\sigma_S^2 \propto I^n. \tag{9.14a}$$

The constant, $n$, may differ among the modalities of sensation.

I chose this function for several reasons. First, relationships between mean and variance within statistical physics often assume the form of Equation (9.14). For example (Jackson, 1968, or other textbooks on statistical mechanics), for a monoatomic ideal gas in thermal equilibrium with a thermal reservoir, and performing no mechanical work, the standard deviation of energy, $\sigma(E)$, is related to mean energy, $\mu$, by the relation

$$\sigma(E)/\mu = 1/(3N/2)^{1/2}, \tag{9.15}$$

where $N$ is the (constant) number of particles in the gas. That is,

$$\sigma(E)^2 \propto \mu^2. \tag{9.15a}$$

As another example, the number, $N$, of photons in a monochromatic beam emitted per unit time by a thermal source kept at constant temperature will fluctuate. The general equation for $\sigma^2(N)$, the mean square fluctuation, was found by Einstein. However, in the Wien approximation we have simply

$$\sigma(N)^2 = \mu. \tag{9.16}$$

Equations (9.15) and (9.16) are specific examples of mean–variance relationships of the form (9.14).

A second reason for selecting Equation (9.14) is that a similar relationship might be expected from any process wherein a total measurement, $I$, is the sum of a number of partial measurements. For example, a length, $ma$, is measured by laying down $m$ times a measuring rod of length $a$. Suppose that each single measurement is regarded as a random variable whose standard deviation is $\sigma_1(a)$. Then the variance of the sum of $m$ measurements, $\sigma(ma)^2$, is equal to $m\sigma_1(a)^2$ by the rule of summing variances of independent random variables (for example, Freund and Walpole, 1980, p. 157 or Weatherburn, 1961, p. 27). That is,[3]

$$\sigma(ma)^2 \propto m = ma/a = I/a,$$

or

$$\sigma(ma)^2 \propto I. \tag{9.17}$$

Total variance varies as the "intensity" ($=$ length here) of the whole, which is just a way of saying that larger quantities are associated with greater fluctuations. The variance of measurements of the separation of two marked points in two different cities will be expected to exceed the variance of measurements of the separation of two marked points both within a given room.

None of the above examples demonstrate the validity of Equation (9.14); however, they illustrate the plausibility of such a relationship.


## THE ENTROPY FUNCTION

Introducing Equation (9.14a) into (9.11),

$$H = \tfrac{1}{2}\ln\left[1 + (\beta'/\sigma_R^2)I^n/t\right], \tag{9.18}$$

where $\beta'$ is a proportionality constant $> 0$. Finally, condensing the constant $\beta'/\sigma_R^2$ into a single constant, $\beta$,

$$\boxed{H = \tfrac{1}{2}\ln(1 + \beta I^n/t), \qquad \text{[natural units]}} \tag{9.19}$$

Of course, $H$ [bits] is obtained by dividing $H$ [natural units] by $\ln 2$. *Equation* (9.19), *then, gives the absolute entropy of m samplings by a sensory receptor taken over an interval of time, t, of a stationary stimulus population of mean intensity, I*. Since $F = kH$,

$$\boxed{F = \tfrac{1}{2}k \ln(1 + \beta I^n / t)} \quad . \tag{9.20}$$

Before looking more deeply into the meaning of $H$ as calculated from (9.19), let us review the primary assumptions that have been used to derive Equations (9.19) and (9.20). Six of them are listed below.

(1) There is a process of sampling by the receptor of its stimulus.

(2) The stimulus population approximates the normal distribution closely enough that the central limit theorem will apply to a sample of almost any size drawn from the stimulus population.

(3) Sensory neurons encode their state of certitude concerning the mean stimulus intensity.

(4) The rate of sampling of a stimulus by its receptor is constant.

(5) A "noise" or reference stimulus distribution is present. This reference stimulus is Gaussian with constant variance.

(6) Stimulus variance at the receptor is a simple power function of the mean stimulus intensity measured at a point external to the receptor.

Essentially, upon the above six assumptions, the entropy function was derived. In some applications of the $H$-function we shall not require one of either assumptions (4) or (6). In later chapters, we shall occasionally add an additional assumption, namely that $\Delta H$, a small difference in $H$, is constant and plays the part of a threshold.

## POPULATION VS. SAMPLE VARIANCE

In order to understand the $H$ concept more clearly, and to understand the limitations of the modeled $H$-function given by Equation (9.19), we had best look at some of the intermediary stages of its development. Looking back at Equation (9.10), we see that for constant $\sigma_R^2$, the value of $H$ is dependent upon $\sigma_S^2/m$, which is the variance of a *population* of means. However, the perceiving organism does not have access to the value of $\sigma_S^2/m$. Rather it must sample the stimulus population and obtain, at best, the value of the variance of a *sample* of the population means. That is, the organism measures $s^2/m$ as an estimator of $\sigma_S^2/m$. In order to develop a more accurate $H$ function, we should have to make allowance for the probability distribution of the sample variance, which we shall not do here.

MAXIMUM $H$ AS POTENTIAL INFORMATION

We recall from Equation (9.10),

$$H = \tfrac{1}{2}\ln\!\left(1 + \sigma_S^2/m\,\sigma_R^2\right). \qquad (9.10)$$

For fixed, $I$, $H$ is seen to be maximum for $m = 1$. However, if the sensory receptors are sensing variances rather than means, no sample variance can be obtained for $m$ less than 2. Nonetheless, for simplicity, let us take

$$H = H_{\max} \qquad \text{for } m = 1. \qquad (9.21)$$

Then $H_{\max}$, being an absolute entropy, represents the greatest amount of information *receivable* by the receptor per stimulus. Remember, though, that $H_{\max}$ is only *received* when the mean signal variance is reduced to zero, leaving only the noise or reference signal variance [recall the $(H_{SN} - H_N)$ idea of Equations (7.18) and (8.14)]. Looking at Equation (9.10), we see that this "extinction" of the mean signal variance, $\sigma_S^2/m$, will only occur for large values of $m$, the number of samplings made by the receptor—that is, for large $t$. What transpires is a gradual reduction in the mean signal variance as $m$ increases—the effects of Fisher's information felt here. We might look at $H_{\max}$, which we have termed an absolute entropy or an uncertainty, as the *potential* of the perceiving system to acquire information. *Potential information is transformed gradually into information as the perceptual act proceeds.*

To broaden the perspective, it is interesting to think back to the quantum physical picture outlined in Chapter 2. Perception of a quantum event occurs as the wavefunction (the square of whose modulus is a probability density function) collapses over time, $\Delta t$. That is, in time $\Delta t$, the variance of the quantum probability density decreases, with the resulting perception of the event. The physiological event occurs continuously, within the "paradigm" of classical physics; the wavefunction –mediated event occurs suddenly, within the paradigm of quantum physics.

THE SENSORY NEURON AS METACHANNEL

The concluding section of Chapter 6 should take on clearer meaning now. We see that the sensory receptor receives a "message" or "statement" from the so-called "outside world."[4] Within the context of the present theory, this statement is never made available to the brain, nor, presumably, to "consciousness." Since the sensory neuronal report, $F$, is equal to $kH$, and $H$ is the entropy or uncertainty or potential to receive information, the neuronal report is proportional to the uncertainty of the receptor about the statement. That is, the neuronal report is a *statement about a statement* or a *metastatement* (Norwich, 1983, 1984).

We see in cartoon fashion in Figure 9.2 a germ of the Berkeleian approach to sensory physiology: The substance of the world seems forever cut off from the mind that perceives it. We seem to be drawn ineluctably into the philosophical core; however, I am determined to delay it, so on to. . . .

## *F* AT THE THRESHOLD

Let us consider the legitimacy of the use of the *H*-function, as obtained from Equation (9.19), for small values of $I$, when used in (9.1),

Receptor                      Neuron                      Brain

FIGURE 9.2  The different worlds of the receptor, sensory neuron, and brain. The "outside world" is seen only by the receptor. The brain receives from the sensory neuron only a report concerning the "uncertainty" of the receptor about the state of the outside world. From these reports about uncertainty, the brain must synthesize its picture of the outside world. The cartoon depicts only the passive phase of perception: from the receptor to the brain. It omits the active phase of perception, which is the effect of the brain on the receptor.

$F = kH(I, t)$. It is well known that when $I$ is less than some value, $I_{thresh}$, which may have to be determined with due attention to the statistical methods of signal detection theory, a stimulus is imperceptible. However, since $H$ has been modeled as a continuous, monotone function of $I$ for all values of $I \geq 0$, $F$ will be greater than zero for all values of $I$ greater than zero. When the perceptual variable, $F$, is interpreted as subjective magnitude, $F > 0$ for $I < I_{thresh}$ is not acceptable. Clearly, some correction is necessary in Equation (9.1) when $I$ is near threshold, particularly when dealing with subjective magnitudes. Simplest would seem to be

$$F = k[H(I, t) - H(I_{thresh}, t)]. \qquad (9.22)$$

This equation would be appropriate if $I_{thresh}$ assumed the form of a masking stimulus. As we see in the next chapter, Equation (9.22) is in accord with the experimental findings of Lochner and Burger (1961).[5] But later we treat thresholds in a manner quite different from the usual, by representing them in terms of the minimum quantities of information required to perceive a stimulus or to discriminate between stimuli; so it is, perhaps, premature to speculate about Equation (9.22). We shall continue to use Equation (9.20), but with caution or not at all in the proximity of $I_{thresh}$. So we have now issued caveats on the use of certain of our model equations both for very small $t$ and for very small $I$.

## INFORMATION-FREE APPROACH

In Chapter 8 (Information) it was stated that we could, probably, proceed with this entropic interpretation of perception without using the concept of information at all. We can now see explicitly how that might be effected. Referring to Equation (9.9), we see that $H$ can be split into its two components generically,

$$H = -\int p_{SR} \ln p_{SR}\, dx + \int p_R \ln p_R\, dx, \qquad (9.23)$$

where $p_{SR}$ is the summated probability density for stimulus and reference. The second integral on the right-hand side, representing the differential entropy for the reference stimulus, is constant, since $p_R$ depends only on the constant, $\sigma_R^2$, which has been taken as constant. Therefore, we can write

$$H = [\text{differential entropy for stimulus + reference}] + \lambda', \quad (9.24)$$

where $\lambda'$ is constant;

$$F = kH = k\,[\text{differential entropy for stimulus + reference}] + \lambda, \quad (9.25)$$

where $\lambda$ is constant; or simply

$$F = kH_{\text{diff}} + \lambda. \qquad (9.25a)$$

$H_{\text{diff}}$ is, of course, decreasing with time due to its argument, $\sigma_S^2/t$. Written in the above form, the theory is, in principle, "information-free," since the differential entropy is not an information.

Equation (9.25) is of great interest to me because it parallels Boltzmann's equation

$$S = -k_{\text{B}}H_{\text{B}} \qquad (9.26)$$

(cf. Equation (6.20)), where $H_{\text{B}}$ is Boltzmann's $H$-function (akin to a differential entropy), $k_{\text{B}}$ is Boltzmann's constant, and $S$ is physical entropy. Equation (9.26), the equilibrium form for which has been derived in Chapter 6 [$S = k_{\text{B}} \ln W$ (Equation (6.21); see Tolman, 1979, p. 135], states that, ignoring additive constants, physical entropy is proportional to Boltzmann's $H$-function *both in and out of equilibrium* (ter Haar, 1966, p. 27). Boltzmann showed that, due to molecular collisions,

$$\frac{dH_{\text{B}}}{dt} \leq 0, \qquad (9.27)$$

thus demonstrating through the use of statistical mechanics that the thermodynamic entropy, $S$, is nondecreasing (recall the second law of thermodynamics). One cannot but note the parallel:

$F$ [due to its dependence on $H(t)$] is necessarily nonincreasing with increasing time.

$S$ [due to its dependence on $H_{\text{B}}(t)$] is necessarily nondecreasing with increasing time.

We return to $H_{\text{B}}$ in Chapter 15.


## CONSERVATION LAWS AND UNIFICATION

The second part of Chapter 1 was devoted to a discussion of the nature of physical laws and their capacity to "unify" the observations of science. The distinction was made between laws of conservation and laws of mechanism, and I should like to pursue that distinction here in terms of sensory science. Chapter 3 consists of a survey of many of the empirical rules (or laws) of sensation and perception. These are rules that have been learned by experience; they are, essentially, codified measurements. Our job in the next few chapters is to *derive* these laws theoretically from Equations (9.19) and (9.20). That is, *we try to derive* all *empirical laws that relate a single, constant stimulus of intensity* $I > I_{\text{thresh}}$, *applied for a duration of time* $t > t_0$, *to a selected perceptual variable, F, using the single theoretical law,* $F = kH$.

Megalomania, perhaps.

Now, it is important to realize that $F = kH$ is a theoretical law of the *conservation type*; it is *not* a mechanistic law. Please recall that the $H$-function was derived from considerations of uncertainties resident in the stimulus. That is, a model of the stimulus was formulated, and an expression for differential entropy was derived from it. We approached it from the point of view of fluctuations in the density of quanta. However, stimuli other than those of the intensity type may give rise to other models for $H$; the use of a fluctuating density of quanta may not always be appropriate. Some other quantity may be sampled by the sensory receptor.

We have seen how $H$ measures the potential to deliver information. Neurophysiologically, the equation $F = kH$ depicts the transformation of that potential stimulus information into the language of the sensory receptors. Consider a constant stimulus applied to a receptor. When $m_1$ samplings have been made, $H = H_1$. When $m_2$ samplings have been made, $H = H_2$. Let $m_2$ be greater than $m_1$. Then $F_1 = kH_1$, $F_2 = kH_2$, so that

$$(F_1 - F_2)/k = H_1 - H_2. \tag{9.28}$$

We specify that the information $H_1 - H_2$ bits is transferred to the receptor, which acknowledges its receipt by signaling $F_1 - F_2$ units of information. When $m_1$ is very small and $m_2$ is very large, so that $H_1 \rightarrow H_{\text{max}}$ and $H_2 \rightarrow 0$, then

$$F_{\text{max}}/k = H_{\text{max}}. \tag{9.29}$$

That is, $F_{\text{max}}$ is proportional to the total stimulus information. If we write, further,

$$\frac{F_1 - F_2}{F_1} = \frac{H_1 - H_2}{H_1}, \tag{9.30}$$

we just state that the difference between any two $F$-values, as a receptor continues to sample its stimulus, designates the fraction of the total available information transmitted to the receptor at any $m$-value or time. So we see that $F = kH$ can be viewed as a kind of conservation law that meters the flow of information from stimulus to receptor. No more than $F_{\text{max}}/k$ units of information may be transmitted from stimulus to receptor.

We observe, though, that no *mechanism* for the transmitted information is specified; we don't know *how* the information passed from stimulus to receptor. We recall from Chapter 1 that laws of mechanism *complement* laws of conservation. The development and use of $F = kH$ in no way supplants the search for the principles of operation of sensory receptors—the electrical and mechanical properties of signal transducers. *A fortiori*, laws of the type $F = kH$ *need* laws of mechanism to provide a base for information transmittal. In the final analysis, knowledge of mechanism will enable us to formulate improved versions of the $H$-function and perhaps tailor the $H$-function to each specific type of receptor. The thrust of the next few chapters, however, will be to show how far we can go *without* knowledge of mechanism, using a common mathematical form of the $H$-function for all modalities of sensation.

## APPENDIX: THE PARABLE OF THE SUPERMARKET

*(A Pedagogical Lamentation on the Elusiveness of Friendship)*

I suppose my motives might be suspect when I go the supermarket with almost no money or plastic at my disposal but with a calculator capable of adding numbers as large as $10^{500}$. I proceed to the fruit section where I note that each species of fruit is piled on its own special table: one table for grapes, one table for apples, etc. I go to one such table and proceed to weigh nearly every item of fruit on the table using the scale provided. I enter the weight into the memory on my calculator and then compute the average weight of a piece of fruit, which I duly record. Before leaving the table, I pick up one piece of fruit at random, reweigh it, and record the weight. I then go on to a second table and repeat the above ritual. I am monopolizing the scales, so I make little grimaces and utter audible expression of annoyance to signify my dissatisfaction with the whole tableful of fruit, in the hopes of assuaging the anger of the woman behind me. What does she know of the methods of science?

I leave the store without buying anything, but brandishing my calculator, and I soon meet a friend on the street. He tells me how happy he is to meet me, but I suspect that he doesn't mean it. Nonetheless, I decide to pose the following problem to him. I provide him with the weights of the two pieces of fruit that I have selected at random, but I do not tell him what kinds of fruit they are. I ask him to guess, for each of the two types of fruit, what the *average weight* of the fruit on the table was, and to estimate the "uncertainty" in his guess of the average. That is, I am really asking him to estimate a sort of standard deviation of his guess of the average.

Well, the first piece of fruit weighted 5120 grams. My friend guesses that this fruit must have been a watermelon or pumpkin, estimates the average weight of the species as 5000 grams and his error as $\pm 2000$ grams. The weight of the second piece of fruit was 45 grams. My friend guesses that it must be a berry of some kind, and estimates the average weight as 50 grams $\pm 20$ grams. His uncertainties about the average weight are, then, 2000 and 20 grams. I suspect that he is burning with curiosity to know the true values of the means, so I kindly relieve his curiosity by telling him what they were. I wish to continue the dialogue by showing my friend what wisdom lay inherent in his choices, but he seems very anxious to go somewhere and I do not wish to detain him. He tells me that we really must get together some time, but I think he doesn't mean it. He leaves before I can teach him the two main lessons to be learned from the guessing game, but I'll tell him next time. Maybe I'll send him a letter . . . .

The first lesson is that when I provided him with the correct answer, his uncertainty "collapsed" (in the language of physics), and he received a quantity of information that depended on the magnitude of his prior uncertainty. We can, in fact, measure this information. The scale that I used in the supermarket had a resolution of about 5 grams; that is, measurements were accurate within a range of $\pm 5$ grams. Consider, now, each of the two pieces of fruit which were, in fact, a pumpkin and a strawberry.

    (i)   Pumpkin:

        estimated error $= \pm 2000$ grams,

        "reference weight" or resolution of the scale $= 5$ grams,

        call 5 grams a "resolvable category,"

        information received $= \log_2(\text{number of resolvable categories}) =$

$$\log_2 2000/5 = 8.64 \text{ bits.}$$

        Perhaps more precisely, since his estimate of error did not take account of the error of the scale, we can combine errors using the rule of addition of variances. Then,

information received $= \frac{1}{2} \log_2[(5^2 + 2000^2)/5^2]$
$$= \frac{1}{2} \log_2(1 + 2000^2/5^2)$$
$$= 8.64 \text{ bits.} \qquad \text{(Pumpkin)}$$

    (ii)   Strawberry:

        estimated error $= \pm 20$ grams,

        reference weight or resolution of the scale $= 5$ grams,

        again, call 5 grams a resolvable category,

        information received $= \log_2(\text{number of resolvable categories}) =$

$$\log_2(20/5) = 2.00 \text{ bits.}$$

        Or, using again the addition of variances,

information received $= \frac{1}{2} \log_2[(5^2 + 20^2/5^2]$
$$= \frac{1}{2} \log_2(1 + 20^2/5^2)$$
$$= 2.04 \text{ bits.} \qquad \text{(Strawberry)}$$

The second lesson, that I did not get the chance to teach my friend, is that he received a greater quantity of information when I provided him with the correct average weight of the pumpkin than when I provided him with the correct average weight of the strawberry. Larger measurements are associated with larger quantities of information. Intrinsically, he knew that when he ascribed a larger error to the pumpkin estimate than to the strawberry estimate. All this mathematical knowledge was actually present in my friend's mind all along. I just helped him to extract it. Socrates understood such matters long ago, as we learn in Plato's *The Meno*.

My friend is probably already regretting having treated me in such a distant manner. He is probably going to call me tonight to apologize. I'll have to remind him that, in this Parable of the Supermarket, we are not forbidden to compare Equations (Pumpkin) and (Strawberry) to Equation (9.10) with $m = 1$:

$$H = H_S - H_R = \tfrac{1}{2}\ln\!\left(1 + \sigma_S^2/\sigma_R^2\right).$$

He'll grow warm and friendly with the acquisition of this wisdom. I'm sure he will.

## NOTES

1. Is this equivalent to the existence of an organism that possesses the ability to perceive a continuum of stimuli, immersed in a world in which stimuli always assume discrete values, like the eigenvalues of a quantum mechanical system?

2. I know, when I look at a light signal, that I do not perceive quantal fluctuations. That is, I am not conscious of such fluctuations. But do the sensory neurons report such fluctuations anyway? I think not. However, even when a sensory neuron fires at a constant average rate, there are moment by moment fluctuations in the constant rate (stationary time series). I shall assume, in the absence of knowledge to the contrary, that these fluctuations in neuronal firing rate do not reflect quantal fluctuations in the stimulus density although, admittedly, future research may show otherwise. Recall, also, that we are confining our discussion, for the most part, to stimuli of the "intensity" type, so phenomena such as "phase locking" in pitch perception are not considered here.

3. This relation, $\sigma(na) \propto \sqrt{n}$, led Cattell (1893) to his well-known conjecture: "The algebraic sum of a number of variable errors tends to increase as the square root of the number . . . ." Recall also the generalization of the above by Guilford (1932) into the "Fullerton —Cattell law," discussed in note 6 Chapter 2. However, it is most

important that the reader make the following distinction. In the development of this entropy theory of perception, we are introducing a mean–variance relationship (Equation (9.14)) *at the level of the stimulus* (for example, a relationship between the mean and variance of the density of odorant molecules). We are *not* introducing any *a priori* relationships between the mean stimulus level and the differential threshold, $\Delta I$, for purposes of obtaining Weber's law. We derive Weber's law from the general equation of entropy (9.19). I am grateful to Professor Harry Lawless for drawing my attention to this situation.

4. Within this entropic view of perception, the meaning of the term "outside world" is not all that simple, as shown in Figure 9.2. Since a direct view of the outside world is denied to us, the best we can do is to formulate a model of this world. This model is one wherein magnitudes of outside-world events are inferred from the neuronal reports of uncertainties.

5. Lochner and Burger (1961) found for loudness that a function of the form

$$F = k( I^n - I^n_{thresh} )$$

was much more accurate in describing experimentally measured data than a function of the form

$$F = k( I - I_{thresh} )^n.$$

We see in Chapter 10 that, in terms of $H$, Lochner and Burger's findings mean that

$$F = k[ H( I,t) - H( I_{thresh}, t)]$$

is better than

$$F = kH( I - I_{thresh}, t).$$

## REFERENCES

Barlow, H. B., and Mollon, J. D. 1982. Psychophysical measurements of visual performance. In *The Senses* (H. B. Barow and J. D. Mollon, Eds.). Cambridge Univ. Press, London.

Cattell, J. M. 1893. On errors of observation. *American Journal of Psychology* 5, 285–293.

Freund, J. E., and Walpole, R. E. 1980. *Mathematical Statistics*, 3rd ed. Prentice–Hall, Englewood Cliffs, NJ.

Haar, D. ter. 1966. *Elements of Thermostatistics*. Holt, Rinehart, & Winston, New York.

Jackson, E. A. 1968. *Equilibrium Statistical Mechanics*. Prentice–Hall, Englewood Cliffs, NJ.

Lochner, J. P. A., and Burger, J. F. 1961. Form of the loudness function in the presence of masking noise. *Journal of the Acoustical Society of America* 33, 1705–1707.

Margineanu, D.-G. 1972. Entropy changes associated with a nerve impulse. *Kybernetic* **11**, 73–76.

Norwich, K. H. 1977. On the information received by sensory receptors. *Bulletin of Mathematical Biology* **39**, 453–461.

Norwich, K. H. 1983. To perceive is to doubt: The relativity of perception. *Journal of Theoretical Biology* **102**, 175–190.

Norwich, K. H. 1984. Why the eye may be found to be a source of light. *Proceedings of the 6th International Congress of Cybernetics and Systems of the WOGSC*, Vol. 2, pp. 831–836.

Rhode, W. S. 1971. Observations of the vibration of the basilar membrane in squirrel monkeys using the Mössbauer technique. *Journal of the Acoustical Society of America* **49**, 1218–1231.

Tolman, R. C. 1979. *The Principles of Statistical Mechanics*. Dover, New York.

Weatherburn, C. E. 1961. *A First Course in Mathematical Statistics*. Cambridge Univ. Press, London.

# 10

# Derivation of the Law
# of Sensation

THE DUAL FORMS OF THE EMPIRICAL LAW OF SENSATION:
FECHNER'S AND STEVENS' LAWS

We proceed, now, in the flow diagram of Figure 1.2, toward the center block: experimental evaluation of $F = kH$. This process occupies several chapters and involves, essentially, the evaluation of the function (9.20)

$$F = \tfrac{1}{2}k \ln(1 + \beta I^n/t). \tag{10.1}$$

In this chapter it is demonstrated, if it is not already apparent to the reader, that Equation (10.1) can be used to derive *both* of the common forms of the "law of sensation," which were described in some detail in Chapter 3. The quest to "unify" the two forms of the law of sensation—the semilog law of Weber and Fechner (WF) with the power law of Plateau, Brentano, and Stevens (PBS)—has been pursued with great vigor throughout the years. Hundreds, if not thousands, of pages have been published in this endeavor. Yet the unification emerges easily from the entropy equation (9.20)/(10.1).

You will recall how the law of sensation (or the "psychophysical law") was discovered. Stimuli of constant intensity, $I$, of constant duration (it is to be hoped), $t'$, were applied to a sensory receptor in an appropriate state of adaptation (e.g., unadapted). The perceptual variable, $F$, was measured, and the data were graphed. From the graphed data, it became apparent that $F$ was sometimes related linearly to the log $I$ (WF law) and that log $F$ was sometimes related linearly to log $I$ (PBS law). These relationships are illustrated in Figures 3.1a and 3.1b. $F$, the perceptual variable, is, on some occasions, taken as the subjective magnitude of the stimulus (e.g., how bright the light seems to be), and, on other occasions, is taken as the impulse frequency in a sensory neuron issuing from the receptor. The conundrum of the law of sensation is that *both* these two laws and *only* these two laws seem to work.

There is a body of papers dealing with different methods for measuring the subjective magnitude: the method of categories, of magnitude estimation, and of magnitude production. One of these (categories) is found by some to favor the semilog law (WF), and another (magnitude estimation) to favor the power law. While the distinction is undoubtedly important, I defer here to my psychophysical colleagues, who are better able to define the distinction. In these pages, I shall lump together all methods of measuring subjective magnitude and refer to them as just that: subjective magnitude.

## DERIVATION OF THE LAW OF SENSATION FROM THE ENTROPY EQUATION

In order to derive the two forms of the law of sensation from Equation (10.1), we set $t = t' = $ constant, and let

$$\gamma = \beta/t'. \tag{10.2}$$

Thus

$$\boxed{F = \tfrac{1}{2}k \ln(1 + \gamma I^n).} \tag{10.3}$$

*Case* $(i)$ where $\gamma I^n \gg 1$.

From Equation (10.3) we have

$$F \simeq \tfrac{1}{2}k \ln(\gamma I^n). \tag{10.4}$$

$$F = \tfrac{1}{2}kn \ln I + \tfrac{1}{2}k \ln \gamma, \tag{10.5}$$

or

$$F = a \ln I + b = a' \log I + b, \tag{10.5a}$$

which is Equation (3.4) stating the WF law (Norwich, 1977). Note that we did not have to begin as Weber did by asserting (Equation (3.1)) that

$$\Delta I/I = \text{constant}$$

(which is true for a limited range of $\Delta I$), nor by setting $\Delta F$ to be constant for a jnd, as Fechner did.

Case $(ii)$ where $\gamma I^n \ll 1$.

Utilizing the Taylor expansion for $\ln(1 + x)$ where $0 < x \le 1$,

$$\ln(1 + x) = x - \left(\tfrac{1}{2}\right)x^2 + \left(\tfrac{1}{3}\right)x^3 - \cdots, \tag{10.6}$$

we find from (10.3)

$$F \simeq \tfrac{1}{2}k\gamma I^n - \tfrac{1}{4}k\gamma^2 I^{2n} + \text{higher order terms.} \tag{10.7}$$

Retaining only the first-order term,

$$F = \tfrac{1}{2}k\gamma I^n, \tag{10.8}$$

which is identical with Equation (3.7) with a different representation of the constant (Norwich, 1977). Taking logs of both sides of Equation (10.8),

$$\log F = n \log I + \log(\tfrac{1}{2}k\gamma) \tag{10.9}$$

*It is clear, I think, that the two forms of the law of sensation emerge as $\gamma I^n$ approaches each of the two extreme values. Between the extremes, one or both of the two forms will appear to be valid (see, for example, Figures 5.1 and 5.2 of Norwich, 1991). The most general law of sensation, which embraces both the WF and PBS laws, is the entropy law (10.3).*

It is seen that as $I$ becomes large so that $\gamma I^n$ is not $\ll 1$, the approximation of Equation (10.9) weakens. Instead of the first-order approximation (10.8) we need at least the second-order approximation (10.7). That is, due to subtraction of the term $\tfrac{1}{4}k\gamma^2 I^{2n}$, "true" $F$ is *less* than $\tfrac{1}{2}k\gamma I^n$. Therefore, in a log–log plot of $F$ vs. $I$, the data points with higher values of $I$ fall *below* the straight line. This result was observed for Stevens' taste data, as shown in Figure 3.1a. This phenomenon, wherein data with larger $I$-values fall below the expected straight line was observed by Atkinson (1982) for many sensory modalities. Conversely, when $I$ becomes small, so that $\gamma I^n$ is not $\gg 1$, the approximation of Equation (10.4) weakens. Therefore in a graph of $F$ vs. log $I$, data points with lower values of $I$ fall *above* the straight line. This result, also, was seen in Stevens' taste data, as shown in Figure 3.1b. However, the most important observation is that between the two extremes, by and large, both the logarithmic law and the power laws (Weber–Fechner and PBS laws) provide good approximations to the data.

The mystery of the dual form of the law sensation would seem to be solved. Moreover, since the common property of all modalities of sensation is to transmit information, we see the *reason* for a common law of sensation. Henceforth, I use Equation (10.3) as the most general and the most meaningful form of the law of sensation.

## OBJECTIONS TO A COMMON LAW OF SENSATION

The opinion has often been expressed that it is unreasonable to expect a single law to govern the operation of many sensory modalities. The most cogent objection I have encountered was put forward by Weiss (1981). Weiss draws our attention to the arbitrary nature of the measuring scale that is used to measure the physical stimulus. Suppose, using one scale of measurement, the stimulus intensity is found to be $I$ units. Suppose, moreover, that this measure of $I$ agreed with the law of sensation,

$$F = f(I). \tag{10.10}$$

However, some other investigator decides to use a different scale of measurement, so that his/her measurement of stimulus is found to be $I'$ units, where $I' = g(I)$, and where $g$ is some function of $I$. For example, it may be that $I' = \log I$. Then, in general,

$$F \neq f(I'). \tag{10.10a}$$

That is, the law of sensation will not be valid when intensity is measured using the latter scale of measurement. Using the above example,

$$f(\log I) \neq f(I).$$

Weiss' arguments are quite correct; but his conclusion—that no universal law of sensation is possible—is too severe. The appropriate conclusion is that there must be rules set forth governing the selection of a scale of measurement for the magnitude of the physical stimulus of a given modality, if that modality is to be governed by a common law of sensation. Within the entropy theory, that rule is given by Equation (9.14a),

$$\sigma_S^2 \propto I^n:$$

the variance of the stimulus signal must vary as the $n$th power of the physical magnitude of the stimulus. If Equation (9.14a) holds for the measure $I$, then, in general, it will fail to hold for $I' = g(I)$. There are, of course, transformations, $g$, that still enable Equation (9.14a); to wit, Weiss' example from audition. That is, if $I$ is sound intensity and $I'$ is sound pressure, then $g$ expresses the physical relation, $I' = I^{1/2}$, and, hence,

$$\sigma_S^2 \propto I^n = \left(I'^2\right)^n = \left(I'\right)^{2n} = \left(I'\right)^m,$$

in agreement with Equation (9.14a). Hence, the law of sensation can be expressed using either intensity or sound pressure units.

However, measuring distance in logarithmic units using a slide rule would violate Equation (9.14a).

## OBJECTIONS TO THE ENTROPIC FORMULATION OF THE LAW OF SENSATION

Only a few objections have been voiced specifically to the entropic form of the law of sensation through the years. People often ask how one can determine *a priori* the magnitude of the quantity $\gamma I^n$ relative to unity, so that one might know which form of the two empirical laws will best hold. Unfortunately, we do not know, *a priori*, the value of the constant, $\gamma$, which is, itself, made up of several constituent constants. The most reasonable approach, in my opinion, is to use the general form of the law, Equation (10.3), rather than either of the two approximations.

One may wonder why nature seems to operate at the "boundary" between the two approximate forms of the entropy law, rather than at one or other of the extremes. Why, for example, does all sensation not occur in the region $\gamma I^n \gg 1$, so that the semilog law (WF) would always be valid, or, conversely, in the region $\gamma I^n \ll 1$ (PBS)? I have no answer to this question, but I feel that it is a very important one. A simple exploration of the function $y = \ln(1 + x)$ in this critical region has been given elsewhere (Norwich, 1991, Figure 5.2).

The entropic law has also been challenged because it does not allow for the saturation of sensory effect at high values of stimulus intensity, $I$. That is, in reality, when $I$ reaches an upper limit, no further increase in $F$ (sensation or neural impulse rate) can occur. Yet no such limit appears in Equation (10.3). While this objection is valid, it is, of course, true that no such limit appears in either of the two empirical laws either.

## OTHER ENDEAVORS TO UNIFY THE TWO FORMS OF THE LAW OF SENSATION

A truly incredible volume of ink has been spent in the attempt to explain the apparent "two laws" of sensation, as evidenced, for example, by Krueger's reviews of the subject. I should like to flag only three of these endeavors—those that have impressed me the most or amused me the most, as the case may be.

The first of these, is the well-known paper by D. M. MacKay (1963), in which the author postulates that a sensory receptor emits a frequency, $f_1$, which is a linear function of $\log(I - I_0)$, where $I_0$ is constant. He then assumes the presence of an internal "organizer" or "effort generator" that emits a "matching" frequency, $f_2$, which is a linear function of $\log(F - F_0)$, where $F_0$ is constant. He assumes, further, that an equilibrium is achieved wherein

$$f_1 = bf_2 + \text{constant}, \qquad (10.11)$$

where $b$ is a weighting factor. He proceeds to show, algebraically, that

$$F - F_0 = a(I - I_0)^n, \qquad a, n \text{ constant}, \qquad (10.12)$$

which is a form of the power law of sensation. MacKay, thus, involves both semilog and power laws into one unified theory.

I confess that I do like the idea of matching frequencies using an internal frequency generator, for reasons that may become clearer toward the end of this book. However, in other respects, I find MacKay's theory wanting. A large number of ad hoc assumptions are invoked, in order to produce a power law of sensation. Moreover, MacKay's theory does not, to my knowledge, generalize; it accounts, in a way, for the psychophysical law and no other law of sensation. In contrast, the entropy equations (10.1)/(10.3) will be found to give rise to a large number of the observed laws of sensation and perception.

The second study of the two empirical laws with which I was much taken is given by Resnikoff (1989), section 2.4.[1] This author shows that there are only two possibilities for the law of sensation ("psychophysical function") which "(1) yield constant relative information gain for 1 jnd responses, and (2) yield relative information that is invariant under changes of scale for the stimulus measure."

The entropy equation (10.3) does, of course, embody function (2), but does not yet contain constraint (1). However, we build (1) into the entropy function as an additional constraint when we come to discuss the Weber fraction.

Finally, leaving laughs last, the most sensational law of sensation may be "Nimh's Law"—so named by M. H. Birnbaum (Nimh, 1976)—which, admittedly, will always fit the data more closely than any other simple mathematical law.

We return to theoretical considerations toward the end of the chapter, but let us proceed now to consider how the parameters of Equation (10.3), our general law of sensation, can be evaluated.

## NUMERICAL EVALUATION OF THE CONSTANTS $k$, $\gamma$, AND $n$

We note that the general law, given by Equation (10.3), contains three parameters, $k$, $\gamma$, and $n$, that must be estimated from experimental data, while each of the component laws, WF and PBS, each have only two parameters. Two parameters are all that are needed to produce a straight line in a semilog plot (WF), and two parameters are all that are needed to produce a straight line on a log–log plot (PBS). The third parameter in the general law is needed, so to speak, to incorporate the slight deviation from a straight line that is observed with either of the two plots. However, the deviation from linearity is often so slight that robust numerical estimates of all three parameters are not possible. The method for parameter estimation that is usually used is the method of curve fitting by the least-squares criterion. When one attempts to curve fit a function of three parameters to data that are nearly linearly arrayed, using an appropriate computer program, it is often observed that two of the parameters tend to "trade off" with each other. That is, one parameter increases its value, perhaps over several orders of magnitude, while a second parameter decreases concurrently. The result of all this variation in parameter values is to leave the sum of squares of residuals nearly constant. The sum of squares does decrease, but the fractional change is not nearly as great as is the fractional change in the values of the parameters. I refer to such parameter values as *nonrobust*.

It is often easy to see the reason for the trading-off behavior of nonrobust parameter values. For example, if one attempts to curve fit the general entropy equation (10.3) to experimental data that span only the region where $\gamma I^n \ll 1$, the computer will not fail to oblige you. It will produce a set of numerical values for $k$, $\gamma$, and $n$. However, you will probably notice that while the sum of squares of residuals decreases only slightly, the values of $k$ and $\gamma$ change dramatically, the one increasing and the other decreasing, while the value of $n$ remains relatively stable. The reason for this behavior can be seen from Equation (10.8), which is the approximation of the general equation for small values of $\gamma I^n$:

$$F = \tfrac{1}{2}k\gamma I^n = \tfrac{1}{2}\varepsilon I^n. \qquad (10.13)$$

We see that the *product* of parameters, $k\gamma$, is regarded by the computer as a single parameter, $\varepsilon$. Therefore, $k$ and $\gamma$ can change *ad libitum* without changing the calculated value of $F$, thus leaving the sum of squares nearly constant. These ideas are illustrated in Tables 10.1 and 10.2, and in the accompanying Figure 10.1.

The upshot of the above is that it is difficult, indeed, to estimate distinct values for $k$ and $\gamma$ from data that relate $F$ to $I$. The value of the exponent, $n$, however, is robust. We have to appeal to other types of data to separate out $k$ and $\gamma$. Nonetheless, for select sets of measured data, where $I$ spans the full physiological range of perceptible values, the data may demonstrate enough deviation from linearity that three distinct parameter values may be found.

Let us consider first the data of Stevens for taste of NaCl solutions (Figure 8 of Stevens, 1969), Figures 3.1a and 3.1b. Suppose that we first use the data of Figure 3.1a and fit $\ln F$ vs. $\ln I$ to a straight line by least-squares regression. Most of us have access to a scientific hand calculator that will do the job easily. From Equation (10.9), the slope of this straight line provides the value for $n$. Suppose, now, we use the data

TABLE 10.1    A Set of Eight Pairs of Numbers Selected
Using Only the Criterion that when $Y$ Is Plotted
against $X$, the Points Will Scatter, Roughly, about a Straight Line.

| $X$ | $Y$ |
|-----|-----|
| 1 | 1.5 |
| 2 | 2.2 |
| 3 | 2.5 |
| 4 | 3.3 |
| 5 | 3.7 |
| 6 | 4.2 |
| 7 | 4.8 |
| 8 | 5.3 |

*Note.* A function of the form given by Equation (10.3) was fitted to these simulated data. The use of such a three-parameter function is not really appropriate to fit data that lie nearly on a straight line. Please see Table 10.2.

of Figure 3.1b, and fit $F$ vs. $\ln I$ to a straight line. From Equation (10.5) we see that the slope of this line is equal to $\frac{1}{2}kn$ and its $F$-intercept is equal to $\frac{1}{2}k \ln \gamma$. Since we have determined the value of $n$ from the first graph, we can obtain the value of $k$ from the slope of the second graph. With $k$ determined, we can calculate the value of $\gamma$ from the intercept of the second graph. However, the system is "overdetermined," since the

TABLE 10.2    Excerpts from Simplex Program Output
Used to Carry Out Curve Fitting of the Simulated
Data from Table 10.1

| Iteration number: | 518 | 776 | 1134 | 1571 |
|-------------------|-----|-----|------|------|
| Sum of squares of residuals | 0.187 | 0.156 | 0.143 | 0.136 |
| $k$ | 21.86 | 42.13 | 88.90 | 164.3 |
| $\gamma$ | 0.1225 | 0.06357 | 0.02959 | 0.01618 |
| $n$ | 0.7575 | 0.707 | 0.6833 | 0.6684 |
| $k\gamma$ | 2.678 | 2.678 | 2.631 | 2.658 |

*Note.* The function fitted was

$$Y = \left(\tfrac{1}{2}\right) k \ln(1 + \gamma X^n).$$

We may observe from this table that the sum of squares of residuals diminished with progressive number of iterations (of course), but the decrease was quite small over 1000 iterations (27%). Over the same 1000 iterations, the value of $n$ changed by only about 12%. However, $k$ and $\gamma$ each changed by a *factor* of 7.57. In fact, $k$ and $\gamma$ "traded off" in value with each other, so that the product, $k\gamma$, remained nearly constant at 2.65, as required by the Taylor series (10.6). The simulated data are plotted in Figure 10.1, together with the "best" and "poorest" fitted functions (sum of squares = 0.136 and 0.187, respectively). It may be seen that, despite the considerable differences in parameter values, the fitted curves are nearly superimposed over the range of the data.

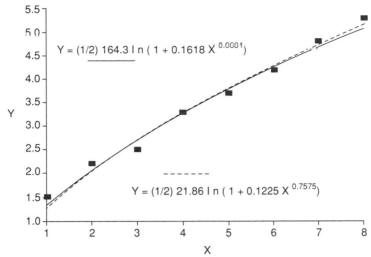

FIGURE 10.1   Numerical example of Table 1. Two curves fit a set of simulated data points nearly equally well, despite the fact that the parameters of the two curves differ considerably. The curves are obtained from a fit to the entropy function (10.3). This demonstrates the difficulties encountered when points that lie nearly on a straight line are fitted by a function of three parameters.

intercept of the first straight line is equal to $\ln(\frac{1}{2}k\gamma)$. The value of this intercept may be checked against the already determined values of $k$ and $\gamma$. Usually some adjustment of values is necessary to obtain a compromise position. When I assign such problems in curve fitting to my students, they usually attack the problem in the manner described above, and emerge with quite reasonable and consistent values for the three parameters.

Alternatively, one can use a computer program that fits nonlinear functions such as (10.3) by a process of "hill climbing," using the least-squares criterion. My own favorite is a downhill simplex routine (not to be confused with the simplex method of linear programming) that will provide a good fit of Equation (10.3) to the data with a few minutes' execution time on a PC. This method was devised by Nelder and Mead in 1965, but good renditions in Fortran and C computer languages can be found in Press *et al.* (1986, 1988), and a clear explanation of the algorithm together with a listing of a simplex program in Pascal is given by Caceci and Cacheris in BYTE magazine (1984).

Equation (10.3) was fitted to Stevens' NaCl-taste data (log $F$ fitted against log right-hand side of (10.3)) by the simplex method, and the result is shown in Figure 10.2. The following parameter values were obtained: $k = 41.31$, $\gamma = 0.09995$, $n = 1.483$.

The value of the exponent, $n$, is, of course, similar to the value one would obtain from a simple regression line to a log–log plot. The value of

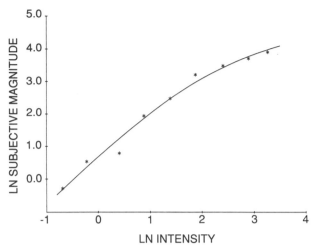

FIGURE 10.2   Data of S. S. Stevens (1969). Natural log of subjective magnitude of taste of sodium chloride solutions plotted against natural log of percent concentration by weight of NaCl. The entropy equation in the form of Equation (10.3) has been fitted to the data, and the resulting curve has been plotted.

$$F = (41.31/2)\ln(1 + 0.09995 I^{1.483}).$$

Compare with the PBS and WF laws, plotted in Figures 3.1a and 3.1b, respectively. Notice how the deviation of the data points from a straight line on the full log plot is embraced naturally by the entropy equation.

the scaling constant, $k$, takes on much more significance to us after we have explored the process of adaptation.

Much of the published data relating $F$ with $I$ do not exhibit enough curvature in a log–log or semilog plot to permit robust estimations of $k$ and $\gamma$. A number do, however, as in the example given above.

Figure 10.3 shows the entropy function fitted to the auditory data of Luce and Mo (1965). The following parameters were obtained by a least-squares procedure: $k = 113.1$, $\gamma = 0.03131$, $n = 0.2896$. Again, the value of the exponent, $n$, is in accord with the value of 0.3 which is usually quoted for audition. Figure 10.4 demonstrates the fit of the entropy equation to Luce and Mo's data on lifted weights. The parameter values are $k = 1040.$, $\gamma = 3.022 \times 10^{-4}$, $n = 1.499$. Data for mean magnitude estimates of sweetness of sucrose were estimated from a graph provided by Moskowitz (1970b), and the results are shown in Figure 10.5. These data are somewhat more approximate than the others. Parameters for the entropy function are $k = 24.6$, $\gamma = 0.0126$, $n = 2.03$. The value for $n$ is a little greater than the value that would have been obtained from the usual log–log plot.

There is magic in the values of the constant, $k$, but to sample its enchantment you must remain apprentice to this sorcerer for at least one

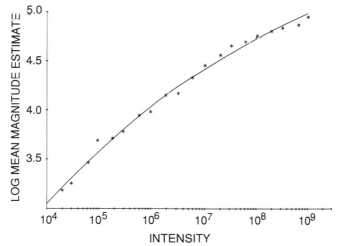

**FIGURE 10.3** Data of Luce and Mo (1965). Natural log of mean magnitude estimate of intensity of a 1000-Hz tone (subject 9) plotted against log of sound intensity. The reader may observe in Luce and Mo's Figure 2 how the data on a log–log plot deviate characteristically from a straight line. The curvature is captured by the entropy equation:

$$F = (113.1/2)\ln(1 + 0.03131I^{0.2896}).$$

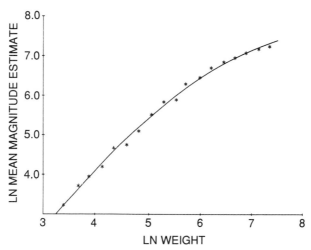

**FIGURE 10.4** Data of Luce and Mo (1965). Natural log of mean magnitude estimate plotted against natural log of lifted weight (subject 6). The deviation of the plotted data from a straight line on a log–log plot for all six subjects is very clearly seen in Luce and Mo's Figure 3. The fitted entropy equation is

$$F = (1040/2)\ln(1 + 0.0003022I^{1.499}).$$

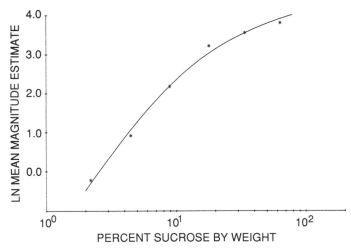

FIGURE 10.5    These data were digitized, approximately, from Moskowitz (1970b), Figure 1. Natural log of sweetness of sucrose is plotted against log percent sucrose by weight. The entropy function is

$$F = (24.6/2)\ln(1 + 0.0126I^{2.03}).$$

The deviation of sucrose data from a straight line is seen, perhaps, even more clearly in Moskowitz's earlier paper of the same year (1970a), Figure 1.

more chapter (or else cheat and jump ahead, but you may find yourself in deep water![2])

## MEASUREMENTS OF TOTAL NUMBERS OF ACTION POTENTIALS

When $F$ is interpreted as the impulse or action potential frequency in a nerve fiber, the integral $\int_0^t F \, dt$ gives the total number of impulses that will be recorded in the interval, $t$, following administration of the stimulus. Integrating Equation (10.1) with respect to $t$,

$$\int F \, dt = \int \frac{1}{2} k \ln(1 + \beta I^n/t) \, dt$$

$$= \frac{1}{2} kt \ln(1 + \beta I^n/t) + \frac{1}{2} k\beta I^n \ln(\beta I^n + t) + \text{constant}. \quad (10.14)$$

We can now evaluate the parameters of the entropy function (10.1) by curve fitting $\int_0^t F \, dt$ to data that relate total number of impulses to stimulus intensity. A recent example of this type of experiment is provided by Duchamp-Viret *et al.* (1990), who measured the response in olfactory bulb neurons to the four stimuli, DL-camphor, anisole, DL-limonene, and isoamyl acetate. The number of impulses in the interval 0–500 ms following onset of the stimulus for "all stimuli together . . . pooled as a function of concentration" were plotted against concentration, in their Figure 9A. Equation (10.14) was fitted to their data, and the result is shown in Figure 10.6. Note that no further increase in total impulses per 500 ms occurs for values of $\log_{10} I$ greater than about $-2$. This saturation effect is not embraced by Equation (10.1), which does not recognize any physiological upper limit for the variable $I$. Otherwise, the curve fit is quite good. Parameter values are $k = 59.0$, $\beta = 6.91 \times 10^4$, $n = 1.15$.

I submit here, in conclusion, a brief and quite approximate analysis of the mechanoreception data of Werner and Mountcastle (1965). I am not sure that their stimuli, which were repeated indentations of skin, qualify as simple "intensities," but the analysis offered below is easy and the results are quite striking.

A tactile probe was used to stimulate the skin of cats and monkeys. A train of 30–50 stimuli of strength, $I$, were delivered at intervals of 3–5 s. Intensity was measured in micrometers of skin indentation. The sensory receptors are mechanoreceptors, and impulses were counted in a single mechanoreceptive fiber. The total number of impulses were counted for a

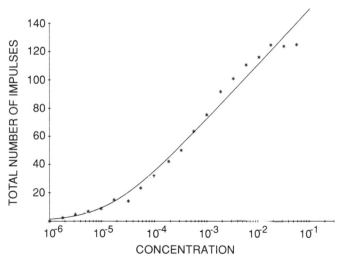

FIGURE 10.6   The integral of the entropy function with respect to time gives the total number of impulses expected over a given time interval. This integral, given by Equation (10.14), has been fitted to the observed total number of impulses counted in the interval 0–500 ms in an olfactory bulb neuron, as reported by Duchamp-Viret *et al.* (1990). The fitted curve (solid line) conforms reasonably well to the data, but will not show "saturation" for high values of concentration. Parameters values for the fitted curve are given in the text.

number of time intervals, such as 20, 50, 100, 250, 500, and 1000 ms. Werner and Mountcastle then plotted the logarithm of the total number of impulses counted against the logarithm of skin indentation in micrometers. Their result was a series of nearly parallel straight lines (their Figure 10). To analyze these data, it is simpler to use an approximate form of the entropy equation, similar to Equation (10.8). Expand (10.1), again, in a Taylor series, retaining only the first term:

$$F = \tfrac{1}{2}k\beta I^{n}/t. \tag{10.15}$$

Suppose that the stimulus begins at $t = 0$, and the first impulse is registered at $t = t_0$. Then we have

$$\int_{t_0}^{t} F \, d\tau = \int_{t_0}^{t} \tfrac{1}{2}k\beta I^{n}/\tau \, d\tau = \tfrac{1}{2}k\beta I^{n} \ln(t/t_0). \tag{10.16}$$

This integral is approximately equal to the total number of impulses in the time interval $t_0$ to $t$. Taking logs of both sides,

$$\ln \int_{t_0}^{t} F \, d\tau = n \ln I + \ln\left[\tfrac{1}{2}k\beta \ln(t/t_0)\right]. \tag{10.17}$$

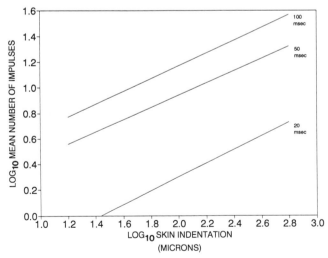

FIGURE 10.7a   Mechanoreceptor data of Werner and Mountcastle (1965, fiber 23, Figure 10) have been represented schematically. Log$_{10}$ of mean total number of impulses in a single mechanoreceptive fiber have been plotted against the log$_{10}$ of stimulus (skin indentation). The result is a series of nearly parallel straight lines. The total duration of the stimulation is indicated at the right-hand side of each line. The slope of the straight lines is, by the entropy theory, equal to the exponent, $n$, in the law of sensation.

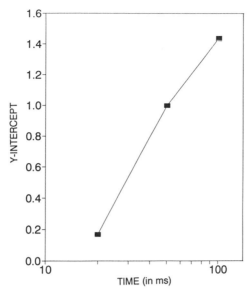

FIGURE 10.7b    The straight lines in Figure 10.6a have the general equation

$\log_{10}$ mean number of impulses $= n \log_{10}$ skin indentation $+ \log_{10} K$.    (10.17)/(10.18)

In this graph, $K$ (not $\log_{10} K$) is plotted against $\log t$, where $t$ is total duration of stimulation. From Equation (10.19), these three points are expected to lie on a straight line, which they do approximate.

We see that if $\ln \int_{t_0}^{t} F \, d\tau$ is plotted against $\ln I$ for a given, fixed value of $t$, the result expected is a straight line whose slope is equal to $n$. The intercept of this straight line is given by

$$\ln K = \ln\left[\tfrac{1}{2} k \beta \ln(t/t_0)\right] = \text{intercept.} \qquad (10.18)$$

Measured values of the quantity, $K$, have been tabulated by Werner and Mountcastle in their Table 1. For $t = t_1$, let $K = K_1$. Then, from (10.18),

$$K = \left(K_1 - \tfrac{1}{2} k \beta \ln t_1\right) + \tfrac{1}{2} k \beta \ln t. \qquad (10.19)$$

Thus, from Equation (10.18), $K = \exp$ (intercept of straight line) is a linear function of $\ln t$, a relationship which can be tested.

Since the impulse rate in Werner and Mountcastle's study equilibrated after about 150 ms (authors' Figure 4), only summation times equal to or less than 150 ms can be used in Equation (10.16). (We could, of course, modify (10.16) to allow for equilibration.) The three straight lines for fiber 24-3 (shown also in the authors' Figure 10), corresponding to $t = 20$, 50, and 100 ms are drawn, approximately, in Figure (10.7a). The $K$-values for these straight lines (obtained from the authors' Table 1) are plotted against $\ln t$ in Figure (10.7b). We see that the three points lie nearly on a straight line, as predicted by Equation (10.18). That is, the entropy equation has shown that the data of Werner and Mountcastle in a log–log plot will lie on a series of parallel straight lines (as found experimentally by these authors), whose slope is equal to the power function exponent and whose intercepts are proportional to $\ln(t/t_0)$. This analysis cannot be pushed too far. Equation (10.15) is only an approximation of (10.1), and no allowance has been made for the spontaneous firing rate of about six impulses per second.

## THE PERCEPTUAL VARIABLE

The variable, $F$, has been termed a "perceptual variable," but what are the criteria for selecting such a variable? I have used, variously, magnitude estimates, category scales, and neural impulse rates. I suppose that I am searching for any quantity that nature appears to use as a measure of entropy, $H$. That definition may not be adequate, but it is the best I can offer at this time. Neither is the list exhaustive. For example, for the sense of audition, neural impulse rate may not, in itself, be an adequate measure of $H$. Intensity of sound is mediated more strongly by the number of nerve fibers that are firing than by the frequency of impulses in a given fiber (Coren and Ward, 1989). Perhaps, in this case, number of fibers firing is an appropriate perceptual variable.[3] For a review of the "Doctrine of Correspondence" (psychophysical to neurophysiological) the reader is referred to Marks (1978, pp. 164–170). We begin to distinguish theoretically between $F$(neuronal) and $F$(psychophysical) in Chapter 13.

Within an evolutionary model, one might say that sensory systems evolve in a manner compatible with the equation $F = kH$. That is, nature, using the evolutionary process, refines *some* physiological mechanism (neural firing rate, number of fibers firing, even electric or magnetic field strengths) which encodes the stimulus entropy. When we have discovered the identity of $F$ by mathematical means for some modality, we may then designate it as a perceptual variable.

## UNIFICATION

We recall Equation (3.17), where a unifying sensory function, $F = F(I, t)$, was hypothesized. This hypothesized function is now identified with the function given by Equation (10.1). The unifying function has now achieved its first goal: by setting $t = t' = $ constant, we obtain, from

Equation (3.18),

$$F = F(1, t'),$$

which is identified with Equation (10.3), which, in turn, is the unified law of sensation.

We observe that by setting $t = $ constant and defining a new constant, $\gamma$, in Equation (10.2), we have effectively removed assumption (4) (Chapter 9), the assumption of constant sampling rate. As we continue to use restricted forms of the $H$-function, obtained by setting one or another variable equal to a constant, we selectively remove a corresponding assumption from the list of six.

## HISTORY

We have spoken briefly about Fechner's law in Chapter 3. This relationship between stimulus and response forms what Fechner termed "outer psychophysics." However, Fechner also wrote about "inner psychophysics," in which he conjectured that in the nervous system there exists internally generated oscillators and that the sensation resulting from some external stimulus had to superimpose itself, in some way, upon these internal oscillations.[4] Such considerations led Delboeuf (1873) to suggest a modification of Fechner's law of the form

$$F = k \log(1 + I/I_n), \tag{10.20}$$

where $I_n$ is produced as a result of internal neurological activity.

Delboeuf's equation is mentioned here because of its clear resemblance to the entropy equation (10.3). One cannot but observe the similarity in Delboeuf's insertion of $I_n$ to the required incorporation of $\sigma_R^2$ in the information equation. Where Delboeuf has used $\log(1 + I/I_n)$, we have used the information $\log(1 + \sigma_S^2/\sigma_R^2)$, which we might write as $\log(1 + I^n/I_R^n)$ [being careful about the interpretation of $I_R$].

We see in Chapter 12 that Bekesy (1930) utilized a similar function in his attempt to account quantitatively for the results of Knudsen on differential sensitivity, $\Delta I/I$, of audition. Bekesy attributed the derivation of the equation to Alfred Lehmann (1905).

The theoretical work of Rushton (1959) using data measured by Fuortes (1959) is also noteworthy. Working with membrane resistance in the eccentric cell in the eye of *Limulus* (crab), Rushton obtained the following equation empirically:

$$R_O - R_I = \tfrac{1}{2} \log_{10}(1 + 25I), \tag{10.21}$$

where $R_I$ is membrane resistance in response to light intensity, $I$, and $R_O$ the resistance in the dark. Rushton goes on to speculate " . . . further, $R_I$ will be a linear function of impulse frequency. . . ." This equation also is of the same general form as the entropy Equation (10.3).

## NOTES

1. Must $c$ always be equal to 1 if Resnikoff's Equation (2.21) is to agree with Equation (2.20)?
2. Such was, of course, the lesson taught by Goethe.
3. Since sound intensities in the range of human hearing vary by a factor of about $10^{10}$, recruitment of fibers is, in itself, unlikely to mediate loudness.
4. For a broad examination of Fechner's contributions, see the recent review by Murray (1993).

## REFERENCES

Atkinson, W. H. 1982. A general equation for sensory magnitude. *Perception and Psychophysics* **31**, 26–40.

Caceci, M. S., and Cacheris, W. P. 1984. Fitting curves to data: The simplex algorithm is the answer. *BYTE* **9**, May, 340–362.

Coren, S., and Ward, L. M. 1989. *Sensation and Perception*, 3rd ed. Harcourt, Brace, Jovanovich, San Diego.

Delboeuf, J. R. L. 1873. Etude psychophysique: Recherches théoriques et expérimentales sur la mesure des sensations et spécialement des sensations de lumière et de fatigue. *Mémoires couronnés et autres mémoires de l'Académie Royale de Belgique*. Hayez, Brussels.

Duchamp-Viret, P., Duchamp, A., and Vigouroux, M. 1990. Temporal aspects of information processing in the first two stages of the frog olfactory system: Influence of stimulus intensity. *Chemical Senses* **15**, 349–365.

Fuortes, M. G. F. 1959. Initiation of impulses in visual cells of *Limulus*. *Journal of Physiology* **148**, 14–28.

Krueger, L. E. 1989. Reconciling Fechner and Stevens: Toward a unified psychophysical law. *Behavioral and Brain Sciences* **12**, 251–320.

Krueger, L. E. 1991. Toward a unified psychophysical law and beyond. In *Ratio Scaling of Psychological Magnitude* (S. J. Bolanowski, Jr., and G. A. Gescheider, Eds.). Erlbaum, Hillsdale, NJ.

Lehmann, A. 1905. *Die körporlichen Äusserungen psychischer Zustände*. Part 3. *Elemente der Psychodynamik* (Translated by F. Bendixen). O. R. Reisland, Leipzig.

Luce, R. D., and Mo, S. S. 1965. Magnitude estimation of heaviness and loudness by individual subjects: A test of a probabilistic response theory. *The British Journal of Mathematical and Statistical Psychology* **18** (Part 2), 159–174.

MacKay, D. M. 1963. Psychophysics of perceived intensity: A theoretical basis for Fechner's and Stevens' laws. *Science* **139**, 1213–1216.

Marks, L. E. 1978. *The Unity of the Senses: Interrelations among the Modalities*. Academic Press, New York.

## References

Moskowitz, H. R. 1970a. Ratio scales of sugar sweetness. *Perception and Psychophysics* **7**, 315–320.

Moskowitz, H. R. 1970b. Sweetness and intensity of artificial sweetener. *Perception and Psychophysics* **8**, 40–42.

Murray, D. J. 1993. A perspective for viewing the history of psychophysics. *Behavioral and Brain Sciences*, **16**, 115–186.

Nimh, Sue Doe 1976. Polynomial law of sensation. *American Psychologist* **31**, 308–309.

Norwich, K. H. 1977. On the information received by sensory receptors. *Bulletin of Mathematical Biology* **39**, 453–461.

Norwich, K. H. 1991. Toward the unification of the laws of sensation: Some food for thought. In *Sensory Science Theory and Applications in Food* (H. Lawless and B. Klein, Eds.), pp. 151–184. Dekker, New York.

Press, W. H., Flannery, B. P., Teukolsky, S. A., and Vetterling, W. T. 1986. *Numerical Recipes: The Art of Scientific Computing*. Cambridge Univ. Press, New York.

Press, W. H., Flannery, B. P., Teukolsky, S. A., and Vetterling, W. T. 1988. *Numerical Recipes in C: The Art of Scientific Computing*. Cambridge Univ. Press, Cambridge.

Resnikoff, H. L. 1989. *The Illusion of Reality*. Springer, New York.

Rushton, W. A. H. 1959. A theoretical treatment of Fuortes's observations upon eccentric cell activity in *Limulus*. *Journal of Physiology* **148**, 29–38.

Stevens, S. S. 1969. Sensory scales of taste intensity. *Perception and Psychophysics* **6**, 302–308.

Weiss, D. J. 1981. The impossible dream of Fechner and Stevens. *Perception* **10**, 431–434.

Werner, G., and Mountcastle, V. B. 1965. Neural activity in mechanoreceptive cutaneous afferents: Stimulus-response relations, Weber fractions, and information transmission. *Journal of Neurophysiology* **28**, 359–397.

# 11

## Sensory Adaptation

THE ENTROPIC INTERPRETATION OF ADAPTATION[1]

We continue, now, in our task of evaluating the fundamental entropy equation (9.20)/(10.1),

$$F = F(I, t) = kH = \tfrac{1}{2}k \ln(1 + \beta I^n / t). \qquad (11.1)$$

We recall from Chapter 3 (The Weber Fraction: The Analogs) the general process that is employed in evaluating the function $F(I, t)$. In order to derive the law of sensation from $F(I, t)$, we set $t = t' =$ constant and obtained Equation (10.3), the general equation embracing both logarithmic and power laws of sensation. Now, in order to explore the principle of adaptation using the same mathematical function, $F(I, t)$, we set $I = I' =$ constant. That is, we explore the behavior of the perceptual variable, $F$, and the entropy function, $H$, when a single, steady stimulus is applied to a sensory receptor for a period of time, $t$. When we deal with stimuli applied for "long" periods of time (for example, $t > 1$ s), as we do in this chapter, $t$ may well refer to either the duration of the stimulus or to the time since onset of the stimulus, since generally these times will be equal. However, in Chapter 13, when we deal with very brief stimuli, $t$ refers unequivocally to the time since stimulus onset. For such brief stimuli, the ratio of time since onset to stimulus duration may exceed unity substantially. For the longer stimuli treated in this chapter the ratio is, effectively, unity.

Since stimulus intensity, $I'$, is constant, we write[2]

$$\lambda = \beta(I')^n = \text{constant}, \qquad (11.2)$$

analogous to (10.2).

Hence the equation

$$F = kH = \tfrac{1}{2}k \ln(1 + \lambda/t), \tag{11.3}$$

analogous to (10.3), describes the change in $F$ with $t$ for a constant stimulus. It is evident from Equation (11.3) that when $t$ is small, $F$ is large, and as $t$ becomes larger, $F$ declines. This behavior describes the process of sensory adaptation (see Chapter 3, Adaptation). It is well known that when $F$ describes subjective magnitude, such as the sensation of taste, this magnitude will sometimes increase briefly after administration of the stimulus, and then decline. We deal with this early rise in sensation in a preliminary way in Chapter 14. Until then, we concern ourselves solely with the declining phase of the adaptation process.

There are both mathematical and physiological limitations governing the range of values taken by the time variable, $t$. We recall from Equation (9.3) that

$$t = m/\alpha,$$

where $\alpha$ is a constant, greater than zero, and $m$ is an integer, greater than zero, representing the number of samples taken by a receptor of its stimulus population. It would seem that when $m = 1$, $t$ takes on its smallest value[3] of $1/\alpha$. At the other extreme, there is almost certainly a maximum value for $m$ that characterizes each type of receptor. Maximum $m$ would represent the greatest number of sampling values (intensity values) that a receptor could retain in its local "memory." Although we do not know from anatomical or physiological considerations exactly how great this number is, we do know that it must exist. For example, it is not likely that your pressure receptors are currently storing the values of pressures applied 15 min ago. That is, the receptor's memory is less than 15 min. Some minimum and maximum for $m$ must exist, but we cannot, at the moment, provide values for these extremes.

If the maximum value for $m$ (and hence, $t$) is great enough, then, from Equation (11.3), $F$ will tend toward $\ln(1) = 0$—the case of complete adaptation, or adaptation to extinction. If, however, the maximum value for $m$ (and hence for $t$) is somewhat smaller, $F$ will fall to some level greater than zero, and will not decrease further, corresponding to the case of incomplete adaptation. *The entropy equation* (11.3) *is valid only to the time when F first reaches its minimum value.* Beyond this equilibration point, we cannot use the entropy equation in its present form.

The theoretical graph of $F$ vs. $t$ is governed, then, by the ln-function (11.3). For small $t$, the function falls steeply, and for large $t$, it falls gently toward zero. The characteristics of the curve differ markedly from those of the exponential function, which is often used, empirically, to describe such adaptation phenomena. The exponential function does not rise as sharply for small $t$, and descends more steeply for larger $t$.

"Adaptation" is often discussed together with "fatigue," some writers making a distinction between the terms. Adaptation, as seen from the entropy perspective, has nothing whatever to do with fatigue.

Since $F = kH$, $F$ is a "mirror" of $H$. As $H$ does, so $F$ does. The entropic view of adaptation may be inferred from the preliminary discussion given in Chapter 8 (the Central Limit Theorem) and Chapter 9 (Maximum $H$ as Potential Information). Referring to Equation (11.3)—when $t$ is small ($m$ small), receptor uncertainty is great and the *potential* to receive information is high; when $t$ is large ($m$ large), receptor uncertainty is reduced, and thus the potential to receive information is low or absent. *Adaptation, therefore, refers to the progressive acquisition of information (eradication of uncertainty).* When the maximum value of $t$ for a given receptor is insufficient to reduce the $H$-function to zero, adaptation will be incomplete. A receptor which has adapted to its fullest extent cannot receive further information. When a receptor has adapted completely, it retains no further uncertainty about its stimulus magnitude, leading to a rather dramatic conclusion: *A receptor cannot perceive*

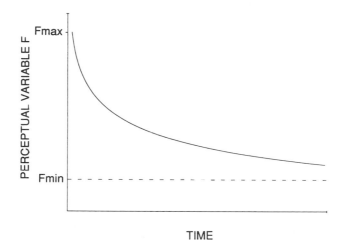

TIME

FIGURE 11.1 Schematic diagram of an adaptation curve. The variable, $F$, represents either impulse frequency in a sensory neuron or subjective magnitude of a stimulus. $F_{max}$ is the maximum value obtainable by $F$. Sometimes one finds an early portion of the curve where $F$ rises with time (not shown here). This early rising phase can be detected neurophysiologically and, occasionally, psychophysically, particularly with the chemical senses. $F_{min}$, the minimum value obtainable by $F$, is often not obtained during the course of the experiment, but rather, must be estimated by means of an asymptote to the curve, as shown in the diagram. When $F_{min}$ is equal to zero, adaptation is said to go to completion.

*a certainty.* If the outcome to an event is completely certain, the receptor cannot perceive it.

The reader will observe that here, as elsewhere, I seem to have anthropomorphized the receptor, relegating to it the capacity to be certain or uncertain, as if it possessed a mind. This view is, however, incomplete. A receptor, as an isolated unit, cannot reasonably be expected to possess the potential for certainty or uncertainty. I return later to this matter, but even then, I am afraid, my views may be considered audacious.

The fall of $F$ with $t$ is illustrated schematically by the curves in Figure 3.2 and Figure 11.1. Again, $F$, the perceptual variable, will be interpreted either as subjective magnitude (magnitude estimates) or as impulse rate in a sensory neuron. However, we see in Chapter 13 that this dual interpretation of $F$ is, at best, an approximation. That is, $F$ (subjective magnitude) is not precisely synchronous with $F$ (impulse rate). In fact the two types of curve are not even necessarily of exactly the same shape, as discussed in note 1 of Chapter 13.

## INFORMATION, RECEPTORS, AND CATEGORICAL JUDGMENTS

From Equation (11.3),

$$\boxed{H = \tfrac{1}{2}\ln(1 + \lambda/t).} \qquad (11.4)$$

We have established, now, the existence of a minimum and maximum value of $t$, which can be designated $t_0$ and $t_{max}$, respectively.[4] Since $H(t)$ is a monotone decreasing function of $t$,

$$H_{max} = \tfrac{1}{2}\ln(1 + \lambda/t_0) \qquad (11.5)$$

and

$$H_{min} = \tfrac{1}{2}\ln(1 + \lambda/t_{max}). \qquad (11.6)$$

Let

$$\Delta H = H_{max} - H_{min}. \qquad (11.7)$$

Then $\Delta H$ is the difference between the receptor uncertainty at the beginning and end of the process of adaptation. It is the reduction in potential information. *That is, $\Delta H$ equals the quantity of information received by the receptor during the process of adaptation.* Since $F = kH$,

$$\Delta H = \Delta F/k. \qquad (11.8)$$

That is, the *excursion* of the adaptation curve divided by the scaling constant, $k$, is equal to the total information received by the receptor during the adaptation process. Moreover, both quantities $k$ and $\Delta F$, on the right-hand side of (11.8) can be measured. Since experimental adaptation data can be fitted to Equation (11.3), we can obtain a value for the constant, $k$; since

$$\Delta F = F_{max} - F_{min}, \qquad (11.9)$$

we can measure $\Delta F$ by taking the difference between the highest and lowest values on the adaptation curve. We can, thereby, measure $\Delta H$ using Equation (11.8) to obtain a value in natural units of information per stimulus. Examples of this technique will follow.

We might just note at this point that there is an approximation to Equation (11.7), which not only permits one to estimate the value of $\Delta H$ from visual inspection of an adaptation curve, but seems to provide some insight into $\Delta H$ as well (cf. Chapter 8, The Central Limit Theorem). Let us assume (rightly or wrongly) that we can use the "Fechner approximation," $\lambda/t_{max} \gg 1$. Admittedly, use of this approximation will sometimes lead us astray. Since $t_0 < t_{max}$, it will also be true that $\lambda/t_0 \gg 1$. Introducing these approximations into Equations (11.5) and (11.6),

$$H_{max} \simeq \tfrac{1}{2}\ln(\lambda/t_0)$$

and

$$H_{min} \simeq \tfrac{1}{2}\ln(\lambda/t_{max}),$$

so that, from Equation (11.7),

$$\Delta H \simeq \tfrac{1}{2}\ln(\lambda/t_0) - \tfrac{1}{2}\ln(\lambda/t_{max}),$$

$$\Delta H = \tfrac{1}{2}\ln(t_{max}/t_0),$$

or

$$\boxed{\Delta H = \ln\sqrt{t_{max}/t_0} .} \qquad (11.10)$$

This equation was demonstrated by the author (Norwich 1981, 1984). It is useful because the right-hand side can be approximately evaluated by simple visual inspection of an adaptation curve. For example, from a curve such as that illustrated in Fig. (11.1) one can estimate (sometimes) the value of $t_0$ at which the curve is maximum and of $t_{max}$ at which the curve is minimum. Sometimes the curve seems to continue falling slowly throughout its duration, so I usually suggest taking $t_{max}$ as the time when the curve has fallen through, say, 90% of its total excursion. The final result of the calculation is not all that sensitive to small changes in $t_{max}$, but is exquisitely sensitive to changes in the estimate of $t_0$. Anyway, a glance at the adaptation curve provides an estimate of the ratio of

$t_{max}/t_0$, and the log of the square root of this ratio equals the information transmitted (or an approximation thereto).

If, moreover, we introduce Equation (9.3) into (11.10), then

$$\Delta H = \tfrac{1}{2} \ln( m_{max}/m_0),$$

where $m$ is the number of samplings made by the receptor. But since $m_0$ is the minimum number of samplings = 1 (say), therefore

$$\Delta H \simeq \tfrac{1}{2} \ln m_{max}. \tag{11.11}$$

That is, information received by the receptor is approximately equal to one-half the logarithm of the greatest number of samplings that can be contained in the memory of the receptor.

The reader will recall from Chapters 4 and 5 that one can also calculate an information per stimulus by means of an experiment on categorical judgments. Quite a lot of labor was expended to derive the quantity $\mathscr{I}(X|Y)$ from the confusion matrix. It was shown that for all modalities of sensation, a maximum of about 2.5 bits of information was transmitted per stimulus, the so-called channel capacity. This 2.5 bits or 1.75 natural units of information corresponded to $2^{2.5} = e^{1.75} \simeq 6$ categories. That is, a human being is capable of distinguishing, without error, "the equivalent of" about six categories of light or sound intensity, concentration of solutions, etc. We now explore the question of the relationship between this quantity of information, $\mathscr{I}(X|Y)$, obtained from measurements of categorical judgments, and the information $\Delta H$, obtained using Equation (11.7) from measurements made on adaptation curves.

The factors limiting the maximum value of $\mathscr{I}(X|Y)$ are usually assumed to reside in the brain. Perhaps the main reason for this assumption is that the number of jnd's distinguishable (range of 20–350) is much greater than the number of absolute categorical judgments (about 6). Since the senses can distinguish many more than 6 jnd's, the limitation in making an absolute judgment about an unknown stimulus must, surely, lie in the brain. And so it may be. But I would like to suggest an alternative. I suggest that the limitation on the quantity of information available for an absolute judgment may be, in the final analysis, due to the limitation in the amount of information provided by the sensory receptors. That is, if the sensory receptors can receive a maximum of $\Delta H$ bits of information per stimulus, then no more than $\Delta H$ bits can be used to make an absolute judgment. Implicit in this suggestion is that, to a degree of approximation, the sensory receptors operate in parallel; for example, the amount of information received by the brain from $n$ olfactory receptors is the same as that received from only one receptor. That is, redundancy (numerosity) in receptors may be necessary to ensure receipt of a stimulus, but once received, the information from the large number is the same as the information from only one receptor. Some psychologists have expressed dissatisfaction with this hypothesis. Ward (1991) has put forward an alternative hypothesis: $N$ receptors acting in parallel and sampling at rate $\alpha$ samples/s may produce the effect of a single adaptation process with sampling at the rate $N\alpha$. Such may be the case, but further work must be done on it.

I submit, anyway, by way of conjecture, that

$$\Delta H = \mathscr{I}(X|Y). \qquad (11.12)$$

The truth of Equation (11.12) is not vital to the integrity of the entropy theory of perception, but we shall see presently that (11.12) does seem to verify when tested on experimental data—which we now proceed to do.


## EXPERIMENTAL TESTS OF THE ENTROPIC THEORY OF ADAPTATION

Let us now test the entropic theory, to the level that we have developed it hitherto, using published data. Gent and McBurney (1978) measured the change in magnitude estimate, $F$, with time, for the sense of taste. Let us select from their paper a medium (0.32 $M$) solution of sodium chloride. I digitized, as carefully as possible, the data from Gent and McBurney's Figure 1. When Equation (11.3) was fitted to the data using a least-squares technique, the following parameter values were obtained:

$$k = 7.634,$$

$$\lambda = 46.04 \text{ s.}$$

The fitted equation was, therefore,

$$F = (7.634/2)\ln(1 + 46.04/t). \qquad (11.13)$$

The results are graphed in Figure 11.2. The fitted curve, while perhaps tolerable, seems to fall a little too slowly at larger times, a feature characteristic of all data in this paper.[5] Gent and McBurney fitted the curves to monoexponential functions.

Using the above parameter values, we can measure the information transmitted per sodium chloride stimulus. From Equation (11.9),

$$\Delta F = F_{\max} - F_{\min} = 8.57 - 1.00 = 7.57, \qquad (11.14)$$

if we consider the adaptation process to be complete at 90 s. The excursion, $\Delta F$, would equal $8.57 - 0 = 8.57$, if we suspect that the adaptation process would proceed to extinction. Therefore, from Equation (11.8), using the smaller of the two values for $\Delta F$, the information

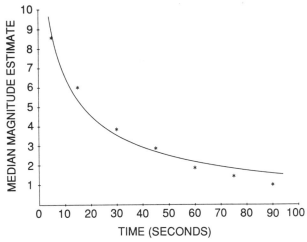

FIGURE 11.2   Data of Gent and McBurney (1978) illustrating psychophysical adaptation. Mean magnitude estimate of 0.32 $M$ solution of sodium chloride plotted against time. The smooth curve is given by the entropy equation (11.13).

transmitted by this solution of medium intensity

$$\Delta H = \Delta F/k = 7.57/7.634 = 0.992 \text{ natural units.}$$

Dividing by $\ln 2$,

$$\Delta H = \Delta F/(k \ln 2) = 1.431 \text{ bits,} \qquad (11.15)$$

a value slightly less than the channel capacity for taste (1.7–2.0 bits). Or, using the larger of the two values for $\Delta F$,

$$\Delta H = 8.57/(7.634 \ln 2) = 1.620 \text{ bits.} \qquad (11.16)$$

Moving now to an example in which $F$ is measured as impulse frequency in a sensory neuron, we examine the data of B. H. C. Matthews (1931). Matthews investigated the response of stretch receptors in the muscles of a frog. He provided stretch or tension stimuli to a small muscle in the upper, outer side of the middle toe of the frog and recorded from the lateral branch of the peroneal nerve. A 2-gram load was applied to the muscle tendon, which was immersed in Ringer's solution, and the resulting impulse frequency plotted against time is shown in the Matthews' Figure 3. The entropy equation for adaptation (11.3) was fitted to the data digitized from this graph.[6] The parameter values obtained were as follows (Table 11.1):

$$k = 54.51,$$
$$\lambda = 16.71 \text{ s.}$$

The fitted equation was, therefore,

$$F = \left(\tfrac{1}{2}\right)(54.51)\ln(1 + 16.71/t). \tag{11.17}$$

From Equation (11.9)

$$\Delta F = F_{max} - F_{min} = 119 - 23 = 96 \text{ impulses/s.} \tag{11.18}$$

From Equation (11.8),

$$\Delta H = \Delta F/(k \ln 2) = 96/(54.51 \ln 2) = 2.541 \text{ bits.} \tag{11.19}$$

Again we find that the value for information transmitted per stimulus is close to the "global" value of about 2.5 bits. Since $2^{2.541} = 5.82$, we see that we remain close to the "magical number 6" categories. Matthews' data and its fitted curve are shown in Figure 11.3. Using the very approximate Equation (11.10) with data from Table 11.1, we have

$$\Delta H \simeq \tfrac{1}{2} \ln(14.05/.228)/\ln 2 = 2.97 \text{ bits.} \tag{11.19a}$$

Continuing with examples where $F$ is measured neurophysiologically, we consider adaptation in the guinea pig auditory nerve, as reported by Yates $et\ al.$ (1985) (see Chapter 3, Adaptation). The responses in auditory nerve ganglion cells to 100-ms tone bursts were measured by these investigators. Adaptation was incomplete; that is, firing rate did not

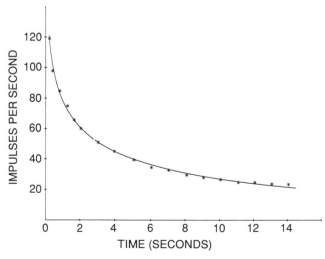

FIGURE 11.3   Data of Matthews (1931), Figure 3, illustrating neural adaptation. Two-gram load applied to a muscle tendon of the frog. The smooth curve is given by the entropy equation (11.17).

TABLE 11.1    Data of Matthews (1931), Figure 3:
Two-Gram Weight Applied to Muscle of Frog

| Time [s] | Impulse frequency [s$^{-1}$] fitted | Impulse frequency [s$^{-1}$] measured |
|---|---|---|
| 0.228 | 117.47 | 118.98 |
| 0.411 | 101.68 | 97.79 |
| 0.826 | 83.28 | 84.63 |
| 1.277 | 72.11 | 74.80 |
| 1.658 | 65.56 | 65.72 |
| 2.059 | 60.24 | 59.86 |
| 3.073 | 50.76 | 50.73 |
| 4.009 | 44.78 | 44.82 |
| 5.068 | 39.74 | 39.36 |
| 6.048 | 36.13 | 34.40 |
| 7.052 | 33.11 | 32.51 |
| 8.091 | 30.53 | 29.44 |
| 9.056 | 28.50 | 27.80 |
| 10.03 | 26.74 | 26.56 |
| 11.08 | 25.07 | 24.62 |
| 12.05 | 23.71 | 24.62 |
| 13.06 | 22.45 | 23.63 |
| 14.05 | 21.36 | 23.33 |

*Note.* Data were fitted to the entropic adaptation equation
(11.3) using a simplex procedure with the least-squares criterion (see Figure 11.3). The number of digits used for a given
entry does not reflect the number of significant figures in the
measurement, a quantity that is not really known to the
author. Function fitted is $F = 0.5*(\text{Parameter } 1)*\ln(1 + (\text{Parameter } 2)/t)$. Value of Parameter 1 = 54.51. Value of
Parameter 2 = 16.71. Sum of squares of residuals = 38.22.

descend to zero. Judging from results of experiment GP53/08:4, the
decline in firing rate was complete by 25 to 30 ms following onset of the
stimulus. To use the graphs in this paper, probability density was interpreted as firing rate, as suggested by the authors. These data (Yates
*et al.*, Figure 5) were digitized and fitted to the entropy equation (11.3).
The values of the parameters were as follows:

$$k = 157.7,$$

$$\lambda = 37.64 \text{ ms.}$$

Thus, the fitted equation was

$$F = \left(\tfrac{1}{2}\right)(157.7)\ln(1 + 37.64/t). \tag{11.20}$$

From Equation (11.9)

$$\Delta F = F_{max} - F_{min} = 284 - 67 = 217. \tag{11.21}$$

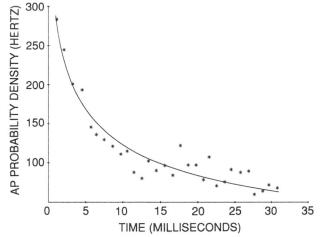

FIGURE 11.4   Data of Yates *et al.* (1985). Neural adaptation in the auditory ganglion cell of a guinea pig to a 100-ms tone burst. $F$ is measured as action potential probability density (Hz), similar to impulse frequency. The smooth curve is given by the entropy function (11.20). To estimate the information transmitted by this adaptation process using Equation (11.10), we observe that $t_{max} \simeq 25$ ms and $t_0 \simeq 1$ ms. Thus, $\Delta H \simeq \ln\sqrt{25}/\ln 2 =$ 2.3 bits of information/stimulus.

From Equation (11.8)

$$\Delta H = \Delta F/(k \ln 2) = 217/(157.7 \ln 2) = 1.99 \text{ bits.} \quad (11.22)$$

The data and fitted curve are shown in Figure 11.4.

In passing, may I draw your attention to the older neurophysiological data on audition by Galambos and Davis (1943), also introduced in Chapter 3. Pure tones were delivered to the ears of cats, and the frequency of impulses was measured in what were believed originally to be single auditory fibers (1943 paper). However, in a note of correction (1948), the authors amended the interpretation of their measurements and attributed them to single unit activity of second-order neurons, rather than first-order neurons, as originally expected. The data of Galambos and Davis were digitized from their graph (Figure 3) and published in Table 2 of Norwich (1981). The entropic equation (11.3) was fitted as closely as possible to their data. The following parameter values were obtained:

$$k = 120.31,$$
$$\lambda = 4.00 \text{ s.}$$

Hence

$$\Delta F = 400 - 80 = 320 \text{ Hz} \quad (11.23)$$

$$\Delta H = 320/(120.31 \ln 2) = 3.84 \text{ bits.} \quad (11.24)$$

Analogous to auditory nerve fiber response to acoustic stimuli, we examine now optic nerve response to visual stimuli. Cleland and Enroth-Cugell (1968) applied square-wave inputs of light to the retina of cats and recorded the impulse frequency of on-center ganglion cells in the cat retina from optic tract fibers. A number of their tracings for different light intensities were provided in the authors' Figure 2, showing the effects of adaptation. Their tracing No. 2 has been digitized, as well as we were able, and the entropy equation for adaptation (11.3) was fitted to the data (Figure 11.5). The exact position of $t = 0$ for these data was hard to determine. I took the liberty here of shifting the origin back and forth by a few milliseconds in order to produce the best curve fit. The values for the parameters were as follows:

$$k = 302.5,$$
$$\lambda = 0.1175 \text{ s.}$$
$$\Delta F \geq 271.0 - 37.6 = 233.4 \tag{11.25}$$
$$\Delta H \geq 233.4/(302.5 \ln 2) = 1.11 \text{ bits.} \tag{11.26}$$

I use " $>$ " because the adaptation process is continuing at 0.42 s, where the graph in Figure 11.5 terminates. Interpretation of these results is not

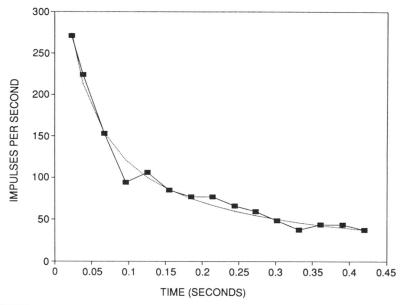

FIGURE 11.5   Data of Cleland and Enroth-Cugell (1968). Neural adaptation in the on-center ganglion cells of the cat to square-wave inputs of light to the retina. The smooth curve is given by the entropy equation (11.3) with $k = 302.5$ and $\lambda = 0.1175$ s.

straightforward. We are decidedly *not* dealing here with independent sensory receptors (see, for example, Dowling, 1987, pp. 35–36). Moreover, the input was not a single step function but a square wave, so that receptors were not totally unadapted at $t = 0$, the time of stimulus onset.

## EXPERIMENTAL TESTS OF THE ENTROPIC THEORY: COMBINED STIMULUS INTENSITY AND ADAPTATION

In Chapter 10, we subjected the entropy equation with $t =$ constant (Equation (10.3)) to various experimental tests, and we confirmed the fact that the WF and PBS laws merge and are contained within the entropy equation. In the preceding section of the present chapter we subjected the entropy equation with $I =$ constant (Equation (11.3)) to a number of experimental tests. We confirmed the adequacy of the equation to fit adaptation data, although in some instances, particularly with magnitude estimates, one would be happier with a closer fit.[5] We also observed that the values of information transmitted per stimulus calculated from adaptation data were compatible with corresponding values calculated from experiments on categorical judgments. Henceforth, it will be assumed that the "channel capacity," whether determined by entropic or category analysis, will be about 2.5 bits of information per stimulus.

Let us proceed, now, and subject the *general* equation of entropy (9.20)/(10.1)/(11.1) to experimental test. That is, we let *both I and t* vary[7] and study the *surface*,

$$F = F(I, t). \tag{11.27}$$

That is, we may regard $I$ and $t$ as two independent variables and $F$ as a dependent variable. The graph of $F$ as a function of $I$ and $t$ will describe a surface. However, for simplicity in presenting the data, we shall take "slices" through the surface for $I = I_1, I_2, I_3$, and present a series of two-dimensional graphs of $F$ vs. $t$.

Let us consider first the older work of Matthews (1931) on stretch receptors, whose experiments were described above. Instead of dealing with only one experiment in which a 2-g force was applied, we now consider, together, three experiments in which forces of 1, 2, and 5 g were applied to the tendon. Each force gave rise to its own, unique adaptation curve. The three sets of data were fitted simultaneously to the general entropy equation (11.1), each set being assigned equal weighting. The total sum of squares was minimized to give values for the three parameters. Data analyzed were taken from Matthews' Figure 15B (in Ringer's solution), which I am assuming, were all obtained from the same preparation (or, at least, are governed by the same set of parameters). The

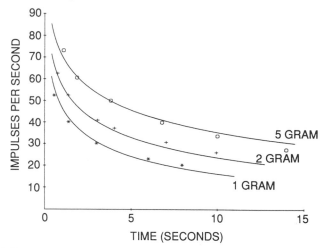

FIGURE 11.6   Data of Matthews (1931), Figure 15B. Frog stretch receptor. All three curves were fitted simultaneously to the same set of three parameters (given in the text). That is, only three adjustable parameters were used, in all, to curve-fit all three curves, or a ratio of one parameter per curve. The fitted entropy function is given by Equation (11.28).

parameter values are:

$k = 32.24,$

$\beta = 17.19$    (cf. $\beta = 54.51$ for the preparation analyzed in Figure 11.3),

$n = 0.9496.$

The results of the three simultaneous curve fits are shown in Figure 11.6. Remember that a *total* of three parameters were used to curve-fit the three sets of data, or a ratio of one parameter per curve. Equation (11.1) is represented explicitly by

$$F = \left(\tfrac{1}{2}\right)(32.24)\ln(1 + 17.19 I^{0.9496}).  \tag{11.28}$$

Calculating the channel capacity using the 5-gram data set,

$$\Delta F = 72.9 - 27.2 = 45.7 \text{ impulses/s}.  \tag{11.29}$$

$$\Delta H = 45.7/(32.34 \ln 2) = 2.04 \text{ bits/stimulus}.  \tag{11.30}$$

The three data sets and the corresponding parameter values are given in Table 11.2.

As a second example of a surface fit to Equation (11.1), and the first example of insect sensation, we consider the sugar receptor of the blowfly. Dethier and Bowdan (1984) stimulated this receptor with sucrose solutions of three different concentrations: 1.0, 0.1, and 0.01 $M$. They measured the frequency of impulses in bipolar neurons in tarsal hairs. In

TABLE 11.2   Data of Matthews (1931), Figure 15B: Three Experiments in Which a 1-, 2-, and 5-g Weight Were Applied, Respectively, to the Muscle of a Frog.

| $t$ [s] | Frequency fitted | Frequency measured | Data set |
|---|---|---|---|
| | | | 1 gram |
| 0.548 | 56.06 | 52.47 | |
| 1.373 | 41.98 | 40.06 | |
| 2.975 | 30.85 | 30.12 | |
| 5.992 | 21.81 | 22.95 | |
| 7.955 | 18.55 | 20.18 | |
| | | | 2 gram |
| 0.746 | 61.55 | 62.48 | |
| 1.354 | 52.22 | 52.43 | |
| 3.036 | 39.97 | 40.82 | |
| 4.021 | 35.87 | 37.10 | |
| 7.030 | 28.12 | 30.61 | |
| 9.944 | 23.66 | 26.02 | |
| | | | 5 gram |
| 1.077 | 69.51 | 72.91 | |
| 1.845 | 60.98 | 60.32 | |
| 3.808 | 49.69 | 49.73 | |
| 6.787 | 40.94 | 39.64 | |
| 10.01 | 35.27 | 33.46 | |
| 13.97 | 30.60 | 27.20 | |

*Note*. The three data sets were curve-fitted *simultaneously* to Equation (9.20)/(10.1)/(11.1) *using the same three parameters for all three curves* (Figure 11.7). The equation is

$$F = \tfrac{1}{2}k \ln(1 + \beta I^n/t).$$

Intensity, $I$, was set equal to 1, 2, and 5, respectively in each of the three curve-fits. The above equation was then fitted to the $F$ vs. $t$ data. Function fitted is $F = 0.5*(\text{Parameter } 1)*\ln(1 + (\text{Parameter } 2)*I\hat{\ }(\text{Parameter } 3)/t)$. Value of Parameter 1 = 32.24. Value of Parameter 2 = 17.19. Value of Parameter 3 = 0.9496. Sum of squares of residuals = 64.50.

this way, three sets of data were obtained showing the adaptation of the sugar receptor. The three sets of data were fitted simultaneously to the general entropy equation (11.1), with weightings in the ratio of 1:3:5 (1.0, 0.1, 0.01 $M$). With parameters evaluated, Equation (11.1) became

$$F = \left(\tfrac{1}{2}\right)(121) \ln(1 + 1.15I^{0.585}/t). \qquad (11.31)$$

The data and fitted surface (curves) are shown in Figure 11.7. Again we note that *all three curves* have been fitted with the *same* three parameter values, or the average ratio of one parameter per curve. Maximum information per stimulus was calculated to be 2.9 bits per stimulus. More details about these curves are given by Norwich and Valter McConville

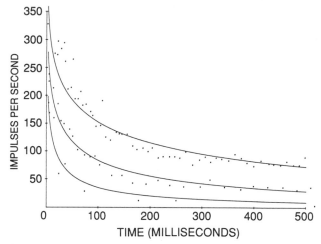

**FIGURE 11.7**   Data of Dethier and Bowdan (1984) for the sugar receptor of the blowfly. For the upper curve, the concentration of the sugar solution was 1.0 $M$ (i.e., $I = 1.0$); for the middle curve, 0.1 $M$ ($I = 0.1$); and for the lowest curve, 0.01 $M$ ($I = 0.01$). Again, all three curves were fitted simultaneously to the same set of three parameters; that is, only three adjustable parameters were used, in all, to fit all three curves, or a ratio of one parameter per curve. The fitted entropy function is given by Equation (11.31).

(1991). In this same paper the reader may find more extensive mathematical tests of the adaptation principle and a simultaneous curve fit to adaptation data from the slit sense organ on the walking leg of the Hunting spider.

We can now understand the near-parallel straight lines of Schmidt (1988, p. 88), introduced in Chapter 3. The logarithm of the neural response of a pressure receptor plotted against the logarithm of the stimulus pressure (for $t$ constant) gives a straight line (power law of sensation). As the state of adaptation increases ($t$ increases), the straight line shifts downward on the graph. The result is a series of nearly parallel straight lines (Figure 3.3). We proceed by expanding the right-hand side of Equation (11.1) in a Taylor series (where $t$ is large enough to make the expansion legitimate), as in Equation (10.7). Retaining only the first-order term,

$$F = \tfrac{1}{2}k\beta I^n/t. \tag{11.32}$$

The receptor can be represented in different states of adaptation by setting $t = t_i = $ constant. Taking logs of both sides of (11.32),

$$\log F = n \log I + \log(\tfrac{1}{2}k\beta) - \log t_i. \tag{11.33}$$

That is, plotting $\log F$ vs. $\log I$ gives a straight line whose slope is $n$ and whose intercept, $\log(\tfrac{1}{2}k\beta) - \log t_i$, slides down as $t_i$ increases, exactly as shown in Figure 3.3. As an exercise, the reader might like to check the theoretical values of the spacing between the straight lines in Figure 3.3. Take $I$ as constant in Equation (11.33), and calculate the expected displacement of each line from the uppermost line using the $t$-values on the right-hand side of the graph. Compare with the observed displacement.

I think that the point is amply illustrated: Equation (9.20)/(10.1)/ (11.1) is capable of allowing for both adaptation and stimulus magnitude changes using the same set of parameter values, when $F$ is measured neurophysiologically. The information transmitted is usually close to the nominal value of 2.5 bits per stimulus.

## MAGICAL NUMBERS FROM THE LAW OF SENSATION

You will recall from our studies in Chapter 10 that it was not always possible to obtain three robust parameters from Equation (10.3) using measurements of $F$ vs. $I$ ($t$ constant) but that we did manage to do so in a number of cases. I suggested that there was magic in the values obtained for the parameter, $k$, and we are now in a position to be appropriately enchanted.

For the sodium chloride data of S. S. Stevens (Figure 10.2), we obtained the value $k = 41.31$. The values of $F_{max}$ and $F_{min}$ can be read directly from the graph: $F_{max} = e^{3.91} = 50.$ and $F_{min} = e^{-0.288} = 0.75$. Hence we calculate $\Delta F$ from this experiment in the same manner as that for an adaptation curve. As in Equation (11.9),

$$\Delta F = 50. - 0.75 = 49.25. \tag{11.34}$$

Using Equation (11.8)

$$\Delta H = 49.25/(41.31 \ln 2) = 1.72 \text{ bits}. \tag{11.35}$$

We observe that this value is quite close to the value of 1.62 bits of information per stimulus obtained by analysis of the taste adaptation data of Gent and McBurney for sodium chloride. It is also close to the value of 1.70 bits per stimulus for $\mathscr{F}(X|Y)$ (sodium chloride) obtained from an experiment on categorical judgments (Beebe-Center $et$ $al.$ 1955).

For the auditory data of Luce and Mo (Figure 10.3), $k = 113.1$.

$$F_{max} = e^{4.96} = 142.6, \qquad F_{min} = e^{3.18} = 24.0.$$

$$\Delta F = 118.6. \tag{11.36}$$

$$\Delta H = 118.6/(113.1 \ln 2) = 1.51 \text{ bits}. \tag{11.37}$$

As much as one would like to supply limits of variability for such calculations, I know of no way to calculate these limits.

From Equation (11.22), the information transmitted in the guinea pig ganglion cell was 1.99 bits. Category experiments on human audition will give values between 1.62 and 2.51 bits per stimulus (Garner, 1953).

For the weight-lifting data of Luce and Mo (Figure 10.4), $k = 1040$.

$$F_{max} = e^{7.25} = 1408, \qquad F_{min} = e^{3.22} = 25.0$$

$$\Delta F = 1408. - 25. = 1383. \tag{11.38}$$

$$\Delta H = 1383/(1040 \ln 2) = 1.92 \text{ bits.} \tag{11.39}$$

I have no corresponding values for $\mathcal{I}(X|Y)$ for comparison but, again, the value is close to the expected global value for channel capacity.

Finally, from Chapter 10, the sweetness-of-sucrose data of Moskowitz gave

$$k = 24.6, \qquad F_{max} = 45., \qquad F_{min} = 0.80.$$

$$\Delta F = 44.2, \tag{11.40}$$

$$\Delta H = 44.2/(24.6 \ln 2) = 2.59 \text{ bits,} \tag{11.41}$$

a little high for taste but, again, these data were quite approximate.

Again, the reader is reminded that data measured to study the law of sensation usually do not permit estimation of three robust parameters, and, therefore, do not usually permit calculation of channel capacities.

## NUMERO, NUMERO, WHEREFORE ART THOU NUMERO?[8]

What function, you might wonder, do numbers have in science? What is the difference, I put to you, between a physicist and an engineer? Well, you may be inclined to answer, the physicist deals with pure science and the engineer with applied science.

While that is true, I believe that there is another more salient distinction referable to their respective uses of mathematics. The engineer uses mathematics to obtain (often) a numerical result: the weight tolerance of a bridge, the characteristics of a circuit. The physicist uses mathematics to obtain (often) a "verbal" or nonnumerical result: energy and mass are, in principle, the same; the universe began from an explosion at a single point; etc. As I stated before, I am writing this material with the world view of the physicist. Therefore, to me, the pages of numbers given above are not end-values in themselves. They are useful only in helping to confirm a position which can be stated in words, namely that a single principle of entropy, F is a measure of H ($F = kH$), seems to account for all stimulus-magnitude and all adaptation experiments in which a single, constant stimulus is used. As we move forward in this book, we see that the scope of this principle is even broader.

# AUDITION: THE TECHNIQUE OF SIMULTANEOUS DICHOTIC LOUDNESS BALANCE (SDLB)

This technique was described in Chapter 3, Adaptation. A tone of constant intensity, $I_a$, is presented to the adapting ear, beginning at $t = 0$. An intermittent tone of variable intensity, $I$, is presented to the opposite or test ear for total duration, $t'$. The subject must adjust the intensity of the intermittent, test tone until its loudness matches that of the steady, adapting tone.

The application of the entropy principle to the SDLB technique is very simple (if not perfectly accurate). Let us assume that both ears of a given subject have identical values for the parameters $k$, $\beta$, and $n$. If the loudness of the test tone is equal to that of the adapting tone then

$$\tfrac{1}{2}k \ln(1 + \beta I^n/t') = \tfrac{1}{2} k \ln(1 + \beta I_a^n/t). \qquad (11.42)$$

Hence

$$I^n/t' = I_a^n/t$$

$$n \log_{10} I - n \log_{10} I_a = \log_{10} t' - \log_{10} t$$

$$10 \log_{10}(I/I_a) = (10/n) \log_{10} t' - (10/n) \log_{10} t. \qquad (11.43)$$

But

$$10 \log_{10}(I/I_a) = \text{decibels of adaptation},$$

so that

$$\text{decibels of adaptation} = (10/n) \log_{10} t' - (10/n) \log_{10} t. \qquad (11.44)$$

Therefore, if we plot decibels of adaptation against $\log_{10} t$, we expect to obtain a straight line whose slope equals $-10/n$, where $n$ is the power function exponent from the power law of sensation.

In the various papers describing experiments of the SDLB type, decibels of adaptation are plotted against $t$ (not $\log t$) and are seen to produce a curve, as shown in Figure 11.8 (data from Figure 3d, 50 s off, 10 s on, of Small and Minifie, 1961). If, however, we replot the data with a $\log_{10}$ $t$-scale instead of a $t$-scale, the data are seen to lie nearly along a straight line, as shown in Figure 11.9. Fitting a straight line to these data, we obtain

$$\text{decibels of adaptation} = -8.816 - 27.98 \log_{10} t. \qquad (11.45)$$

Comparing (11.44) with (11.45) we have

$$(10/n) = 27.98, \qquad n = 0.36. \qquad (11.46)$$

This value for $n$ is quite close to the expected value for the power function exponent for sound intensity at 4000 Hz, the frequency used by

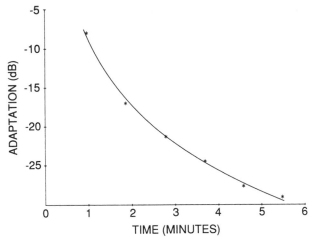

FIGURE 11.8 Data of Small and Minifie (1961), Figure 3d, 50 s off and 10 s on: simultaneous dichotic loudness balance. Data are plotted here in the usual way: decibels of adaptation are plotted against time. The data fall on a curve.

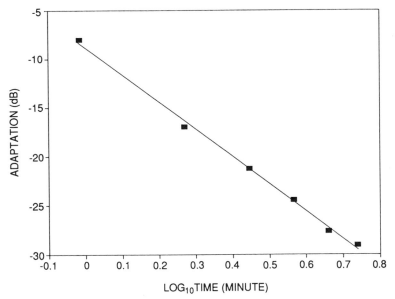

FIGURE 11.9 Same data as in Figure 11.8. However, decibels of adaptation are now plotted against the log of time. The data tend to lie on a straight line. Then $-10/$slope of line gives the power function exponent. The intercept with the line $\log t = 0$ gives the "on time," in principle.

Small and Minifie. We are not quite so accurate, however, when we test the intercept. Again comparing (11.44) with (11.45),

$$(10/n) \log_{10} t' = -8.816. \qquad (11.47)$$

Inserting the value of $n$ from (11.46),

$$\log_{10} t' = (-8.816)(0.36)/10 = -0.317$$

$$t' = 0.482 \text{ min} = 29 \text{ s}. \qquad (11.48)$$

However, the experimental "on time" for this graph was only 10 s. Other graphs obtained from SDLB experiments gave somewhat closer estimates of $t'$. But one must remember that Equation (11.42), from which these computations were made, assumed that the test ear was always completely unadapted, which was not the case experimentally. I think that the predictions made by the theory are reasonable.

Loudness adaptation does not occur, or is not prominent, monaurally, as discussed by Scharf (1978, p. 219). Yet adaptation of one ear with respect to another is prominent. Such an effect can be explained if $k$ or $\beta$ for audition were slowly increasing functions of time. For example, $\beta/t$ might tend to remain constant. We may observe, though, that Equation (11.43) can be obtained from Equation (11.42) even if $k$ and $\beta$ are time-varying parameters, provided that $\beta$[left ear] = $\beta$[right ear], etc.

The reader is encouraged to carry out more of these SDLB analyses, and perhaps to refine Equation (11.42). The mathematical analyses are quite straightforward, requiring only a regression line. Don't forget: "decibels of adaptation" are negative numbers as we calculate them.


## CONCLUDING REMARKS

I have presented rather a new view of the process of sensory adaptation. Eschewing the more traditional ideas such as the association of adaptation with fatigue, I have represented adaptation as the process of acquisition of information. As adaptation proceeds, information is gained progressively. When adaptation is complete, we cease to sensate[9] because we have received all possible information from a particular stimulus. We might extend this idea beyond simple stimuli of the intensity type. When an image is fixed in constant position on the retina, the image fades or "grays out" (Troxler's effect). Perhaps this is another example of the principle: *To perceive is to receive information; in the absence of new information, sensation desists.* Troxler's effect has, recently, been simulated by a "silicon retina" as an adaptation process (Mahowald and Mead, 1991).

Another view of adaptation as gain in information was presented by Keidel *et al.* (1961).

In the process of deriving Equation (11.3), we have held $I$ constant and set $\lambda = \beta I^n =$ constant in Equation (11.2). In so doing, we have removed assumption 6 from the set of six assumptions listed in Chapter 9.

Equation (11.3) was descended from its ancestor,

$$H = \tfrac{1}{2}\ln\left[1 + \sigma_S^2/\left(m\sigma_R^2\right)\right]. \tag{9.10}$$

You will recall that stimulus population variance, $\sigma_S^2$, was divided by $m$, the number of samplings made by the receptor since the time of introduction of the stimulus, to provide a reduced variance, $\sigma_S^2/m$, by virtue of the central limit theorem. That is, the receptor was modeled as an averaging device. Hence adaptation as reduction of uncertainty. However, mathematically, we obtain the same equation (9.10) if we associate each sampling with the population variance, $\sigma_S^2$, and regard the reference variance, $\sigma_R^2$, as increasing with the number of samplings. For example, by the rule of addition of variances, we may obtain $m$ times the error squared after $m$ measurements: hence $m\sigma_R^2$. Perhaps the reader prefers to model the sampling process in this manner, but I find it less comprehensible.

Our fundamental equation of adaptation (11.3) is in logarithmic form, but for all except the smallest values of $t$, the $F$-function can be expanded in a Taylor series (cf. Equation (11.32)), in the usual way, to give a power function. Retaining only the first term of the series, we have

$$F = \tfrac{1}{2}k\lambda t^{-b}, \tag{11.49}$$

where $b = -1$. It is of interest that in recent years, insect physiologists have been curve-fitting adaptation curves by power functions of the form of (11.49), but usually with fractional values for the constant $b$, such as $b = -0.31$ (Chapman and Smith, 1963; Thorson and Biederman-Thorson, 1974; Mann and Chapman, 1975). In reanalyzing some of their data, our research group has found that better curve-fits are sometimes obtained using $b = -1$. See, for example, the analysis of the data of Bohnenberger (1981) as presented by Norwich and Valter McConville (1991). You will recall that our value, $b = -1$, arose originally from the "null conjecture" of linear sampling rate, expressed by Equation (9.3). There is, of course, no reason why $b$ should not be retained as an additional parameter; it's just that there is, perhaps, not sufficient evidence to support abrogation of the null conjecture.

Finally, a remark about the synchrony of the process of adaptation with the time interval of exposure to the stimulus. My original conjecture (Norwich, 1981) was that the neurophysiological adaptation process (which we have analyzed above) was synchronous with the exposure of the receptor to the stimulus environment. That is, as the receptor sampled, so the neuron fired. Nature, however, was not to be this simple.

Experiments carried out by L. Ward (1991) have shown that the sampling process (at least for vision) is completed exceedingly rapidly. In the order of 1 ms, human perceivers have obtained nearly the full complement of information from a flash stimulus, as measured later in an experiment on categorical judgments. In contrast, however, the neurophysiological adaptation curve may *begin* at about 1 ms, and proceed for many milliseconds, as seen from the guinea pig data of Cleland and Enroth-Cugell (1968). It is as if the retina takes a "photograph" of the flash using a very rapid "shutter," and this photograph is later scanned by the more slowly reacting nervous system. The scanning comprises the sampling process which is responsible for adaptation to the stimulus. But the above is pure conjecture.

## NOTES

1. We confine the discussion of adaptation to changes in the perceptual variable, $F$, with time. That is, we are not concerned here with changes in threshold that accompany adaptation.
2. I am resisting the temptation to represent the constant $\beta I^n$ by the Greek letter $\tau$, even though it has the dimensions of time. $\tau$ is too easily misread as $t$.
3. It is arguable that $m$ may not take on values less than 2 in Equation (11.3). Remember that, fundamentally, Equation (11.3) comes from Equation (9.12). *If* the receptor is utilizing sample variances as estimators of $\sigma_S^2$, then at least two samples are needed. Then $m \geq 2$.
4. We use $t_0$ fairly frequently, so I selected "$t_0$" rather than the longer "$t_{min}$."
5. When one allows explicitly for a threshold value of $\Delta H$, as given by Equation (14.4), the rate of decline of the theoretical curve is found to match the observed data much more closely.
6. The digitization performed here and elsewhere in this book was usually carried out using a digitizing site mounted on a Hewlett-Packard plotter (which was also used to draw many of the graphs). A computer program was written which facilitated the process and permitted digitization from log or linear scales.
7. We actually carried out a similar exercise at the end of Chapter 10, when we studied the total number of impulses recorded over a period of time.
8. *Wherefore?* Means *why?* or *for what reason?* Juliet was not searching for Romeo from her balcony! Refer to commentary on Shakespeare's play.
9. The Oxford English Dictionary recognizes the intransitive verb, *sensate*, as an obsolete form. However, I recommend its revitaliza-

tion for use in the field of sensation and perception. *He ceased to sense while under anesthesia* seems less satisfactory than *He ceased to sensate while under anesthesia*.

## REFERENCES

Beebe-Center, J. G., Rogers, M. S., and O'Connell, D. N. 1955. Transmission of information about sucrose and saline solutions through the sense of taste. *Journal of Psychology* **39**, 157–160.

Chapman, K. M., and Smith, R. S. 1963. A linear transfer function underlying impulse frequency modulation in a cockroach mechanoreceptor. *Nature* **197**, 699–700.

Cleland, B. G., and Enroth-Cugell, C. 1968. Quantitative aspects of sensitivity and summation in the cat retina. *Journal of Physiology* **198**, 17–38.

Dethier, V. G., and Bowdan, E. 1984. Relations between differential threshold and sugar receptor mechanisms in the blowfly. *Behavioral Neuroscience* **98**, 791–803.

Dowling, J. E. 1987. *The Retina: An Approachable Part of the Brain.* Belknap Press of Harvard Univ. Press, Cambridge, MA.

Galambos, R., and Davis, H. 1943. The response of single auditory-nerve fibers to acoustic stimulation. *Journal of Neurophysiology* **6**, 39–57.

Galambos, R., and Davis, H. 1948. Action potentials from single auditory-nerve fibers? *Science* **108**, 513.

Garner, W. R. 1953. An informational analysis of absolute judgments of loudness. *Journal of Experimental Psychology* **46**, 373–380.

Gent, J. F., and McBurney, D. H. 1978. Time course of gustatory adaptation. *Perception and Psychophysics* **23**, 171–175.

Keidel, W. D., Keidel, U. O., and Wigand, M. E. 1961. Adaptation: Loss or gain of sensory information? In *Sensory Communication* (W. A. Rosenblith, Ed.), MIT Press/Wiley, New York.

Mahowald, M. A., and Mead, C. 1991. The silicon retina. *Scientific American*, **May** 76–82.

Mann, D. W., and Chapman, K. M. 1975. Component mechanisms of sensitivity and adaptation in an insect mechanoreceptor. *Brain Research* **97**, 331–336.

Matthews, B. H. C. 1931. The response of a single end organ. *Journal of Physiology* **71**, 64–110.

Norwich, K. H. 1981. The magical number seven: Making a "bit" of "sense." *Perception and Psychophysics* **29**, 409–422.

Norwich, K. H. 1984. The psychophysics of taste from the entropy of the stimulus. *Perception and Psychophysics* **35**, 269–278.

Norwich, K. H., and Valter McConville, K. M. 1991. An informational approach to sensory adaptation. *Journal of Comparative Physiology A* **168**, 151–157.

Scharf, B. 1978. Loudness. In *Handbook of Perception*, Vol. IV. *Hearing* (E. C. Carterette and M. P. Friedman, Eds.). Academic Press, New York.

Schmidt, R. F. 1978. Somatovisceral sensibility. In: *Fundamentals of Sensory Physiology* (R. F. Schmidt, ed.). Springer-Verlag, New York.

Small, A. M., Jr., and Minifie, F. D. 1961. Effect of matching time on perstimulatory adaptation. *Journal of the Acoustical Society of America* **33**, 1028–1033.

Thorson, J., and Biederman-Thorson, M. 1974. Distributed relaxation processes in sensory adaptation. *Science* **183**, 161–172.

Ward, L. M. 1991. Informational and neural adaptation curves are asynchronous. *Perception and Psychophysics* **50**, 117–128.

Yates, G. K., Robertson, D., and Johnstone, B. M. 1985. Very rapid adaptation in the guinea pig auditory nerve. *Hearing Research* **17**, 1–12.

# 12

## Differential Thresholds, Weber Fractions, and JND'S

### THE ANALOGS

Before pressing into this rather detailed chapter, let's take a minute for purposes of orientation. In the flow diagram, Figure 1.2, we are still within the center block: evaluation of $F = kH$. As I have reiterated at various times, this book is largely about the unification of the laws of sensation. I am endeavoring to show that the single equation, $F = kH$, with a single, explicit mathematical form for the $H$-function, will encompass all sensory phenomena involving the variables steady $I$, $F$, and $t$ for a single stimulus. While we could possibly improve our curve-fitting, upon occasion, by modifying the $H$-function in some *ad hoc* manner, that is not really the issue. The important matter is that *one* function permits us to account for (nearly) *all* observed sensory effects in a quantitative manner, and from this *one* function we can derive (nearly) *all* the empirical laws that have been formulated during the past 130 years. Unification is not a game to be played for the exercise, or for its own sake (to say "I climbed the mountain"). Unification is pursued for the physical and biological insight provided by the unifying equation, as we discussed in Chapter 1, as well as for its predictive value.

We recall the analog to the ideal gas law that was suggested in the first and third chapters:

$$V \quad T \quad P$$
$$\Uparrow \quad \Downarrow \quad \Downarrow$$
$$t \quad I \quad F$$

(i) $$P \propto T \quad \text{or} \quad P = f(T, V')$$

(Charles' law): pressure is a monotone increasing function of $T$ with $V = V' = $ constant, analogous to

$$F = F(I, t')$$

(Law of sensation): $F$ is a monotone increasing function of $I$ with $t = t' = $ constant.

(ii)    $$P \propto 1/V \quad \text{or} \quad P = f(T', V)$$

(Boyle's law): pressure is a power function of $V$ with $T = T' = $ constant, analogous to

$$F = F(I', t)$$

(Law of adaptation): $F$ is a power function of $t$ (for larger $t$) with $I = I' = $ constant.

In this chapter we come to the third equation:

(iii)    $$\Delta T/T \propto \Delta P \cdot (1/T),$$

with $\Delta P$ held constant.

We now show that

$\Delta I/I \propto \Delta F \cdot (1/I)$ with $\Delta F$ held constant (well, almost!).

No. There is no profound connection (of which I am aware) between the ideal gas law and the entropy law. I am just trying to illustrate, particularly for readers who are unfamiliar with the methods of physics, how a single equation can contain within itself the explanation for many, apparently diverse physical phenomena. I am trying to encourage the reader, in this way, to think of the law of sensation, the principle of adaptation, and the Weber fraction as different views of the same principle of perception: to perceive is to gain information.

## THE WEBER FRACTION

The Weber fraction, $\Delta I/I$, was introduced in Chapter 3, The Weber Fraction: The Analogs, and that material should probably be reviewed at this time. We require a detailed understanding of virtually every paragraph in that section as we proceed through the following theoretical derivation of the mathematical function for $\Delta I/I$.

The mathematical technique that will be employed is to replace the differentials in a differential equation by their finite differences (e.g., replace $dx$ by $\Delta x$), the inverse of the process used by Fechner (Equations (3.2) and (3.3)), who replaced finite differences by the corresponding differentials. We are already in possession of an integrated function, the

$H$- or $F$-function, and we proceed to the corresponding differential equation; Fechner began with a differential equation and integrated to obtain his "$F$-function."

Luce and Edwards (1958) supported by Krantz (1971) and others attempted to show that Fechnerian integration was in error and that jnd's could not, in general, be summated using Equations (3.11) and (3.12). In the present discussion, we confine $\Delta x$ to be small in comparison with $x$, and the objections expressed mathematically on page 225 of the paper by Luce and Edwards do not apply. It is important to understand and to observe that total jnd's calculated from Equations (3.11) and (3.12) is, indeed, nearly the same value as that obtained by adding jnd's one on top of the other, the method recommended by these authors (Luce and Edwards, p. 233). The reader is referred to Figures 3.5a and 3.5b, showing the data of Lemberger (1908), dealing with differential thresholds for sugars. These data were taken from Table 4 of Lemberger's paper, which is reproduced here, in part, in Table 12.1 (last few points omitted). In Chapter 3, with reference to Figure 3.5b, and using Equation (3.12), we calculated the total number of jnd's from $I$ = threshold to $I$ = 18.75% solution to be 21 jnd's. However, as may be seen from Table 12.1, Lemberger actually made 22 measurements of $\Delta I/I$ by adding jnd's one on top of the other. That is, $(\Delta I)_1$ extended from 0.44 to 0.60% solution; $(\Delta I)_2$ extended from 0.60 to 0.82% solution, etc. So the 22 measurements, extending from 0.44 to 18.75%, comprised exactly

TABLE 12.1   Data of Lemberger (1908): Weber Fraction for Sucrose

| Measured differential threshold (concentration of solutions in percent) | Weber Fraction | Measured differential threshold (concentration of solutions in percent) | Weber Fraction |
|---|---|---|---|
| 0.44–0.60 | 0.3636 | 5.08–5.833 | 0.1482 |
| 0.60–0.82 | 0.3666 | 5.833–6.75 | 0.1572 |
| 0.82–1.125 | 0.3720 | 6.75–7.75 | 0.1481 |
| 1.125–1.40 | 0.2444 | 7.75–8.916 | 0.1505 |
| 1.40–1.63 | 0.1643 | 8.916–10.35 | 0.1608 |
| 1.63–1.85 | 0.1350 | 10.35–11.97 | 0.1565 |
| 1.85–2.13 | 0.1514 | 11.97–13.90 | 0.1612 |
| 2.13–2.45 | 0.1502 | 13.90–16.17 | 0.1633 |
| 2.45–2.825 | 0.1531 | 16.17–18.75 | 0.1596 |
| 2.825–3.267 | 0.1561 | | |
| 3.267–3.775 | 0.1558 | | |
| 3.775–4.39 | 0.1629 | | |
| 4.39–5.08 | 0.1572 | | |

Note. German, "Saccharose" translated as "sucrose."

22 jnd's. This value agrees exceedingly well with our value of 21 jnd's obtained using Equation (3.12). However, the values of $\Delta I$ were small compared with $I$. When $\Delta I$ approaches $I$ in value, one must, indeed, heed the warning of Luce *et al.*

The above having been said, we proceed with the derivation of the theoretical function for the Weber fraction, $\Delta I/I$, which issues directly from Equation (9.19),

$$H = \tfrac{1}{2}\ln(1 + \beta I^{n}/t). \tag{12.1}$$

It is assumed that in experiments for determining Weber fractions, all stimuli are applied for the same interval of time, $t'$, so that we may again introduce Equation (10.2)

$$\gamma = \beta/t'. \tag{12.2}$$

Thus

$$H = \tfrac{1}{2}\ln(1 + \gamma I^{n}). \tag{10.3}/(12.3)$$

Differentiating $H$ with respect to $I$,

$$\frac{dH}{dI} = \frac{\tfrac{1}{2}\gamma n I^{n-1}}{1 + \gamma I^{n}}. \tag{12.4}$$

Replacing $dH$ and $dI$ by the corresponding finite differences, and rearranging the equation,

$$\Delta I = \frac{2\Delta H(1 + \gamma I^{n})}{\gamma n I^{n-1}} = \frac{2\Delta H}{n}\left[I + \frac{1}{\gamma I^{n-1}}\right]. \tag{12.5}$$

Dividing both sides by $I$,

$$\boxed{\Delta I/I = \frac{2\Delta H}{n}\left[1 + \frac{1}{\gamma I^{n}}\right].} \tag{12.6}$$

The above equation still makes no physiologically meaningful statement; it simply relates a change, $\Delta I$, in stimulus intensity, to a corresponding change, $\Delta H$, in entropy. There is nothing yet to render $\Delta I/I$ interpretable as a Weber fraction. We are interested in the *stimulus change per jnd*. Therefore, it is necessary to add an additional assumption to the list of six assumptions given in Chapter 9. I recommend

(7) The subjective magnitudes of all jnd's are equal.

The reader will recall that this assumption was originally due to Fechner (Equation (3.2)). We do not, however, require the full complement of seven assumptions for a description of the Weber fraction because, due to the introduction of Equation (12.2), we have, effectively, dropped assumption (4). Assumption (7) can, if desired, be relaxed (please see "$\Delta H$ as Threshold," below).

In the discussion that follows, we associate each stimulus of magnitude, $I$, with a unique quantity of information, the information that it could transmit to the receptor if the receptor were completely unadapted to the stimulus; that is, the potential information of the stimulus. This concept was introduced in the previous chapter, augmented by note 5 in that chapter. There is, further, a double-stimulus approximation discussed below ("On the Physical Meaning of $\Delta I$").

Letting the constant subjective magnitude of the jnd be $\Delta F$, we can divide both sides of Equation (12.6) by this quantity to give

$$\frac{\Delta I/\Delta F}{I} = \frac{2\Delta H/\Delta F}{n}\left[1 + \frac{1}{\gamma I^n}\right], \qquad (12.7)$$

or, since

$$\Delta F = k\Delta H, \qquad (12.8)$$

$$\frac{\Delta I/\Delta F}{I} = \frac{2}{kn}\left[1 + \frac{1}{\gamma I^n}\right]. \qquad (12.9)$$

The expression $(\Delta I/\Delta F)/I$, introduced in Chapter 3, then, represents the Weber fraction in a complete fashion: fractional change in stimulus intensity per jnd. However, we shall usually use the form (12.6). $\Delta H$ is the *informational differential threshold*. Note that we have now incorporated both of Resnikoff's requirements (Chapter 10).

With $\Delta H(=\Delta F/k)$ taken as the constant informational cost of a jnd by assumption 7, above, Equation (12.6) is a simple expression giving $\Delta I/I$ as a function of $I$. Equation (12.9), by the way, is about as close as we get to the third analog of the ideal gas ((iii) above).

Equation (12.6), (12.7), or (12.9) define a theoretically derived function that describes the observed shape of many Weber fraction curves. For smaller $I$, the second term on the right-hand side dominates and $\Delta I/I$ is large. We must be careful, though, because as the fraction becomes large, $\Delta I \to I$, and the finite difference approximation weakens. As $I$ becomes greater, the second term on the right-hand side approaches zero, and $\Delta I/I$ approaches $2\Delta H/n$. That is,

$$\text{Weber constant} = 2\Delta H/n. \qquad (12.10)$$

The general form of the function (12.6) is illustrated in Figure 12.1. The early, rising portion of the curve is derived from the term $\gamma I^n$, so it might be called the *power function component*; the later plateau in the curve, corresponds to Weber's law, Equation (3.1),

$$\Delta I/I = \text{constant},$$

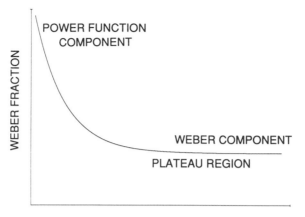

STIMULUS INTENSITY

FIGURE 12.1    Weber fraction, $\Delta I/I$, vs. stimulus intensity, $I$. Illustrates the basic shape of the curve measured for various sensory modalities. $\Delta I/I$ is large for small values of $I$ (even though $\Delta I$ is quite small). This component of the curve has been labeled "power function component" because it is described in Equation (12.6) by means of an $I^n$-term. Some investigators have recorded only this part of the curve and report a monotonically decreasing value for $\Delta I/I$. For larger values of $I$, $\Delta I/I$ approaches a constant. This component has been called the "Weber component" because Weber believed that $\Delta I/I$ was universally constant. Curves of exactly this shape are seldom measured, but were, in fact, recorded by Knudsen and Riesz for audition. The general shape is also found for taste receptors of insects. It is described by Equations (12.6) and (12.16). A more usual shape for the Weber fraction curve is shown in Figure 12.2.

so it might be called the *Weber component*. The shape of these curves, early fall followed by plateau, is of the type measured by Riesz (1928) for audition. Equation (12.6) cannot, however, describe the *terminal rise* in the curve, the rise observed for larger values of $I$, as seen, for example, in the curves measured by König for vision (Figure 3.6), or Holway and Hurvich for taste of sodium chloride (Figure 12.2).

I can trace the history of the use of equations like (12.6) back as far as 1907, when a very similar equation was used empirically by Nutting:

$$\Delta I/I = P_m + (1 - P_m)(I_0/I)^n. \qquad (12.11)$$

It was also used, in the same form, by Knudsen (1923) and an equation of exactly the same type as (12.6) was used empirically by Riesz (1928). In the present work, Equation (12.6) was, of course, derived from the general equation of entropy (12.1).

Békésy (1930) modeled the neural excitation process to obtain the equation

$$E = b \log\left(1 + \frac{a}{c}J\right), \qquad (12.12)$$

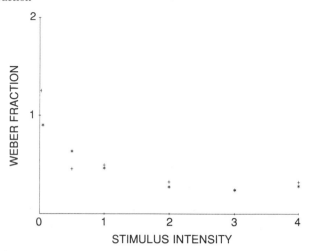

FIGURE 12.2   $\Delta I/I$ vs. $I$ for taste of sodium chloride. The oft-cited data of Holway and Hurvich (1937). Although no curve has been drawn in, the data conform to a curve of the type shown in Figures 3.5a and 3.6.

where $E$ is "excitation" (potential), $c$ is tissue salt concentration, $J$ is sound pressure, and $b$ is constant, as is $a/c$. This equation is very close to our equation of entropy. Békésy gives credit to Alfred Lehmann (1905)[1] for the original derivation of Equation (12.12). Békésy then derived from Equation (12.12) our Equation (12.6), with $n = 1$ and, referring to Knudsen's auditory data, showed that the measured Weber fraction for frequencies of 200 and 1000 Hz were well fitted by this equation. Békésy's model is summarized by Harris (1963). In Chapter 3, we followed Ekman's derivation of the $n = 1$ equation (Equation (3.10)) and we learned that this equation may date back as far as Fechner himself.

Equation (12.4) can be cast into a new and useful form. From Equation (12.3),

$$1 + \gamma I^n = e^{2H}.\tag{12.13}$$

Since

$$\tfrac{1}{2}\gamma n I^{n-1} = \tfrac{1}{2}(n/I)(\gamma I^n)$$

$$= \tfrac{1}{2}(n/I)(e^{2H} - 1).\tag{12.14}$$

Introducing Equations (12.13) and (12.14) into (12.4),

$$\frac{dH}{dI} = \frac{1}{2}(n/I)\frac{e^{2H} - 1}{e^{2H}}$$

or

$$\frac{dH}{dI} = \frac{1}{2}(n/I)(1 - e^{-2H})\;.$$

(12.15)

Again, going over into the $\Delta$-form,

$$\Delta I/I = \frac{2\Delta H}{n}\left[\frac{1}{1 - e^{-2H}}\right]\;.$$

(12.16)

This interesting equation gives the Weber fraction in terms only of the variable, $H$, or since $H = F/k$, in terms of $F$. For example, for audition, $\Delta I/I$ is given solely in terms of loudness. Note that as loudness, $H$, becomes large, $\Delta I/I \to 2\Delta H/n = Weber's\ constant$. As loudness decreases, $\Delta I/I$ becomes larger, as seen in Figure 12.1 (Riesz type). Equations (12.6) and (12.16) are mathematically equivalent.

Equation (12.15) is, perhaps, the most natural *differential equation for the entropy*. This equation can be solved, by separating the variables, to give the entropy function, $H$ (Equation (12.1)). The constant $\gamma$ emerges as a constant of integration.

## DERIVATION OF THE POULTON–TEGHTSOONIAN LAW

This law (PT law henceforth), in which exponent plotted vs. stimulus range defines a rectangular hyperbola, has been described in Chapter 3, The Poulton–Teghtsoonian Law, Equation (3.27), and this is the perfect time to review it. I think there is no better example of the power of the entropy equation than its ability of produce the PT law in its totality, including the value of the constant. The law can actually be obtained, in part, by very simple means, which I give first, followed by a second, somewhat more lengthy derivation which provides the complete form of the law.

First, rather simply, writing the $H$-function in the "Fechner" or semilog approximation (Equation (10.5)),

$$H = \tfrac{1}{2}n \ln I + \tfrac{1}{2}\ln \gamma.$$

(12.17)

We recall that this approximation is valid only for $\gamma I^n \gg 1$. Let us take two values for $I$, one close to the physiological maximum, $I_{high}$, and one close to the minimum value for which (12.17) is valid, $I_{low}$. Then

$$H_{high} = \tfrac{1}{2}n \ln I_{high} + \tfrac{1}{2}\ln \gamma,$$

(12.18a)

and

$$H_{\text{low}} = \tfrac{1}{2}n \ln I_{\text{low}} + \tfrac{1}{2}\ln \gamma. \qquad (12.18b)$$

Then

$$\delta H = H_{\text{high}} - H_{\text{low}}, \qquad (12.19)$$

or

$$\delta H = \tfrac{1}{2}n \ln I_{\text{high}}/I_{\text{low}}, \qquad (12.20)$$

from which, if $I_{\text{low}}$ is "low enough," we have approximately,

$$n \cdot \ln(\text{range of intensities}) = 2\,\delta H. \qquad (12.21)$$

We see that Equation (12.21) does describe the PT law (Equation (3.27)) formally, without, however, providing a value for the quantity $2\delta H$ on the right-hand side. The reader can evaluate $\delta H$ using Equation (12.19) with the assumption that $H_{\text{high}} \gg H_{\text{low}}$.

The second derivation achieves the same end using the concept of the jnd. Let us return to Equation (3.14):

$$\delta N = N_{\text{plateau}} = \frac{\ln 10}{\text{Weber constant}} \log_{10}(I_{\text{high}}/I_{\text{low}}), \qquad (12.22)$$

where $\delta N$ is the number of jnd's contained beneath the plateau or Weber region of the Weber fraction curve. In the above equation we insert Equation (12.10), giving

$$\delta N = \frac{n \ln 10}{2\Delta H} \log_{10}(I_{\text{high}}/I_{\text{low}}). \qquad (12.23)$$

Let $H_{\text{high}}$ now be defined as the entropy of the maximum physiological stimulus, calculated from Equation (12.3) (no approximation is used). Define $H_{\text{low}}$ as the entropy, calculated from Equation (12.3) of the stimulus whose intensity marks the lower end of the plateau region of the Weber fraction. As before (12.19),

$$\delta H = H_{\text{high}} - H_{\text{low}}, \qquad (12.24)$$

but with the quantities on the right-hand side defined differently (now with respect to a plateau). Then, since $\Delta H$ is the constant entropy span of one jnd (by assumption (7)),

$$\delta N = \delta H/\Delta H. \qquad (12.25)$$

That is, we could "fit in" $\delta H/\Delta H$ distinguishable stimuli beneath the plateau (see also note 3). Equations (12.23) and (12.25) now each provide expressions for $\delta N$. Equating the right-hand sides of these two equations, and canceling $\Delta H$ from both sides,

$$\delta H(\text{natural units}) = \frac{n \ln 10}{2} \log_{10}(I_{\text{high}}/I_{\text{low}}). \qquad (12.26)$$

Now, $\log_{10}(I_{\text{high}}/I_{\text{low}})$ is the quantity defined for Equation (3.27) as the $\log_{10}$ range of stimuli spanning the entire Weber fraction curve. Here we define this quantity as the range of stimuli spanning the plateau region of the Weber fraction curve. Rearranging Equation (12.26),

$$(n)(\log_{10} \text{ range}) = 2\delta H/\ln 10, \qquad (12.27)$$

so that we have, again, nearly derived Equation (3.27) except for the value of $\delta H$. The advantage, however, in this second derivation, through the medium, as it were, of the Weber fraction, is that we can provide *a priori*, an approximate value for $\delta H$.

The clue lies in Equation (12.25). Since $\Delta H$, the informational value of the jnd, is constant, $\delta H$ is proportional to $\delta N$, the total number of jnd's under the plateau of the Weber fraction. But we learned, by experience, that the number of jnds beneath the plateau is not a bad approximation of the *total* number of jnd's, threshold to maximum physiological stimulus. For example (Chapter 3, The Weber Fraction: The Analogs), in the analysis of Lemberger's data on the differential threshold of taste, there are 19.8 jnds beneath the plateau, and 21 jnd's under the whole of the analyzed curve (3 final values omitted). In general, fewer than 30% of the total jnds lie to the left of the plateau,[2] so that

$$\delta N_{\text{pleateau}} \text{ is less than but approximately equal to } \delta N_{\text{total}}. \quad (12.28)$$

Therefore, from Equation (12.24), $\delta H$, which is defined equal to $\delta H_{\text{plateau}}$, is less than but approximately equal to $\delta H_{\text{total}}$. But since $H_{\text{low}}$ is small,

$$\delta H_{\text{total}} \simeq H_{\text{high}}, \qquad (12.29)$$

and $H_{\text{high}}$ has been shown to be a measure of the channel capacity of the modality, particularly in those senses that adapt completely (Chapter 11). Therefore, with an element of approximation

$$\delta H_{\text{total}} \simeq 2.5 \text{ bits} = 1.75 \text{ natural units of information}, \quad (12.30)$$

where the 2.5 bits is the universal channel capacity ($\simeq \log_2$ of the "magical number" 6). (The same value can be inserted for $\delta H$ in Equation (12.21) to complete the first derivation of the PT law.)

Inserting this value for $\delta H$ into Equation (12.27),

$$(n)(\log_{10} \text{ range}) = \frac{(2)(1.75)}{\ln(10)} = 1.52, \qquad (12.31)$$

which is the PT law in a form very close to that discovered empirically by Teghtsoonian using data assembled by Poulton. Since the value used for $\delta H$ was a little too small (we used just the range of stimuli spanned by the plateau region rather than the total stimulus range), we could really expect that the "correct" value for the constant would be 15–30% larger than 1.52. The near-perfect agreement with Equation (13.27) is probably fortuitous.

Note that Equation (12.31) is expected to be valid across the modalities, because of the nearly constant value of the information content of a stimulus: 2.5 bits = 1.75 n.u. That is, Equation (12.31) is an intermodality law. Whether it is an *intra*modality law, holding within a modality where $n$ changes, for example with frequency, remains to be thought through.

## INFORMATION PER STIMULUS FROM WEBER FRACTIONS

In order to derive the PT law, we inserted an average value for the information per stimulus (channel capacity) of 2.5 bits per stimulus. It is instructive, now, to proceed without using the average value, but rather to calculate the stimulus information for each modality. There's nothing really new here; we are just turning the problem around. Putting Equation (12.26) into words, we have

$$\text{Information per stimulus (bits)} = \frac{\ln 10}{2\ln 2} \text{ (power function exponent)}$$

$$\cdot (\log_{10} \text{ stimulus range of plateau}).$$

$$(12.32)$$

If we now eliminate ($\log_{10}$ stimulus range of plateau) using Equation (12.22),

Information per stimulus (bits)

$$= \frac{1}{2\ln 2} \text{ (power function exponent)(jnds beneath plateau)}$$

$$\cdot (\text{Weber constant}).$$

$$(12.33)$$

Since both of the above two equations utilize the plateau region of the Weber fraction, and the plateau is, in practice, often difficult to define, it would be useful to find an equation for stimulus information that does not require definition of the plateau. Such an equation was derived by the author (Norwich, 1987):

Information per stimulus (bits)

$$= \frac{\ln 10}{2 \ln 2} (\text{power function exponent})(\log_{10} \textit{total stimulus range})$$

$$- \frac{1}{2 \ln 2} \ln \left[ \frac{\text{Weber fraction just above threshold}}{\text{Weber fraction at maximum stimulus}} \right]. \quad (12.34)$$

However, in eliminating the need to define the plateau in Equation (12.34) we may have gained very little. We must now evaluate the Weber fraction close to threshold, where measurements are not very accurate. Moreover, in the derivation of (12.34), the usual $dI \rightarrow \Delta I$ has been used, which is barely acceptable for larger $\Delta I$.

Willy nilly, Equations (12.32), (12.33), and (12.34) are evaluated for three modalities: taste, vision, and audition in Table 1 of Norwich (1987). I think that all three equations fare reasonably well in providing values for information transmitted per stimulus, but Equation (12.34) seems to be the weakest.


INVARIANTS IN MEASURING DIFFERENTIAL THRESHOLDS

We recall from Chapter 3 that measurement of the magnitude of the jnd was dependent upon the statistical criterion selected by the experimenter (Figure 3.7). That is, there is no unique measurement of the size of the jnd. One might, then, ask how quantities such as "total number of jnd's beneath plateau" can be used as a variable in an equation. The answer lies in Equation (3.14):

$$(\delta N)(\text{Weber constant}) = \ln 10 \cdot \log_{10}(\text{range of stimuli}). \quad (3.14)$$

The right-hand side of this equation is independent of the measurement of the jnd. The left-hand side contains the product $(\delta N)$(Weber constant). This product is, then, an invariant, which is independent of the statistical criterion used to measure the jnd. Remember that the Weber constant is equal to the value of $\Delta I / I$ under the plateau. As the criterion for measurement of the jnd becomes more lax (for example, the 75% criterion of Chapter 3, The Weber Fraction: The Analogs, becomes, say, 50%), the magnitude of the jnd, $\Delta I$, decreases so that the total number of jnd's $\delta N$, increases. But the product $(\delta N)(\Delta I)$ remains invariant. That is, $\delta N$ can enter as a variable into a general equation governing sensory function as long as it is multiplied by a "balancing" factor, such as $\Delta I$ or the Weber constant.

## ON THE PHYSICAL MEANING OF $\Delta I$

One should understand clearly the distinction between $\Delta I$ and $\sigma$, as we have used them. $\Delta I$ represents a change in the *mean* value of the intensity of a stimulus signal. $\sigma^2$ represents a steady-state fluctuation in the *instantaneous* value of a stimulus and is brought about by quantum effects and internal biological variations [as discussed in Chapter 9, "Relationship between Variance and Mean" (refer also to note 3 of Chapter 9)]. We, as investigators, can control $\Delta I$; we have no direct control over $\sigma^2$.

There is another very important distinction that must be made—this one concerning the manner or mode in which $\Delta I$ is produced by the experimenter. This distinction is made very clearly for the case of audition by Viemeister (1988, Figure 1) and for vision by Cornsweet and Pinsker (1965, Figure 2). In one mode, the subject must detect which of two stimuli, $I$ or $I + \Delta I$, is the most intense. In a second mode, the subject must detect a brief change, $\Delta I$, in a continuously administered stimulus. It is the second of the two modes that is encoded by our mathematical derivation of the Weber fraction. That is, we incremented $I$ by $\Delta I$ and took account of the corresponding increment in $H, \Delta H$ to obtain Equation (12.6). The method of Riesz is related to, but not exactly the same as, the second mode. (See also Chapter 12, "The Exponent $n$ at Various Auditory Frequencies.") My colleagues and I have treated the first mode mathematically, in a preliminary manner, in a series of publications cited below. However, in this book, we are concerned exclusively with the second of the two modes.

In both modes, in effect, two stimuli are administered, the second stimulus to a subject who may be in a partially adapted state. This state of partial adaptation is *not* allowed for in our derivation of Equation (12.6), which may introduce an error.

## THE TERMINAL, RISING PORTION OF THE WEBER FRACTION CURVE

A number of investigators have reported measurements showing that the graph of $\Delta I/I$ vs. $I$ either approaches a plateau (Figure 12.1) or declines monotonically with increasing $I$, and we have treated this case theoretically in Equations (12.6) or (12.16), corresponding to the second mode of stimulus administration. However, measurements of $\Delta I/I$ more usually show a terminal rise. That is, rather than descending to a plateau, the curves fall in a gentle arc and then rise again at higher values of $I$ (see Figure 3.6). This characteristic shape of the curve is common to many modalities of sensation. An explanation for this terminal rise, based on the first mode of stimulus administration, was the substance of a Masters thesis submitted by my student, Kristiina Valter McConville (1988). The theory was also reviewed by Norwich (1991). However, because of its complexity, and because the values of the parameters $t_0$ and $\beta$ required to make the theoretical equations match the observed experimental data differed from the values of these parameters required in other equations, I have decided to omit the derivation here. So, for the moment, we continue to regard the terminal rise of the Weber fraction as a bit of a mystery, or, perhaps due to a saturation effect as one approaches the maximum physiological stimulus.

## $\Delta H$ AS THRESHOLD

The use, in this chapter, of the quantity $\Delta H$ to define a fixed quantity of information transmitted for each jnd may be viewed as a modernized version of Fechner's conjecture of constant $\Delta F$ (difference in subjective magnitude) for a jnd.[3] We have, in effect, used $\Delta H$ as a *threshold for discrimination*.[4] However, it is not, by any means, certain that $\Delta H = \Delta F/k = $ constant is a valid statement.

A very clever technique for measuring the subjective magnitude of the jnd was devised by Stevens (1936) in a paper that is seldom cited. Stevens measured loudness (subjective magnitude) as a function of sound intensity, and he used Riesz's data (1933) to obtain total jnd's as a function of sound intensity. He was then able to plot total jnd's against loudness and found the relation (using $F$ for loudness and $N$ for number of jnd's)

$$F = KN^{2.2}, \qquad K \text{ constant} \qquad (12.35)$$

or

$$\frac{dF}{dN} \rightarrow \frac{\Delta F}{\Delta N} = 2.2KN^{1.2}. \qquad (12.36)$$

That is, taking $\Delta N = 1$ jnd, the increment in subjective magnitude, $\Delta F$, increased as $N^{1.2}$. That is, $\Delta F$ was not constant for hearing.

However, the jury is still out on this matter. I would like to see Stevens-type, dual experiments performed with the same subjects: the first experiment $F$ vs. $I$ and the second $\Delta I$ vs. $I$ to give $N$ vs. $I$. Such dual experiments should be performed for a number of sensory modalities. From each pair of experiments one could obtain plots of $N$ vs. $F$, which would speak to the issue of the constancy of the jnd. Assumption 7 ("The Weber Fraction," above) can be replaced by any equivalent statement of the form: $\Delta F = $ experimentally determined function of $I$, giving rise to a variation of Equation (12.6).

## WORKING TOWARD A COMMON SET OF PARAMETERS

It would be desirable, for each modality, to obtain a unique set of average values for at least the parameters $n$, $\beta$, $t_0$, and $\Delta H$. Armed with these values (plus the value of one additional parameter which we introduce in the next chapter) one could, in principle, predict the results of all experiments for each modality that involve only a single, constant stimulus, applied for a specified period of time. However, there are problems associated with the computation of these parameter values from published experimental data. Investigators conduct experiments using varied techniques and do not always report all relevant experimental conditions. Moreover, if an investigator does not use a particular theory as a guide to experimental design, he or she will not always control all variables critical to the evaluation of the theory, or even report all relevant data. *Theory is as necessary to the experimenter as experimental results are to the theorist.*

It is exceedingly difficult to bring together experiments performed by different investigators at different epochs, under different sets of standards, and emerge from this amalgam, with a consistent set of parameters for a given modality. However, we shall try. Let us consider the sense of taste of sodium chloride or saline solution. We have already analyzed several types of experiment involving the taste of sodium chloride solution:

(1) The "law of sensation" studies of Stevens (Figure 10.1) gave the value $n = 1.483$, using Equation (10.3). This value is a little higher than that usually cited for $n$. We later use $n = 1.0$.

(2) The total number of jnd's for the sense of taste of sodium chloride for the 75% correct criterion can be estimated from the data of Holway and Hurvich using the usual Equations (3.11) or (3.12). We obtained the value of 9.35 jnd's, which seems rather small. Since the information per jnd is assumed to be constant, this information, $\Delta H$, may be estimated from the equation

$$\Delta H \simeq \frac{\text{maximum information content of a stimulus}}{\text{total number of jnds}} \simeq \frac{1.18}{9.35} = 0.126 \text{ n.u.}$$

That is, the value of the "channel capacity" for the sense of taste tends to be about 1.7 bits or 1.18 natural units of information.

We add several more parameter values in the next chapter.


## PREDICTION: EFFECT OF ADAPTATION ON EQUAL LOUDNESS CONTOURS

Adaptation is expected, from informational considerations, to produce divergence of equal loudness contours for reasons which can be seen directly from Equation (12.16). When loudness, $F$, is constant, then, from (12.16), since $H = F/k$ and $\Delta H = \Delta F/k$,

$$\Delta I \propto I \Delta F. \tag{12.36}$$

That is, if two tones are separated by a small constant loudness difference, $\Delta F$, the corresponding difference in the physical intensity of the two tones will vary directly with the intensity of the lower tone (or, approximately with the mean physical intensity of the two tones). We can compare two sets of two tones, the first given to an unadapted ear and the second to an adapted ear, where both (mean) loudness, $F$, and difference in loudness, $\Delta F$, is the same for both adapted and unadapted cases. Let $I_u$ be the (mean) sound intensity for the unadapted ear and $I_a$ be the (mean) sound intensity for the adapted ear. Then, from Equation (12.36),

$$\Delta I_a \propto I_a \Delta F$$

and

$$\Delta I_u \propto I_u \Delta F.$$

Then, dividing these equations,

$$\Delta I_a/\Delta I_u = I_a/I_u. \tag{12.37}$$

But, by the definition of adaptation, $I_a > I_u$. That is, it requires greater sound intensity to produce loudness, $F$, in the adapted ear than in the unadapted ear. Therefore, $\Delta I_a > \Delta I_u$. That is, we can predict that equal loudness contours will diverge, with adaptation to sound.[5]

In fact, measurements made by Békésy (1929) (reprinted in an English language version, 1960) confirm the theory (Figure 12.3). Two tones of 800 Hz were presented to an unadapted ear. From his graph, we can determine that these tones were of sound pressures of about $8.0 \times 10^{-3}$ and $7.0 \times 10^{-2}$ dynes/cm$^2$. The ear was then adapted to a tone of high intensity and long duration at 800 Hz. Two more tones were then presented to the adapted ear, of sound pressures $3.2 \times 10^{-1}$ and $9.8 \times 10^{-1}$ dynes/cm$^2$. The loudness of these two tones matched the loudness of the previous two tones, so that both $F$ and $\Delta F$ were equal. We note, however, that

$$\Delta I_a = 9.8 \times 10^{-1} - 3.2 \times 10^{-1} = 6.6 \times 10^{-1},$$

while

$$\Delta I_u = 7.0 \times 10^{-2} - 8.0 \times 10^{-3} = 6.2 \times 10^{-2},$$

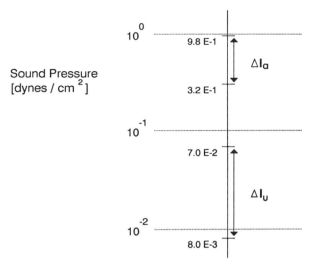

FIGURE 12.3 Data of Békésy (1929, Figure 1, at 800 Hz; and 1960, Figure 7-1). $\Delta I_u$ and $\Delta I_a$ represent changes in sound pressure of a tone delivered to an unadapted and an adapted ear, respectively. The lower boundary of $\Delta I_u$ sounds equally as loud as the lower boundary of $\Delta I_a$, and the upper boundary of $\Delta I_u$ sounds as loud as the upper boundary of $\Delta I_a$. That is, a tone at $8.0 \times 10^{-3}$ dynes/cm$^2$, presented to the unadapted ear, sounds as loud as a tone of $3.2 \times 10^{-1}$ dynes/cm$^2$, presented to the adapted ear. Similarly $7.0 \times 10^{-2}$ dynes/cm$^2$ (unadapted) is as loud as $9.8 \times 10^{-1}$ dynes/cm$^2$ (adapted). In units of dynes/cm$^2$, $\Delta I_a > \Delta I_u$.

where $I$ is measured here in units of sound pressure. That is, $\Delta I_a > \Delta I_u$ as predicted.

## SUMMARY

Amid the swirl of equations in this chapter, one tends to forget that our aim in this endeavor is not *this* algebraic relation or *that* numerical calculation, but rather to extract from the whole a tiny kernel of wisdom. The kernel probably centers around the concept of constant $\Delta H$ as an informational threshold, or informational differential limen.

The equation $F - kH$ did not play a large role in this chapter, making only a cameo appearance in Equations (12.7)–(12.9) and showing up for the finale on equal loudness contours. We used, exclusively, Equation (12.1),

$$H = H(I, t).$$

We introduced the condition that $\Delta H$, a small, constant quantity of information, was necessary to make a distinction between two stimuli of different intensity. Using this theme in several variations, we were able to derive an expression for the Weber fraction, $\Delta I/I$, as a function of $I$ and $t$. Equation (12.6) is probably its most practical form, giving the Weber fraction as a function of stimulus intensity. But Equation (12.16) has some theoretical interest in that the Weber fraction is shown to be a simple exponential function of stimulus entropy.

Cornsweet and Pinsker (1965), for the sense of vision, were able to produce experimentally two distinct types of Weber fraction curve, depending on how they presented their differential stimuli (mode I or mode II described above). They could generate either a curve of the type shown in our Figures 12.1 and 12.2 (Cornsweet and Pinsker's Experiment II) or a totally flat curve (Cornsweet and Pinsker's Experiments I and III), by varying their experimental methods. In using the entropy theory to derive Equation (12.6), we have reproduced the experimental conditions of Cornsweet and Pinsker's Experiment II (our mode II) and have, consequently, derived theoretically the type of curve they observed. We *incremented* intensity, $I$ to reach $I + \Delta I$ ($L$ to reach $L + \Delta L$ in Cornsweet and Pinsker's nomenclature), corresponding to an increment in entropy from $H$ to $H + \Delta H$.

Through the medium of the theory of the Weber fraction, we were able to derive the Poulton–Teghtsoonian law, nearly from first principles, including the value of the constant. We were also able to demonstrate a property of equal loudness contours. We learned that while the jnd does not have a unique magnitude, if multiplied by a balancing factor, it does give rise to an invariant form.

The informational differential threshold, $\Delta H$, can, by its definition, be "stacked." That is $N \times \Delta H$ = channel capacity, where $N$ is equal to the total number of jnd's.[4]

We observed in this chapter, for a second time, that the power function exponent, $n$, has appeared in equations (for the Weber fraction) that have, ostensibly, nothing to do with the power law of sensation. (Where was the first occasion when $n$ appeared outside of the power law?[6])

Since this chapter was largely bereft of the variable, $F$, there was no need to appeal to experiments in which sensation was measured numerically. Although the exponent, $n$, was in that manner born, it has now been shown to be a parameter which can be measured without reference to magnitude estimation. As we proceed, we shall find $n$ arising again and again in expressions having nothing to do with subjective magnitude: equations for simple reaction time, for threshold detection, etc.

We derived, from the primary $H$-function, Equation (9.19)/(12.1), expressions for the Weber fraction, bringing now three classes of sensory law under the umbrella of this fundamental equation; the law of sensation, the principle of adaptation, and now the differential threshold. We completed the analogs with the ideal gas law. However, we continue, now, to derive still more sensory laws from the seminal Equation (9.19)/(12.1).

NOTES

1. The equation is derived neurophysiologically as Eq (1.1) of Lehmann's book (in German) and appears in another context on p. 250.

2. By calculating $R$ = jnd's beneath plateau/total jnd's, the reader can establish for himself/herself that $R \geq 0.7$. In fact $R$ is often greater than 0.85. There is, admittedly, a subjective element involved in the calculation. It depends on where an ill-defined plateau is considered to begin and end, as well as on just how great the physiologically maximum stimulus is taken to be.

3. The reader may also have noted that the $F = kH$ relation has not been used hitherto in this chapter, except briefly in Equations (12.7)–(12.9). $\Delta F$ is, of course, equal to $\Delta H/k$, so we have replaced Fechner's $\Delta F$ = constant by $\Delta H$ = constant.

4. We have used the relation $\Delta H = H_{max}/N_{max}$, which is an approximation. That is, $\Delta H$ multiplied by the number of such $\Delta H$'s ($N_{max}$ of them) is approximately equal to the total range of $H$, zero to $H_{max}$.

5. In Figure 1 of their chapter, Keidel *et al.* (1961) indicate the opposite: "Steps of equal loudness correspond to smaller steps of sound pressure in the adapted than in the unadapted ear." However, it is possible that the authors refer to steps measured in logarithmic coordinates.

6. The first occasion in which we encountered the power function exponent in a place other than the power law of sensation was when it appeared, unexpectedly, as a part of the Weber–Fechner law, Equation (10.5).

## REFERENCES

Békésy, G. v. 1929. Zur theorie des Hörens. Über die eben merkbare Amplituden-und Frequenzänderung eines Tones. Die Theorie der Schwebungen. *Physikalische Zeitschrift* **30**, 721- 745

Békésy, G. v. 1930. Über das Fechnersche Gesetz und seine Bedeutung für die Theorie der akustischen Beobachtungsfehler und die Theorie des Hörens. *Annalen der Physik* **7**, 329–359.

Békésy, G. v. 1960. *Experiments in Hearing.* Translated and edited by E. G. Wever, McGraw-Hill, New York.

Cornsweet, T. N., and Pinsker, H. M. 1965. Luminance discrimination of brief flashes under various conditions of adaptation. *Journal of Physiology* **176**, 294–310.

Harris, J. D. 1963. Loudness discrimination. *The Journal of Speech and Hearing Disorders* Monograph Supplement Number 11, 1–63.

Holway, A. H., and Hurvich, L. M. 1937. Differential gustatory sensitivity to salt. *American Journal of Psychology* **49**, 37–48.

Keidel, W. D., Keidel, U. O. and Wigand, M. E. 1961. Adaptation: Loss or gain of Sensory Information?. *In Sensory Communication* (W. A. Rosenblith, ed.). M.I.T. Press and Wiley & Sons, New York (jointly).

Knudsen, V. O. 1923. The sensibility of the ear to small differences of intensity and frequency. *Physical Review, Series 2* **21**, 84–102.

Krantz, D. H. 1971. Integration of just-noticeable differences. *Journal of Mathematical Psychology* **8**, 591–599.

Lehmann, A. G. L. 1905. *Die körporlichen Äusserungen psychischer Zustände*. Part 3. *Elemente der Psychodynamik* (Translated by F. Bendixen). O. R. Reisland, Leipzig.

Lemberger, F. 1908. Psychophysische Untersuchungen über den Geschmack von Zucker und Saccharin (Saccharose und Krystallose). *Pflügers Archiv für die gesammte Physiologie des Menschen and der Tiere* **123**, 293–311.

Luce, R. D., and Edwards, W. 1958. The derivation of subjective scales from just noticeable differences. *Psychological Review* **65**, 222–237.

McBurney, D. H., Kasschau, R. A., and Bogart, L. M. 1967. The effect of adaptation on taste jnds. *Perception and Psychophysics* **2**, 175–178.

McConville, K. M. V., Norwich, K. H., and Abel, S. M. 1991. Application of the entropy theory of perception to auditory intensity discrimination. *International Journal of Biomedical Computing* **27**, 157–173.

Norwich, K. H. 1987. On the theory of Weber fractions. *Perception and Psychophysics* **42**, 286–298.

Norwich, K. H. 1991. Toward the unification of the laws of sensation: Some food for thought. In *Sensory Science: Theory and Application in Foods* (H. Lawless and B. Klein, Eds.), pp. 151–183. Dekker, New York.

Nutting, P. G. 1907. The complete form of Fechner's law. *Bulletin of the Bureau of Standards* **3** (No. 1), 59–64.

Poulton, E. C. 1967. Population norms of top sensory magnitudes and S. S. Stevens' exponents. *Perception and Psychophysics* **2**, 312–316.

Riesz, R. R. 1928. Differential intensity sensitivity of the ear for pure tones. *Physical Review, Series 2* **31**, 867–875.

Riesz, R. R. 1933. The relationship between loudness and the minimum perceptible increment of intensity. *Journal of the Acoustical Society of America* **4**, 211–216.

Stevens, S. S. 1936. A scale for the measurement of a psychological magnitude: loudness. *Psychological Review* **43**, 405–416.

Teghtsoonian, R. 1971. On the exponents in Stevens' law and the constant in Ekman's law. *Psychological Review* **78**, 71–80.

Valter, K. M. 1988. *The Entropy Theory of Perception as Applied to Intensity Discrimination of Auditory Pure Tones*. M.Sc. thesis, University of Toronto.

Viemeister, N. F. 1988. Psychophysical aspects of auditory intensity coding. In *Auditory Function: Neurobiological Bases of Hearing* (G. M. Edelman, W. E. Gall, and W. M. Cowan, Eds.). Wiley, New York.

# 13

## Simple Reaction Times and The Blondel–Rey Law

### INTRODUCTION

The process of deriving empirical sensory laws from an entropic or information theoretical base, namely Equation (9.19), will be continued. However, I now deal with those processes that lie at the limits of my understanding. I present matters here as well as I am able, but there are gaps in my comprehension.

We recall that *reaction time* is the time between the onset of a stimulus and the beginning of an overt response. *Simple reaction time* requires that a subject press a key or button immediately upon detection of a stimulus. An excellent introduction to reaction times is given by P. Rabbit (1987). Simple reaction time with Piéron's empirical laws have been introduced in Chapter 3, Simple Reaction Time, and the Blondel–Rey (–Hughes) law, together with the Bloch–Charpentier law, were introduced in the same chapter, Threshold Effects. Now is a good time to review these various experimentally discovered laws, as well as (Chapter 3, The Very Approximate Law of Olfactory Thresholds) the approximate law of Laffort, Patte, Etcheto, and Wright on olfactory thresholds, and (Chapter 3, The Ferry–Porter Law and the Talbot Law) the Ferry–Porter law. These various empirical or phenomenological laws may seem to be strange bedfellows, unlikely to be directly related to one another. However, it transpires that the laws are, indeed, closely linked theoretically and mathematically. The same fundamental equation of entropy seems capable of generating all of them with some degree of success.

There have been at least two full books published in the English language that are dedicated to the study of reaction times, one authored by Welford (1980) and the other by Luce (1986). The present chapter has very little in common with those works, emphasizing, as it does, the unification of reaction time phenomena with other sensory effects and the derivation of general laws of perception, not yet taking into account the matter of interindividual differences.

Cattell (1886) perceived that simple reaction time decreases with increasing stimulus intensity. Thus, for example, it requires less time to react to a bright light than to a dim one. Piéron captured this idea by using a host of empirical equations, one of which is given by Equation (3.26). It might be thought that this phenomenon (decreased reaction time with increased stimulus intensity) could be accounted for by the principle of *energy summation* or *temporal summation/integration*. For example, the intensity of light can be expressed as power, measured in watts which are joules per second. Then the product of intensity with time is equal to the light energy propagated in that time. The light receptor may summate this energy, permitting a reaction when the summated energy reaches some threshold value. There are, however, problems with the energy summation hypothesis. It does not, to my knowledge, lead to graphs of simple reaction time vs. stimulus intensity of the correct form. It will not, for example, allow a derivation of the Piéron laws for simple reaction time (or, at least, I am not aware of such a derivation). Moreover, energy summation does not seem to generalize easily to the chemical senses. It does lead to a crisp explanation for the Bloch–Charpentier law, Equation (3.22), for light and sound, but runs into difficulty with stimuli above threshold.

In the present chapter we replace the principle of energy summation by the principle of information summation, an idea which we have begun to develop in the previous chapter. After exposure to a stimulus, information begins to accumulate within the perceptual unit (a structure we shall formulate progressively). When summated information reaches the threshold value of $\Delta H$, reaction can take place and conscious sensation can occur. This concept of an informational differential threshold, $\Delta H$, is extended from Chapter 12, where it was utilized as the quantity of information needed to discriminate between two stimuli of different intensities. Now it is to be used as the quantity of information needed to react. Many of these ideas were introduced by Norwich *et al.* (1989). As in Chapter 12, we do not really require the $F = kH$ relation. Two new concepts of a fundamental nature will be introduced in this chapter: the time delay factor, $\xi$, and the informational distinction between neuronal and behavioral adaptation processes.

## DERIVATION OF AN EQUATION GIVING SIMPLE REACTION TIME AS A FUNCTION OF STIMULUS INTENSITY

We make use of the now-familiar concept that after presentation of a steady stimulus there ensues an adaptation process, and that as adaptation proceeds, entropy ("potential information") falls, and information is gained. Adaptation registers neurally in the afferent neurons, and adaptation to a stimulus with constant intensity is described by the $H$-function (9.19),

$$H = \tfrac{1}{2}\ln(1 + \beta I^n/t) = H(I,t). \tag{13.1}$$

As always, $t_0$ is defined as the time at which $H$ reaches its maximum value, and $H$ decreases for $t > t_0$. Let $\Delta H$ be the decrease in entropy between the times $t_0$ and $t_r > t_0$. That is,

$$\Delta H = H(I,t_0) - H(I,t_r). \tag{13.2}$$

If $\Delta H$ is the minimum quantity of information required to make a simple reaction to the stimulus of intensity, $I$, then $t_r$ is equal to or less than the simple reaction time. We speak later about the neuromuscular time lags which effectively guarantee that $t_r$ is less than simple reaction time, but, for the moment, let us ignore this time lag.

Introducing Equation (13.1) into (13.2),

$$\Delta H = \tfrac{1}{2}\ln(1 + \beta I^n/t_0) - \tfrac{1}{2}\ln(1 + \beta I^n/t_r). \tag{13.3}$$

Solving for $t_r$,

$$t_r = \left( \frac{1}{t_0\, e^{2\Delta H}} - \frac{1 - e^{-2\Delta H}}{\beta I^n} \right)^{-1}. \tag{13.4}$$

$t_r$ is taken as a function of $I$; $\Delta H$ is taken as a constant threshold information.

Interestingly, while $t_r$ looks as if it depends on four independent parameters, $\beta$, $t_0$, $n$, and $\Delta H$, it depends, in fact, on only three independent parameters, which may be seen as follows. Let $t_{r\,\min}$ be the minimum possible value of $t_r$. This minimum value will occur when the denominator on the right-hand side of Equation (13.4) is maximum, which will, in turn, occur when $I$ is maximum. Letting $I \to \infty$ in (13.4),

$$\boxed{ t_{r\,\min} = t_0\, e^{2\Delta H} }. \tag{13.5}$$

Let $I_{\min}$ be the minimum value of $I$ for which a response is possible (threshold value of $I$). As $I \to I_{\min}$, $t_r \to \infty$. That is, for $I = I_{\min}$, the denominator of the fraction on the right-hand side of Equation (13.4) approaches zero:

$$\frac{1}{t_0\, e^{2\Delta H}} - \frac{1 - e^{-2\Delta H}}{\beta I_{\min}^n} = 0.$$

Solving for $I_{\min}$,

$$I_{\min} = \left( \frac{t_0(e^{2\Delta H} - 1)}{\beta} \right)^{1/n},$$

(13.6)

or, equivalently,

$$\frac{t_0 \, e^{2\Delta H}(1 - e^{-2\Delta H})}{\beta} = I_{\min}^n,$$

(13.6a)

or, introducing Equation (13.5),

$$\frac{(1 - e^{-2\Delta H})}{\beta} = \frac{I_{\min}^n}{t_{r\,\min}}.$$

(13.6b)

Introducing Equations (13.5) and (13.6b) into (13.4),

$$t_r = \left[ \frac{1}{t_{r\,\min}} - \frac{1}{t_{r\,\min}} \left( \frac{I_{\min}}{I} \right)^n \right]^{-1},$$

or

$$t_r = \frac{t_{r\,\min}}{1 - (I_{\min}/I)^n}.$$

(13.7)

Equations (13.4) and (13.7) are mathematically equivalent, but from (13.7) we can see that $t_r$ depends only on three independent parameters, $t_{r\,\min}$, $I_{\min}$, and $n$.

We note, again, the appearance of the power function exponent, $n$. The ubiquitous $n$ seems to pervade all equations governing sensory function.

Equation (13.7), then, is put forward as the equation of entropy giving simple reaction time, $t_r$, as a function of stimulus intensity, $I$. We see that as $I$ increases in value, $t_r$ becomes smaller, the universally observed relationship between stimulus intensity and reaction time.

Let us return, now, to the thorny issue of the claim that the quantity $t_r$ has upon simple reaction time. Is $t_r$ the simple reaction time? $t_r$ is, by definition, the time taken for the $H$-function, measurable in an appropriate afferent neuron, to decline through a range $\Delta H$ natural units of information. This adaptation process occurs before reaction to a stimulus can occur. But, presumably, after the information, $\Delta H$, has been transmitted to the brain, a signal must be sent via the motor neurons from brain to muscle, after which the subject can signal her/his response. It would seem reasonable, therefore, to define $t_R$ as the simple reaction time (from stimulus onset to the motor act of pressing a button), and to act

$$t_R = t_r + t_{\text{lag}}. \tag{13.8}$$

$t_r$ is, then, the time for the adaptation curve to register (in sensory neurons) a decline, $\Delta H$, in entropy, and $t_{\text{lag}}$ is the delay time taking account of conduction time to the cerebal cortex, through motor neurons and synapses to muscle, and the contraction of muscle. Welford (1980) divides $t_R$ further into four divisions, and Halpern (1986) further analyzes $t_R$ into components that are significant for the human sense of taste. It would seem that $t_{\text{lag}}$ is an appreciable interval of time, so that

$$t_R > t_r. \tag{13.9}$$

If we introduce Equation (13.8) into (13.7),

$$t_R = \frac{t_{r\,\text{min}}}{1 - (I_{\text{min}}/I)^n} + t_{\text{lag}}, \tag{13.10}$$

giving $t_R$, a measurable quantity, as a function of $I$, with four independent parameters, the previous three plus $t_{\text{lag}}$. However, all attempts to curve-fit Equation (13.10) to simple reaction time data, using values of $t_{\text{lag}}$ that are greater than zero, have failed. Various investigators in different laboratories have tried to provide such a curve-fit, using simple reaction times to visual, auditory, and gustatory stimuli, but none has succeeded. Values obtained for the parameters are nonphysiological ($t_{\text{lag}}$ or $n$ negative) and are inconsistent between different sets of data. On the other hand, when $t_{\text{lag}}$ is taken to be zero, as in Equation (13.7), the results are usually quite satisfactory, as shown below. It is as if conduction in motor neurons occurred with infinite speed, which is, of course, absurd. It is particularly bizarre because Helmholtz introduced the measurement of reaction time specifically as a means of measuring neuronal conduction time, precisely the element that is here being ignored. The mystery may be linked to the findings of Libet (1985), as discussed by Norwich et al. (1989).

Equation (13.7) fits simple reaction time data very well (the reader may wish to look ahead at Figures 13.1 and 13.2). Because it is highly unlikely that neuronal conduction time can really be ignored, and because an additive $t_{\text{lag}}$ as in Equation (13.10) just does not agree with measured data, I suggest, tentatively, the modification shown in Box 13.1. This modification would allow for a time lag due to conduction time, while preserving the algebraic form of Equation (13.7). The "true" or neuronal values of $t_0$ and $\beta$ are diminished from their values as mea-

BOX 13.1    An Approach to the Problem of Conduction Time

Suppose that neuronal conduction time is introduced by means of a multiplicative factor, rather than by an additive term as in Equations (13.8) and (13.10):

$$t_R = t_r + t_{\text{lag}}. \tag{B.1}$$

That is, we let

$$t_0 \text{ (neuronal)} = \xi t_0 \text{ (simple reaction time)}; \tag{B.2}$$

and

$$\beta \text{ (neuronal)} = \xi \beta \text{ (simple reaction time)}, \tag{B2a}$$

where $0 < \xi < 1$. Then $t_0$ (srt) and $\beta$ (srt) are the values of $t_0$ and $\beta$ obtained by measuring motor or efferent responses in simple reaction time (Tables 13.1 and 13.2), while $t_0$ (neuronal) and $\beta$ (neuronal) are the values of these parameters as they would emerge from analysis of adaptation data obtained from afferent neurons. When $I$ is dimensionless, that is, measured in units relative to threshold, both $t_0$ and $\beta$ have the dimensions of time, so that Equations (B.2a) and (B.2b) suggest that there is a change in *time scale* between the *neuronal station* and the *behavioral station* (afferent neuron and simple reaction time).

The advantages of the transformation (B.2) and (B.2a) are as follows:

(i) In explaining that $t_{r\,\text{min}}$ (neuronal), as obtained by Equation (13.5), becomes $\xi t_0 \, e^{2\Delta H}$, which is less than $t_{r\,\text{min}}$(srt), which makes sense due to conduction delays.

(ii) In showing why an equation of the form of (13.7) fits simple reaction time data so well despite conduction time delays. That is, replacing $t_0$ by $\xi t_0$ in Equation (13.5) results in $t_{r\,\text{min}}$ being replaced by $\xi t_{r\,\text{min}}$ in Equation (13.7). $\xi t_{r\,\text{min}}$ is simply curve-fitted as a single parameter. The delay is "built into" the parameter, so to speak.

(iii) In showing why $I_{\text{min}}$ (neuronal), as obtained from Equation (13.6), remains the same as $I_{\text{min}}$ (srt) when $t_0$ and $\beta$ are replaced by $\xi t_0$ and $\xi \beta$, respectively, which makes sense, because minimum intensity for reaction should be independent of any time lags.

Since only $t_{r\,\text{min}}$ and not $I_{\text{min}}$ changes under the transformation, Equation (13.7) is transformed into

$$t_r(\text{neuronal}) = \frac{\xi t_{r\,\text{min}}}{1 - (I_{\text{min}}/I)^n} = \xi t_r(\text{srt}). \tag{B.3}$$

Equations (B.2) and (B.2a) are, then, equations postulated purely *ad hoc*, in order to account for a neural conduction time lag. They may be of use in converting time-dependent parameters $t_0$ and $\beta$ measured in an experiment on simple reaction time for use in a situation where conduction lag does not evidently occur.

The value of $\xi$ will vary depending on which station is used to determine $t_0$ and $\beta$. For simple reaction time, I am guessing that $\xi \simeq 0.5$. That is, about 50% of the minimum reaction time is due to neuromuscular conduction time and 50% is due to the neuronal adaptation process. This value of $\xi$ seems to give tolerable results when used with simple reaction times to visual stimuli and sodium chloride taste stimuli. Psychophysical or behavioral adaptation (decrease in subjective magnitude) also lags considerably behind neuronal adaptation. I put it to the reader to suggest a value for $\xi$ for behavioral adaptation relative to neuronal adaptation.

The disadvantage to the use of Equation (B.2) and (B.2a) is that the resulting Equation (B.3) is not readily interpretable in terms of current understanding of the physiology of the nervous system. Moreover, since $\beta$ is increased for reaction time by Equation (B.2a), apparent sampling rate is slowed. If fact, all time-dependent processes are slowed as we go from receptor to behavior, resulting in a spreading out of the curve of simple reaction time along the time-axis—a kind of relativistic time dilatation. Rosenblith and Vidale (1962, Figure 14) observed this phenomenon in responses to auditory stimuli. Behavioral response times (reaction times) spanned at least 100 to 300 ms, cortical response times spanned about 10 ms (see text as well as Figure 14), while earliest electrical responses in the auditory nerve spanned only about 2 ms. There is a mystery here, and Equations (B.2) and (B.2a) only transcribe the mystery into mathematical language. This "time dilatation" with approximate preservation of the amount of information transmitted is demonstrated explicitly in Figures 14.1a and 14.1b.

sured in reaction time data, using a multiplicative reduction or diminution factor, but the diminution factors are identical. The true or neuronal values are given by Equation (B.2) and (B.2a). All is not roses with this altered formulation, but it is the best I can suggest at the moment.

In the analysis that follows, we use Equation (13.7) with $t_r$ identified with the measured simple reaction time. However, if we attempt to obtain from reaction time data a value for $t_0$ that is compatible with data from sensory neurons, we probably have to use a diminution factor, $\xi$, as suggested in Box 13.1.

## DERIVATION OF ONE OF THE EMPIRICAL EQUATIONS OF H. PIÉRON

Piéron carried out extensive experimentation on simple reaction times for many sensory modalities. He fitted his data to many equations of convenience (Piéron, 1914, 1920). Frankly, I haven't even attempted to derive most of these algebraic forms from the informational equation. However, the one empirical equation that he presented in his text (Piéron, 1952) is easily derived from Equation (13.7), so I present the derivation here.

Piéron's empirical equation for simple reaction time is (Equation (3.26))

$$t_r = CI^{-n} + t_{r\,\min}, \tag{13.11}$$

where $C$ is constant. To derive it, we consider the case where

$$(I_{\min}/I)^n \ll 1. \tag{13.12}$$

The denominator of the fraction on the right-hand side of Equation (13.7) can then be expanded in a binomial series:

$$\left[1 - (I_{\min}/I)^n\right]^{-1} \simeq 1 + (I_{\min}/I)^n + \cdots \tag{13.13}$$

retaining only the first-order term. Hence, Equation (13.7) becomes

$$t_r \simeq t_{r\,\min}\left[1 + (I_{\min}/I)^n\right].$$

That is,

$$t_r = (t_{r\,\min}I_{\min}^n)I^{-n} + t_{r\,\min}, \tag{13.14}$$

which is identical with Piéron's Equation (3.26)/(13.11). Moreover, we can identify Piéron's constant, $C$, with the constant $t_{r\,\min} \cdot I_{\min}^n$. However, we must not forget that the derivation was based upon the approximation (13.12).

## THE CONSTANT $\Delta H$ FOR SIMPLE REACTION TIME

We do not know from *a priori* consideration the value of $\Delta H$, the minimum quantity of information necessary to react. However, I am prepared to put forward a conjecture based on a suggestion made several years ago by L. M. Ward in a personal communication. The conjecture is that $\Delta H$, the minimum quantity of information required to react to a stimulus, and, hence, the absolute informational threshold for detection of the stimulus, is equal to $H_{\max}$, the channel capacity for that stimulus, as measured in a *neuronal* adaptation process. That is, $\Delta H$ for reaction

= (magical number) $\simeq$ ln(6) = 1.75 natural units, or about 2.5 bits. I am making this conjecture because, as we see in the coming pages, it permits us to make accurate predictions for the senses of taste, vision, and hearing. However, the conjecture will force us, for the first time, to make a definite distinction between neuronal and behavioral adaptation processes.[1]

## EVALUATION OF THE INFORMATIONAL EQUATION FOR SIMPLE REACTION TIME

We proceed now to evaluate Equation (13.7) for two modalities: audition and vision. Later (see "Compiling a Common Set of Parameters for Taste of Sodium Chloride") we shall also evaluate Equation (13.7) for the sense of taste of sodium chloride.

### Audition

The data of Chocholle (1940) were analyzed. Subjects were requested to press a button as soon as possible after a tone was sounded.[2] The subjects were tested over a large range of sound intensities and over a wide range of frequencies. For a given frequency, reaction time, of course, was observed to decrease with increasing stimulus intensity. Chocholle's data for a 1000-Hz tone are listed in Table 13.1. $I$ is given in relative units of sound pressure (lowest pressure = 1.00).

TABLE 13.1   Data of Chocholle, Subject I, 1000-Hz Tone

| Sound pressure | Reaction time(s) measured | Reaction time(s) theoretical |
|---|---|---|
| $1.00 \times 10^5$ | 0.110 | 0.117 |
| $3.20 \times 10^4$ | 0.110 | 0.118 |
| $1.00 \times 10^4$ | 0.112 | 0.118 |
| $3.20 \times 10^3$ | 0.118 | 0.119 |
| $1.00 \times 10^3$ | 0.124 | 0.121 |
| 320 | 0.129 | 0.124 |
| 100 | 0.139 | 0.129 |
| 31.6 | 0.148 | 0.138 |
| 10.0 | 0.161 | 0.157 |
| 3.16 | 0.192 | 0.203 |
| 2.51 | 0.218 | 0.220 |
| 2.00 | 0.248 | 0.243 |
| 1.58 | 0.276 | 0.275 |
| 1.26 | 0.312 | 0.320 |
| 1.00 | 0.398 | 0.394 |

*Note*. Theoretical values were calculated from Equation (13.18).

The data were fitted to Equation (13.7) using the least-squares criterion, and the following parameter values were obtained:

$$t_{r\,\min} = 0.117 \text{ s}, \tag{13.15}$$

$$I_{\min} = 0.449, \tag{13.16}$$

$$n = 0.439. \tag{13.17}$$

With these parameter values in place, Equation (13.7) becomes

$$t_r = \frac{0.117}{1 - \dfrac{0.449^{0.439}}{I^{0.439}}} = \frac{1}{8.55 - 6.01I^{-0.439}}. \tag{13.18}$$

Chocholle's data together with the fitted function (13.18) are shown in Figure 13.1. We note that the values for $t_{r\,\min}$ and $I_{\min}$ are nominal, falling a little below the smallest measured values for $t_r$ and $I$, respectively. The value obtained for $n$, the power function exponent, is 0.439, close to, but less than, the value of about 0.6 expected from psychophysical experiments. A similar result was reported by Marks (1974).

Using the conductive delay factor suggested in Box 13.1, $\xi = 0.5$,

$$t_{r\,\min}(\text{neuronal}) = \xi t_{r\,\min}(\text{srt}) = (0.5)(0.117) = 0.059 \text{ s}, \tag{13.19}$$

using Equation (B.3). Alternatively, we can write from purely neuronal

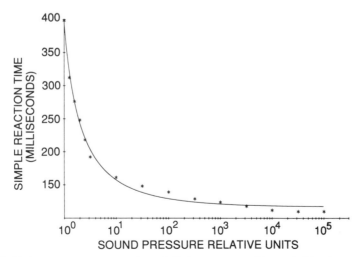

FIGURE 13.1    Data of Chocholle (1940) (Subject 1, 1000 Hz tone). Simple reaction time to an auditory stimulus. The data are listed in Table 13.1. The smooth curve was generated by Equation (13.18).

considerations, $t_0 = 0.002$ s (from Yates *et al.*, 1985, Figure 5), and $\Delta H = 1.75$ natural units, using the "channel capacity" conjecture, so that

$$t_{r\,min}(\text{neuronal}) = t_0\,e^{2\Delta H} = (0.002)\,e^{(2)(1.75)} = 0.066 \text{ s.} \quad (13.20)$$

## Vision

The data of Doma and Hallett (1988) were used. Subjects were required to track a target visually. The latency between the time the target moved and the time the eye moved was taken as a measure of reaction time. Subjects were tested over a range of light intensities,[3] for light of various wavelengths. Doma and Hallett's data for yellow–green light (564 nm) are given in Table 13.2. Again, the intensities are in relative units.

The data were fitted to Equation (13.7), which provided the following parameter values:

$$t_{r\,min} = 0.149 \text{ s,} \quad (13.21)$$

$$I_{min} = 0.0332, \quad (13.22)$$

$$n = 0.288. \quad (13.23)$$

TABLE 13.2    Data of Doma and Hallett, Yellow–Green Light, 564 nm

| Intensity of light | Reaction time(s) measured | Reaction time(s) theoretical |
|---|---|---|
| 100 | 0.163 | 0.165 |
| 31.6 | 0.173 | 0.173 |
| 10.0 | 0.185 | 0.184 |
| 3.16 | 0.208 | 0.203 |
| 1.00 | 0.239 | 0.238 |
| 0.794 | 0.244 | 0.248 |
| 0.631 | 0.262 | 0.260 |
| 0.501 | 0.277 | 0.274 |
| 0.398 | 0.291 | 0.291 |
| 0.316 | 0.305 | 0.312 |
| 0.251 | 0.335 | 0.337 |
| 0.200 | 0.364 | 0.369 |
| 0.158 | 0.414 | 0.411 |
| 0.126 | 0.475 | 0.476 |
| 0.100 | 0.543 | 0.547 |

*Note.* Theoretical values were calculated from Equation (13.24).

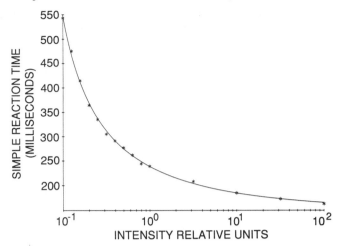

FIGURE 13.2   Data of Doma and Hallett (1988) (yellow–green light at 564 nm). Simple reaction time to a visual stimulus. The data are listed in Table 13.2. The smooth curve was generated by Equation (13.24).

When these parameter values are inserted into Equation (13.7), we obtain

$$t_r = \frac{1}{6.71 - 2.52 I^{-0.288}}. \qquad (13.24)$$

Doma and Hallett's data and the fitted function (13.22) are shown in Figure 13.2.

Again, the parameters $t_{r\,\min}$ and $I_{\min}$ take on proper values, just below the corresponding smallest measured values for $t$ and $I$, respectively. The value of $n$ is 0.288, very close to the commonly quoted value of 0.3.

We observe that the power function exponent, $n$, appears both in Equation (13.7) and in its approximation, Piéron's equation (13.11) and (13.14). People have often mused about the enigmatic appearance of an exponent of about the magnitude of the "Stevens" exponent appearing in an equation for simple reaction time. We can now understand why it appears in this position.

## THE INFORMATIONAL BASIS OF REACTION TIMES

The above discussion is, of course, predicated on the assumption that a fixed quantity of information, $\Delta H$, must be transmitted before a subject can react. Note that evaluation of two parameters, $t_{r\,\min}$ and $I_{\min}$, does not permit us to solve for unique values of the three parameters, $\beta$, $t_0$, and $\Delta H$. Nonetheless, as we see in our forthcoming analysis of the Blondel–Rey law, there is good evidence that the same set of parameters will describe both types of experiment. We also find below, that at least for the sense of taste of sodium chloride, we seem fairly close to having a single set of parameter values that will describe and predict all experimental findings.

Here, as is the case with the many other sensory equations developed in this book, no allowance is made for interindividual differences. Rather, a single equation is derived to represent a typical, or perhaps averaged, result.

Please recall that here, as elsewhere, we are utilizing a kind of conservation law for information. When $\Delta H$ units of information have been collected, a response is possible, etc. No mechanism for the mediation of reaction is provided. The shorter reaction time observed for a more intense stimulus follows from the properties of the $H$-function. Referring to Equation (13.1),

$$\frac{\partial H}{\partial t} = \frac{-\beta/(2t^2)}{1/I^n + \beta/t}, \tag{13.25}$$

so that for a given $t$, the larger $I$ becomes, the greater the value of the derivative $|\partial H/\partial t|$, and, hence, the more rapidly $H$ declines. *That is, stimuli of greater intensity transmit information at a greater rate than stimuli of lower intensity.*

The history of information theory as a means of explaining reaction time began some time ago when information theory was young. Hick (1952) analyzed the *choice reaction time* (cf. simple reaction time). A subject is required to make one selection from among $m$ choices, for example by pressing one lit key from among 10 keys. The choice reaction time was found to be proportional to $\log(m + 1)$, or, approximately, to the information required to press the correct key, giving rise to *Hick's law.* Hyman (1953) and Hellyer (1963) showed that the time required for a subject to react to a complex task is a linear function of the number of bits of information involved in the task. Colin Cherry, in his fascinating book (1957) describes and illustrates an experiment demonstrating Hick's law that the reader can try for herself/himself. The experiment is attributed to J. C. R. Licklider. A simpler experiment is suggested by Coren and Ward (1989), Demonstration Box 2-3. We can watch Hick's law at work by analyzing the data of Merkel (1885), as reported by Coren and Ward, p. 39. Merkel's data are plotted in Figure 13.3. It is seen that choice reaction time increases as the number of response alternatives increases. The smooth curve was generated by the fitted function

$$\text{choice reaction time} = 270.74 \ln(1 + m), \tag{13.26}$$

where $m$ is the number of response alternatives.

An interesting application of information theory is found in the papers of E. T. Klemmer (1956, 1957). Klemmer showed that simple reaction

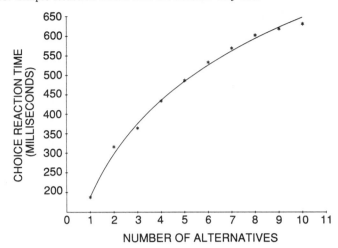

FIGURE 13.3    Data of Merkel (1885), demonstrating Hick's law. Choice reaction time is plotted against number of alternatives. The smooth curve is the logarithmic function given by Equation (13.26): if $m$ is the number of alternatives, choice reaction time varies as $\log(1 + m)$.

time varies with the subject's uncertainty *about the time of stimulus occurrence*.

Our present use of information in the analysis of simple reaction times differs from the above. We generate simple reaction time curves based on the assumption that $\Delta H$ units of information are required for a reaction, where $H$ is a function purely of stimulus intensity. In the quantized view of stimulus signals, more intense signals not only present greater uncertainty about the mean value of the signal, but yield or give up their uncertainty more rapidly upon sampling than do less intense signals (Equation (13.25)). In summary,

Hick:    Subjects react more rapidly to simpler tasks because less information is required to make a decision.

Norwich:    Subjects react more rapidly to more intense stimuli because information can be collected more rapidly.

## COMPILING A COMMON SET OF PARAMETERS FOR TASTE OF SODIUM CHLORIDE

Let us examine the constant, $\beta$, as it appears in Equation (9.19)/(13.1). The term $\beta I^n/t$ is added to unity, so that it is a dimensionless quantity. That is, $\beta$ has the dimensions of $t/I^n$. When intensity, $I$, is measured in relative units, it, too, is dimensionless, and in this case $\beta$ will have the dimensions of time. However, when $I$ is measured in more common laboratory units, such as moles per liter, the dimensions of $\beta$ become more complicated (Appendix). In this section, we work with simple, relative units of concentration of sodium chloride, so that $\beta$ will have the dimensions of time and, specifically, be in units of seconds. There is no curve-fitting in this section. We are trying to establish a *plausible* set of parameter values.

There is evidence that the "time scale" or "time range" of adaptation-dependent processes increases as one proceeds from the primary sensory afferents, through cortical events, to the behavioral or psychophysical report of the subject. For example, an adaptation process that requires, say, 60 milliseconds to go to completion in an auditory ganglion cell may require 60 seconds to go to completion behaviorally. Such a change in time scale is allowed for the $\xi$-factor $(0 < \xi < 1)$ introduced in Box 13.1. That is, $t_0$ and $\beta$, as measured, say, in an adaptation process in a ganglion cell, become $t_0/\xi$ and $\beta/\xi$, respectively, in a behavioral (psychophysical) adaptation process (decreasing subjective magnitude with increasing time). Conversely, we can use the $\xi$-factor to convert the value of $t_0$ found in an (behavioral) experiment on simple reaction time to a neuronal $t_0$-value.

$$t_0(\text{neuronal}) = \xi t_0(\text{behavioral}) \tag{13.27a}$$

and

$$\beta(\text{neuronal}) = \xi\beta(\text{behavioral}). \tag{13.27b}$$

For time in general,

$$t(\text{neuronal process}) = \xi t(\text{behavioral process}). \tag{13.28}$$

The result of such a transformation of variables is to leave invariant the quantity of information transmitted by an adaptation process measured at any station between primary afferent neuron and muscle effector (e.g., vocal activity providing psychophysical report), which may be seen mathematically as follows. Between time, $t_0$, and any time, $t$,

$$H(\text{neuronal}) = \tfrac{1}{2}\ln(1 + \beta I^n/t_0) - \tfrac{1}{2}\ln(1 + \beta I^n/t). \tag{13.29a}$$

Using Equations (13.27) and (13.28)

$$H(\text{behavioral}) = \tfrac{1}{2}\ln(1 + \xi\beta I^n/(\xi t_0)) - \tfrac{1}{2}\ln(1 + \xi\beta I^n/(\xi t)). \tag{13.29b}$$

The latter two equations are identical since $\xi$ cancels in Equation (13.29b);

therefore,

$$H(\text{neuronal}) = H(\text{behavioral}). \tag{13.30}$$

That is, it is possible to measure the same quantity of information from a neuronal process as from a behavioral (psychophysical) one. Moreover, from Equations (13.27a) and (13.27b),

$$\beta(\text{neuronal})/t_0(\text{neuronal}) = \beta(\text{behavioral})/t_0(\text{behavioral}). \tag{13.27c}$$

That is, the ratio $\beta : t_0$, whether measured neuronally or behaviorally, will be constant. The above approach will suffice for current purposes, but for further work we must seriously regard the matter of note 1, wherein the informational content of the two adaptation processes can differ.

Let us turn our attention now to $\Delta H$, which is an informational threshold. We learned in Chapter 12 that $\Delta H = \Delta F/k$ corresponded to that constant quantity of information transmitted with a change in subjective magnitude of one jnd. While $\Delta H$ was constant for each subject, the magnitude of $\Delta H$ was not fixed, but varied with the criterion used by the investigator to *define* the jnd. In the case of the Weber fraction for the taste of sodium chloride solution measured by Holway and Hurvich, we found $\Delta H = 0.126$ natural units.

The value of $\Delta H$ required for reaction to a stimulus, or the absolute detection of a stimulus, need not be equal to a quantity of arbitrary magnitude determined by the method of the investigator. Rather it can be determined by an average or mean, independent of any criterion imposed by the investigator (other than pressing the button). We postulated above the $\Delta H$ for absolute detection is approximately equal to the entire information capacity of the modality, or the channel capacity, represented by $H_{\max}$. As we have seen, this value has been cited as about 2.0 bits for taste, 2.5 bits for audition, etc.[4]

Finally, then, the proposed universal values for taste of sodium chloride.

There is very wide variation in the values of $n$ cited for taste of sodium chloride, extending from about 0.5 to 1.4. I have selected here $n = 1.0$, but I encourage the reader to experiment with other values of $n$. Other parameter values will change as $n$ is changed. Accordingly, $\Delta H$ (absolute detection) $\simeq 2.0$ bits $\rightarrow 2\ln 2 = 1.39$ natural units of information. $\Delta H$ for discrimination of the jnd was taken as 0.126 natural units, the value we used in Chapter 12. There is, of course, an arbitrary element to $\Delta H(\text{jnd})$, as discussed earlier.

The problem is, then, to find a value for $t_0$ (neuronal), which is the time following stimulus onset at which a neuronal adaptation curve will have its maximum amplitude (action potentials per second). Pfaffmann

(1955) studied the response of neurons in the chorda tympani of the cat, dog, and rat, and reported: "The activity of the chorda tympani initiated by applying taste solutions to the tongue is typically an asynchronous discharge of impulses. For an electrolyte like sodium chloride, the latency of the discharge is of the order of 30 msec; ... ." This value, however, is too great to permit the informational calculation of simple reaction times that are in accordance with the measurements made by Bujas for human beings in 1935. A value of $t_0 = 0.015$ s or smaller was necessary; $t_0 = 0.015$ s was adopted.

By inspection, because it tends to give the right answers, I selected $\beta/t_0 = 15$, when intensity, $I$, is measured in units relative to threshold $= 1$. Therefore, $\beta = 0.225$ s.

A proposed universal set of parameters for the taste of sodium chloride is, then

$$n = 1.0 \qquad \beta = 0.225 \text{ s} \qquad t_0 = 0.015 \text{ s.}$$

$$\Delta H(\text{absolute detection}) = 1.39 \text{ n.u.}$$

$$\Delta H(\text{discrimination of jnd}) = 0.126 \text{ n.u.} \qquad (13.31)$$

Using this parameter set, I submit, we can generate most, if not all, of the sensory functions of tasted sodium chloride solutions. Let's check it out.

Computing the value of the Weber constant

From Equation (12.6), the value of the Weber constant is given by $2\Delta H/n$. Substituting from (13.31) values for $\Delta H$ and $n$,

$$\text{Weber constant} = (2)(0.126)/1.0 = 0.25. \qquad (13.32)$$

This value compares favorably with the approximate value obtained from Holway and Hurvich's data, as shown in Figure 12.2.

Computing the equation relating simple reaction time to stimulus intensity

From Equation (13.5), dividing by $\xi$ to go from neuronal to behavioral,

$$t_{r\,\min} = (t_0/\xi)\, e^{2\Delta H} = (0.015/0.5)\, e^{(2)(1.39)} = 0.48 \text{ s.} \qquad (13.33)$$

From Equation (13.6),

$$I_{\min} = \left( \frac{(t_0/\xi)(e^{2\Delta H} - 1)}{\beta/\xi} \right)^{1/n}.$$

$\xi$ cancels, so that

$$I_{min} = \left( \frac{0.015(e^{(2)(1.39)} - 1)}{0.225} \right)^{1/1.0} = 1.0 \text{ relative units.} \quad (13.34)$$

When the above values for $t_{r\,min}$ and $I_{min}$ are inserted into Equation (13.7), the resulting curve can be compared with the experimental data of Bujas (1935). The predicted curve is not bad at all. A better fit to the data is obtained by making a small adjustment in the values of the parameters (best made manually rather than by least squares) so that

$$t_{r\,min} = 0.342 \text{ s,} \quad (13.33a)$$

$$I_{min} = 0.98 \text{ relative units.} \quad (13.34a)$$

The resulting curve, together with the data of Bujas, is plotted in Figure 13.4. Note that Equation (13.7) cannot be properly fitted to the data by a least-squares criterion *applied to the ordinate only* (that is, computing sums of squares of errors using "errors" in simple reaction time only, and ignoring "errors" in stimulus intensity), because of the extreme sensitivity of the curve fit to the data point with the lowest intensity.

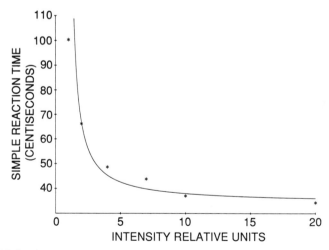

FIGURE 13.4  Data of Bujas (1935). Simple reaction time to a gustatory stimulus (sodium chloride solution). Intensity of the stimulus is plotted in concentration units relative to threshold = 1. The smooth curve is plotted using Equation (13.7) with $t_{r\,min} = 0.342$ s and $I_{min} = 0.98$ units, very close to the values obtained from the universal parameter set for taste of sodium chloride, Equation (13.31). The smooth curve has *not* been curve-fitted to the data by a least-squares method (please see main text).

Tiny errors in the abscissa of this data point changed the parameters of the curve fit greatly.

Further analyses of Bujas' data have been given by Norwich (1991).

Calculating the Weber fraction as a function of stimulus intensity

From Equation (12.6),

$$\Delta I/I = (2\Delta H/n)\left(1 + \frac{1}{(\beta/t)I^n}\right). \tag{13.35}$$

Substituting Holway and Hurvich's $t = 10$ s, as well as values for $\beta$, $\Delta H$, and $n$ from (13.31),

$$\Delta I/I = \frac{(2)(0.126)}{1.0}\left(1 + \frac{1}{(0.225/10)I^{1.0}}\right). \tag{13.35a}$$

If the above function is evaluated for $I = 1$ (threshold) to $I = 160$ (about 4 $M$ solution), the result is an approximation to the findings of Holway and Hurvich. The theoretical curve actually falls somewhat more rapidly than Holway and Hurvich's curve (Fig. 12.2), similar to the curve of $\Delta I/I$ for sucrose observed by Lemberger (Fig. 3.5a). If the reader wishes to check the match of the theoretical curve to Holway and Hurvich's data, I recommend changing concentration to molar units in the manner shown in the Appendix. Threshold $\simeq 0.025$ $M$ so that $\lambda = 40$. However, we are lucky, indeed, to even have an approximation here. We have used the neuronal value of $\beta$ (what value of $\xi$ should be used?) and have utilized Equation (12.6), a mode II equation, to describe Holway and Hurvich's experiments which were, in fact, conducted according to mode I (refer to Chapter 12, On the Physical Meaning of $\Delta I$).

Calculating the information transmitted by an adaptation process over $t$ seconds

Transmitted information for a hypothetical neuronal adaptation process is given by

$$H = \tfrac{1}{2}\ln(1 + \beta I^n/t_0) - H_{min}. \tag{9.19}/(13.1)$$

Setting $I =$ some intermediate value for concentration, say 10. relative units (corresponding approximately to 0.1 $M$), and selecting values for $\beta$ and $n$ from (13.31),

$$H = \tfrac{1}{2}\ln\left(1 + (0.225)(10)^{1.0}/0.015\right) - H_{min}$$
$$= 2.51 - H_{min} \text{ natural units.}$$

I do not know, *a priori*, the value of $H_{min}$ for neuronal adaptation to a sodium chloride solution, so I can go no further. A value of $H_{min} \simeq$ 1.3 n.u. would leave $H$ at about the right value. That is, one would expect that the steady-state firing rate of the neuron would be about one-half of its maximum firing rate.

Calculating the subjective magnitude as a function of time in an adaptation process

Let us recast the adaptation data of Gent and McBurney that we analyzed in Chapter 11 into relative concentration units. The 0.32 $M$ solution becomes 12.8 in units relative to threshold ($\simeq 0.025$ $M$). The value of $n$ obtained by Gent and McBurney for sodium chloride for their subjects was 0.5. Then we must select the value of 12.86 s for $\beta$, so that $\beta I^n$ becomes $(12.86)(12.8)^{0.5} = 46.$ s, which is the value we obtained by curve fitting (see Chapter 11). If $\beta = 15t_0$ (see above Equation (13.31)), then $t_0 \simeq 1$ s for the taste of sodium chloride. Psychophysically, taste intensity curves tend to rise for a few seconds (i.e., taste intensity builds for this time interval), so the calculated value of $t_0$ is, perhaps, tolerable.

Again, we are not curve fitting in this section. Rather we are trying to establish a plausible set of values characterizing the sense of taste of sodium chloride in all its manifestations, and the set suggested by Equation (13.31), with allowance made for the range of measured values of $n$, does seem to merit consideration.

## THE LAWS OF BLONDEL AND REY, OF HUGHES, AND OF BLOCH AND CHARPENTIER

While the intensities of stimuli for reaction time are at and above threshold, the intensities of stimuli used to demonstrate the law of Blondel and Rey, etc. are precisely *at* threshold. "How long," they asked, "must a stimulus of intensity $I'$ be held so that the stimulus is just perceptible?" However, despite this shift in the scale of intensity values, from the point of view of the entropy theory, the Blondel–Rey and its associated laws utilize the same variables and parameters as those used to define simple reaction time: stimulus intensity, $I$; duration of stimulus, $t$; as well as $\beta$ and $n$, $t_0$, and $\Delta H$. It seems reasonable that $\Delta H$, the minimum quantity of information required to perceive a stimulus in a Blondel–Rey experiment, would be the same quantity, $\Delta H$, needed to react in a simple reaction time experiment, since if you can detect the stimulus you can react to it. However, there is room for error in reasoning here.

Anyway, algebraically, the Blondel–Rey equation should be exactly the same as the equation for simple reaction time, with the terms rearranged, since all variables and parameters are the same. Here the unifying capacity of the entropy equation is in clear evidence. Let us just rearrange the terms in Equation (13.7) while introducing (13.5):

$$(I_{\min}/I)^n = 1 - t_0 e^{2\Delta H}/t_r. \tag{13.36}$$

In keeping with the nomenclature of Equation (3.25), let us replace $t_r$ by $t$, and $I_{\min}$ by $I_\infty$ (which has the same meaning), and $I$ by $I_{\text{thresh}}$. Then

$$I_\infty/I_{\text{thresh}} = \left(1 - t_0 e^{2\Delta H}/t\right)^{1/n} \tag{13.37}$$

or

$$I_{\text{thresh}}/I_\infty = \left(1 - t_0 e^{2\Delta H}/t\right)^{-1/n}. \tag{13.38}$$

When

$$t \gg t_0 e^{2\Delta H}, \tag{13.39}$$

we can expand the right-hand side of Equation (13.38) in a binomial series and drop terms of order higher than the first:[5]

$$\boxed{I_{\text{thresh}}/I_\infty = 1 + t_0 e^{2\Delta H}/(nt).} \tag{13.40}$$

If we now set the constant, $t_0 e^{2\Delta H}/n$ equal to $a$, we have

$$I_{\text{thresh}}/I_\infty = 1 + a/t, \tag{13.41}$$

which is the algebraic form of the Blondel–Rey law, Equation (3.25).

We have not really completed the derivation of the Blondel–Rey law (and its auditory analog which we have called "Hughes' law"), because the variable, $t$, which appears in Equation (13.41) represents time since stimulus onset, while $t$ in Equation (3.25) represents the duration of the flash. These two times are not equal, the former, time since stimulus onset at which information $\Delta H$ is transmitted via a *neuronal* adaptation function, will be greater than the latter, the duration of the flash. Therefore, the Blondel–Rey constant has been derived to be *not less than*

$$a = t_0 e^{2\Delta H}/n \tag{13.42}$$

$$= t_{r \min}/\text{power function exponent}. \tag{13.43}$$

*That is, the Blondel-Rey constant, in our unified system of equations for sensation, is approximately equal to the ratio of the minimum reaction time to a visual signal to the power function exponent ("Stevens exponent") for vision.* We can test the theory partially for at least one set of data, the simple reaction time data of Doma and Hallett (Table 13.2). Using the value of $t_{r \min} = 0.149$ from Equation (13.21) multiplied by the conduction factor, $\xi = 0.5$ (taking us from behavioral to neuronal adaptation), and power function exponent for a point source on dark background $= 0.5$ (Coren and Ward, 1989, Table 2.11), we have from Equation (13.43)

$$a = (0.5)(0.149)/0.5 = 0.149 \text{ s}, \tag{13.44}$$

or, from first principles, $t_0(\text{neuronal}) \simeq 0.002$ s (value from audition[6]); $\Delta H = 1.75$ n.u.;

$$a = t_0\, e^{2\Delta H}/n = 0.13 \text{ s}. \tag{13.45}$$

Since $t(\text{stimulus duration}) < t(\text{since onset}) = bt$, where $b < 1$, "true $a$" $= a/b > a$, referring to Equation (13.41). The range of values measured for the Blondel–Rey constant is given by Williams and Allen (1977, p. 43) as 0.055 to 0.35, so the values calculated by Equations (13.44) and (13.45) are in accord with the measured values.

Now, we may recall from Chapter 3 that Blondel and Rey observed that their law *contained* the law of Bloch and Charpentier. That is, in Equation (13.41), when $t$ is very small, the second term on the right-hand side dominates, so that

$$I_{\min}/I_\infty = a/t,$$

which is the Bloch–Charpentier law. Therefore, since we have *derived* Equation (13.41), we can do the same thing, thereby also deriving the Bloch–Charpentier law. Right?

Well, almost right. Don't forget that we have used inequality (13.39) in order to derive (13.41). If we let $t$ become too small, that is, if we use stimulus durations that are too brief, we violate this inequality. Again, taking $t_0 \simeq 0.002$ s and $\Delta H = 1.75$ n.u., we have $t_0\, e^{2\Delta H} = 0.066$ s, so that by (13.39) we must have $t > 0.066$ s and preferably $t \gg 0.066$ s for validity of our derivation, while the Bloch–Charpentier law is, apparently, valid experimentally for flashes much briefer than 0.066 s. Again, we must make allowance for the fact that $t > t_{\text{flash}}$.

## THE BLONDEL–REY LAW AND THE FERRY–PORTER LAW

We have seen in the previous section how we were able to transform the equation for simple reaction time into the Blondel–Rey law by simple algebraic manipulation. When the variables are the same and the parameters are the same, the laws must be mathematically identical. We try the same trick with the Ferry–Porter law, but we are in deep water—perhaps too deep. We deal here not with a single stimulus, but with multiple, sequential stimuli (flashes), which the entropy equation (13.1) was not constructed to handle. Between flashes, there is a process of dark adaptation, which is beyond our theoretical grasp at this moment. We must continue to deal with the variable, $t$, which is the time since stimulus onset rather than the flash duration. And we attempt to derive the curve for pure cone vision in the central fovea, although we lack definitive knowledge of the relevant $\Delta H$-values. However, the game can be fun anyway. If you would like to follow me where angels would, no doubt, fear to tread, please read on.

Again, a change in nomenclature. Let us represent $I_{thresh}$ simply as $I$. Then, Equation (13.40) becomes

$$I/I_\infty = 1 + t_0 \, e^{2\Delta H}/(nt).$$
(13.46)

When

$$t_0 \, e^{2\Delta H}/(nt) \ll 1$$
(13.47)

(cf. Equation (13.39)), then, using a Taylor series, we can approximate the right-hand side of Equation (13.46) by an exponential function:

$$I/I_\infty = \exp\left[\left(\frac{t_0 \, e^{2\Delta H}}{n}\right)\frac{1}{t}\right].$$
(13.48)

Taking logs of both sides,

$$\ln I - \ln I_\infty = \left(\frac{t_0 \, e^{2\Delta H}}{n}\right)\frac{1}{t},$$

or

$$(1/t) = \left(n/t_0 \, e^{2\Delta H}\right)\ln I - \left(n/t_0 \, e^{2\Delta H}\right)\ln I_\infty.$$
(13.49)

Ignoring, for the moment, the distinction between $t$ and flash duration, we write, for a flashing light with equal times for "on" and "off,"

$$\text{frequency} = 1/(2t).$$
(13.50)

$$\text{critical fusion frequency [CFF]} = \left(n/2t_0 \, e^{2\Delta H}\right)(1/\log_{10} e)\log_{10} I$$
$$- \left(n/2t_0 \, e^{2\Delta H}\right)\ln I_\infty.$$
(13.51)

This equation, then, does give the correct algebraic form of the Ferry–Porter law,

$$\text{CFF} = c_1 \log I + c_2,$$
(3.30)

and provides theoretical values for the constants, $c_1$ and $c_2$.

Informationally, Equation (13.51) states that a minimum time, $t$, must pass in order that a flash of intensity, $I$, may transmit a quantity of information, $\Delta H$. If this criterion is met, the flash can be discriminated, or seen "crisply." If the duration of time is less than $t$, the minimum "quantum" of information, $\Delta H$, will not be transmitted, and the flash either will not be visible or will merge with the next flash. A complete informational treatment of the Ferry–Porter law must take account not just of a single flash, but of the repetitive sequence of flashes and the process of dark adaptation between flashes. Such analysis is beyond the current scope of the theory. A complete theory must also take into account the distinction between duration and time since onset.

The slope of the straight line defined by Equation (13.51), obtained by plotting CFF against $\log_{10} I$, can be evaluated in one of two ways: $t_0 e^{2\Delta H}$ can be evaluated from reaction time data, or from first principles.

(i) Using data from simple reaction time with Equations (13.5) and (13.21),

$$t_0 e^{2\Delta H} = \xi t_{r\,\min} = (0.5)(0.149) = 0.0745 \text{ s}.$$

The $\xi$ carries us from behavioral to neuronal. Again taking $n = 0.5$, the slope of the straight line in a Ferry–Porter plot =

$$(n/2t_0 e^{2\Delta H})(1/\log_{10} e) = 7.73 \text{ s}^{-1} \text{ (srt)} \qquad (13.52a)$$

(ii) From first principles, $t_0 e^{2\Delta H} = 0.002 e^{(2)(1.75)} = 0.066$ s, so that

$$(n/2t_0 e^{2\Delta H})(1/\log_{10} e) = 8.72 \text{ s}^{-1} \text{ (first principles)}. \qquad (13.52b)$$

Hecht (1934) suggested that the observed values for slope tend to cluster about $11 \text{ s}^{-1}$ for images on the central fovea (no statistics were given), so the theoretical values are quite close.

We note that, in theory as well as by experiment, the slope of the straight line in the Ferry–Porter law plotted using common logs is approximately equal to the reciprocal of the Blondel–Rey constant (comparing Equations (13.40) and (13.51) and noting that $2 \log_{10} e \simeq 1$).

Again, here as elsewhere, we are plagued by the necessity of merging the results of experiments that are not quite compatible. We should value the results of a study on simple reaction times to light restricted to a narrow beam on the fovea, or $5°$ peripheral to the fovea, in order to calculate the slopes of Ferry–Porter plots made for the same retinal locus.

We observe that Equation (13.51) is valid, strictly speaking, only for values of $t$ permitted by inequality (13.47); that is, $t$ of the order of 0.13 s or greater (Equation (13.45)), corresponding at most to 3 Hz (!?). However, the Ferry–Porter law is observed experimentally to be valid for frequencies as high as about 50 Hz. That is, the theoretical equation (13.51) is valid over a range of frequencies much greater than we had any legitimate reason to expect. The theoretician's problem is usually quite the opposite of this: one can often not find experimental verification over the range of values for which an equation was derived. Resolution of this paradox may lie in the same quarters as before: $t_{\text{flash}} < t = t_{\text{neuronal}}$.

The above theoretical derivation of the Ferry–Porter law is very brief, requiring only about one page of development beyond the Blondel–Rey law. The reader is reminded, however, that this is a kind of conservational derivation, dealing with limits upon the rate at which information from a photon beam can be transmitted to a photoreceptor. A good deal of study has been made, and is being made, of the excellent papers of E. Hisdal, in an effort to improve the theory as it is presented here. The brevity of the theory, as put forth above, may be taken to imply that the author is ignoring the truly prodigious number of scientific papers dealing with flickering lights and the mechanism of flicker fusion phenomena. These papers have not been ignored: the diffusion theory of Ives (1922), the photochemical theory of Hecht and Verrijp (Hecht and Verrijp, 1933; Hecht, 1934, 1937), the multiple-stage models of Kelly (1961), and many more recent efforts. The reader is reminded that the informational approach *does not compete* with these models of mechanism; it *complements* the models of mechanism. The informational approach provides restrictions or guidelines governing the development of mechanisms of any perceiving system. *Mechanisms* of perception and sensation must develop (evolve?) within the limitations imposed by information transfer.


## BRIGHTNESS ENHANCEMENT

"Brightness enhancement" refers to "an increase in the brightness of an intermittent light over that of a steady light of the same luminance" (Graham, 1965). I have not even attempted to treat this phenomenon mathematically. Let me just remind the reader that within the informational or entropy theory, *variance* of light samples, rather than their mean, is the determinant of brightness. Therefore, a flickering light could, at appropriate frequencies of flicker, indeed, appear brighter than a steady light of the same luminance, since the flicker can in principle increase the variance of samples from the light beam.


## OLFACTORY THRESHOLDS

To conclude this chapter, we make a very approximate derivation of what is, in fact, a very approximate law, given by Equation (3.29). Taking common logs of both sides of Equation (13.6) and multiplying through by $n$ gives

$$n \log_{10} I_{\min} = \log_{10}\left[t_0(e^{2\Delta H} - 1)/\beta\right]. \qquad (13.53)$$

Is there any reason to think, now, that the quantity of the right-hand side of this equation should be approximately constant for all odorants?

We could argue the matter on theoretical terms, but I think the result would be inconclusive. The best one can say at the moment is that *if* $t_0(e^{2\Delta H} - 1)/\beta$ is constant, then

$$-n \log_{10} I_{\min} = \text{constant}. \tag{13.54}$$

Using the definition of $p_{\text{ol}}$ from Equation (3.28), we have

$$(n)(p_{\text{ol}}) = K, \tag{13.55}$$

which provides a derivation of Equation (3.29), the approximate law discovered experimentally by Laffort, Patte, and Etcheto, with support by Wright.

## CONCLUSIONS

In this chapter, we have pushed the entropy theory to its current limits to derive, among other sensory phenomena, simple reaction time as a function of stimulus intensity, the Blondel–Rey–Hughes law, the Bloch–Charpentier law, and the Ferry–Porter law (in part only).

One of the promising results of this chapter, I think, is the set of parameters characterizing the taste of sodium chloride (Equation (13.31)). A time-lag factor, $\xi$, may have to be employed (or a more cleverly formulated device that will allow for conduction delays), but, by and large, this parameter set has permitted us to account, in a quantitative way, for the results of nearly all sodium chloride taste experiments known to this author that involve a single, pure NaCl stimulus. It will be instructive to see if this data set will be capable of predicting the results of experiments not yet performed or unknown to this author. The theory presented does not seem to be capable of explaining the increase in simple reaction time with increasing taste stimulus duration reported by Kelling and Halpern (1983).

Perhaps the chief complexity introduced in this chapter relates to time scales. There were two distinct problems:

(i) Relating the time scale of behavioral events (such as simple reaction times) to the time scale of neuronal events (such as the adaptation in impulse rate at a ganglion cell). These scales have been related by means of the factor $\xi$, introduced in Box 13.1. The use of this factor is not completely satisfactory from the theoretical point of view, but it does seem to work.

(ii) Relating the time scale of neuronal events to the time scale of stimulus events (that is, time since onset to duration of stimulus). One must be mindful of the lessons taught in this regard by Ward (1991) psychophysically and by Wasserman and Kong (1974) neurophysiologically. Nonetheless, the algebraic forms of the laws of Blondel–Rey,

Bloch–Charpentier, and Ferry–Porter have emerged, *complete with theoretical derivations of their respective constants,* when "time since onset" replaces "duration of stimulus" in the respective equations

As we press the variables $I$ and $t$ through their complete physiological range of values, the question of the constancy of the parameters must be examined. If the parameters $n$ or $\beta$ were found to be functions of $I$, the formulation of the $H$-function as it was given in Chapter 9, would have to be reexamined. Whether $t_0$ is a function of $I$ is a moot point. Burke *et al.* (1987) found psychophysically for sodium chloride, quinine sulfate, and citric acid stimulation of the anterior tongue that "Higher intensity ratings were associated with faster onset times...," while Travers and Norgren, recording electrophysiologically in the nucleus of the solitary tract in rats (1989, Figure 2), seemed to show the opposite for sodium chloride stimulation of the anterior tongue and nasoincisor ducts.

We are approaching the end of our experimental evaluation of the entropy theory. Only some brief remarks on the exponent, $n$, remain for the next chapter. Although we have encountered the current limits to the theory in this chapter, one should not forget the extraordinarily wide range of observed sensory effects that have been captured by the theory: General sensory principles expressed by the law of sensation, the principle of adaptation, the Weber fraction, and simple reaction time; and the derivation of a host of special empirical laws, which we shall not enumerate here.

## APPENDIX: CHANGING THE UNITS OF THE PARAMETER $\beta$

Since $\beta$ occurs always in the combination $\beta I^n/t$, and $\beta I^n/t$ is dimensionless [occurring, as it does, in $\log(1 + \beta I^n/t)$], the dimensions of $\beta$ are those of $t/I^n$. That is, if we alter the units in which either $I$ or $t$ are measured, we must alter the value of the constant, $\beta$, accordingly.

Consider particularly a change in the units of $I$ from $I$ to $I'$. Suppose the change in units is governed by the constant, $\lambda$, so that

$$I' = \lambda I.$$

Then,

$$\beta I^n = \beta'(I')^n = \beta'(\lambda I)^n = (\beta'\lambda^n)I^n.$$

That is,

$$\beta' = \beta/\lambda^n.$$

For example, for taste of sodium chloride, with $n$ chosen as 1.3, if $I$ is measured in molar units, and $I'$ is measured in units relative to threshold = 1 unit, then $\lambda \simeq 100$ (since threshold is approximately 0.01 $M$).

Thus,

$$\beta' = \beta/100^{1.3}.$$

That is

$\beta$ (with $I$ in relative units) = 0.0025 $\beta$ (with $I$ in molar units).

$\beta$ (with $I$ in relative units) will have the dimensions of time.

## NOTES

1. The adoption of $\Delta H$ for reaction = $H_{max}$ compels us to make a distinction between the neuronal and behavioral adaptation processes, which we have hitherto regarded as "equivalent," adopting the symbol $F$ to represent both. When we analyze behavioral adaptation data, such as those of Gent and McBurney (1978), we find examples of perceptible stimuli that transmit fewer than $H_{max}$ bits of information, which would not be possible if $H_{max}$ were the threshold for absolute detection. Hence my insistence that $H_{max}$ units of information be transmitted by the corresponding *neuronal* adaptation curve. Thus we have postulated a distinction between the two types of adaptation process: the neuronal process transmits a minimum of $H_{max}$ units of information, while the behavioral process may reflect the transmission of less information. Evidence in support of this position may be found in Figures 11.6 and 11.7, which each depict neuronal adaptation curves for stimuli of three different intensities. In each of the three curves of Figure 11.6, ($F_{max} - F_{min}$) has about the same value. Similarly, in each of the three curves of Figure 11.7, ($F_{max} - F_{min}$) has about the same value. That is, the curves do not adapt to extinction. Since information, $\Delta H$, is equal to ($F_{max} - F_{min})/k$, approximately the same quantity of information is transmitted by the three stimuli of different intensities that generated each of the three curves. The three curves have different amplitudes, signifying different stimulus intensities, but transmit nearly the same quantity of information.
2. There are many variations in the way experiments to measure simple reaction time are carried out. For example, ready signals may indicate an impending stimulus (Kohfeld, 1969; Botwinick and Storandt, 1972).
3. The term "light intensity" is being used rather glibly here, where proper photometric units should be used. Preferable in most instances would be *illuminance* (millilamberts) or, perhaps, *retinal illuminance* (Trolands).
4. There are at least two problems that issue from the use of the absolute informational threshold, $\Delta H$. One is that the threshold

intensity, $I_\omega$, cannot, strictly speaking, be determined by eliciting an infinite reaction time. It can be determined, classically (e.g., Galanter, 1962), as the weakest stimulus that can still be detected ("reacted to") 50% of the time. Modulating factors can be allowed for using signal detection theory. Alternatively, one can use *neural-quantum theory* (e.g., Stevens, 1961, pp. 806–813). The second problem deals, perhaps, with even more profound issues. The two informational thresholds, $\Delta H$ (discrimination of jnd) and $\Delta H$ (absolute detection), have been found to differ substantially in magnitude of information. However, we can argue that $\Delta H$ (absolute detection), is, in a sense, the first or lowest jnd—that is, it is the amount of information needed to discriminate the smallest perceptible signal from the zero signal. Why should this jnd require a greater quantity of information than subsequent jnd's? There is something unique about the "first" jnd which I cannot, at this moment, understand.

5. We note that Equations (13.40) and (13.41) are independent of the parameter $\beta$, depending only on the parameters $n$, $t_0$, and $\Delta H$.

6. We note that in writing Equations (13.44) and (13.45) no distinction has been made between the parameters characterizing photopic and those characterizing scotopic vision.

## REFERENCES

Botwinick, J., and Storandt, M. A. 1972. Sensation and set in reaction time. *Perceptual and Motor Skills* **34**, 103–106.

Boynton, R. M. 1961. Some temporal factors in vision. In *Sensory Communication* (W. A. Rosenblith, Ed.) MIT Press/Wiley, New York.

Bujas, Z. 1935. Le temps de réaction aux excitations gustatives d'intensité différente. *Societé de Biologie, Comptes Rendus* **119**, 1360–1364.

Burke, D., Akontidou, A., and Frank, R. A. (1987). Time-intensity analysis of gustatory stimuli: Preliminary assessment of a new technique. *Annals of the New York Academy of Sciences* **510**, 210–211.

Cattell, J. M. 1886. The influence of the intensity of the stimulus on the length of the reaction time. *Brain* **8**, 512–515.

Cherry, C. 1957. *On Human Communication: A Review, Survey, and a Criticism*. MIT Press, Cambridge, MA.

Chocholle, R. 1940. Variations des temps de réaction auditifs en fonction de l'intensité à diverses fréquences. *l'Année Psychologique* **41**, 65–124.

Coren, S., and Ward, L. 1989. *Sensation and Perception*, 3rd ed. Harcourt Brace Jovanovich, San Diego.

Doma, H., and Hallett, P. E. 1988, Rod-cone dependence of saccadic eye-movement latency in a foveating task. *Vision Research* **28**, 899–913.

Galanter, E. 1962. The detection problem. In *New Directions in Psychology*, Holt, Rinehart & Winston, New York.

Gent, J. F., and McBurney, D. H. 1978. Time course of gustatory adaptation. *Perception and Psychophysics* **23**, 171–175.

Graham, C. H. (Ed) 1965. *Vision and Visual Perception*. Wiley, New York.

Halpern, B. 1986. Constraints imposed on taste physiology by human taste reaction time data. *Neuroscience and Behavioral Reviews* **10**, 135–151.

Hecht, S. 1934. Vision. II. The nature of the photoreceptor process. In *A Handbook of General Experimental Psychology* (C. Murchison, Ed.). Clark Univ. Press, Worcester, MA.

Hecht, S., and Verrijp, C. D. 1933–1934. Intermittent stimulation by light: III. The relation between intensity and critical fusion frequency for different retinal locations. *Journal of General Physiology* **17**, 251–268.

Hecht, S. 1937. Rods, cones and the chemical basis of vision. *Physiological Review* **17**, 239–290.

Hecht, S. 1943. Vision. II. The nature of the photoreceptor process. In *A Handbook of General Experimental Psychology* (C. Murchison, Ed.). Clark Univ. Press, Worcester, MA.

Hellyer, S. 1963. Stimulus-response coding and the amount of information as determinants of reaction time. *Journal of Experimental Psychology* **65**, 521–522.

Hick, W. E. 1952. On the rate of gain of information. *Quarterly Journal of Experimental Psychology* **4**, 11–26.

Hisdal, E. 1965. Information content of a beam of photons. *Journal of the Optical Society of America* **55**, 1446–1454.

Hyman, R. 1953. Stimulus information as a determinant of reaction time. *Journal of Experimental Psychology* **45**, 188–196.

Ives, H. E. 1922. A theory of intermittent vision. *Journal of the Optical Society of America* **6**, 343–361.

Kelling, S. T., and Halpern, B. P. 1983. Taste flashes: Reaction times, intensity, and quality. *Science* **219**, 412–414.

Kelly, D. H. 1961. Visual responses to time-dependent stimuli. II. Single channel model of the photopic visual system. *Journal of the Optical Society of America* **51**, 747–754.

Klemmer, E. T. 1956. Time uncertainty in simple reaction time. *Journal of Experimental Psychology* **51**, 179–184.

Klemmer, E. T. 1957. Simple reaction time as a function of time uncertainty. *Journal of Experimental Psychology* **54**, 195–200.

Kohfeld, D. L. 1969. Effects of ready-signal intensity and intensity of the preceding response signal on simple reaction times. *American Journal of Psychology* **82**, 104–110.

Libet, B. 1985. Unconscious cerebral initiative and the role of conscious will in voluntary action. *Behavioral and Brain Sciences* **8**, 529–566.

Luce, R. D. 1986. *Response Times and their Role in Inferring Elementary Mental Organization*. Oxford Univ. Press, New York.

Marks, L. 1974. On scales of sensation. *Perception and Psychophysics* **16**, 358–376.

Norwich, K. H., Seburn, C. N. L., and Axelrad, E. 1989. An informational approach to reaction times. *Bulletin of Mathematical Biology* **51**, 347–358.

Norwich, K. H. 1991. Toward the unification of the laws of sensation: Some food for thought. In *Sensory Science: Theory and Applications in Foods* (H. Lawless and B. P. Klein, Eds.). Dekker, New York.

Pfaffmann, C. 1955. Gustatory nerve impulses in rat, cat and rabbit. *Journal of Neurophysiology* **18**, 429–440.

Pfaffmann, C., Bartoshuk, L. M., and McBurney, D. H. 1971. *The Handbook of Sensory Physiology*. Vol. IV. *Chemical Senses.2. Taste* (Lloyd M. Beidler, Ed.). Springer, New York.

Piéron, H. 1914. Recherches sur les lois de variation des temps de latence sensorielle en fonction des intensités excitatrices. *l'Année Psychologique* **20**, 17–96.

Piéron, H. 1920–1921. Nouvelles recherches sur l'analyse du temps de latence sensorielle et sur la loi qui relie ce temps à l'intensité de l'excitation. *l'Année Psychologique* **22**, 58–142.

Piéron, H. 1952. *The Sensations*. Yale Univ. Press, New Haven.

Rabbit, P. (1987). Reaction times. In *The Oxford Companion to the Mind* (R. L. Gregory with O. L. Zangwill, Ed.) Oxford Univ. Press, Oxford.

Rosenblith, W. A., and Vidale, E. B. 1962. Neuroelectric events and sensory communication. In *Psychology: A Study of a Science* (Sigmund Koch, Ed.), Vol. 4, McGraw–Hill, New York.

Stevens, S. S. 1961. Is there a quantal threshold? In *Sensory Communication* (Walter A. Rosenblith, Ed.). Wiley, New York.

Travers, S. P., and Norgren, R. 1989. The time course of solitary nucleus gustatory responses: Influence of stimulus and site of application. *Chemical Senses* **14**, 55–74.

Ward, L. M. 1991. Informational and neural adaptation curves are asynchronous. *Perception and Psychophysics* **50**, 117–128.

Wasserman, G. S., and Kong, K-L. 1974. Illusory correlation of brightness enhancement and transients in the nervous system. *Science* **184**, 911–913.

Welford, A. T. 1980. *Reaction Times* (A. T. Welford, Ed.). Academic Press, London.

Williams, D. H., and Allen, T. M. 1971. Absolute thresholds as a function of pulse length and null period. In *The Perception and Application of Flashing Lights*. Adam Hilger/Univ. Toronto Press.

Yates, G. K., Robertson, D., and Johnstone, B. M. 1985. Very rapid adaptation in the guinea pig auditory nerve. *Hearing Research* **17**, 1–12.

# 14

## Odds and $n$'s, and the Magical Number $\mathrm{Log}\,(2\pi)$ Bits of Information

RETROSPECTIVE: THE GENEALOGY OF $F = kH$

With this chapter, we come to an end of the "Validation" block in the flow diagram of Figure 1.2. It is, perhaps, useful to take inventory of what has been accomplished.

Equation (2.6), $F = kH$, has been put forward by way of a postulate, relating the perceptual variable, $F$, to the entropy, $H$. Using a simple model of the stimulus signal, we derived

$$H = H(\beta, n; I, t) = \tfrac{1}{2}\ln(1 + \beta I^n/t). \qquad (9.19)$$

Combining Equations (2.6) and (9.19) gave us

$$F = F(k, \beta, n; I, t) = \tfrac{1}{2}k\ln(1 + \beta I^n/t). \qquad (9.20)$$

In Chapters 10 through 13, we subjected Equations (9.19) and (9.20) to a series of mathematical operations and, bearing in mind the interpretation of $H$ as an information, derived a host of laws of sensory science that had earlier been observed experimentally purely as empirical rules. We also derived theoretically a number of laws that have not been observed experimentally but might well be in the future. Schematically, much of these chapters might be summarized as in the "Genealogy" chart that follows (p. 248–9).

*F* JUST ABOVE THRESHOLD FOR DETECTION: DISTINCTION BETWEEN *F*(PSYCHOPHYSICAL) AND *F*(NEURAL)

We continue here our discussion of "*F* at the threshold," begun in Chapter 9. The equation $F = kH$ must be scrutinized at small values of

# THE GENEALOGY OF $F = kH$

## Constrain $F$ [$t$ constant]

$$F(\beta, n; I, t) = kH \xrightarrow[\substack{\beta \text{ moderate} \\ \text{to large}}]{t \text{ constant}} \quad \begin{array}{l} \text{FECHNER'S LAW} \\ \text{Equation (10.5)} \end{array} \left.\begin{array}{l} \\ \\ \\ \\ \\ \end{array}\right\} \begin{array}{l} \text{LAW OF} \\ \text{SENSATION} \end{array}$$

$$\xrightarrow[\substack{\beta \text{ moderate} \\ \text{to small}}]{t \text{ constant}} \quad \begin{array}{l} \text{POWER LAW} \\ \text{Equation (10.8)} \end{array}$$

## Integrate $F$ with respect to $t$

$$\int_0^t F(\beta, n; I, \tau)\, d\tau \longrightarrow \text{Observed measurements of total number of action}$$
potentials in time, $t$.

## Constrain $F$ [$I$ constant]

$F(\beta, n; I, t) \xrightarrow{I \text{ constant}}$ Observed psychophysical and neural adaptation functions.

## Difference between $H$-values

$$H_{t_{\text{high}}} - H_{t_{\text{low}}} = \frac{\Delta F(\beta, n; I, t)}{k} \xrightarrow[t_{\text{low}} \text{ to } t_{\text{high}}]{I \text{ constant}} \quad \text{Adaptation phenomena:}$$

CHANNEL CAPACITIES
from psychophysical
and neuronal data.

## $F$ evaluated for both ears simultaneously

$$F(\beta, n; I, t') = F(\beta, n; I_a, t) \qquad \text{(Equation (11.42))}$$
$$\longrightarrow \text{Equation governing SDLB (auditory adaptation).}$$

## $F$ unconstrained

$$F(\beta, n; I, t) \xrightarrow{I \text{ and } t \text{ both vary}} \begin{array}{l} \text{Simultaneous curve fits to multiple} \\ \text{sets of data using a single value} \\ \text{for } \beta \text{ and a single value for } n. \end{array}$$

$$\boxed{\Delta H \geq \text{constant for discrimination}}$$

## THE GENEALOGY OF $F = kH$—*Continued*

**Differentiate *II***

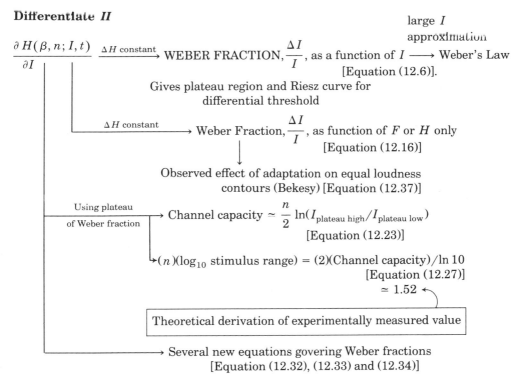

large $I$
approximation

$\dfrac{\partial H(\beta, n; I, t)}{\partial I}$ $\xrightarrow{\Delta H \text{ constant}}$ WEBER FRACTION, $\dfrac{\Delta I}{I}$, as a function of $I$ $\longrightarrow$ Weber's Law

[Equation (12.6)].

Gives plateau region and Riesz curve for
differential threshold

$\xrightarrow{\Delta H \text{ constant}}$ Weber Fraction, $\dfrac{\Delta I}{I}$, as function of $F$ or $H$ only
[Equation (12.16)]

Observed effect of adaptation on equal loudness
contours (Bekesy) [Equation (12.37)]

Using plateau
of Weber fraction $\longrightarrow$ Channel capacity $\simeq \dfrac{n}{2} \ln(I_{\text{plateau high}}/I_{\text{plateau low}})$
[Equation (12.23)]

$\hookrightarrow (n)(\log_{10} \text{stimulus range}) = (2)(\text{Channel capacity})/\ln 10$
[Equation (12.27)]
$\simeq 1.52$

Theoretical derivation of experimentally measured value

$\longrightarrow$ Several new equations govering Weber fractions
[Equation (12.32), (12.33) and (12.34)]

**$H(\beta, n; I, t)$ used purely algebraically**

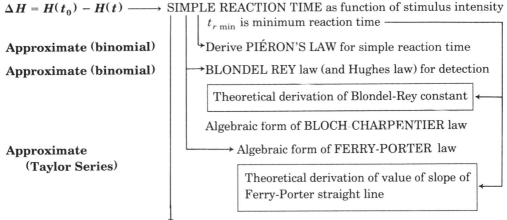

$\Delta H \geq$ constant for reaction OR conscious perception (detection)

$\mathbf{\Delta H = H(t_0) - H(t)}$ $\longrightarrow$ SIMPLE REACTION TIME as function of stimulus intensity

$t_{r \min}$ is minimum reaction time

**Approximate (binomial)** $\hookrightarrow$ Derive PIÉRON'S LAW for simple reaction time

**Approximate (binomial)** $\longrightarrow$ BLONDEL REY law (and Hughes law) for detection

Theoretical derivation of Blondel-Rey constant

Algebraic form of BLOCH-CHARPENTIER law

$\longrightarrow$ Algebraic form of FERRY-PORTER law

**Approximate
(Taylor Series)**

Theoretical derivation of value of slope of
Ferry-Porter straight line

If approximately constant parameters for odorants $\longrightarrow (n)(p_{\text{ol}}) \simeq$ constant

$H$. The theory, as developed in Chapter 13, requires that a minimum quantity of information, $\Delta H$, be received by the receptor before the perceiver (psychophysically) reaches the threshold of detection. Clearly, then, for $H < \Delta H$ at the receptor, we must have $F$(psychophysical) = 0. We seem to be led to the position

$$F(\text{neuronal}) = k'H(\beta; I, t), \qquad (2.6)/(14.1)$$

but

$$F(\text{psychophysical}) = kH(\beta/\xi; I, t/\xi), \qquad \text{if } H(\beta; I, t) \geq \Delta H,$$

$$= 0 \qquad\qquad \text{otherwise}, \qquad (14.2)$$

where $\xi$ is the time dilatation factor introduced in Equation (13.28).[1] Equation (14.2) is written in contradistinction to

$$F(\text{psychophysical}) = k\left[ H(I - I_0, t) \right], \qquad (14.3)$$

where $I_0$ is the stimulus intensity for threshold detection. There is no support for Equation (14.3) that is evident within entropy theory.

If $\Delta H$ were a "crisp" constant, involving sensory neurons acting precisely in concert, the relationship between $F$(neuronal) and $F$(psychophysical) would be as sketched in Figures 14.1a and 14.1b. However, such a model is simplistic. We have been proceeding, hitherto, using the simplifying assumption that many sensory neurons act precisely in parallel to produce the conscious or psychophysical effect. Allowing for slight asynchrony in the behavior of the parallel sensory neurons, and slight variation in the magnitude of the threshold (say $\Delta H \pm \varepsilon$, where $\varepsilon \ll \Delta H$), we would then expect a somewhat blurred peak to the psychophysical adaptation curve, as shown in Figure 14.1c. In this way we can account in a qualitative manner for the early rise found in adaptation curves of the psychophysical type.

In Figure 14.1c, we have a semi-quantitative explanation for the well-known Broca–Sulzer effect: at high light intensity (luminance) levels, the momentary brightness shortly after a flash of brief duration (0.03 to less than 1. s) appears greater (as much as fivefold) than the brightness of a maintained light stimulus (1 s or more) of the same intensity as the flash. The curve of Figure 14.1c is of the same form as those in Figures 5 and 6 of Broca and Sulzer's original paper (1902), which we can now interpret as adaptation curves. In fact, applying Equation (11.10) for adaptation data to the Broca–Sulzer curves of greater amplitude (far from threshold) provides an estimate of information transmitted per stimulus. For example, for Figure 5 we have, approximately,

$$\text{information} = \log_2\sqrt{0.5/0.03} = 2 \text{ bits/stimulus}.$$

Again, we have used duration of stimulus as an approximation of time since onset of stimulus, the variable used in the entropy equation.

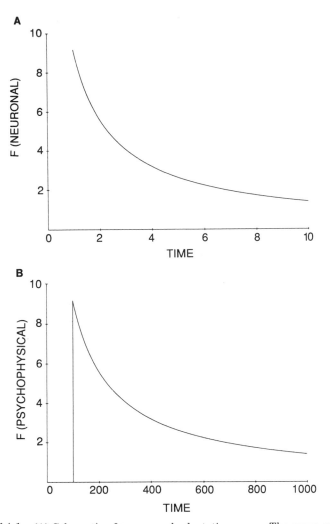

FIGURE 14.1 (A) Schematic of a neuronal adaptation curve. The curve was generated by Equation (11.3), $F = kH = \frac{1}{2}k \ln(1 + \beta I'^n/t)$, with $k = 10$ and $\beta I'^n = 1.5$. $t_0$, the earliest neuronal response, occurs at 1 unit of time. $\Delta H$, the total information transmitted by this adaptation process, can be determined using the methods discussed in Chapter 11. The information transmitted by the portion of the curve illustrated is, then, equal to $-\frac{1}{2}\ln[(1 + 1.5/10)/(1 + 1.5/1)] = 0.388$ natural units. (B) Psychophysical adaptation curve derived from the neuronal curve of (a) by use of a "time dilatation" factor, $\xi = 0.01$ (see Box 13.1). That is, using Equations (B.2) and (B.2a) from Box 13.1, we write $\beta$(psychophysical) $= (1/\xi)\beta$(neuronal) $= 100\beta$(neuronal), and $t_0$(psychophysical) $= 100t_0$(neuronal). Therefore, this curve was generated by Equation (11.3) with $k = 10$ and $\beta I'^n = 1500$, beginning with $t_0 = 100$ time units. We note that the psychophysical adaptation curve is identical in shape to the neuronal curve, but shifted forward in time, and spread out in time. We note also that the psychophysical curve does not begin until information, $\Delta H$, has been transmitted by the neuronal curve. That is, $t_0$(psychophysical) $> 10$ time units. The information transmitted by the psychophysical process is equal to $-\frac{1}{2}\ln\{1 + (1.5)(100)/1000\}/\{1 + (1.5)(100)/100\}] = 0.388$ natural units, as before. (A) and (B) are in keeping with the experimental findings: neuronal adaptation processes occur rapidly following stimulus onset, while psychophysical processes (conscious awareness of the stimulus) are delayed in time and dilated in time (cf. Chapter 13). Both types of adaptation curve, when analyzed by the methods of Chapter 11, yield the same value for transmitted information.

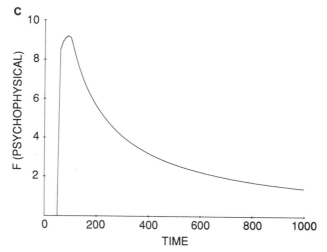

**C**

FIGURE 14.1 *Continued* (C) Recalling that no conscious awareness of the stimulus begins until the neuronal adaptation process has transmitted its capacity of $\Delta H$ units of information, and allowing that the psychophysical adaptation process relies on inputs from a number of neurons, there may be a range of thresholds, $\Delta H \pm \varepsilon$, which would have the effect of blunting the curve of (b) to give this effect. Curves of this type have been observed experimentally (e.g., Broca–Sulzer effect).

Equation (14.2) is still, in itself, not adequate because it presupposes that when the receptor finally receives information, $\Delta H$, the psychophysical response "jumps" suddenly from zero (imperceptible stimulus) to $kH(I, t/\xi)$, which may be substantially greater than zero. Such jumps at threshold are not in keeping with experience. We require, therefore, something like[1]

$$F(\text{psychophysical}) = k[H(\beta/\xi; I, t/\xi) - \Delta H], \quad \text{if } H(\beta/\xi; I, t/\xi) \geq \Delta H$$
$$= 0 \qquad \qquad \text{otherwise,} \qquad (14.4)$$

in keeping with Equation (9.22) and with the findings of Lochner and Burger (1961). This equation looks complicated because we are using neuronal $\beta$- and $t$-values with the time-expansion factor, $\xi$; but the equation just states that

$$F = k(H - \text{threshold}), \quad \text{if } H \geq \text{threshold}$$
$$= 0 \text{ otherwise.} \qquad (14.4\text{a})$$

This equation is struck by way of conjecture, because it eliminates the "jump start" of sensation and it seems to encompass much that we have learned about neuronal/psychophysical information receipt. There are, however, insufficient data available to test and refine the equation. So I leave it with the reader as the state of the art in the autumn of 1992.

## EXPANDING THE HORIZONS BEYOND "INTENSITY" AND "DURATION"

The sole independent variables used in the current theoretical development are intensity of the stimulus (regarded as constant) and time since onset of the stimulus. The cardinal dependent variable, the entropy, $H$, has been regarded as a function of these two variables only. While I think most readers would agree that the initial mathematical development has been complicated enough with just these two independent variables, there would also be tacit agreement that the experience of sensation and perception is considerably broader than single, monochromatic step functions.

There are many directions in which the entropic view of perception might be extended. We have seen in the previous chapter, for example, how simple reaction time is affected not only by the entropy of stimulus intensity, but also by the entropy of stimulus onset time (Klemmer's "foreperiod variability"). We have also seen that the entropy of the complexity of a task (Hick) affects reaction time. So the entropy of stimulus intensity is just one dimension of a multidimensional phenomenon.

We have regarded the "law of sensation," $F = F(k, \beta, n; I)$ [$t$ constant], as a function involving only three fixed parameters, $k$, $\beta$, and $n$, which is an egregious oversimplification. Even if we confine our attention to single, constant stimuli of physical magnitude, $I$, disregarding masking stimuli and the like, three fixed parameters will not suffice. Marks and Warner have shown brilliantly (1991) how *context* affects $F$, not just marginally, but emphatically, where context refers to the ensemble or set of possible stimulus values. Lockhead (1992) emphasized the importance of "assimilation" [subject's values of $F$(psychophysical) tend to reflect the value of $F$ in the trial just preceding]. So the constrained dependency of $F$ on just three parameters and two independent variables constitutes only a simplified beginning. I believe that the $F = kH$ concept will mature only when investigators carry it with them into the laboratory and design experiments to test and expand it.

In Chapter 17, we explore various other extensions and applications of the entropy concept of perception.

## THE EXPONENT $n$

I must confess to a certain antipathy[2] toward this exponent, $n$. I believe I have harbored this feeling of ill will ever since I found it necessary to introduce the exponent by means of the empirical equation (9.14). After all, one of the reasons for developing the $H$-function was to be able to replace a host of empirical equations with equations that were logically derived. And here, at the very base of the logical derivation, is just the sort of equation I was trying to get rid of.

"But no matter," I reasoned slyly. "I'll just hide the unsavory little $n$, multiplied and divided by a hoard of other parameters (you've heard of the 'lumped parameter model'; everybody uses them) in a new, synthesized parameter called '$\theta$' or '$\Lambda^2$' (Greek letters always lend an air of authority to your parameters), and no one will ever see the $n$ again!" But, as the fates would have it, the little demon, $n$, kept escaping from its parametric prison. No sooner would I bury it in a compound parameter[3] ($kn = a$, Equation (10.5, 10.5a)), then it would resurrect itself to stand alone in the Weber fraction (Equation (12.6)), and announce its primacy on the plateau of the Weber fraction in Equation (12.27):

$$n \cdot \ln(\text{range of plateau}) \simeq 2\delta H \simeq 3.5 \text{ natural units}, \qquad (14.5)$$

or

$$\text{range of plateau} \simeq e^{3.5/n}. \qquad (14.6)$$

I would hide its light under a bushel in Equation (13.6), making $I_{\min}$ the primary variable, only to find that the $n$ had immolated its bushel to appear again as a stand-alone parameter in the equation for simple reaction time (Equation (13.7)), and in Piéron's equation (13.14).

Would no one rid me of this troublesome power? I laid awake nights plotting, but my graphs came to naught.

If Equation (9.14) had been born of the marriage of logical ancestors, I would have no objection to the numerousness of its progeny. But the birth of $n$ in the illegitimate cauldron of empirical iniquity rankled me to my puritanical roots, as I suffered again its brazen countenance in the form of a fundamental variable in the Blondel–Rey constant (Equation (13.42)).

How far could $n$ drift from its humble origins in the power law of sensation? At least as far as the slope of the straight line in the Ferry–Porter law (Equation (13.51)). And, of course, the approximate law of olfactory thresholds would have to be

$$n \cdot p_{ol} = K. \qquad (13.55)$$

Well, if we cannot displace $n$, then more power to it! Let's explore various appearances of the exponent $n$ to see if its numerical values are consistent with each other. In particular, let's explore the values of $n$ measured for the sense of hearing.

# THE EXPONENT $n$ AT VARIOUS AUDITORY FREQUENCIES

We have learned that there are values of the exponent, $n$, that are characteristic of each of the modalities of sensation. The measured value of $n$ is, moreover, modulated within a modality by numerous factors such as the mode of measurement [magnitude estimation vs magnitude production (e.g., Meiselman *et al.*, 1972)] and the duration of the stimulus (e.g., Ueno, 1976, shows that $n$ for vision falls by a factor of about 40% for brief stimuli). The value of $n$ for intensity of pure tones also changes with the frequency of the tone tested. In classical psychophysics, $n$ can be measured only by carrying out an experiment relating subjective magnitude to physical magnitude (law of sensation). However, because of the appearance of the exponent, $n$, in many of the equations of the entropy theory, we are afforded the means of estimating the value of $n$ by various techniques that do not involve subjective magnitudes. One of the potential applications of the entropy theory of perception is this objective (or more objective) means it provides for the evaluation of the power function exponent. Comparing the psychophysical with the entropic evaluation of $n$ for audition provides a further experimental test of the validity of the entropy theory.

Let us examine three ways by which $n$ can be measured at different auditory frequencies.

## Measuring $n$ for Pure Tones Psychophysically at Many Frequencies

One could, of course, proceed as follows. At 1000 Hz, measure subjective magnitude, $F$, corresponding to many different physical magnitudes (sound intensities), $I$; plot $\ln F$ vs. $\ln I$, and calculate $n(1000)$. Then repeat the process at 2000 Hz to obtain $n(2000)$, etc. Equivalently, one can take advantage of charts and tables of equal loudness contours, such as those provided by Robinson and Dadson (1956), a technique that was used by Lochner and Burger (1962). In this method, one measures $F$ vs. $I$ only once: for 1000 Hz, giving $n(1000)$. Represent these measured $F$-values as $F(I_{1000})$ (see *sone* vs. *phon*, Evans, 1982). For example, when $I_{1000} = 80$ dB, $F(I_{1000}) = F(80$ dB$) = 15$ sones of loudness (say). Using the equal loudness contours, one can then find for 2000 Hz the intensities, $I_{2000}$, for which loudness is equal to $F(80$ dB$)$. This sounds more complicated than it really is. A glance at Table 14.1 should clarify the issue. Anyway, in this manner, we can plot a graph of $\ln F(I_{2000})$ vs. $\ln I_{2000}$, whose slope is equal to $n(2000)$. In similar fashion, we can obtain values of $n$ for all frequencies in the physiological range of hearing, using only one set of measurements of loudness. A graph of $n$ vs. tone frequency measured using equal loudness contours is given in

TABLE 14.1   Plotting Loudness Against Intensity for
Different Frequencies Using Equal Loudness Contours

| $I_{1000}$ (dB) | $I_{2000}$ (dB) | $F(I_{1000})$ |
|---|---|---|
| 10 | 7 | Loudness 1 |
| 20 | 17 | Loudness 2 |
| ⋮ | ⋮ | ⋮ |
| 120 | 110 | Loudness 12 |

*Note.* The third column lists loudness measured to correspond
with the sound intensities listed in column 1 (for 1000 Hz). The
second column lists (for 2000 Hz) sound intensities that are
equally as loud as those corresponding in column 1, obtained
from a graph or table of equal loudness contours. We could
proceed in this fashion to construct a column for every frequency desired in the physiological range. Plotting the loud-
nesses in the right-hand column against each of the other
columns in the table, in turn, provides a set of curves, each
defining the law of sensation at a certain frequency.

Figure 14.2. The slopes (values of $n$) were found by curve-fitting using a
simplex program.

Measuring $n$ for Pure Tones Using the Weber Fraction

The Weber fractions measured by Riesz (1928) for audition are well
described by Equation (12.6), which gives values of $\Delta I/I$ as a function of
$n$. In fact, Equation (2) of Riesz, which he used empirically to describe his
data, is identical with our Equation (12.6):

$$\Delta I/I = (2\Delta H/n) + (2\Delta H/n\gamma)(1/I)^{n}. \quad (12.6)/(14.7)$$

Riesz, using the symbol $E$ for our $I$, wrote

$$\Delta E/E = S_\infty + (S_0 - S_\infty)(E_0/E)^{r}. \quad (14.8)$$

By comparing Equations (14.7) and (14.8) we see that Riesz's $r$ is
equivalent to our $n$. Riesz gave empirical equations for each of $S_\infty$, $S_0$,
and $r$ as functions of frequency, $f$. We include these empirical equations
here for the sake of completeness.

$$S_\infty = 0.000015 f + 126/(80 f^{0.5} + f), \quad (14.9)$$

$$S_0 = 0.3 + 0.0003 f + 193/f^{0.8}, \quad (14.10)$$

and, most importantly,

$$n = r = \frac{244000}{358000 f^{0.125} + f^2} + \frac{0.65 f}{3500 + f}. \quad (14.11)$$

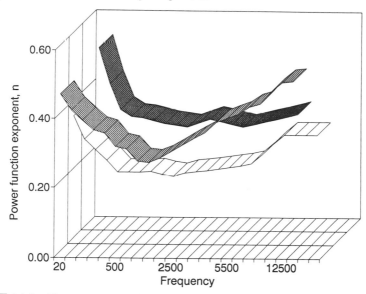

FIGURE 14.2    The exponent, $n$, for audition, plotted against frequency of pure tones, by three independent methods. (i) Front curve. Riesz measured differential thresholds (Weber fractions) for a range of auditory frequencies. He fitted his data empirically to an equation that we identify as our Equation (12.6), giving differential thresholds as a function of $n$. Hence, we can plot $n$ as a function of frequency. (ii) Middle curve. Chocholle measured simple reaction times for a range of auditory frequencies. By fitting his data to our Equation (13.7), we can find a value of $n$ for each frequency. (iii) Rear curve. $n$ is measured psychophysically for pure tones of 1000 Hz. $n$ is calculated for other frequencies using equal loudness contours.

Since Riesz measured the Weber fraction for a wide range of frequencies, $f$, we can, using Equation (14.11), obtain values of $n$ at any frequency within this range.[4] These values of $n$ are plotted against frequency in Figure 14.2.

Just a word on Riesz's place in history. Despite the relatively early date of his work (1928), Riesz's results for a single frequency have definitely been reproduced by later investigators. In particular, the reader is referred to Harris (1963, Experiment III: A Repetition of Riesz), and to the comparison of six groups of investigators shown by McConville *et al.* [1991, Figure 4(b)]. There is, however, some debate about whether $\Delta I/I$ changes as radically with frequency as Riesz's data indicate. Riesz used a method of beats to determine $\Delta I$, while other investigators have used a pulsed tone method (such as method II of Chapter 12). The latter method may have produced the muting of the frequency effect that Riesz had discovered. The pulsed tone results are contrasted clearly with the beat results as shown by Gulick *et al.* [1989, Figure 10.9(a)].

I also remind the reader that the mathematical method used to derive the theoretical expression for the Weber fraction in entropy theory,

Equation (12.6), utilized a small change in intensity, $\Delta I$, without introducing any adaptation effect ($t$ was held constant). That is, it was a quasi-static method and as such, it matched Riesz's experimental method rather closely, which probably accounts for the nearly exact matching of the numerical results.

## Measuring $n$ for Pure Tones Using Simple Reaction Times

We may see from Equation (13.7) that simple reaction time is expressed in terms of the parameter, $n$. Therefore, by measuring simple reaction time as a function of $I$ for each frequency of interest, 50 Hz, 100 Hz, ... we obtain, by curve fitting, measures of $n(50)$, $n(100)$. ... Fortunately, Chocholle (1940) published just such data giving simple reaction time vs. intensity for many frequencies. Equation (13.7) was curve-fitted to Chocholle's data at each frequency, using a simplex optimization program, and the resulting graph of $n$ vs. frequency is shown in Figure 14.2.

From the "ribbon graphs" in Figure 14.2, one can see that the exponent, $n$, varies in value across the range of auditory frequencies, and the graph of $n$ vs. frequency is quite similar when measured directly by psychophysical means, by means of differential thresholds, or by means of simple reaction times. There are differences between the curves, but I think that the general concurrence of $n$-values constitutes a very powerful experimental test of the entropy theory. Moreover, as stated above, it opens the door to more objective measurements of $n$ for audition using techniques that do not involve the use of subjective magnitudes.

## AN INTENSITY–FREQUENCY FORMULATION OF THE ENTROPY EQUATION FOR AUDITION

Our objective in this section is to try to discover an equation that gives two subjective measures, loudness and pitch, as a function of the independent variables intensity and frequency using the informational approach. To my knowledge, no mathematical relationship has been discovered by anyone, experimentally or theoretically, which achieves this goal. We do not achieve the goal here either. However, I present a rather natural reinterpretation of the entropy equation (9.20) that may carry some promise for an avenue of approach.

A steady pure tone can be described completely only when its amplitude, frequency, and phase have been defined. The intensity of the tone is related to its amplitude, and this is the only feature of the tone we have considered hitherto. However, a rather natural way to incorporate frequency into our entropic formulation is to regard $t$, the time variable, not as the time since onset of the auditory stimulus, but rather as an approximation of *the duration or periodicity of the dominant waveform*. In its simplest interpretation, this periodicity would correspond to that of Schouten's *residue* but, in principle, it need not be even that restrictive. We shall not stop here to define Schouten's residue theory of pitch perception. It is discussed very clearly by Wightman and Green (1974). Following this line of reasoning, we can redefine $t$ as $\Delta t$, the period of the residue or other dominant waveform. Thus, the entropy equation (9.20) takes on the new form

$$F = \tfrac{1}{2}k \ln(1 + \beta I^n / \Delta t). \tag{14.12}$$

Then, if $\Delta t$ is the reciprocal of the fundamental frequency, $\nu$, we have

$$F = \tfrac{1}{2}k \ln(1 + \beta I^n \nu). \tag{14.13}$$

Equation (14.13) probably produces more problems than it solves, but it is not without some saving graces. For $\nu$ constant, it reduces to

$$F(\text{loudness}) = \tfrac{1}{2}k \ln(1 + B_I I^n), \tag{14.14}$$

where $B_I$ is constant, not changing with $I$. This equation, then, describes the psychophysical law in the usual manner. It would not describe auditory adaptation phenomena, either monaural or binaural. For $I$ constant, Equation (14.13) becomes

$$F(\text{pitch}) = \tfrac{1}{2}k \ln(1 + B_\nu \cdot \nu), \tag{14.15}$$

where $B_\nu$ is constant, not changing with $\nu$. $F(\text{pitch})$, then, is given as a function of frequency, $\nu$, to the first power. This function is, in fact, precisely that found for pitch in experiments reported by Lindsay and Norman (1977):

$$\text{pitch} = 2410 \log_{10}(1 + 1.6 \times 10^{-3}\nu). \tag{14.16}$$

One can interpret $\nu$ as the frequency of Schouten's residue, but perhaps there is a more general interpretation of $\nu$, as demanded by modern theories of pitch (again referring to Wightman and Green, 1974). One must look for a physiological mechanism capable of extracting both intensity and pitch information from the combined equation (14.13). We recall that each equation, such as (14.13), that governs the transmission of information, is of necessity associated with a mechanism for transmission (Chapter 1). I leave these questions with the reader. Perhaps Equation (14.13) is just a curious transmogrification of Equation (9.20).

## DE-ADAPTATION

We have analyzed, in some depth, how the process of adaptation to a constant stimulus can be represented within the entropy theory, as a process of acquisition of certainty. However, not a word has been said about the informational process that takes place after cessation of the steady stimulus, resulting in loss of certainty and reversion, eventually, to a status of maximal uncertainty. This latter process might be called "de-adaptation." In studies of vision, it is "dark adaptation." Not a word has been written about this phase of sensation because I do not yet understand it. All attempts I have made to date to encompass the de-adaptation phase into the general theory have failed.

Related to the problem of de-adaptation is the problem of modifying the entropy equation to handle a time-varying stimulus. Some investigators have introduced stimuli in the form, for example, of sinusoids (Bohnenberger, 1981) and have measured the neuronal response. My students and I have not been able to predict the response to such time-varying stimuli from the response to the step input. I should add that it is possible to construct rather complicated and arbitrary criteria whereby a sensory receptor can determine whether a change in mean signal intensity (or variance) is due to random fluctuation in a steady signal (stationary time series) or due to a real change in the mean. The trick is to find a *simple* criterion.

## THE "MAGICAL" NUMBER 7: WHENCE AND WHY?

The "channel capacity" of a one-dimensional stimulus, as we have seen, is usually about 2.5 bits of information per stimulus, as determined in an experiment involving categorical judgments. For judgments of simple stimulus intensities, channel capacity seldom exceeds 2.5 bits and is often less. Since $2^{2.5} = 5.7$, the magical number is probably closer to 6 than 7 for our purposes. One of the most encouraging results of entropy theory has been the extraction of the maximum information per stimulus from simple adaptation data and the demonstration that this maximum stimulus information is very nearly equal to the corresponding channel capacity for that modality. A rather exciting possibility emerged in Chapter 13, when we were able to demonstrate that the threshold for intensity detection (*not* the threshold for intensity discrimination) was probably equal to the maximum information per stimulus. That is, the maximum information must be received by the neuron and signaled by $F$(neuronal) (Figure 14.1a) *before* the stimulus can be detected. Hence $F$(psychophysical) is displaced forward in time, as shown in Figure 14.1b. So we now do make a distinction between $F$ as measured neuronally and $F$ as measured psychophysically, but we do not yet have the whole picture.

However, whence arose the mysterious $\log_2 6 \simeq 2\frac{1}{2}$ bits of information? What is the theoretical meaning of this information capacity–information threshold? It is tempting to define this quantity of information (about 1.75 natural units) from Equation (12.27)/(14.5):

Maximum information per stimulus

$$= \tfrac{1}{2}n \cdot \ln(\text{range of plateau of Weber fraction}), \quad (14.17)$$

where, as always, *range* is equal to *maximum intensity of plateau* divided by *minimum intensity of plateau*. For example, for the sense of taste, range $\simeq 100$, and $n \simeq 1$, so that *maximum information per stimulus* is approximately equal to $(\tfrac{1}{2})(1) \cdot \ln(100) = 2.3$ natural units (which is a little high for taste). However, Equation (14.17) leaves something to be desired. It expresses the maximum information in terms of quantities, such as range and exponent, which are not elementary quantities.

Is maximum information per stimulus characteristic of the human species, or is it a limit imposed on all perceiving organisms? In a recent study by Norwich and McConville (1991), maximum stimulus information was calculated for insects and arachnids from adaptation data, and the values obtained were similar to the values found in the human species. If we encountered an intergalactic visitor, would its perception be limited to the same quantity of information per stimulus?

I have not been able to produce a perfectly general derivation of the magical number 6, despite the many years I have pondered it. There is, however, an interesting, although restricted, derivation that I would like to introduce.

I ask that you let your mind be plastic and stretch your thinking to encompass the idea of a hypothetical visual "perceptor," an abstract entity capable of perceiving light stimuli of low intensities. I am avoiding the term visual "receptor" because that term would admit a photoreceptor of the type found in a laboratory photometer or light meter, and I am interested in a unit which can perceive; that is, which can make a selection from among alternatives (Chapter 2) and signal its uncertainty in accordance with an entropy function. In particular, I ask that you consider a very sensitive visual perceptor, one that can detect even a single photon of light.

Let us use Equation (9.10) with $m$, the number of samplings, equal to 1.

$$H = \tfrac{1}{2} \ln\!\left(1 + \sigma_S^2/\sigma_R^2\right), \quad (14.18)$$

where $\sigma_S^2$ and $\sigma_R^2$ are the variances of the external light signal and the internal reference signal, respectively.[5] Since the distribution of photons in illumination of low intensity will be governed by the Poisson distribution, and the smallest nonzero mean is one photon, and since for the Poisson distribution, variance is equal to the mean, therefore variance is equal to one photon. If we approximate the Poisson distribution for discrete variables by a probability density function for continuously distributed variables, the variance must then take on the dimensions of the square of the random variable.[6] Let the continuous random variable be light energy, which occurs in bundles of energy, $h\nu$, by the quantum theory, where $h$ is Planck's constant and $\nu$ is the frequency of the light wave. Thus

$$\sigma_S^2 \simeq (h\nu)^2 \qquad (14.19)$$

corresponds to unit variance. Notwithstanding the fact that the Poisson distribution with unit mean is not well represented by the normal distribution, we introduce Equation (14.19) into (14.18) to obtain

$$H = \tfrac{1}{2} \ln\!\left[1 + (h\nu)^2/\sigma_R^2\right]. \qquad (14.20)$$

We now ask: What is the maximum value obtainable by $H$ (that is, the maximum stimulus information)? It would seem at first that we can make $\sigma_R^2$ indefinitely small, so that $H$ could become indefinitely large. However, on the quantum scale, our liberties are sometimes checked.

Just to be clear, the numerator, $(h\nu)^2$, represents the variance of the signal or stimulus or external photon (light quantum) and the $\sigma_R^2$ in the denominator represents the variance of the reference or "noise" or internally generated photon. We recall from Chapters 7 and 9 why the reference signal is held to be necessary when we deal with continuously distributed variables, although one might argue here whether our variables are discrete or continuous.

We invest our visual perceptor with no short-term memory; it can have no "recall" of the arrival of a reference photon in the past. Therefore, the signal photon and the reference photon must arrive at the perceptor simultaneously, since only in the presence of a reference signal can information be measured. This simultaneity will provide us with a restriction on the maximum possible value of $H$.

Since $\sigma_R^2$, like $\sigma_S^2$, is the square of an energy, we suppose that the reference signal, too, is carried by a single photon, or light quantum. Let us set

$$\sigma_R^2 = (\Delta E)^2. \qquad (14.21)$$

This equation, while seemingly a change in symbol, makes a statement of some physical significance. It states that the variance of the distribution of the reference signal, when applied to a single photon, is equal to the square of the "uncertainty" in the magnitude of the energy comprising this photon. Introducing Equation (14.21) into (14.20),

$$H = \tfrac{1}{2} \ln\!\left[1 + (h\nu)^2/(\Delta E)^2\right]. \qquad (14.22)$$

Now, the photon, or light quantum, is made up of a group of light waves that add together constructively and destructively to produce a *wave packet* that travels through space at the speed of light. Our photon of energy $h\nu$ will be made up by a wave packet which spans a length,

$$\Delta x = c \cdot \Delta t, \tag{14.23}$$

where $c$ is the speed of light and $\Delta t$ is the time taken by light to travel the distance, $\Delta x$. Bohm has shown[7] that $\Delta x$ must be at least as great as the wavelength, $\lambda$, of the photon, where, from the elementary properties of light waves,

$$\lambda = c/\nu. \tag{14.24}$$

That is

$$c \cdot \Delta t \geq c/\nu, \tag{14.25}$$

or

$$\nu \geq 1/\Delta t, \tag{14.26}$$

so that the frequency of the signal photon is equal to or greater than the reciprocal of the time taken by the wave packet to pass a given point in space. Since we seek the conditions for the near-simultaneous occurrence of two events (arrival of two wave packets: signal and reference), we therefore select the smallest possible value of $\Delta t$, corresponding to the largest possible value of $1/\Delta t$, which is equal to $\nu$, by Equation (14.26). Inserting

$$\nu = 1/\Delta t \tag{14.27}$$

into Equation (14.22),

$$H = \tfrac{1}{2} \ln\left(1 + \frac{h^2}{(\Delta E \cdot \Delta t)^2}\right). \tag{14.28}$$

We note that the expression $(\Delta E \cdot \Delta t)$ refers to the reference photon. $\Delta E$ is the uncertainty in its energy, and $\Delta t$, the time interval of spread of the wave packet of the signal photon, is also the time interval of spread of the wave packet of the reference photon, if the two packets are to arrive nearly simultaneously at the perceptor. Now, we know from Heisenberg's Uncertainty Principle[8] that

$$\Delta E \cdot \Delta t \geq h/(2\pi), \tag{14.29}$$

so that

$$\frac{h^2}{(\Delta E \cdot \Delta t)^2} \leq 4\pi^2. \tag{14.30}$$

Inserting the latter inequality into Equation (14.28), we have

$$H \leq \tfrac{1}{2} \ln(1 + 4\pi^2).$$ (14.31)

That is,

$$H \leq 1.850 \text{ natural units}$$
$$= 2.67 \text{ bits of information.}$$ (14.32)

The theoretical magical number is then

$$2^{2.67} = 6.36 \text{ categories,}$$ (14.33)

corresponding well to the empirical value of about 6.

Since $(1 + 4\pi^2)$ is quite close to $(2\pi)^2$, Equation (14.31) states that $H$, the maximum information obtainable by perceiving a stimulus of one photon, is given by

$$H \simeq \log_2 2\pi \text{ bits,}$$ (14.34)

or, in natural units,

$$e^H = 2\pi.$$ (14.35)

What does the above restriction on $H$ mean, physically? Referring to Equation (14.28), it means that if you try to increase the value of $H$ (maximum stimulus information) by decreasing the energy, $\Delta E$, of the reference signal,[9] you will find that $\Delta t$, the spread in time of the wave packet carrying the reference photon, will, of necessity, increase by Heisenberg's Principle, thereby frustrating your efforts to increase $H$. Referring to Figure 8.2 and Equation (14.22), we see that, very roughly, $H$ is the number of times the variance, $(\Delta E)^2$, can "fit into" the variance, $(h\nu)^2$, that is, the number of times the reference variance fits into the signal variance. Any attempt to increase $H$ either by increasing $(h\nu)^2$ or by decreasing $(\Delta E)^2$ will always fail.

How realistic is the above argument? Certainly, the visual perceptor is an entirely abstract concept, perhaps bearing no relationship to any real perceptual system. Constraining the argument to one signal photon is restrictive. Approximating the discrete Poisson distribution by the continuous Gaussian distribution is suspect. And, finally the insistence on a memoryless system, where signal and reference photons must arrive within the same time interval ($\simeq 1/\nu \simeq 10^{-15}$ s) would seem to remove the argument from the usual time scale of biological events. Nonetheless, the exercise compels us to examine the problem of maximum information carefully and demonstrates the critical nature of the reference signal. If we regard the light as composed of discrete particles, perhaps we might dispense with the reference photon, since we can calculate information for discrete events without necessarily subtracting a reference signal. But if light is regarded as continuous or wave-like, we must deal with continuous distributions, and the reference signal is required for calculating information. Once in place, the reference signal limits the maximum information transmission. The exercise is also worthwhile because it is as close as we have come to providing a mechanism for an elementary perceptual event. Electrons, scattered by the incoming photons, could be detected... but we have not come so far as to suggest a mechanism for generation of the reference signal, so our *perceptual unit* is incomplete.

## A BRIEF HISTORY OF THE "COMPLETE" LAW OF SENSATION

We borrow the term "complete" from Nutting (1907), and indirectly from Lehmann (1905) who referred to Fechner's law as "unvollständig," or incomplete.

Our Equation (10.3) was, of course, derived as an equation of entropy. But we have seen that an equation of similar algebraic form has been postulated as a law of sensation by various earlier investigators. Except for Békésy, I can find no evidence that these investigators were aware of each other's work.

In 1873, Delboeuf expanded Fechner's law to obtain Equation (10.20), which is a special case of our Equation (10.3), with $n = 1$.

In 1905, Lehmann wrote a neurophysiological equation of the same form as Delboeuf's.

In 1907, Nutting adopted Equation (12.11) as an empirical equation representing the Weber fraction for light. Equation (12.11) is of the same form as our entropic Equation (12.6). By integrating, Nutting obtained an equation very similar to our Equation (10.3) for the law of sensation of light. Nutting's process was the inverse of our own: We began with the law of sensation and differentiated to obtain the Weber fraction. Nutting's equation for brightness, given below, is constructed so that $F = 0$ when $I$ lies at the threshold level for detection:

$$F = F_0 \log\left[1 + P_m(I^n \cdot I_{\text{thresh}}^{-n} - 1)\right]. \tag{14.36}$$

In 1930, Békésy adopted the neurophysiological equation of Delboeuf–Lehmann, Equation (10.3) with $n - 1$ (please refer to Chapter 12).

In 1959, Ruston used the Delboeuf–Lehmann–Békésy equation empirically, with the addition of a constant (Equation (10.21); see Chapter 10).

In 1977, I derived Equation (10.3), a further generalization of the Delboeuf–Lehmann–Békésy equation, from entropic considerations (please see Chapter 9).

Are there other members of this strange family of *inconnus*?

NOTES

1. Actually, $H(\beta; I, t)_{\text{neuronal}} = H(\beta/\xi; I, t/\xi)_{\text{psychophysical}}$. The two $H$-functions have the same value because both $t$ and $\beta$ have been divided by the same factor, $\xi$, in the function on the right-hand side. Recall that in the $H$-function, we use only the ratio $\beta/t = (\beta/\xi)/(t/\xi)$. This idea is illustrated in Figures 14.1a and 14.1b.

2. Yes, I think that theoreticians can emote toward mathematical entities in much the same manner that normal people express emotions toward other human beings.

3. I particularly objected to its seeking refuge in my initials.

4. The symbol $f$ is used here for frequency, because it is the symbol used by Riesz. However, in the remainder of the chapter, we use the symbol $\nu$.

5. We recognize that the stimulus signal originates externally, or outside the organism, while the reference or "noise" signal originates internally, or within the organism.

6. We let the continuous probability density function be $p(E)$, where $E$ is the energy of incident light. The mean has the dimensions [energy] and the units $h\nu$, and the variance has the dimensions [energy$^2$] and the units $(h\nu)^2$.

7. Bohm (1989) has shown (pp. 92 et seq) that "whenever the light quantum [photon] is observed under conditions in which it is not absorbed, it cannot be localized to a region smaller than $\lambda$ [that is, one wavelength or time $1/\nu$]." The quantities in parentheses are mine, not Bohm's. To be rigorous here, we need a model of the perceptor's mechanism of simultaneous detection of the signal and reference photons. For example, if the photons each scatter an electron, detection of the scattered electrons could not localize the width of the wave packets to a region less than one wavelength. This restriction is important in our argument, since it, in concert with the Uncertainty Principle, ultimately fixes the magnitude of the maximum information transmissible.

8. Bohm (1989, Chapter 5.11) states that Equation (14.29) may be used only "in any process in which a quantum is transferred from radiation field to matter (or vice versa)." Aharonov and Bohm (1961) caution against the use of Equation (14.29) inappropriately to express "a further uncertainty relation between the *duration* of a measurement and the *energy transfer* to the observed system." Also, the Uncertainty Principle is sometimes written with a divisor of $4\pi$ instead of $2\pi$, which would increase our theoretical value for the magical number by a factor of nearly 2.

9. Actually, $(\Delta E)^2$ is the variance of the reference signal, but by decreasing the variance, you decrease the mean (from the Poisson distribution).

# REFERENCES

Aharonov, Y., and Bohm, D. 1961. Time in the quantum theory and the uncertainty relation for time and energy. *Physical Review* **122**, 1649–1658.

Bohm, D. 1989. *Quantum Theory*. Dover, New York. Published originally in 1951 by Prentice-Hall.

Bohnenberger, J. 1981. Matched transfer characteristics of single units in a compound slit sense organ. *Journal of Comparative Physiology A* **142**, 391–402.

Broca, A., and Sulzer, D. 1902. *Journal de Physiologie et de Pathologie Générale*. **4**, 632–640.

Chocholle, R. 1940. Variations des temps de réaction auditifs en fonction de l'intensité à diverses fréquences. *l'Année Psychologique* **41**, 65–124.

Evans, E. F. 1982. Basic physics and psychophysics of sound. In *The Senses* (H. B. Barlow and J. D. Mollon, Eds.). Cambridge Univ. Press.

Gulick, W. L., Gescheider, G. A., and Frisina, R. D. 1989. *Hearing: Physiological Acoustics, Neural Coding, and Psychoacoustics*. Oxford Univ. Press, New York.

Harris, J. D. 1963. Loudness discrimination. *The Journal of Speech and Hearing Disorders*, Monograph Supplement **11**, 1–63.

Lehmann, A. G. L. 1905. *Die körperlichen Äusserungen psychischer Zustände*. Part 3. *Elemente der Psychodynamik* (Translated by F. Bendixen). O. R. Reisland, Leipzig.

Lindsay, P. H., and Norman, D. A. 1977. *Human Information Processing*, 2nd ed. Academic Press, New York.

Lochner, J. P. A., and Burger, J. F. 1961. Form of the loudness function in the presence of masking noise. *Journal of the Acoustical Society of America* **33**, 1705–1707.

Lochner, J. P. A., and Burger, J. F. 1962. Pure-tone loudness relations. *Journal of the Acoustical Society of America* **34**, 576–581.

Lockhead, G. R. 1992. Psychophysical scaling: Judgments of attributes or objects? *Behavioral and Brain Sciences* **15**, 543–558.

Marks, L. E., and Warner, E. 1991. The slippery context effect and critical bands. *Journal of Experimental Psychology: Human Perception and Performance* **17**, 986–996.

Meiselman, H. L., Bose, H. E., and Nykvist, W. F. 1972. Magnitude production and magnitude estimation of taste intensity. *Perception and Psychophysics* **12**, 249–252.

Norwich, K. H., and Valter McConville, K. M. (1991). An informational approach to sensory adaptation. *Journal of Comparative Physiology A* **168**, 151–157.

Nutting, P. G. 1907. The complete form of Fechner's law. *Bulletin of the Bureau of Standards* **3**, 59–64.

Riesz, R. R. 1928. Differential intensity sensitivity of the ear for pure tones. *Physical Review Series 2* 867–875.

Robinson, D. W., and Dadson, R. S. 1956. A re-determination of the equal-loudness relations for pure tones. *British Journal of Applied Physics* **7**, 166–181.

Ueno, T. 1976. Luminance-duration relation in reaction time to spectral stimuli. *Vision Research* **16**, 721–725.

Wightman, F. L., and Green, D. M. 1974. The perception of pitch. *American Scientist* **62**, 208–215.

# 15

## Boltzmann and Berkeley

BOLTZMANN: $F = kH$ AND $S = -k_B H_B$

We now begin our philosophical climb up the left-hand side of the flow diagram in Figure 1.2. Although the equations are few, one requires some understanding of the ideas presented earlier in the book dealing with statistical mechanics, information theory, and the foundations of the entropy theory of perception.

The $H$-function we have been using in our sensory studies is an $H$-function of the type introduced by Shannon. $H$ (suitably constructed) can be interpreted as the uncertainty that precedes an event or as the information gained upon perceiving the outcome of the event. However, the manner in which we have utilized the $H$-function is quite different from the manner in which it has been used in communications science and in psychology. As we observed in Chapter 5, information theory as used in the latter disciplines is *nonunique* in character—that is, other measures of information are not interdicted—and *extrinsic* in its application. Extrinsic implied that the $H$-measure is used as a tag or label on a given channel, which might state, for example, "This channel has transmitted 100 bits of information." It was extrinsic to the physical operation of the channel in that no equation governing the physics of the channel contained the labeled $H$-measure as a variable. The extrinsic property of the $H$-function as used in communications science and psychology is best understood in contradistinction to the intrinsic property of the $H$-function as used in physics. In Chapter 6, we studied, in very preliminary fashion, the use made by Boltzmann of the $H$-function. If $H_I$ denotes the uncertainty of the human perceiver about which microstate is assumed by an ensemble of molecules, then Boltzmann could have written[1]

$$S = k_B H_I. \qquad (6.20)/(15.1)$$

That is, physical or thermodynamic entropy is equal to Boltzmann's constant (named in his honor after his death) multiplied by the $H_I$-function. Boltzmann's use of the $H$-function is both unique (no other function will do) and intrinsic. It is intrinsic because the $H$-measure *does* enter directly into an equation governing the physical state of matter.

The point of examining these concepts is to help put our fundamental equation,

$$F = kH, \qquad (2.6)/(15.2)$$

into some sort of perspective. The use of the entropy, $H$, in this equation is intrinsic, in the manner used by Boltzmann. The mathematical form of the $H$-function is unique: no mathematical function for $H$ differing substantially from Equation (9.19) will likely possess its power to embrace all the sensory processes examined in Chapters 10 through 15. It should be absolutely clear that the intrinsic manner in which the entropy/information concept enters our equations in this entropy theory of perception differs radically from the extrinsic use of entropy/information in communications science and psychology. Our use of the information concept in the analysis of psychophysical experiments is completely different from the manner which Garner and Hake described in their well-known paper in 1951.

In order to draw perceptual theory even closer to statistical mechanics, let us look a little more deeply at the famous mathematical function known as *Boltzmann's H-function*, $H_B$, which was introduced in Chapter 9. Boltzmann defined this function by means of the equation

$$H_B = \int \cdots \int f \ln f \, \delta v_\mu, \qquad (15.3)$$

where $\delta v_\mu$ is an element in $\mu$-space, as described in Chapter 6. The quantity, $f$, is the density of particles in $\mu$-space, that is the number of particles per unit volume of $\mu$-space. In fact, it can be shown (Appendix) that in an equilibrium state, apart from an additive constant,

$$H_B = -H_I, \qquad (15.4)$$

so that, from Equation (15.1)

$$S = -k_B H_B. \qquad (9.26)/(15.5)$$

Let us now compare Equation (15.5) with (15.2), referring to Table 15.1. We see that in both cases, the variable on the left-hand side of the equation ($S$ or $F$) represents a quantity which is measurable in the

TABLE 15.1   Comparing $H_B$ (Boltzmann's $H$) with $H$ (Shannon's $H$), and $S$ (Physical Entropy) with $F$ (Perceptual "Entropy")

| Entropy | $H$-function | Evolution of $H$ | Evolution of entropy |
|---|---|---|---|
| $S = -k_B H_B + \text{constant}$ | $H_B = \int f \ln f \, dv_\mu$ | $\dfrac{dH_B}{dt} \leq 0^*$ | $\dfrac{dS}{dt} \geq 0^\dagger$ |
| $F = kH + \text{constant}$ | $H = -\int p \ln p \, dx$ | $\dfrac{dH}{dt} \leq 0^\ddagger$ | $\dfrac{dF}{dt} \leq 0^\S$ |

*Note.* Discussion in main text. From the right-hand column, the evolution of physical or thermodynamic entropy in time proceeds in the opposite direction from the evolution of perceptual "entropy" (the quantity usually called the "perceptual variable"). $S$ and $F$ are analogous quantities.
  *As a consequence of molecular collisions;
  †Expression of the second law of thermodynamics;
  ‡As a consequence of the central limit theorem;
  §Expression of the principle of sensory adaptation.

laboratory: thermodynamic entropy in one case and, for example, neuronal impulse rate in the other. On the right-hand side, $k_B$, which is Boltzmann's constant, is (presumably) an immutable constant of nature, while $k$ is a constant that is quite different when applied in different contexts or in different sensory systems. $H_B$ is defined by Equation (15.3), while $H$ is defined by Equation (9.23), the symbol $p_{SR}$ being represented as $p$ for simplicity. The additive "constants" come from the discussion in the Appendix in one case and from Equation (9.25a) in the other.

Apart from minus signs, the difference between the two $H$-functions ($H_B$ and $H$) stems from the difference between the quantities $f$ and $p$. $f$ is the density of particles in $\mu$-space, while $p$ is the probability density of particles in what is usually regarded as configuration space (that is, ordinary, Euclidean, three-dimensional space). $H_B$ is usually taken as a measure of *disorder* (Chapter 9), while $H$ is related to the measure of *uncertainty*. If particles are clustered together in $\mu$-space, so that some cells are densely packed, while others are empty, the system is regarded as being in an ordered state, and the value of $H_B$ tends to be large. If we view $\mu$-space as the union of configuration space with "velocity space," the ordered state represents a concentrated gas in configuration space (for example, all molecules of the gas in one corner of a room), and a region of thermal nonequilibrium in velocity space. *Boltzmann's H-theorem* showed for molecular collisions that

$$\frac{dH_B}{dt} \leq 0. \qquad (9.27)/(15.6)$$

That is, $H_B$ can never increase. Therefore, an ordered state, with larger

$H_B$, will tend to evolve into a more disordered state with smaller $H_B$. Since $S = -k_B H_B$, we have (since $k_B > 0$) as a consequence of the minus sign,

$$\frac{dS}{dt} \geq 0, \tag{15.7}$$

which states the well-known rule that physical or thermodynamic entropy tends always to increase.

Now the $H$-function, *as we have employed it* in sensory perception, also begins at its maximum value (maximum uncertainty about the mean stimulus intensity) and then, if the perceptual process continues, decreases as a consequence of the central limit theorem. That is

$$\frac{dH}{dt} \leq 0. \tag{15.8}$$

However, since $F = +kH$ (no minus sign this time),

$$\frac{dF}{dt} \leq 0. \tag{15.9}$$

So physical entropy and the perceptual variable evolve in time in opposite directions. $S$ and $F$ are analogous variables. They are both laboratory-determined entropies that serve as measures of their respective $H$-functions. These items are summarized in Table 15.1.

Letting our imagination loose, we might evoke a comparison between the evolution of the universe and the evolution of a percept. The universe, it is thought, began with a big bang in a state of low physical entropy and is evolving ("adapting") toward a state of high physical entropy. In making a percept, we begin in a state of high informational entropy and ("evolve") adapt toward a state of low informational entropy. That is, the process of perception is a "big crunch."

## GEORGE BERKELEY: THE RELATIVITY OF PERCEPTION

... it does[2] not appear to me, that there can be any motion other than *relative*: so that to conceive motion, there must be at least conceived two bodies, whereof the distance or position in regard to each other is varied. Hence if there was one only body in being, it could not possibly be moved. This seems evident, in that the idea I have of motion does necessarily include relation.

The reader can, perhaps, identify the writer. My classes, when I read this passage, never fail to identify the writer as Albert Einstein. Einstein introduced what we now call the "special theory of relativity" in a paper entitled "On the Electrodynamics of Moving Bodies," published in 1905.

The above quotation, however, is taken from Section 112, part I, of "On the Principles of Human Knowledge," by George Berkeley, published in 1710, 195 years before Einstein's famous paper [refer, for example, to the volume annotated by M. R. Ayers (1975)]. Einstein, of course, carried the idea much further, and virtually reformulated our ideas of space and time in rigorous mathematical terms. Moreover, he was probably totally unaware of Berkeley's statement (at least I can find no evidence that he had read it) and not particularly sympathetic to Berkeley's theories of perception. Is it not, however, an arguable point that Berkeley was the first modern relativist?[3]

While I hope, in the future, to explore the link between $H_B$ and $H$ in more detail, it was not, as I have said earlier, by analogy to $S = -k_B H_B$ that $F = kH$ was written.[4] The $F = kH$ relationship emerged in my mind from considerations of the philosophy of George Berkeley.

Berkeley (1685–1753) cannot properly be condensed into a portion of a chapter, which is, nonetheless, all the space we may allow him here. Born in Ireland, educated in Trinity College, Dublin, he became a Fellow of that college in 1707. Berkeley made numerous contributions to philosophy. Perhaps best known of his works are "An Essay towards a New Theory of Vision" (1709), and "Principles..." first published the following year. It is with the latter opus that we are concerned.

Berkeley's ideas on perception cannot be appreciated fully without some understanding of the theories of John Locke, which preceded him. Locke proposed the existence of a single "substance" that constituted the essence of matter. The particles of which this substance was composed gave rise to perceivable properties such as solidity and motion, called *primary qualities*, and other properties such as color and sounds, called *secondary qualities*. Berkeley, however, denied the reality of the substance or substratum that could be postulated but never directly perceived. Berkeley functionally replaced the substance of a body or object by a Spirit, or an active being "possessing a will."[5] If the spirit or mind were to be removed, the body or object would then cease to exist. But let us permit Berkeley to speak for himself.

For as to what is said of the absolute existence of unthinking things without any relation to their being perceived, that seems perfectly unintelligible. Their *esse* is *percipi*, nor is it possible they should have any existence, out of the minds or thinking things which perceive them. **(Principles, Part I, Section 3)**

Some truths there are so near and obvious to the mind, that a man need only open his eyes to see them. Such I take this important one to be, to wit, that all the choir of heaven and furniture of the earth, in a word all those bodies which compose the mighty frame of the world, have not any subsistence without a mind, that their being is to be perceived or known; that consequently so long as they are not actually perceived by me, or do not exist in my mind or that of any other created spirit, they must either have no existence at all, or else subsist in the mind of some eternal spirit: it being perfectly unintelligible and involving all the absurdity of abstraction, to attribute to any single part of them an existence independent of a spirit. To be convinced of which, the reader need only reflect and try to separate in his own thoughts the being of a sensible thing from its being perceived.

**(Principles, Part I, Section 6)**

It is very obvious, upon the least inquiry into our own thoughts, to know whether it be possible for us to understand what is meant, by the *absolute existence of sensible objects in themselves, or without the mind*. To me it is evident those words mark out either a direct contradiction, or else nothing at all. ... It is on this therefore that I insist, to wit, that the absolute existence of unthinking things are words without a meaning, or which include a contradiction.

**(Principles, Part I, Section 24)**

*Esse* is *percipi*, wrote Berkeley. To be is to be perceived. Without a perceiver, there can be no existence. From Section 7, Part I: "Now for an idea to exist in an unperceiving thing, is a manifest contradiction; for to have an idea is all one as to perceive: that therefore wherein colour, figure, and the like qualities exist, must perceive them; hence it is clear there can be no unthinking substance or *substratum* of those ideas." So much, he thought, for Locke.

If to be is to be perceived, does the tree cease to exist when I cease to perceive it? No, replies Berkeley in Section 48. "For though we hold indeed the objects of sense to be nothing else but ideas which cannot exist unperceived; yet we may not hence conclude they have no existence except only while they are perceived by us, since there may be some other spirit that perceives them, though we do not. Wherever bodies are said to have no existence without the mind, I would not be understood to mean this or that particular mind, but all minds whatsoever. It does not therefore follow from the foregoing principles, that bodies are annihilated and created every moment, or exist not at all during the intervals between our perception of them."

Does God (the "eternal spirit") play the role of Perceiver-in-Residence, retaining the universe in existence even when you and I may slumber? Berkeley is not absolutely clear on this point. He followed his Principles by a set of Three Dialogues Between Hylas and Philonous. Hylas doubts, while Philonous argues spiritedly for the principle of relative perception. It is not necessary to have read the Principles to appreciate the verbal sparring of Hylas and Philonous. In Sections 251–252 of the Dialogues, Philonous advances a theory of a kind of two-tiered existence: "When things are said to begin or end their existence, we do not mean this with regard to God, but his creatures. All objects are eternally known by God, or which is the same thing, have an eternal existence in his mind; but when things before imperceptible to creatures, are by a decree of God, made perceptible to them, then are they said to begin a relative existence, with respect to created minds."

In this book, we are concerned with the second of Philonous' existences: relative existence with respect to created minds. God does not enter our secular equations explicitly as a Variable, nor do I believe that Berkeley ever intended Him in that role.

Berkeley was, perhaps, the first person whose Weltanschauung, or worldview, was completely dominated by what we in the twentieth century call the concept of relativity. He clearly foresaw the Einsteinian view of relativity of motion (the "principle of relativity"), as evidenced by Section 112, and he also comprehended in his *esse* is *percipi* "the relativity of existence."

I have never been able to refute the Berkeleian position that no meaning can be assigned to "existence" except within the mind of a perceiver. Moreover, I have always felt that as we, in the sciences, approach the core of the issue of perception, whether by the avenue of biology, psychology, or physics, we shall find Berkeleian relativity awaiting us. Specifically, whether describing the effects of a light flash through psychophysics, or the space–time trajectory of the quantum of light through physics, our equations of perception will contain, immanent within them, Berkeley's relativity of existence. I began thinking about these problems as a student, in 1959, and I have carried them with me ever since.

In the course of the preceding few pages we have probed Boltzmann's equations a little deeper, and we have tried to capture the gist of Berkeley's Principles. Still, you may have no sense, yet, of how Boltzmann's and Berkeley's ideas might merge. There is only a thin strand which might unite the two, a strand that I try to extend in the course of the next chapter.

## APPENDIX: THE NEAR-EQUIVALENCE OF $H_B$ AND $H_I$

$H_I$ has been defined for the equilibrium state by

$$H_I = \ln W, \tag{6.19}$$

and $H_B$ by the equation

$$H_B = \int \cdots \int f \ln f \, \delta v_\mu. \tag{15.3}$$

If we represent the integral by a summation, then

$$H_B = \sum_{i=1}^{n} f_i \ln f_i \, \delta v_\mu, \tag{A15.1}$$

where $n$ is the total number of cells in $\mu$-space. From the definition of $f$,

$$f_i = N_i / \delta v_\mu, \tag{A15.2}$$

where $N_i$ is the number of particles in the $i$th cell (cf. Chapter 6). Combining the latter two equations,

$$H_B = \sum_{i=1}^{n} (N_i / \delta v_\mu) \ln(N_i / \delta v_\mu) \cdot \delta v_\mu$$

$$= \sum_{i=1}^{n} N_i \ln N_i - \sum_{i=1}^{n} N_i \ln \delta v_\mu.$$

Recalling that

$$\sum_{i=1}^{n} N_i = N, \tag{6.18}$$

$$H_B = \sum_{i=1}^{n} N_i \ln N_i - N \ln \delta v_\mu. \tag{A15.3}$$

As found in Equation (6.23),

$$\ln W \simeq - \sum_{i=1}^{n} N_i \ln N_i + N \ln N. \tag{A15.4}$$

Since

$$H_I = \ln W, \tag{6.19}$$

we see from Equations (A15.3) and (A15.4) that if $n$ and $N$ are constant, then

$$H_I \simeq -H_B, \tag{A15.5}$$

ignoring additive constants. Therefore, from Equation (6.20),

$$S = -k_B H_B. \tag{9.26}$$

NOTES

1. Although Boltzmann *might have* written this equation in exactly this form, he did not do so. The $H_I$-function, as we have defined it, was not "invented" until after his death.

2. I changed *doth* to *does* to try to disguise the century of writing.
3. I am discounting Galileo for this honor, since what is termed "the Galilean principle of relativity" does not break with our intuitive notions of space. The historians of science may berate me here.
4. Moles (1966), pp. 22–23, anticipated the $S = -k_B H_B \Leftrightarrow F = kH$ relationship when he observed the similarity between Boltzmann's $S = k_B \log W$ and Weber–Fechner's $F = k \log I$.
5. An interpretation of M. R. Ayers (1975).

## REFERENCES

Berkeley, G. 1975. *Philosophical Works* (Introduction and notes by M. R. Ayers) Dent, London.
Garner, W. R., and Hake, H. W. 1951. The amount of information in absolute judgments. *Psychological Review* **58**, 446–459.
Moles, A. 1966. *Information Theory and Esthetic Perception*. Univ. Illinois Press, Urbana.
Tolman, R. C. 1979. *The Principles of Statistical Mechanics*. Dover, New York.

# 16

# Physiological Consequences of the Relativity of Perception

## PERCEPTION OF THE STATES OF MATTER: A PERSONAL REMINISCENCE

The problem, as I perceived it, was how to introduce the abstract philosophical ideas of an eighteenth century philosopher into the scientific laboratories of the twentieth century. In particular, how did the anatomy and physiology of sensory perception reflect the Berkeleian notions of the relativity of existence? I did not query *whether* they did, only *how* they did. Somehow, the organism invests the world about it with the property of existence since, if there are no perceiving organisms, there is no world (using the second of Philonous' states of existence and leaving God out of our equations). What constraints does this biocentric view place on the organs which mediate the process of perception? I was not successful in publishing my earliest thoughts on this subject (1965) until nearly two decades later.

The first paper on relative perception that I succeeded in having published (in 1972) was a somewhat truncated form of my 1965 effort, and was entitled "The Tactile Discrimination of Complex Systems." In this paper, the idea of "sensory receptor" is replaced by the idea of "sensory system," for purposes of exploring how the states of matter are perceived. What anatomical–physiological system is required in order to perceive by tactile means the states of solidity, liquidity, and elasticity?

In order to perceive by tactile means whether an object is solid, it was argued, a human perceiver will prod the object with her/his fingertip, pressing the object at first gently and then more firmly. When the object is pressed gently, and found not to yield to digital pressure, can the perceiver conclude that the object is solid? It would depend on his or her personal definition of " solidity," but generally, the answer would be no. A gel, for example, might not yield to very gentle digital pressure, but would not qualify for classification as a solid. If the substance being explored for solidity, such as my desk top as I write these words, does not yield under much firmer digital pressure, it will qualify as a solid. Now, as one presses firmly on the solid surface with her/his fingertip, there is compression of the tissues in the fingertip. Skin, subcutaneous tissue, and blood vessels are compressed until the solid object is placed in close apposition to the terminal phalanx (bone) of the finger. It would seem that we perceive solidity of state only when we invoke the solid tissue of the body. The tactile discrimination of the state of solidity is made only when the external object and the solid elements of the perceiving system are made contiguous. In brief, we need a solid to perceive a solid. Or, turning the matter around to express it from a biocentric point of view, we invest the world with the property of solidness only by possessing the anatomical property of solidness. By extrapolation, we might state that one can never perceive a degree of hardness in excess of the hardness of bone in the finger (cf. Mohs' scale of hardness). It might also be argued that organisms without solid elements in their bodies cannot be capable of perceiving, by tactile means, the state of solidity.

Similar considerations can be extended to the tactile perception of the state of liquidity. Consider the experiment of Meissner (cited by Ruch and Fulton, 1960, p. 314), where the finger is immersed into a vessel of mercury. Meissner showed that the sense of pressure does not issue from the submerged portions of the finger, but only at the interface between air and mercury. Now, where the finger is immersed in the liquid mercury, the immersed portion is compressed and, presumably, the volume of the immersed part is reduced. The reduction in volume will occur because blood and possibly interstitial fluid will be displaced proximally within the digit (that is, in a direction away from the tip). At the boundary between the submerged and nonsubmerged portions of the digit, tissue is deformed slightly, which activates the mechanoreceptors. The point of this discussion is that when the perceptual apparatus is regarded as a *system*, of which the mechanoreceptors are only one part, it may be seen that the liquid elements of the fingertip must "interact" with the liquid (mercury) in order to enable the perception of the state of liquidity. A slightly more extensive argument is provided in the original paper.

In similar fashion, one might expect that only by virtue of elastic elements, such as found in muscle tendons, can one perceive the property of elasticity as found, say, in an elastic band. And, although it is not a state of matter, to perceive the magnitude of a force, one must oppose the force with a force of equal and opposite magnitude, as required by Newton's third law.

The above examples do not define a perceptual principle "crisply." Rather, they are suggestive. They suggest that not only the sensory receptor with its neural connections, but a host of other anatomical components as well, all play critical roles in the perception of the states of matter. They suggest that we deal with an entire perceptual system, rather than just with a sensory receptor. The term *perceptual unit* has already been introduced (Chapter 13), and we come to use the term to mean *the smallest and simplest configuration of anatomical structures required to mediate the process of perception in some modality*. We see even at this stage that the perceptual unit comprises more than just the receptor–neuron complex, since bone and even blood play their part in perception of the states of matter. The composition of the perceptual unit will depend on exactly what is meant by a "modality"; for example, does the perception of the solid state qualify as a modality?

However, the states of matter examples, I think, convey a more profound message. They demonstrate, albeit in a rudimentary way, a manner in which the perceived world exists "relative to" the perceiving organism. We can say, as above, that only by the interplay of solid tissue with solid matter can solid matter be perceived. Or, we can say that solid matter can only exist *relative to* the perceiving organism if the latter is constructed of solid elements. However, this idea cannot be pushed too far in its present, elementary state. Can we not, as human beings, perceive, or "gain mental apprehension of"[1] infrared radiation, even though we cannot see it directly with our eyes? Can we not, using machines, gain apprehension of the hardness of materials that exceeds the hardness of our own tissues? Does "perception" only mean mental apprehension by direct exposure? And what does "direct" mean? More questions than answers. For me, however, these states of matter examples served just to convey a sense of reciprocity between the perceiver and the perceived and were only a first glimmer of the required anatomical–physiological mandate for Berkeleian perceptual relativity.

I must mention that this idea of reciprocity probably predates Berkeley and is found, embryonically, in the works of the philosopher Baruch Spinoza (1632–1677). Wrote Spinoza (1951) in *The Ethics*, Part II, Proposition XVI, Corollary II: "It follows, secondly, that *the ideas, which we have of external bodies, indicate rather the constitution of our own body* than the nature of external bodies. I have amply illustrated this in the Appendix to Part I." (My italics.)

For the sake of completeness, I refer the reader also to the book by G. Spencer Brown (1969) entitled *Laws of Form*. Much have I travailed with this book in an effort to determine whether the author renders into mathematical form some of the ideas of the reciprocity between perceiver and perceived that have been introduced in the states of matter examples. There is always a tendency for the undirected reader to rush foremost into the least mathematical chapters of a book (as I fear people will do to the current chapter of my own book). This tendency should be resisted, because the sense of comprehension that may be engendered by such activity is specious. So I recommend that only after paying one's dues by studying Spencer Brown's calculus in the early chapters of the book, particular attention be paid to Chapter 12, and especially his "fourth experiment." Note also his Introduction, p. xvii.

The reader is also referred to the paper on active touch by J. J. Gibson (1962).

## ORIGIN OF THE ENTROPY THEORY

The states of matter argument was suggestive of the manner in which Berkeleian relativity of perception interfaced with biology, but it did not suggest to me a mathematical formalism by which one might proceed. If neuronal activity was the language spoken by sensory receptor to brain, then afferent neuronal language must, I felt, be the scientific language of Berkeleian philosophy. If that were the case, though, afferent neuronal language (say neural impulse frequency) must, in some way, express the relativity of the perceived world to the perceptual unit. Such a state of relativity might be true at a trivial level, in that different sensory receptors may be in different states of adaptation, and their respective afferents firing at different rates accordingly, but I was seeking a connection that was a little more profound.

Some years passed as I reviewed one scheme after another for importing the property of "relativity" to afferent neurons. Mathematical models came cheaply, but those models that "went through" could not be purchased. That is, the early models did not breathe life into the study of perception. The realization that information theory came off the shelf, fully equipped with a relative component took rather a long time to crystallize in my mind. When dealing with discrete variables, the entropy, $H$, is a function of the *a priori* probabilities, $p_i$, in accordance with Equation (2.1). Thus, different perceivers with different values for these *a priori* probabilities would obtain different amounts of information by perceiving the outcome of an event. You may recall the example from Chapter 2 (Information: Defined) about the biased coin that would fall heads 2/3 of the time. The perceiver who was aware of the bias received less information from the outcome of the toss of this coin than the perceiver who believed that the coin was a fair one. So information received was relative to the assumed set of probabilities, $p_i$.

If information theory were the mathematical medium by which Berkeleian relativity was to be linked to the biological process of perceiving, then the relative variable, information must be carried by the afferent neuron, which relays sensory messages to the brain. Designating the neuronal firing rate by $F$ (which is how the letter $F$ came originally to be selected), it was then necessary that $F$ be a mathematical function of $H$. I selected the linear function as the simplest functional dependence. Hence, $F = kH$.

It remained for $H$ to be modeled. In the discrete case (which is not too realistic in the macroscopic biological world), it would be necessary for $H$ to be a function of the *a priori* probabilities, $p_i$ (see next section). In the continuous case, $H$ must be a function of the two probability densities, $p_S$ and $p_N$ (for pure signal and noise, respectively). The relative nature of perception, and hence the full weight of Berkeley's philosophy, falls on these probability densities. The manner in which these probability densities have been treated should now be well known to the reader, who has studied the earlier chapters. The resulting model has enjoyed, I think, some success in the analysis of experimental data. However—and this is where our current interest lies—any factor that affects these probabilities, be it physical, emotional, pathological, will affect the neural response to external stimuli and, therefore, will determine the mind's sensory picture of the world.

It must be noted here that information theory, in the manner we have used it, is *a* theory compatible with the fundamental Berkeleian attitude of perceptual relativity, although, admittedly, it does not encompass all details of Berkeley's philosophy. However, information theory is not necessarily *the only* theory capable of mediating Berkeley's ideas. The entropy theory is *a* mathematical theory of perception.

We might look back now and make a somewhat more educated study of Chapter 9 (The Sensory Neuron as Metachannel) and of Figure 9.2. The so-called external world ("so-called" because we can only infer its existence by activity of the mind) provides a *message* that is received by the sensory receptors. However, the neuronal report to the brain is a *metamessage*, which is a message about a message, detailing only the uncertainty of the receptor + neuron about the state of the world. The mind constructs an idealistic world analogous to the idealistic (substance-free) world of Berkeley. The mind depends for its existence on the integrity of the perceptual unit, a concept which we continue to build, but the reader is cautioned not to expect miracles here. However, the mind, which is the end point in the perceptual process (cf. Von Neumann and the collapse of the wave function), seems forever separated from the "objective" world, which it (the mind) creates for itself out of building blocks which are just metastatements.

Wasn't it a lot easier just manipulating equations for simple reaction time, sensory adaptation and the like?

I am afraid to push on too far in this vein lest the reader think that this is a treatise on metaphysics, which was never intended. I am just trying to indicate the intimate relationship that subsists, connecting Berkeleian philosophy with our mathematical theory of perception, and the rather subjective nature of the world that accompanies the theory. Admittedly, we have dealt only with a rather limited range of perceptual phenomena: the sensation of stimuli of the intensity type. Nonetheless, having replaced the objective by the subjective, we should now be prepared for certain consequent changes in scientific worldview that may not be completely in accord with our previous notions of "common sense." For example, what meaning can be assigned to the existence of the universe prior to the emergence of percipient agencies?

The primary purpose of this section was to demonstrate the lineage of $F = kH$ from Berkeley's philosophy "to be is to be perceived." However, we have also seen how the $F = kH$ concept relates closely to Boltzmann's $S = -k_B H_B$ (Table 15.1) and how smoothly the $H$-concept merges with the quantum mechanical view of collapsing the wave function (Chapter 2). $F = kH$ thus provides a degree of unification of various branches of science. That is,

Berkeley's relativity of perception $\to F = kH \to S = -k_B H_B$:

the slender strand alluded to at the end of the previous chapter.


## GENERATION OF SIGNALS BY THE PERCEPTUAL UNIT: THE DISCRETE MODEL

We recall from Chapter 2 ("The Gist of the Entropic Theory of Perception") the example of a perceiver who perceives only discrete stimuli. This model was not, of course, meant to be taken too seriously, but it served as introduction to the continuous model, which we have developed throughout the book. Let us now pick up the simple, discrete model again, as a means of exploring a problem of some epistemological concern.

Consider the hypothetical case of an organism which can perceive only stimuli of some modality that have the discrete intensities, $I_1, I_2, \ldots, I_q$, and that these $q$ intensities occur with a priori probabilities $p_1, p_2, \ldots, p_q$, respectively. We suppose, further, that information transmission is noise-free and hence that each stimulus intensity gives rise to a single response (not a range of responses as in the discrete model studied in Chapter 2, note 6). The organism's perceptual $H$-function is then given by

$$H = -\sum_{i=1}^{q} p_i \log p_i, \qquad (16.1)$$

and its perceptual variable is, as usual,

$$F = kH, \qquad (16.2)$$

where $H = H(p_i)$. The "psychophysical law" has degenerated, since (as long as the $p_i$ remain constant) regardless of the physical intensity of the stimulus, the expectation of exactly $q$ intensities gives rise to the same value of the $H$-function, using Equation (16.1) and, therefore, to the same value of $F$. That is, in this strange organism, all stimuli seem, subjectively, equally intense. It can determine only whether or not a stimulus (of some sort) has been given. The $F$-value is controlled, however, by $q$, the total number of discrete intensities within the organism's sensorium. The adaptation function has also degenerated to a delta function, or perhaps to a step function; perception occurs abruptly with the identification of one stimulus from among $q$ possibilities. Subjectively, the perceiver apprehends a sudden flash of invariant intensity, which then adapts to zero instantaneously. Although the above may seem somewhat unrealistic, the entropic principle governed by $F = kH$ still remains: magnitude of the perceptual variable is proportional to the entropy or uncertainty, $H$, which is, in turn, a function of the *a priori* probabilities, $p_i$.

We note that while all stimuli will seem equally intense subjectively for a constant set of $p_i$-values, the subjective magnitude will change if the values of $p_i$ are changed.

The trappings of the $H$-function (which constitute the basis for the extensive experimental testing that occupied five chapters of the book) have now been stripped off completely, to permit examination of the bare epistemological core. Given the probability set, $p_i$, the organism receives a fixed quantity of information, $H$, from each percept. But how did the organism obtain values for the probabilities, $p_i$, in the first place? Or, expressed in another way, *How is it determined how much information the organism should receive by perceiving each stimulus?*

(i) One answer to this question is that Nature Provides. That is, just as natural forces have, somehow, produced the organism including its sensory receptors, Nature (defined as some agency external to the perceptual unit) will also instill into these receptors values for its *a priori* probabilities, thus fixing the information content of each percept.

There is nothing really wrong with this answer from a mathematical point of view. The problem centers around the physical meaning of the $H$-function. If it is regarded purely as a mathematical function, in accordance with which a receptor–neuron complex operates, then all goes well. If, however, the $H$-function signifies the magnitude of the quality which human beings calls "uncertainty," then the mere installation of the $p_i$-values by Nature, like the setting of a series of switches, will not do. If Nature is setting the switches, then Nature understands the distribution of $p_i$-values; Nature is uncertain; and Nature forms part of the perceptual unit, which is a contradiction.[2]

But all this is highly metaphysical. I concede that (i) will do the job. However, I am not content with it. I do not regard Nature (i.e., some agency outside of the perceptual unit) as playing an explicit role in each act of perception.

(ii) A second answer to the question above in italics, and the one that I favor, is that Nature stays out of the process of perception and that the values for $p_i$ are, somehow, *self-instilled* into the perceptual unit. Since they are established by the unit itself, the unit itself is the "uncertain agency."

The reader may object that I am unreasonably and spuriously anthropomorphizing the perceptual unit, that people and animals can become uncertain, but not a set of neurons and receptors. My reply is that "the buck stops here." No longer are we at liberty to relegate the seat of human mental states upward, to higher and higher cerebral centers that must remain, because of their inherent complexity, unlocalized and undefined. We seek here the smallest anatomical–physiological unit capable of *autonomously* expressing the human state of uncertainty.

So we seek, but can we find?

The perceptual unit itself, without aid from an external agency, must be capable of changing the values of the $p_i$ (subject, of course, to the normalization constraint that the sum of $p_i$ must equal unity), thereby altering the amount of information received from each percept and changing the subjective apprehension, $F$, of the perceptual event. Here, again, is a reflection of Berkeleian relativity of perception to the perceiver and a denial of absolute quantities (such as the amount of information) in the perceived entity.

How, then, does the perceptual unit determine the set of values for $p_i$ that will generate the "correct" information content of each stimulus? I submit that, at least for this hypothesized organism, there is no correct value for information content, but rather, the unit sets the values of $p_i$ to produce a value for information content that is consistent with the unit's own model of the world. The process is much the same as setting values for $p_1$ and $p_2$ for a coin, values that are consistent with the perceiver's model of the coin (fair coin, $2/3$ and $1/3$ biased coin, etc.).

If the perceptual unit does set its own probabilities relative to its own expectation or model of the world, how does it carry out this process? This question, of course, leads us to the mechanism of sensation, which is a subject that has been studiously avoided hitherto. However, without entering deeply into the problem, we can still say that the adjustment will be carried out by either digital or analog means. A digital adjustment would imply, again, a process of switch setting in order to fix the unit's computational device to the proper probability settings. I regard this as an unlikely mechanism, although not impossible. For reasons whose basis may become clearer in the next section, I favor an analog method for setting the *a priori* probabilities. I suggest that the perceptual unit actively generates signals of the modality in question in accordance with its own, intrinsic, view or model of the world and that this self-generation process is carried out in such a manner that the signals serve as stimuli that can be detected and perceived by the same perceptual unit. That is, if, in the world model of the perceptual unit, signals of intensity, $I_1$, occur 100 $p_1$% of the time, signals of intensity, $I_2$, occur 100 $p_2$% of the time ... signals of intensity, $I_q$, occur 100 $p_q$% of the time, the unit will generate signals with intensities at these frequencies. Since the self-generated signals are then detected and perceived by the unit, each signal or stimulus will "transmit" information determined by $H(p_i)$ and will produce the subjective sensory effect, $F(p_i)$. The subjective magnitude, $F(p_i)$, is then consistent with the world model of the perceptual unit. When externally produced stimuli are then perceived, their subjective magnitude (always the same value in this model) is matched to the number and probability of internal stimuli. The cycle is then complete, and the organism perceives intensities that are consistent with its own model of the external world, a world which it can never know "objectively." The shadow of Berkeley.

I suggest (and I recognize that this view is not traditional) that if the external signal were not a member of the recognized stimulus set, $I_1 \ldots I_q$, it would not be perceived by the organism. It must be suspected to be perceived. To perceive is to doubt. In this model of perception, doubt, suspicion, or *interrogation* of the world is carried out by means of self-generated signals.

The reader may now understand my partiality toward the model of D. M. MacKay (Chapter 10, Other Endeavors ... ), which uses a matching model with elements similar to the one above as a means of equating Fechner's and Stevens' laws. The analog model above is also reminiscent of models suggested by Hochberg (1970), and Neisser (1976, "The Perceptual Cycle").

The sequence of perception in view (i) above consists of two phases. In the first phase, Nature sets the switches, in some fashion, to provide values for the probabilities, $p_i$. In the second phase, the stimulus is perceived at subjective level, $F$, established in accordance with Nature's $p_i$-values.

The sequence of perception in view (ii) above also consists of two interrelated phases, which I call the *active phase* and the *passive phase* (Norwich, 1982). The active phase consists of the setting up of uncertainty; for example, the generation of an internal signal by the perceptual unit for purposes of fixing the $p_i$-values. This phase may be thought of as a *calibrating* or *tuning* phase. The passive phase consists of the resolution of the uncertainty introduced by the active phase through apprehension of an external stimulus, with the consequent production of the perceptual response of magnitude, $F$. In a manner of speaking, the active phase asks a question, and the passive phase provides the answer. The active phase is interrogative; the passive phase is assertive.

Although the concept of self-generated signals or stimuli has been introduced here by means of an example of an organism that perceives only discrete intensities and whose sensory processes operate strictly on an $F = kH$ basis, I believe that the general idea of self-generated stimuli can be approached by a number of avenues of thought (see, for example, Norwich, 1982, 1983, 1984). We approach it by still another avenue in the next section. I also believe that any physiological model of perception predicated upon the general concept of Berkeleian perceptual relativity will contain elements by which the perceiving system determines actively, to an extent, what it will perceive in the "outside world."[3]

## GENERATION OF SIGNALS BY THE PERCEPTUAL UNIT: THE CONTINUOUS MODEL

In the continuous model developed in Chapter 9, the stimulus signal is regarded as a continuous variable, and discrete probability functions are replaced by probability density functions. Uncertainty about discrete stimulus values was replaced by uncertainty about the mean stimulus intensity. In order to calculate $H$ using Equation (9.19), we no longer required a set of *a priori* probabilities or even knowledge of a specific probability density function. The process of sampling the continuum, analyzed by means of the central limit theorem, seemed to provide a value of signal variance, which was all we needed in order to calculate the $H$-function and, hence, the value of $F$. Have we, therefore, escaped from the need for active participation by the perceiving system? I think not.

We recall from Equations (9.18) and (9.19) that

$$\beta = \beta'/\sigma_R^2, \qquad \beta' \text{ constant} > 0, \tag{16.3}$$

so that

$$H = \tfrac{1}{2} \ln\left[1 + (\beta'/\sigma_R^2)I^n/t\right]. \tag{9.18}/(16.4)$$

That is, the value of $H$ depends on the value of $\sigma_R^2$, which is the variance of a reference signal. This reference signal played the part of noise in the context of communications theory. We have seen in Chapter 7 and in Figure 7.1 the necessity of introducing a reference signal if one wishes to calculate the amount of information transmitted by a continuous signal. Therefore, $\sigma_R^2$ is a necessary part of the perceptual entropy equation.

I have made various attempts to calculate the order of magnitude of $\sigma_R^2$ from available data but none of the attempts is satisfactory. So I can take the reader no further in this direction. In principle, however, $\sigma_R^2$ may be much smaller than $\sigma_S^2$; that is, the reference signal may be very much less intense than the external signal.

As we discovered in our explorations in Chapter 9, these reference signals arise, not in the "outside world," but rather within the system that *measures* the external signal, and a function of the reference signal is to limit or restrict the amount of information that can be obtained from the external signal. They may be real signals or just an obfuscating, calibrating, or information-limiting effect. However, both in source (internal) and in function (calibrating), these reference signals are similar to the hypothesized signals that were generated by the perceptual unit of the organism that perceived only discrete stimulus intensities. Hence we should be aware—and perhaps I am not emphasizing it sufficiently—that whenever we use the fundamental Equation (9.20),

$$F = \tfrac{1}{2} k \ln( 1 + \beta I^{n}/t ),$$

we are representing the perceptual variable, $F$, as a function of the perceiver-dependent variable, $\beta$. In principle, any alteration of the value of $\beta$ (which contains $\sigma_R^2$) by the perceiver will alter the sensory impressions that the perceiver obtains from the outside world. If $\beta(\sigma_R^2)$ is adjusted by the perceptual system using the process of generating real signals, then the magnitude of sensation of external stimuli is, likewise, governed by these self-generated signals. Therefore, one can reason either from the overly simplified model of an organism that perceives only discrete signals or by using a somewhat more realistic model of an organism that can perceive continuously distributed signals and, in either case, find some logical support for the existence of internally generated stimulus signals.

I would posit, therefore, that all perceptual units actively generate signals of the type which they perceive (Figure 16.1), and that the interaction between the self-generated signal and the external signal is, in part, responsible for the phenomenon of "awareness" that we associate, *by definition*, with the perceptual unit. That is, to be conscious of an environmental stimulus implies that the perceiver is challenging its environment with a similar stimulus. We have noted that a perceiver must generate a force to perceive a force; that a solid element in the digit seems necessary to perceive the solid state, and so on, for other states of matter. I would extend this principle to include the sense of hearing: the auditory perceptual unit must generate audible sound if it is to perceive sound. And I would extend it to include the sense of vision: the visual perceptual unit must generate visible light if it is to perceive light signals. But shall I write "et cetera"? Does the olfactory perceptual unit generate perceptible odor? Does the gustatory unit generate tastable elements? These ideas are certainly at variance with current physiological thought.

In 1965 I submitted a paper to three journals, sequentially. In this paper I put forward ideas quite similar to those expressed in the latter paragraph, although argued from a more philosophical viewpoint. The paper was rejected by all three journals. Prediction from purely theoretical arguments was simply not accepted. Wrote one referee "There is absolutely no *evidence* that the retina generates light or that the ear generates sound" (my italics).

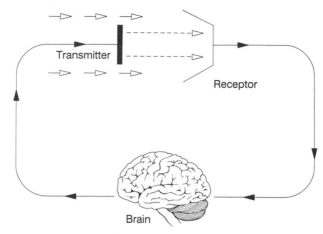

FIGURE 16.1   Hypothesized active and passive phases of perception (self-generated and externally generated stimuli respectively). Active: Self-generated stimuli are issued in response to efferent neuronal signals originating (probably) in the brain and innervating internal (physiological) transmitters (open arrowheads with dashed shafts). Passive: External stimuli arrive from the outside world (open arrowheads with solid shifts). Both types of stimuli are received by the sensory receptors. Solid arrowheads designate neuronal pathways.

However, the years rolled by, and microphones of very small dimensions were produced and placed in the ear canals of human subjects. In 1981, P. M. Zurek reported in the *Journal of the Acoustical Society of America*, "One typically does not think of the human ear as a sound-producing organ. It came as no small surprise, therefore, when a miniature probe microphone placed in my right ear canal registered a continuous narrow-band signal of nearly-constant amplitude." So, it transpired that the ear really *does* generate sound. Interestingly, the mechanism for these emissions may have been predicted by T. Gold in 1948.

Were these emissions of sound from the ear—issuing, it turned out, from the cochlea—the self-generated stimuli required by the entropy theory of perception? I resubmitted the paper, modernized somewhat, and with its Berkeleian profile kept judiciously low, to the *Journal of Theoretical Biology*, one of three journals to have rejected it originally, and the only one in which the editor of 1965 was still in place. By decision of the editor, the late Dr. James Danielli, the paper was finally published, some 18 years after its original submission.[4]

So the ear does generate sound, but does the eye generate light (Norwich, 1984)? The idea that light may issue from the eye (*extramission*) can be traced back at least as far as Alcmaeon of Croton in the fifth century BCE (Lindberg, 1976). Plato, and possibly Empedocles, utilized this concept in their theories of vision. Plato's concept of visual perception seems to involve rays of light both entering and emanating from the eye. The *Timaeus* of Plato, with translation and commentary by F. M. Cornford (1937, sections 45B–46A), gives a clear account of Plato's views. However, the reasoning of the philosophers of old was quite different from our reasoning within the entropy theory.

In 1879, Fick, a physiologist, suggested that human vision toward the infrared end of the spectrum may be affected by thermal radiation issuing from the eye itself. Later reference to Planck's blackbody radiation equation, however, cooled such speculation, showing that infrared effects would be minimal. In modern times, the idea of spontaneous excitation of rods within the retina has been lent some credence. The term *dark light* has been used to refer to this sort of endogenous excitation, which seems to be regarded as a type of noise (Pirenne and Marriott, 1959).

No experimental evidence of which I am aware supports the conjecture that the visual perceptual system (not necessarily the retina) generates light actively in a systematic way *as a necessary part of the visual process*. Various vision researchers have assured me that no such activity takes place as a regular part of the physiological process of vision. Still, I believe that it does and I let the conjecture stand.

## NOTES

1. See definition of *perception* in Chapter 2.
2. One cannot but think of Equation (6.21), $S = k_B \ln W$, where $W$ is the number of microstates and $S$ is physical entropy. Is $S$ simply a mathematical consequence of $W$, or, since $\ln W$ is a measure of human uncertainty, is $S$, somehow, dependent on human uncertainty? Most physicists, I suspect, would take the former attitude, preserving pure objectivity in physics.
3. I feel obliged to keep putting the adjective *outside* in quotation marks, because if perception is truly relative, the outside world and inside world are not obviously distinct. The outside world, or *object-language* is a model created by our minds, which speak only in *metalanguage*.
4. Please see the footnote on the first page of the 1983 paper in the *Journal of Theoretical Biology*, 1983, **102**, p. 175.

## REFERENCES

Berkeley, G. 1975. *Philosophical Works* (Introduction and notes by M. R. Ayers) Dent, London.

Cornford, F. M. 1937. *Plato's Cosmology*. Kegan Paul, Trench, Trübner, London.

Gibson, J. J. 1962. Observations on active touch. *Psychological Review* **69**, 477–491.

Gold, T. 1948. Hearing. II. The physical basis of the action of the cochlea. *Proceedings of the Royal Society of London Series B* **135**, 492–498.

Hochberg, J. 1970. In *Attention: Contemporary Theory and Analysis* (D. I. Mostovsky, Ed.), pp. 99–124, Appleton–Century–Crofts, Meredith Corp., New York.

Lindberg, D. C. 1976. *Theories of Vision from Al-Kindi to Kepler*. Univ. Chicago Press, Chicago.

Neisser, U. 1976. *Cognition and Reality: Principles and Implications of Cognitive Psychology*. Freeman, San Francisco.

Norwich, K. H. 1972. The tactile discrimination of complex systems. *International Journal of Systems Science* **3**, 225–228.

Norwich, K. H. 1982. Perception as an active process. *Mathematics and Computers in Simulation* **24**, 535–539.

Norwich, K. H. 1983. To perceive is to doubt: The relativity of perception. *Journal of Theoretical Biology* **102**, 175–190.

Norwich, K. H. 1984. Why the eye may be found to be a source of light. *Proceedings: 6th International Congress of Cybernetics and Systems, Paris, France*, pp. 831–836.

Ruch, T. C., and Fulton, J. F. 1960. *Medical Physiology and Biophysics*. 18th ed. Saunders, Philadelphia.

Pirenne, M. H., and Marriott, F. H. C. 1959. The quantum theory of light and the psycho-physiology of vision. In *Psychology: A Study of a Science*. Vol. I. *Sensory, Perceptual, and Physiological Formulations* (S. Koch, Ed.), p. 340. McGraw-Hill, New York.

Spencer Brown, G. 1969. *Laws of Form*. Allen & Unwin, London.

Spinoza, Baruch. 1951. *The Chief Works of Benedict de Spinoza* (Translated from the Latin by R. H. M. Elwes), Vol. II. Dover, New York.

Zurek, P. M. 1981. Spontaneous narrowband acoustic signals emitted by human ears. *Journal of the Acoustical Society of America* **69**, 514–523.

# 17

## Extrapolations
## and Speculations

*You shall not be required to finish the work, but neither
are you free to desist from it.*
Rabbi Tarfon: Ethics of the Fathers, 2:15, circa 70 CE

This chapter of speculation should be regarded as an intellectual
dessert (French, *desservir*, to clear the table). Like a dessert, it should
never, ever be eaten before the main course. Like a dessert, it should not
be partaken of by those with restricted diets. Like a dessert, it should be
digested in a relaxed and unhurried fashion, with the mind at ease and
the body at rest. Like a dessert, it should be eaten sparingly and should
confer a degree of joy.

## REALITY

The first portion of this book was largely devoted to the study of the
mathematical capabilities of the $F = kH$ equation, and the second portion was directed toward the philosophical underpinnings of the theory
which gave rise to the equation. The material was presented, chronologically, backward, since it was the idealist world view, the concept of the
relativity of perception, which, in my mind, gave rise in the first place to
the mathematical theory. I chose this chronological reversal because, as
mentioned, I retain a view of my more typical reader as one who would
rather study the science before the philosophy. The extent to which we
have deviated from Marr's philosophy (Chapter 1) should be clearly
appreciated. We do, indeed, examine the "validity"[1] of what the senses
tell us; we do not, strictly speaking, regard the senses as telling us "what
is there;" and we have, certainly, toiled with the "molecules of perception." We have worked only with percepts of the simplest kind: steady
stimuli of the "intensity" type, leaving much of the world of sensation
and perception yet to be explored with the new $H$-concept.

Beginning with a somewhat restricted form of Berkeley's philosophy of perception, we have mapped the Berkeleian world view onto the anatomical–physiological elements of a hypothesized perceptual unit, so that the perceptual unit becomes an organ for the enactment or realization of this subjective world view. Most people are quite happy with the objective world of science that has sufficed for many centuries. What can we make of a world which is relative to you and, concurrently, to me? Is your "outside" world the same as mine? In what sense is the outside world unique or "real?" As we combine our subjective molecular percepts, how do our minds produce cohesive models of the external world? For example, how does the bright stimulus + hard stimulus + cold stimulus unite in our minds to produce, say, an ice cube? This question has, of course, been asked many times. Of fundamental importance is the extent to which the external world may be said to exist relative to the *community of perceivers* rather than relative to each individual mind or perceiver. Berkeley seemed just to assume that the universe could exist relative to a collective mind (yours or mine or both); but on a physiological scale, how does my perceptual unit allow for your perceptual unit?

If we utilize $F = kH(I, t)$ purely as a mathematical entity, without querying its philosophical base (as some of my colleagues encourage), we emerge with a functional, predictive system and even one that confers a degree of unity within sensory science and among the respective sciences (remember the unifying property of $PV = RT$). The problem arises when we ask ourselves about the *reality* of the world that underlies the $F = kH$ relation (remember how the derivation of $PV = RT$ supported the molecular theory of matter). Our problem, here, is very similar to that currently facing quantum mechanicians. Quantum mechanics provides the mathematical machinery for calculating what is observed, and the machinery works flawlessly. However, when we inquire what the equations of quantum mechanics *mean*, the answers are not so readily forthcoming. We are led to ask a very fundamental question about the nature of science: Is the job of the mathematical sciences primarily one of prediction—of striking a set of operational equations that produce verifiable results? Or is the aim of science to "understand" what these equations mean and to grasp the essence of reality?

## THE PERCEPTUAL UNIT

Slowly, slowly, we have been formulating the nature of this unit, the smallest structure capable, *in itself*, of perceiving or being aware. We are not capable of completing the formulation, but we must not refrain from trying. It is the stopped buck. It, in itself, is what perception is all about. The onus of creating awareness may not devolve upon some remote and unreachable cerebral structure, nor may we assume it to "emerge" somehow from the interaction of a myriad of simple, unperceiving elements.

If we assume the attitude that the mathematical equation constitutes the ultimate scientific reality, then we may reduce the perceptual unit to its simplest form. It may consist solely of a receptor–neuron complex. The neuron transmits impulses at rate, $F$, in proportion to an $H$-function that begins at its maximum and decreases progressively with time. When the current stimulus terminates, natural processes built into the receptor reset the variable $m$ or $t$ back to zero, perhaps even by digital processes. The receptor "sleeps." When a new stimulus arrives, the receptor "awakens," $H$ again assumes its maximum value, and the process repeats.

However, if we take the attitude that the $H$-function represents something real, and that changes in the magnitude of $H$ represent changes in that reality, the perceptual unit becomes less simple. We have interpreted the quantity, $H$, as a measure of uncertainty. With this real interpretation of $H$, the perceptual unit which assumes the value, $H$, is most uncertain near the beginning of the act of perceiving and becomes less uncertain as the act proceeds. We have seen in the previous chapter how the magnitude of the perceptual unit's uncertainty can be self-instilled by means of self-generated stimuli or extramission—that is, stimuli produced by the perceptual unit it *self*. The key word is *self*. I am only uncertain if $I$ know of multiple possibilities. So the element omitted from our discussion in Chapter 16 is the element of self. How can the perceptual unit determine that the extramitted stimulus does arise from within itself?[2] Much is written about the identification of structural self immunologically, but little is written about the identification of sensorineural self. I suggested (Norwich, 1983) that the self-generated signal might be identified by its cyclicity. That is, if the perceptual unit were fabricated as a closed loop, then a signal generated at some point, $P$, in the closed loop would initiate a self-generated signal, whose neurological report would return to the same point, $P$. The time that elapsed between the initiation of the signal and the neurological report would identify the stimulus as probably of origin within the self.

Must the external and internal stimuli arrive nearly simultaneously, as in the photon example of Chapter 14, or is there a local perceptual-unit-memory, so that there is recall of internal stimuli of the past?

The proof of the pudding may be in the creating. Can we construct a model—an analog rather than a computer model[3]—of a system with active and passive elements (externally and internally generated stimuli)? Such a hardware model should also produce its $H$-function by analog means. That is, some physical process (not a digital calculation) should have $H$ as its output. I have been searching for such a model, particularly by looking at the analogy between $H$ and $S$ (Chapter 15), because free energy is a function of $S$ and it is the free energy that will empower the analog model.

Would such a model of the perceptual unit, if it were created, be capable of perception or awareness on some rudimentary level? We lack a test for "awareness" analogous to the Turing test for machine thinking. In any case, we could not interrogate a single perceptual unit to determine its state of mind. It would be difficult or impossible to determine whether a primordial perceptual unit, capable, say, of perceiving lights of different intensities, were aware in some way. The unit will require a motor component to allow it to effect a response before one could seriously consider a test of awareness.

I am also concerned about the lack of an element of *motivation* in the hypothesized perceptual unit. At the simplest level, the motivation to perceive is to obtain pleasure or to avoid pain. Yet we have discovered no elements within our model of perception that could be identified with pleasure–pain. Is there a component in the mathematical model that has been overlooked? Is the theoretical structure of the perceptual unit not yet rich enough? Do pleasure–pain emerge only when we consider groups or networks of perceptual units?

The entropy theory is a bottom-up theory. That is, we are trying to comprehend higher perceptual functions by building upon a fundamental, complex perceptual unit. We have not engaged in neural networking, in which very simple, axon–synapse–dendrite processes operate in great numbers to produce "emergent" effects that, it is hoped, will explain higher cognitive processes. In the entropy approach, the core of awareness lies in one, discrete structure; in the current networking approach awareness may emerge from the interaction of many unaware components. There is a clear difference in philosophy between the two approaches.

## ILLUSIONS: THE NECKER CUBE AS ENTROPIC MULTIVIBRATOR

A feature of this chapter on extrapolations is that we finally break the fetters that bound us to elemental stimuli of the intensity type, to consider the principle of entropic perception applied at higher and higher levels: perception of speech, perception of other creatures, perception of the laws of physics.

We did make mention earlier of the Troxler effect, whereby an image which is held to a constant position on the retina will appear to fade out. This phenomenon may be an example of the adaptation principle—decrease to zero of the $H$-function for a whole image—with consequent reduction of $F$ to zero. In other words, we can perceive an image as long as some uncertainty about its nature or quality remains. However, when

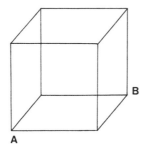

**FIGURE 17.1**   The Necker cube. Face A and face B will alternately appear to be closer to the viewer in three-dimensional space as he or she regards the two-dimensional projection. A very simple explanation for this phenomenon in terms of the entropy theory is suggested in the text.

all information has been extracted, the image fades. One cannot perceive a certainty.

One might also consider the type of fine eye movements called *microsaccades*. Even when a subject tries to keep his eyes as still as possible, small movements of the extraocular muscles occur every second or so and tend to shift his gaze by 5–10 minutes of arc. Do these eye movements function as the discouragers of certainty, guaranteeing a continually changing retinal image in order to prevent a Troxler fade-out?

It is interesting, in this regard, to consider illusions of the Necker cube type (Figure 17.1). The three-dimensional interpretation of this drawing by a viewer tends to shift between two alternatives: A-face front or B-face front. There is a very simple explanation for this phenomenon within the entropy theory. We perceive one three-dimensional interpretation until little uncertainty remains; for example, the A-face is forward without much doubt. But "without much doubt" suggests that the image will be destroyed, because we cannot perceive a certainty. Thence, the second three-dimensional interpretation supervenes. But when the B-face is forward without much doubt, the first interpretation, which has de-adapted somewhat, supervenes, and so on: an entropic multivibrator. Adaptation, in this process, need not proceed to extinction as in the Troxler effect.

## COCHLEAR IMPLANTS

These cochlear prostheses have been developed during the past 25 years as an aid for the deaf (e.g., Gulick *et al.*, 1989). They consist of a small microphone similar to those found in hearing aids. The output voltage of the microphone is led to a processor, whose output, in turn, is transmitted to small wires beneath the skin, just behind the pinna of the ear. These wires carry electrical signals through the middle ear to the cochlea, where a small piece of metal serves as a stimulating electrode. Current from this electrode passes through the cochlea, excites some of the residual auditory nerve fibers, and returns through a ground electrode. There are many types of cochlear implants (extracochlear, intracochlear, single channel, and multiple channel). It is significant that these implants *do* help many people perceive sound. In some cases, the patient will experience only a nondescript sound, which may, nonetheless, serve as a warning of danger. In some cases, speech perception is actually improved somewhat.

However, armed with the concepts of the entropy theory of perception, and fortified by the idea of the perceptual unit which embraces both active and passive elements, we are led to suspect that the current cochlear prostheses contain only half the number of elements needed for true auditory perception. The cochlear implants contain the passive elements of the perceptual unit, but not the active elements. To be truly effective in aiding sound perception, a cochlear prosthesis must be able to generate sound as well as to receive it. This is a tall order, and it is not clear how to implement it. Are there efferent neurons (those leading from the brain toward the ear) that might serve to activate a source of low-intensity sound, and so complete the perceptual unit? I wonder.

## THE RELATIVITY OF EXISTENCE

If *esse* is *percipi*—to be is to be perceived—and if perception is relative, then it would seem that "existence" is relative as well. The world exists relative to the perceiving organism. We have been flirting with this theme throughout the past few chapters, but let us pick up the thread again.

The earthworm possesses a rather rudimentary nervous system by mammalian standards. Its perceptual system seems quite capable of maintaining the earthworm in the habitat in which it lives: the ground. If I asked the question "Is the earthworm aware of, or conscious of, the existence of the planet Mars?" I should probably receive, nearly universally, a reply to the negative.[4] Earthworms just don't know anything about Mars. They cannot see the planet; they cannot touch it. And no matter how many hours I spend trying to teach the worm about the existence of this planet, whose reddish corpus I see clearly hovering above me, the worm will not (likely) become the wiser. There is nothing in the structure of the worm's nervous system that would convince us human beings that it could ever be conscious or aware of the existence of the planet Mars.

However, I would argue that the previous sentence does not go far enough. If Mars is not perceivable by the earthworm, then *Mars does not exist with respect to the earthworm.* The universe that exists relative to the earthworm does not extend beyond the matrix of soil which it makes its habitat and does not include Mars.

Well, what's the difference really, you must be asking, between the two statements:

(i) The worm cannot be aware of the existence of Mars,

and

(ii) Mars does not exist with respect to or relative to the worm?

Purely semantics, you may say.

There is a difference, however (although vermiform readers may declare the whole question nonexistent). Statement (i) is part of the classical world view of an objective universe. I look up in the sky and see Mars; I look down in the earth and see the worm. Both Mars and the worm exist in an absolute sense; the worm just doesn't know about Mars. Statement (ii) is made within a system of relative existence. Mars and the worm both exist with respect to me, but Mars does not exist with respect to the worm. The fundamental views of science are different, and the consequences of these views are different. To wit, consider the theory of evolution.

## THE EVOLUTION OF EVOLUTION

By the *theory of evolution* I mean the totality of the hypothesized process whereby the universe expanded, perhaps from a big bang that occurred at a single "point in space,"[5] to form galaxies of stars, the planet earth, early forms of animal life, and finally(?) the human species. The first component is often referred to as *physical evolution* and the second as *organic* or *biological evolution.* The big bang is still our best bet as the beginning of the process of physical evolution, and natural selection provides a simple, easily visualized mechanism for biological evolution. The problem with this classical theory of evolution, from big bang to *Homo sapiens,* is that the process of evolution is presumed to occur within the framework of an absolutely existing universe, not a relatively existing universe. What meaning can be assigned, within a relative world view, to the existence of the universe in its early evolutionary form before the emergence of creatures that were capable of perceiving it? If existence is relative to a perceiver, what meaning can be ascribed to a physical process (for example, stellar evolution) that occurred before the emergence of the perceiver?

What line of reasoning led to the conceptualization of the big bang theory? Simply that observation of the motions of the galaxies showed that each galaxy was receding from all others. From knowledge of their present locations and present velocities, one can *extrapolate* backward in time to show that at an approximately determinable epoch, some 10–20 billion years ago (were 1 billion is taken as 1000 million), all the matter in these galaxies occupied the same point in space.[5]

There is some additional evidence to support the big bang theory. If the matter that existed in the early moments following the big bang were partially in the form of radiation,[6] then, it was deduced, this radiation should still be present, disseminated throughout the universe and should be largely in the microwave region of the electromagnetic spectrum. In simple language, all around us there should be microwave radiation that does not emanate from leaky microwave ovens, or from police speed traps, but which issued from the big bang. This prediction was made in 1948 by R. Alpher and R. Herman based on theoretical studies they had made earlier with George Gamow (see, for example, Weinberg, 1979, or Narlikar, 1977). In fact, in 1965, isotropic radiation in the microwave region was detected by A. Penzias and R. Wilson of the Bell Telephone Laboratory. Thus there is some confirmatory evidence in support of the big bang hypothesis.

Therefore, there are two channels of evidence that the universe preceded, by aeons, the advent of intelligent perceivers.

By way of analogy, suppose you arrive at an auditorium for a meeting to find the assembly on its feet singing the seventh line of the national anthem. You reason that you arrived after the meeting had been called to order and that the first six lines had been sung before you arrived. But you are not absolutely sure. The assembly may have risen to its feet the instant you arrived and begun singing the anthem at line seven (the chorus) in order to expedite the proceedings. However, you recall that the meeting was to have begun at 8 o'clock, and you arrived at 8:01. There was just time between 8:00 and 8:01 for the assembly to have risen and sung the first six lines of the anthem. The dual lines of reasoning tend to convince you that the proceedings were afoot when you arrived. While you were ruminating about such trivia, you managed to miss the first item of business.

In 1992, a third channel of evidence in support of the big bang was reported by the COBE (Cosmic Background Explorer) group in the United States in the form of angular anisotropy in the background radiation that may have allowed for formation of galaxy clusters under influence of gravitational forces.

In summary, then, there is evidence that systematic cosmological activity occurred prior to the emergence of percipient beings. That is, we can extrapolate our current model of the universe backward in time to obtain a consistent picture of prehistory. We cannot, however, formulate any model of the universe that existed more than 20 billion years ago, "before" the big bang. The theory of relativity teaches us that time, itself, cannot be measured through a singularity such as the hypothesized primordial explosion. Equations break down as certain quantities tend to zero or infinity, and no meaning can be assigned to "time" before the big bang. So, while some evidence supports a universe that preexists the perceiver, this preexistence is not of infinite duration. Cosmologically, it *may be*[7] possible to project into the future by times orders of magnitude greater than we can project into the past. Perhaps 15 billion years is the epoch of (or the "now" of) perception.

However, there are other dimensions to this problem of extrapolation backward in time. We have assumed that laws of physics formulated by modern man preexisted him. Thus we have assumed, for example, the validity of general relativity as a theory of gravitation (or Newton's law of gravitation) acting on the receding galaxies, of the uniqueness of Planck's constant, etc., prior to the emergence of the organisms who were first capable of formulating them. The big bang hypothesis is a consequence of the conjecture that the laws of nature are independent of the beings who were first capable of perceiving these laws. However, do the laws of physics themselves change with the emergence of man?

Let us consider Darwinian or organic evolution, which is believed to have occurred during at least the past 3.4 billion years.[8] A process of natural selection, operating to select random mutations that were favored to survive in their environment, is believed to be responsible for transforming very elementary life forms, progressively, into present complex forms, including man. Indisputably, it is a marvelous theory, *but is Darwinian evolution a complex enough theory to survive in the environment of perceptual relativity, or must the theory, like its elements, evolve to produce higher forms?*

I remind my faithful reader that what I present now is, as the chapter title promises, purely speculation.

We recall that within the entropy theory there are two phases: an active and a passive phase. The active phase serves to establish uncertainty and the passive phase to remove it. The active phase asks a question about the perceived world, and the passive phase answers this question. While we have developed this theory within the bounds of elementary sensory experience, I propose that we now generalize it to include perception of the world at all levels of complexity. The perceptual process is, then, one of formulating questions and obtaining answers to these questions. However, there is not much purchase in enunciating a principle in this somewhat weakened form, so I propose a stronger and more Audacious Formulation (AF):

> *If an organism lacks the capability to pose a (well-formulated) question about some feature of a world, that feature of its world cannot exist relative to this organism.*

This generalization issues by induction (warranted or unwarranted) from the simpler cases of sensory perception that we have analyzed mathematically. The word "feature" that appears in the AF is not crisply defined, nor is the term "well-formulated," so that this preliminary formulation is not adequate, in itself, for the construction of a mathematical model. The interrogative or questioning element of the process of sensation consisted (in its analog form) of the generation of signals such as light or sound. The assertive phase consisted of finding these signals in the world of the perceiving organism. Within the simpler sensory context, then, the AF above in italics states that if an organism cannot, itself, generate light signals (interrogative), its immediate sensory world cannot contain light-generating elements (assertive). Even simpler, if an organism is lacking in solid elements (interrogative), its relative world will be found to be lacking in solid elements (Chapter 16). The AF is a generalization of these simpler, purely sensory functions that we have analyzed previously.

It has often been observed that we learn about an age (historically) or about a people (anthropologically) from the questions they ask. However, the AF goes much further.

Einstein expressed his amazement that the world was intelligible at all.[9] The AF responds to this amazement by making intelligibility a precondition for existence of the world in the first place.[10]

We have substituted the term *intelligibility* for the phrase *the ability to pose a (well-formulated) question*, which appeared in the AF, and for the active, interrogative, or uncertainty-generating phase of perception. But remember the kinship that we established between the words *intelligible* and *perceivable* in Chapter 2: both words imply the fashioning of a set of alternatives and the choosing between (interlego) these alternatives. The English adjectives intelligible and perceivable represent scientifically related concepts.

We have also shifted from considerations of existence relative to an individual to consideration of *existence relative to a species*.

By the AF, the world exists relative to us with characteristic features (such as the laws of physics) because we have been able to interrogate it with respect to these features. Note that the AF has been formulated in such a way that it is the *capability* (in the physiological sense) to interrogate the world about some feature, such as a law of nature, that determines the existence of this feature. Thus, we do not expect that the laws of nature would change relative to *Homo sapiens* during the floruit of this seemingly stable species. The postulated relatively existing universe is subjective insofar as it depends for its existence on the perceiver, but it still retains a degree of objectivity since the perceiver cannot fabricate the world at his whim. Stated another way, the world of the perceiver may contain only those elements which (s)he can interrogate, but *which* of these elements will be found to characterize the world is not under control of the perceiver.

The AF was suggested in order to codify, albeit in a preliminary way, the concept that the world as we know it cannot exist relative to a creature of differing "intelligence" which is not capable of questioning it in the manner that we are. Thus, again, Mars, as an orbiting planet, does not even exist relative to the ape (and *a fortiori* to the earthworm), who cannot interrogate its trajectory in the heavens.

One could say, also, that the earthworm has an existence relative to the human perceiver, but the human being has no existence relative to the earthworm, as distinct, say, from a rock or other impediment to its movement. However, I do not favor such a statement because it seems to give the human being preferred status with respect to the worm. Putting chauvinism aside, I prefer to say that each percipient creature can exist within the world of another, in some fashion.

How can one envisage "parallel" worlds for two creatures who perceive at different levels? Visualization may not be possible, but perhaps we many approach the matter by analogy. Suppose that somewhere within our three-dimensional world there exists a world of two-dimensional creatures who are confined forever to life in a (two-dimensional) surface (Figure 17.2). These creatures have positively no concept of a third dimension, living out their whole lives confined to a surface having length and height, but no depth. We can read about the adventures of

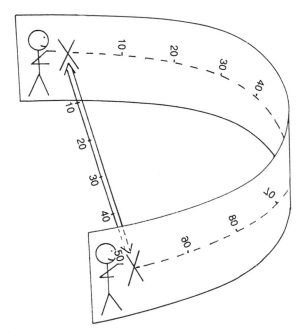

FIGURE 17.2   Two-dimensional figures measure the shortest distance between two $X$'s in their space, and find the distance to be 100 cm. However, a three-dimensional creature (not drawn) finds that the shortest distance between the same two $X$'s in his space is only 50 cm. Intended as a metaphor only, to show how one world can exist within another and the laws of nature (of geometry here) can differ radically between worlds.

such creatures in E. A. Abbott's *Flatland* or A. K. Dewdney's *Planiverse*. Without attempting to be too scientific here, we can perceive the flat creature by "looking" at him in his surface, while he can perceive us only if we intersect his surface, such as by poking our finger through it. Suppose that such a two-dimensional creature wishes to measure the shortest distance between two $X$'s that are fixed in his space. He extends a straight, two-dimensional measuring rod in such a way that the rod passes through the centers of both $X$'s. The first $X$ is located on the scale of the measuring rod at point $X_a$, and the second $X$ at the point $X_b$. The shortest distance between the two $X$'s is, then, equal to $|X_a - X_b|$. Now, unknown and unknowable to the flat creature, his two-dimensional space curves into the third dimension in such a way that the separation of the $X$'s in three-dimensional space is much smaller than his shortest two-dimensional separation, as shown in the figure. That is, *relative* to ourselves in three-dimensional space, the shortest distance between the two $X$'s is, say, 50 cm, while *relative* to the flat creature, the shortest distance is, say, 100 cm. Perhaps in this way we can get some idea of how (i) each creature can exist within the world of the other in some limited fashion and (ii) how the reality of their respective worlds can differ.

The above is all prolegomenon to the Darwinian question: What less intelligent life form served as the ancestor of *Homo sapiens*? Within our current theoretical framework the answer is not quite as simple as it is in classical Darwinism. In accordance with the AF, we can no longer envisage an anthropoid, deficient relative to *Homo sapiens* in percipience and intelligence, occupying our same universe, while lacking the ability to interrogate it fully. Such an ancestor of modern man would have had to live in a universe whose structure and function was less complex than the one we know—less complex by some measure of the reduction in its intelligence (questioning power). This concept challenges our imagination: *The universe itself changes as the creature "evolves."* That is, the past that we calculate, by extrapolating our current universe backward in time to an epoch preceding the appearance of *Homo sapiens* would not be the past that was actually experienced by our evolutionary forerunners. Not only the organism would have changed, but the entire universe relative to that organism.

Expressed in another way, it may not be a legitimate question to ask how the predecessor of *Homo sapiens* evolved within our current universe, because the question itself implies the existence of a set of physical laws that were not in existence or operation until *Homo sapiens* had appeared. To approach the study of evolution within this new, relative framework, we must ask such outrageous questions as: "What was the physics understood by an australopithecine ape?"

The unearthing of fossils of earlier life forms does not negate the new approach to evolution. These life forms exist within our own model of the universe in much the same way that the earthworm exists. However, the world experienced by these earlier life forms may have been quite different from the world that we model by extrapolating *our* current world backward in time. There are, in a sense, multiple pasts: one consistent with the world view of *Homo sapiens*, others consistent with the world views of "earlier" creatures.

Can we, then, legitimately project our world backward in time in a continuous fashion, or will the worlds of our evolutionary ancestors be connected with our own only by a series of discrete jumps past discontinuities? Each organism is associated with its own unique world, operating in accordance with a consistent set of scientific rules, which constitute the answers to the questions that the organism is capable of asking. These worlds may not merge continuously as the organism evolves, giving rise to a jump sequence in evolution (saltation).

Crazy. Admittedly. But, as Niels Bohr once pondered, is it crazy enough? Can the classical, physical–biological evolutionary scheme produce the mind that developed quantum theory (upon whose principles much of physical evolution is explained)? Yes, if you believe that the mind discovered the theory but did not produce it. No, if you believe that the mind is part of the theory, which could, therefore, not have preexisted. The relativity of perception has been extended far beyond the insulated garden of simple sensory experience where it was earlier cultivated.

Evolution "beyond" man? If so, then such creatures can ask questions that we cannot ask. It would not be their ability to *answer* difficult questions that would set them apart from us, so much as the ability to *ask* such questions as we cannot conceive.

Extraterrestrials? Perhaps they exist. But if they share our universe, our science, they are of common intelligence with us.

A good deal has been said about the entropy theory providing informational constraints, but not specifying the mechanism of operation of our sensory receptors. This property of the theory permits us to make a prediction about extraterrestrial life forms. If they exist, and if "perception" carries the universal property of progressive reduction of entropy, then the psychophysical laws governing the operation of their sensory receptors will not differ substantially from our own.

## THE ANTHROPIC PRINCIPLE

A new cosmological principle has gained prominence during the past decade. In 1974, Brandon Carter, then of Cambridge University, coined the term *Anthropic Principle* (Greek, *anthropos*: man). This principle has served as a balance against the Copernican Principle, which states that no part of the universe is more privileged than any other. Copernicus, of course, displaced the idea that the earth is the center of the universe, by the heliocentric theory, which relegated earth the status of "just an ordinary place." The Anthropic Principle shifted the emphasis back slightly toward the observer on earth. In Carter's words, "What we can expect to observe must be restricted by the conditions necessary for our presence as observers." The Anthropic Principle is classified as Strong and Weak.

The Weak Anthropic Principle (WAP) was suggested by R. H. Dicke in 1961. It may be stated (Breuer, 1991):

> Because there are observers in the universe, the universe must possess properties which permit the existence of these observers.

That is, the observer's position is, in a sense, privileged, thus inveighing somewhat against Copernicus.

The Strong Anthropic Principle (SAP) was hypothesized by Carter in 1973. As stated by Breuer:

> The structure of the universe and the particulars of its construction are essentially fixed by the condition that at some point it inevitably produces an observer.

The SAP has been stated in somewhat stronger terms by Tony Rothman (1987) in a delightful article in Discover magazine (articulate, dramatic, and humorous):

> Most scientists interpret the SAP to mean that the universe must be nearly as we know it or life wouldn't exist; conversely, if life didn't exist, neither would the universe.

Note how close this formulation of the SAP is to the principles of relativity of perception and relativity of existence. The pull-out from Rothman's article (although not appearing verbatim within the text of the article) states:

> ...Its (the Anthropic Principle's) extreme form says the laws exist *because* we behold them, making man the creator, not just the measure, of all things.

The first two formulations, by Breuer, stand firmly on the side of an objective universe, even if that universe will "inevitably" produce an observer. However, the two formulations cited from Rothman's article lean decidedly toward a subjective universe, an idea that upsets some otherwise dispassionate scientists. Accordingly, I entertain some fears that the contents of the previous section on the evolution of evolution may cause apoplexy in the vascularly vulnerable.

The Anthropic Principle is a fascinating subject. The interested reader is referred also to the 700-page tome by Barrow and Tippler. Many celebrated physicists, such as J. A. Wheeler, have supported the principle. Wheeler's Participatory Anthropic Principle is expressed by Barrow and Tippler as: "Observers are necessary to bring the Universe into being."

I have introduced the Anthropic Principle at his point because it seems, at least superficially, to be allied to the principle of relativity of perception. Most books dealing with the Anthropic Principle give casual references to Berkeley's philosophy. I do not even attempt to expound further on the subject here. The reader is referred to the excellent monographs cited.


## QUANTUM THEORY AND PERCEPTION

Quantum theory was introduced early in this book (Chapter 2) to show that it was readily amenable to analysis by information theory. Prior to the act of observation, a physical system exists in a combination of states represented by a wavefunction (cf. many possible outcomes to an event engendering uncertainty). Observation (I prefer perception) of the outcome collapses the wavefunction (cf. perceiving the outcome of an event leads to loss of uncertainty or gain in information).

We can now regard the process of establishing the wavefunction as the active or interrogative phase of perception and the process of collapsing the wavefunction as the passive or assertive phase of perception.

Quantum mechanics seems like a more natural medium in which to apply the entropy theory than classical mechanics, in which energy, momentum, etc. are distributed continuously. In quantum mechanics, the passive phase of perception is accomplished abruptly. In classical mechanics, the passive phase of perception occurs slowly, and seemingly continuously, distributing itself through an extended process, which we regard in the spinning of a top or the motion of a pendulum.

We as "mesoscopic" creatures (Greek, *mesos*: middle), that is, half-way between microscopic or atomic scale and truly macroscopic or stellar scale, happen to dwell in the realm of classical mechanics. We are flanked by atomic events on one side and astronomical events on the other. Is it the case that continuity of perception, or the apparent continuity, is a feature only of this middle land?

From the viewpoint of the entropic theory of perception, the smallness of the scale of quantum events is not the cardinal feature distinguishing these events from mesoscopic events; rather it is the inability of us mesoscopic creatures to perceive the occurrence of quantum events continuously. For example, we perceive the effect of the electron striking a screen, but we cannot perceive the electron continuously in its trajectory toward the screen because such continuous perception would require scattering a stream of photons from the tiny electron, which cannot be done. Hence we have before-the-event uncertainty and after-the-event perception, giving rise to a discrete form of the $H$-function. However, macroscopic events, such as astrophysical events, can also not be perceived continuously by mesoscopic creatures, for a number of possible reasons. "Terrestrial" reasons include the large time scale of astrophysical events, visibility only in short or long wavelength electromagnetic radiation that can be captured on film but not witnessed directly by eye, rotation of the earth on its axis, etc. More fundamental reasons for intermittent perceivability include eclipse of a planet as it revolves about its sun and self-eclipse of a binary star. The mesoscopic luxury of continuous perception with sensory adaptation is forfeit and, therefore, it is not outrageous to expect in this macroscopic realm effects of a quantum nature.

The idea of macroscopic quantization is discussed in a paper by Daniel Greenberger (1983).

## SUMMARY

The above are purely speculations and extrapolations beyond the core of the entropic thesis. I would like to leave you with the following thoughts.

It is possible to construct a mathematical theory of perception which is consistent with the idealist philosophy of George Berkeley. This theory may not be the unique "incarnation" of Berkeley's ideas, and it certainly does not incorporate his theology, but it does seem to capture the spirit of his idea of the relativity of perception. The fundamental mathematical formalism of the entropic theory of perception is contained by the simple equation, $F = kH$. This equation is noteworthy for a number of reasons. First, and most obviously, it is mathematically and conceptually similar to Boltzmann's equation, $S = -k_B H$, suggesting (but not yet proving) a link between the physical entropy, $S$, of a system and the perceivability of the system. The equation is also noteworthy for its utilitarian value in understanding and unifying sensory processes. When the informational entropy, $H$, is evaluated as an explicit function of stimulus intensity, $I$, and time, $t$, the equation $F = kH$ allows us to derive mathematically nearly all of the laws of sensory science involving the variables $F$, $I$, and $t$, which have been discovered empirically, or by measurement, over the past one and a third centuries. It also permits us to predict the results of many experiments in psychophysics and sensory physiology that have not yet been performed. We are empowered to obtain, by mathematical analysis of our experiments, knowledge that was previously unavailable to us. The explicit form of the $H$-function permits us to incorporate the information concept into sensory science in a manner not previously possible. For example, channel capacities can be calculated in a very simple manner from neurophysiological adaptation data. The $H$-function gives rise to the various sensory laws not by specifying their physical mechanism but by utilizing the quantity of information transferred as a constraint, in the manner of a law of conservation.

We have not, in these pages, exhausted the analysis of sensory experiments that can be performed involving the single, steady stimulus and variables $I, F, t$. It is to be hoped that the reader can now carry out the theoretical analysis of many of these experiments using the methods presented. Moreover, many investigations which may have been executed purely to search and find may now be hypothesis-driven. That is, it should be possible to predict results before measurements are actually made. The reader is reminded, however, that in a global theory, as this one purports to be, we strive for one or two equations that describe all natural phenomena to a high degree of approximation and to replace scores of unrelated equations each of which may describe a single phenomenon with great precision. The importance of controlling and reporting the time variables has been emphasized. For fine theoretical analysis, one should know the duration of the stimulus, the time since stimulus onset, and the extent of prior adaptation. We have also been led to the point where correlation between neural and behavioral events can be made mathematically, albeit in preliminary fashion.

$F = kH$ was suggested as a mathematical representation of Berkeley's ideas, but when the equation was analyzed carefully from a physical point of view, it was found to require for its implementation two processes: an active process whereby uncertainty or doubt was instilled into the perceiving system and a passive process whereby uncertainty was removed. The active process was a kind of interrogative or questioning process, and the passive process a kind of assertive process. If the perceptual process was to be self-contained, not requiring the intervention of an external agency, then both active and passive processes must be accommodated by the perceiving system. Therefore, perceptual autonomy required the existence of a perceptual unit, which mediated both active and passive components. This perceptual unit is, by definition, the simplest self-contained structure capable of the act of perception. The passive component of the perceptual unit contains the sensory receptor, and it was suggested that the active component consists of a mechanism for self-stimulation of the sensory receptor. The concept of the perceptual unit was built progressively throughout the latter part of the book, but the building process was not completed.

Since the equations of the entropic theory are the physical embodiment of the Berkeleian philosophy from which they took origin, the theory carries in its genetic base, so to speak, the relativity of the perceived world to the perceiver. *To a certain extent*, the perceiver determines the nature of the world he perceives. In the final chapter, we let loose the fetters that were restraining us to the limited sphere of sensation of steady signals of the intensity type and speculated about perception of the world at a higher cognitive level: perception of planets and worms, perception of the laws of physics. As we extended the principle of relativity of perception from the single sensory receptor to the whole organism and, ultimately, to the whole species, it was necessary to generalize the active–passive, or interrogative–assertive, function of the receptor to an interrogative–assertive function of the species as a whole. One possibility for such a function is the AF given above. Perceptual relativity at the level of the species demands a reexamination of the Darwinian principle of evolution.

At the higher cognitive level, perceptual relativity leads us to a position that is nearly indistinguishable from that of the Strong Anthropic Principle. That is, considerations that have issued from biology have led to about the same position as speculations that have issued from cosmology, ending the book with a strong statement for the unification of science.

## NOTES

1. *Objectivity* is a better word than *validity* here.
2. I cannot be consciously aware that a given stimulus is self-generated, because the self-generated stimulus is only a component of a complex that, in its totality, is necessary to produce awareness of a stimulus.
3. A digital or computer model would demonstrate nothing of importance. We are now looking for a physiochemical mechanism (one of the few places in this book where mechanism comes into play) that will *act out* or *live* the role of the perceptual unit. We are trying to create a functional unit that can exhibit some rudimentary aspects of awareness.
4. *Nearly* universally, because some people tend to ask for an indefinite number of clarifications of the question and others just question my sanity for asking.
5. If we regard the universe as closed or finite, in the manner suggested by Einstein's general theory of relativity, the "point" in space at which all matter was collected should more properly be taken as all the space in the universe. Similarly, the expansion that succeeded the big bang should more properly be conceived as an expansion of all space, not just an expansion of matter within space.
6. Radiation is a form of energy, but we recall from Einstein's $E = mc^2$ relation that energy and matter can interconvert, one to the other.

7. The longevity of the universe depends on the *critical cosmic density*, for which the reader is referred to the literature.
8. There are remains of simple organisms such as bacteria and blue–green algae in rocks 3400 million years old (Clarkson, 1986).
9. "One might say 'the eternal mystery of the world is its comprehensibility.' ... The fact that it [the world of our sense experiences] is comprehensible is a miracle." Albert Einstein (1954).
10. We are giving the redoubtable professor no less than he gave us. To deal with the extraordinary coincidence that gravitational and inertial mass are found to be exactly equal, Einstein created the general theory of relativity, in which the two masses are, effectively, constrained to be equal. To deal with the extraordinary coincidence that the universe, as perceived by man, just happens to be intelligible to man, we are creating the principle that intelligibility is a necessary condition for existence of the universe.

# REFERENCES

Abbott, E. A. 1972. *Flatland: A Romance of Many Dimensions*. Barnes & Noble, New York.

Barrow, J. D., and Tipler, F. J. 1986. *The Anthropic Cosmological Principle*. Oxford Univ. Press, New York.

Breuer, R. 1991. *The Anthropic Principle: Man as the Focal Point of Nature* (Translated from the German by H. Newman and M. Lowery). Birkhäuser, Boston.

Clarkson, E. N. K. 1986. *Invertebrate Palaeontology and Evolution*, 2nd ed. Allen & Unwin, Boston.

Dewdney, A. K. 1984. *The Planiverse: Computer Contact with a Two-Dimensional World*. Poseidon Press, New York.

Einstein, A. 1954. Physics and reality. In: *Ideas and Opinions*. Crown Publishing Co., New York.

Greenberger, D. M. 1983. Quantization in the large. *Foundations of Physics* **13**, 903–951.

Gulick, W. L., Gescheider, G. A., and Frisina, R. D. 1989. *Hearing: Physiological Acoustics, Neural Coding, and Psychoacoustics*. Oxford Univ. Press, New York.

Narlikar, J. 1977. *The Structure of the Universe*. Oxford Univ. Press, Oxford.

Norwich, K. H. 1983. To perceive is to doubt. The relativity of perception. *Journal of Theoretical Biology* **102**, 175–190.

Rothman, T. 1987. A 'What you see is what you beget' theory. *Discover*, **May**.

Weinberg, S. 1977. *The First Three Minutes*. Bantam Books, New York.

# Glossary of Symbols

The book spans a number of disciplines: physics, information theory, psychophysics . . . . By and large, the set of symbols characteristically used in a given discipline have been retained, which has led to some replication of nomenclature. For example, $N_i$ has been used to represent the number of phase points in the $i^{\text{th}}$ cell in phase space (as is common in physics), while $N_0$ has been used for Avogadro's number (also common in chemistry and physics), $N(x; \mu, \sigma)$ represents the normal distribution with mean and variance, $\mu$ and $\sigma$, respectively (as is usual in statistics), and $N$ is also used (psychophysically) to represent the total number of jnd's between two intensity levels. The use of a particular symbol will usually be readily apparent from its context, so the replication should not cause any problem.

The listing of symbols below is fairly complete. The number in parentheses which appears after the definition of a symbol refers to a representative equation in which the symbol appears.

*Greek*

$\alpha$     proportionality constant (9.3).

$\beta$     Lagrangian multiplier (6.28).

$\gamma$     constant $= \beta/t'$ (10.2).

$\delta$     as in $\delta x$, used to indicate a small change in the quantity $x$; $\delta v_\mu$: small cell in $\mu$-space. Also used to indicate *the variation in*.

$\varepsilon$     constant (10.13).

$\lambda$     mean of a Poisson distribution (7.2)
      constant $= \beta(I')^n$ (11.2).

$\mu$     mean of a probability distribution;
      $\mu$-space ("$\mu$" for "molecule"): a multidimensional space used in statistical mechanics.

$\nu$     frequency (sometimes represented as $f$).

$\sigma^2$    variance of a distribution:
$\quad$ $\sigma_S^2$: variance of pure signal;
$\quad$ $\sigma_N^2$: variance of noise signal;
$\quad$ $\sigma_R^2$: variance of reference signal.

$\tau$,    time: dummy variable (10.16).

$\xi$,    time dilatation factor: introduced in Box 13.1, multiply by $\xi$ to convert time scale from behavioral to neuronal.

*Italics and Roman*

$a$    represents a constant:
$\quad$ proportionality constant in Fechner's law (3.4)/(10.5a), and in MacKay's (10.12);
$\quad$ base of logarithm in note 5, Chapter 2;
$\quad$ in law by Ekman (3.10),
$\quad$ in Ferry–Porter law (3.30);
$\quad$ in Blondel-Ray law (3.25).

$\ln A$    Lagrangian multiplier (6.28).

$b$    represents a constant:
$\quad$ Fechner's law (3.4)/(10.5a), MacKay (10.11), Ferry–Porter law (3.30).

$C, c$

$\quad$ $c$    represents a constant:
$\quad$ component of $n$ (3.5), law by Ekman (3.10),
$\quad$ $C$    Piéron's law (3.26);
$\quad$ specific heat per mole;
$\quad$ channel capacity (8.21);

$E, e$

$\quad$ $e$    base of natural logarithms;
$\quad$ $E(\ )$ expectation (4.19).

$F, f$

$\quad$ $f$    frequency (same as $\nu$): MacKay (10.11), Riesz (14.9) to (14.11);
$\quad$ density of points in $\mu$-space (15.3);

$\quad$ $F$    perceptual variable: sometimes taken as subjective magnitude, sometimes as neural impulse rate [rate of generation of action potentials in afferent neurons).

$\Delta F$    change in $F$: usually means change corresponding to one jnd.

$G$    used to extremize the $H$-function (4.7).

$H, h$

$\quad$ $h$    Planck's constant (14.19);
$\quad$ $H$    entropy.

$\Delta H$    change in $H$: threshold value of entropy
$\quad$ (i)  to permit discrimination (jnd);
$\quad$ (ii) to permit detection or absolute threshold.

$\mathscr{H}$    entropy relating to single outcome (4.14), (4.15).

$H(X)$    source entropy (4.19).

$H(Y)$    receiver entropy.

$H(X|Y)$
$\quad$ conditional entropy (4.20).

$H(X, Y)$
$\quad$ joint entropy (4.22).

$H_I$    information theoretical entropy: subscript $I$ to eliminate ambiguity when the symbol is used within the context of a physical (statistical mechanics) system (6.19).

$\mathscr{I}$    information.

$\mathscr{I}_m$    mutual information (4.16).

$\mathscr{I}(X|Y), \mathscr{I}(Y|X)$
$\quad$ average mutual information (4.21).

$I$    intensity of a stimulus: e.g., concentration for a taste stimulus, square of mean sound pressure for an auditory stimulus.

$I_\infty = I_{min}$
   absolute threshold (3.23), (13.6), (13.36).

$I_{thresh}$   threshold intensity—a function of stimulus duration: for stimulus duration $\to \infty$, $I_{thresh} \to I_\infty$.

$K, k$

   $k$   scaling constant $> 0$ relating $F$ to $H$ in fundamental equation $F = kH$;

     integration constant (3.7);

   $k_B$ Boltzmann's constant (6.20);

   $K$   intercept of straight line (10.18);

     in law of olfactory threshold (13.55).

$m$    number of samplings made by a receptor of its stimulus population since the onset of the stimulus (9.2), (9.3).

$N, n$

   $n$, exponent of power law of sensation: introduced in (3.8), (10.8);

     number of moles of a gas (1.1);

     number of categories in an experiment on categorical judgment (Chapter 5);

     number of discrete intensities (Chapter 9);

     size of a sample as used in the Central Limit Theorem;

     total number of cells in $\mu$-space (A15.1)

   $N$   total number of jnd's: $N_{I_a}^{I_b}$ is number of jnd's between intensities $I_a$ and $I_b$;

     sum of elements in a stimulus-response matrix;

     total number of phase points (6.25);

     noise (8.21);

   $N_i$   number of phase points that lie in the $i^{th}$ cell in $\mu$-space;

   $N_0$   Avogadro's number;

   $N(x; \mu, \sigma)$

     the normal distribution: variable $x$, mean $\mu$, and variance $\sigma^2$;

   $N_{jk}$   element in a stimulus–response matrix: number of times that stimulus $j$ is given and identified as stimulus $k$;

   $N_{j\cdot}$, sum of elements in the $j^{th}$ row of a stimulus–response matrix (4.24);

   $N_{\cdot k}$, sum of elements in the $k^{th}$ column of a stimulus–response matrix (4.23).

PBS law
   Plateau–Brentano–Stevens law.

PT law
   Poulton–Teghtsoonian law (3.27), (12.31).

$P, p$

   $p$ probability: used in many ways;

   $p(x_j)$ probability of transmitting the symbol $x_j$;

   $p(y_k)$ probability of receiving the symbol $y_k$;

   $p(x_j, y_k)$ joint probability that $x_j$ is transmitted and $y_k$ is received;

   $p(x_j|y_k)$ conditional probability that signal $x_j$ was transmitted given that $y_k$ was received;

   $p(y_k|x_j)$ analogous to above;

   $p(\mathbf{x} = x_i)$ probability that a random variable, $\mathbf{x}$, will take on the value $x_i$ (7.1);

   $p_{ol}$   $-\log_{10} I_\infty = -\log_{10}$ (absolute threshold of a stimulus): used for olfactory stimuli;

$P(x_j, y_k)$ probability of occurrence of $x_j$ and $y_k$ if $x_j$ and $y_k$ are independent events;

$P$     pressure of a gas (Chapter 1)

signal power (8.21).

$Q, q$    quantity of heat;

Range ratio of highest physiological (non-painful) stimulus intensity to the absolute threshold stimulus intensity (3.27);

$r$       same as exponent, $n$ (symbol of Riesz);

$R$      gas constant (Chapter 1).

$R_0, R_I$

membrane resistance (10.21).

$S, s$    physical entropy and physical entropy per mole, respectively (6.13).

$S_0, S_\infty$ values of the Weber fraction in Riesz's terminology (14.8).

$T, t$

$t$ time: usually designates the time since stimulus onset: occasionally (when so-flagged) it designates the duration of the stimulus;

$t_s$    time between samples (9.2);

$t_0$    time following the onset of the stimulus at which an adaptation curve reaches its maximum amplitude (11.5);

$t_r$    simple reaction time (13.4), (13.7);

$t_R$    candidate for simple reaction time (13.8);

$t_{r\,\min}$ minimum simple reaction time (13.5).

$U, u$   internal energy and internal energy per mole, respectively.

$V$      volume of a gas (Chapter 1).

$v_x, v_y, v_z$

cartesian velocity coordinates.

WF law

Weber–Fechner law.

$W$     thermodynamic probability: number of microstates corresponding to a given macrostate; frequency bandwidth (8.20).

$\mathscr{W}$     work done by a system.

$w_i$     energy level of the $i^{\text{th}}$ phase cell.

$x, y, z$ cartesian spatial coordinates.

$x_j$     transmitted symbol.

$y_k$     received symbol.

$Z, z$

$z$ number of photons (7.2);
$Z$ partition function (6.30).

# Index